In Search of Knowledge and Happiness
Genaro Andrade

Copyright © 2020 Genaro Andrade

All rights reserved. No part of this book may be reproduced or transmitted in any form or by any means, electronic or mechanical, including photocopying, recording or by any information storage and retrieval system, without permission in writing from the publisher.

Infinite Knowledge Press—Lincoln, CA
ISBN: 978-1-7357008-0-9
Library of Congress Control Number: Pending
Title: *In Search of Knowledge and Happiness*
Author: Genaro Andrade
Available formats: eBook | paperback distribution

Dedication

I dedicate this book to my wife of many years, to our two kids and their spouses, to our precious loving four, possibly five, grandkids and future grandkids, to my dad and mom. Furthermore, I dedicate this book to the rest of my family, including my brothers, and sisters, all nine of them, as well as my uncles, aunts, cousins, nephews, and nieces.

Acknowledgements

To My Guardian Angel

You came into my life when you were a one-year-old baby, but with each passing day, I learned to love you more and more. I will never forget when we were all sitting at the table having supper. You used to make funny facial expressions. It was hilarious. You made everyone laugh and I thank you for that because as adults sometimes we forget to laugh and have fun.

Furthermore, I remember going for walks with you, you always run in front of me as fast as you could. You were fearless. There were no obstacles for you that you couldn't overcome, nothing stopped you from getting what you wanted, so don't ever change.

After a while you completely won my heart, knowing that you are here on earth makes my days that much brighter. You light up my life. You are my sunshine. You are always happy; you are always smiling and every time I see your smile, I have no other choice but to smile back because your smile and your happiness is contagious. Every time I feel sad or lonely, I think about your precious smile and I instantly feel much better. You give me hope and the strength to keep going forward.

You are a true angel. You are my guardian angel. You are a treasure at the end of the rainbow, you are the light at the end of the tunnel and because of that, I love you. My granddaughter.

To My Parents

My parents are getting older by the minute. My father is ninety-four and my mother is eighty-nine years old. I'm glad that God let them live this long. It has been a blessing for everyone in my family. Nevertheless, it breaks my heart not being able to do more for them. The only thing left for me to do is to love them and try to enjoy their company for as long as they are here.

It's been four years since I noticed that they were slowing down quite a bit. They used to go out for long walks without any problems, but now, they look fragile and tired. It is obvious that they are in pain as they walk. They get tired easily and cannot walk without feeling some type of pain. My mother's left leg is in poor condition, she has arthritis in her knee, and it hurts when she walks.

My father also looks weaker by the day. He doesn't have much strength in his legs, and I can see that he is really struggling when he tries to get up from his chair. My father has Parkinson's disease, which causes his left hand to shake violently. I understand this happens as people age, there is no escaping it.

When I was a little boy, I was taught to love and honor my parents. In fact, it's one of the Ten Commandments from the bible. I try to follow the Ten Commandments because I know that if I do, I would be honoring God, my parents, and myself. I know deep inside that if I follow the Ten Commandments, that everything is going to be alright. I believe that if every person follows the Ten Commandments, then this world would be a better place.

I love my Mother unconditionally because she is a good human being. She loves all her children the same and she cares for people in general. She was always there for me, whether I needed her help or not, day or night, rain, or shine. As far as I can remember I rarely ever asked her for anything, especially for any monetary favors. On the rare occasions when I did ask her for a small loan, she never said no to me or any of her children. I never did take advantage of her good nature because that is not who I am. She was, and still is a loving and caring human being, but most importantly, she loves her children equally no matter what. Mom, I cannot say enough good things about you because you are a symbol of what moms are meant to be...loving, caring and unselfish. God, Mom, and Dad I love you all, and thanks for giving me life.

I love my Father too, but in a completely different way than I love my mother. My Father was different from my mother in many ways, and to this day, he is still different, maybe because he is a man, who knows? He is a macho type of guy who ruled us with an iron fist. I remember him telling me on several occasions that if I didn't do my chores that there would be consequences to pay and when I didn't do them, there were consequences to pay. I will not go into details about the punishing part. All you really need to know is that I learned that there were two different sides of my Father. There was the macho man side, but a softer side as well.

I acquired many good qualities from my Mother. For example, I learn about human kindness, compassion, and honesty. I also learned from her about staying humble no matter what happens in our lives.

I believe that everything happens for a reason and I'm glad that I was able to learn from both of my parents. I learned from my Father about being tough when you must be tough, I learned from my Father about the hard part of life, but I also learned about the softer side of him.

I like to believe that in his own way of doing things, he did love his family too, just like my Mother. He did love us in his own macho way. One of the biggest assets which my dad had, and one that I can remember was that he was always protective of us. He did show me that side of him on several occasions.

A Poem for My Wife

You are the woman who fuels my flame, the woman who supports my failures, my accomplishments, and my goals. You are the woman that I love so tenderly. You are a special woman, a loving mother, a caring and loving human being who puts the needs of others ahead of your own and because of that. I will love you forever.

Contents

Acknowledgements v
To My Guardian Angel v
To My Parents vii
A Poem for My Wife ix

Introduction xv

Chapter 1: Understanding How Our Brains Work 1
The Human Brain Part 1 5
The Human Brain Part 2 7
Our Plasticity Brain 8
Our Brain Continues to Learn as We Get Older 10
Neurotransmitters 11

Chapter 2: The Power of the Mind Part 1 13
The Power of the Mind Part 2 15

Chapter 3: Searching for Knowledge 18
Accumulation of Knowledge Is a Long Journey 20
Using Our Knowledge to Help Others 22

Chapter 4: Searching for Happiness Part 1 24
Searching for Happiness Part 2 27
The Secret to Finding Happiness 30

Chapter 5: Our Feelings and Emotions Part 1 32
Our Feelings and Emotions Part 2 35
Our Feelings and Emotions Part 3 37

Chapter 6: Getting to Know Our True Inner-Selves 41
Learning to Love Ourselves 52
Finding Harmony within Ourselves 57
Do One Thing at a Time and Do It Right 60

Chapter 7: The Conscious Mind 64
The Subconscious Mind 65
The Power of Auto Suggestion 68
The Best Medicine for the Soul 71

Chapter 8: Judging Others 74

Chapter 9: Positive and Accurate Thoughts 76
Affirmative Thoughts 78
Words of Encouragement 81
Negative Thoughts 81
Organizing Our Thoughts 86
Letting Go of Our Negative Thoughts 88
Letting Go of Our Past Failures 89

Chapter 10: Our Hidden Talents 92

Chapter 11: What to do With Stressful Situations 94
Excessive Worry Can Kill Us 97
Excessive Hate and Anger Can Kill Us Too 99
Anxiety is a Silent Killer 102

Chapter 12: Our World as We Know it Now 108
The Ugly Side of Our World 109
Work Related stress 111

Chapter 13: The Power of True Love 113

Chapter 14: Life in the Fast Lane 118
As We Get Older 122

Chapter 15: Replacing Old Ideas with New Ideas 129
Keeping an Open Mind 130

Chapter 16: Self-Confidence 134
Self-Control, Self- Discipline 137

Chapter 17: Who Do We Trust? 143
The Power of Imagination 146
Overcoming Our Weaknesses 148
Healthy Boundaries, are They Important? 152

Chapter 18: Our Human Abilities 156
Changing Our Behaviors.. 158
Why Do We Have Fears? 161

Chapter 19: The Miracle of a Smile... 170
Paradise 173
Focusing on Living Rather Than Dying 174
The Sun 175

Chapter 20: We Can Accomplish More by Working as a Team... 178
Preying on Others 179
Every Day is a New Day Full of Wonders................................... 181
Our Beautiful and Enigmatic World 183
How to Become Successful in Life... 188

Chapter 21: Photography 193
Good Luck, Bad Luck 198
Honesty 200
Overcoming Our Obstacles 202

Chapter 22: Our Irrational Beliefs 206
Why Do We Think, and Act the Way We Do?............................ 210
Encouraging Our Children to Learn New Things Every Day 212
Our Mental State of Mind 217

Chapter 23: Simplifying Our Lives.. 222
How to Reach Our true Potential 228
Taking Advantage of Every Opportunity..................................... 230
Why do we do the things that we do?... 232
How to Be Happy and Successful at Work 239

Chapter 24: We Have the Power to Control the Outcome of Our Actions.241
Love will heal our minds and bodies from diseases 246
Should We Let Other People Influence Our Thoughts and Ideas? 251
Seeing Through the Illusions 253

Chapter 25: A Positive and Healthy Attitude 255
Inspiring Other to Do Better 258
In Need of Appreciation.. 261
The Power of Suggestion 263
When My Motivation Is Not Present 268

Chapter 26: A Death in the Family.. 270
Dealing with Our Feelings and Emotions after a Loved One Dies... 272
Why Are We So Resistant to Changes? 274
A Healthy Body Equals a Sharp Mind 278
Our Physical Bodies Must Stay Active 280

Chapter 27: Replacing Our Old Habits with New Habits 283
Replacing Our Old Beliefs with New Beliefs 286
We should not Be Afraid of Failing 288
Failure Can Be a Good Thing for Kids 291
Constructive Criticism... 293

Chapter 28: Delicious Super Foods for The Brain 295
Toxic Relationships... 299
Signs of A Non-Toxic Relationship 302
Loving Feelings... 304

Chapter 29: Our Wondering and Inquisitive Mind 306
What Are We Passionate About? 310
Never Give Up, Never Surrender 314
Learning to Express Ourselves... 319
Finding Harmony within Ourselves 321

Chapter 30: What Is our Degree of Tolerance? 325
How Do We Measure Success?.. 326
Who Is God?... 329
Is God Responsible for Our Suffering? 329
Does God Communicate with Us? 330

Chapter 31: Fog in our Brain... 332
Curiosity 336
A Plan of Action 339
Greed, Money, and Power 341
How to Position Ourselves for Success... 344

Chapter 32: It's Time to Expose our Hidden Talents 346
Staying Motivated with Positive Thinking.................................... 349
Reaching for the Stars 352
What Is Holding Us Back from Achieving Our Goals?............. 354
About the Author... 363

Introduction

The topics in this book will show you how the human brain works and how it stores information into the subconscious mind. The subconscious mind is different from the conscious mind. The subconscious mind is a storage memory compartment. In other words, it's the hard drive. The conscious mind means we are aware of what we are doing in the moment.

In this book you will learn how to use your imagination. You will learn to develop and use all your skills and abilities. Skills and abilities that you didn't know you had before. In this book, you will experience incredible thrills as you learn to push your mind into higher levels of awareness. Your mind will be better equipped to handle the daily challenges when you push yourself. In this book you will learn that your mind will become aware of new arising situations, and with the help of your mind, you will be able to solve them very quickly. In this book, you will learn to take your life back, regain your confidence and be in total control of your actions.

You will learn how to use your imagination. You will discover that you have tremendous abilities that you didn't know you had. You will discover that you have an incredible imagination waiting to be unlocked.

In this book, you will learn about your feelings and emotions and what the difference is between them. You will learn about how your thoughts are processed, and how they impact your life for better or for worse. You will learn to take control of your thoughts and use them to your advantage. You will learn how to get rid of your negative thoughts and convert them into positive thoughts. You will learn to create positive thoughts instead of self-destructive thoughts. You will learn to integrate your thoughts and to think in a way which is going to benefit you rather than harm you.

In this book, you will learn to transform negative energy into positive energy. You will learn that decision-making does not have to be stressful. You will learn not to take the path of least resistance; you will learn that you can still find happiness despite your problems. You will learn to take full responsibility for your actions. You will learn to expand your knowledge tenfold. You will learn to create new values for yourself, for your family, and for others.

In this book, you will learn to motivate yourself and to stop making excuses for yourself. You will learn to push your mind to higher levels of awareness. Your will learn that your mind is equipped with the necessary tools to help you thrive. Your mind will become aware of arising problems and you will be ready to face new challenges. You will discover new trends and new solutions. You will regain confidence in yourself and regain complete control of your life.

This book has been in the making for over forty years. Yes, I know forty years is a long time to write a book. However, I wanted to make sure that this book was going to be something special. I wanted to write a book that everyone who reads it can benefit tremendously. I wrote this book based on my past experiences and the accumulation of knowledge which I acquired over the past fifty-years.

It was important for me to include as much of my knowledge which I learned into this book. I had to experience everything that life had to offer me first, and as a result, I learned many valuable lessons throughout my life. I will explain some of those lessons throughout this book.

At the beginning, I was writing for myself, but as the years went by, I realized that it was selfish on my part, so I decided to let others read it. It's important to ensure that these words reach and touch the hearts and minds of other people, and I hope that it will help them change their lives forever.

It's not only my intention to share this motivational book with the public, but with my children, grandchildren, family members and friends. I believe that everyone can benefit from reading it and I'm hoping that I can help others avoid the same costly mistakes that I made throughout my life. Do not get me wrong, most of my decisions were good sound decisions. However, there were a few not so good decisions as well. Making mistakes is important because it will allow us to learn from them. So, go ahead and make your own mistakes, I will not stand in your way, I will not take that away from you or anyone else. However, you must know that some mistakes cannot be reversed, so I am hopeful that you will be able to avoid them.

I was not always the best listener, I was not always perfect, no one is, however we don't need to be genius to know when to use common sense or when not to do something dangerous which is going to implicate our lives.

I learned many lessons from different people throughout my life. One of the first lessons which I learned was that I needed to be patient when dealing with people, and this in turn helped me to understand why people behave the way they do. I study their behaviors, what they did and how they did it. I learned why people like to do certain things and dislike others. I also learned that people can be nice, or they can be mean and obnoxious. In fact, I learned that as human beings, we are capable of many good things, but we are also capable of doing many bad things.

I studied psychology for many years. It was a source from where I gained vast amounts of knowledge, and I must say that I'm not an expert on psychology, but it did help me tremendously as far as understanding human behaviors. Psychology helped me to understand how we think as human beings, and how we react when confronted with anger or in an uncivilized manner.

Furthermore, I learned from studying and watching others. I also read hundreds of books in my lifetime because my desire to learn was bigger than myself. I was never satisfied. I was always looking for something new to learn. I had an insatiable thirst for knowledge. Even today, my desire to acquire new information has not diminished one bit. It is strong as ever.

Chapter One

Understanding How Our Brain Works

Understanding the human brain is perhaps one of the most difficult tasks that anyone can endure. We all know that the human brain is an amazing and complex organ, but at the same time, it was designed to accomplish many incredible tasks. Our brain is like a supercomputer which has not been invented yet. It's an extremely complicated human machine designed by our creator.

How does our brain work? First, I want to make it crystal clear that our brain is different from our mind. Our brain is like the power plant that supplies the electricity which we use to power up our light bulbs and every other electronic devices that we have. Similarly, our mind is drawing the energy that it needs from our brain in order to work properly. Now! Imagine if our brain suddenly dies, then our mind will stop working all together. We need to realize that our mind controls everything, is going to help us to develop self-discipline and self-control. Furthermore, our mind is going to help us to control our emotions, our feelings, our thoughts, and our actions. More about our mind later.

The human body and brain were given to us by our creator, but it's after us to learn how to use them. We have the capacity and the power to do it, but unfortunately, most of us do not know how to tap into the power of the brain yet. We owe it to ourselves to learn. Develop and train our minds. We must learn to take control of our thoughts if we want to grow as super humans. Allowing our brain to dictate our actions is the easiest thing to do, but there's no merit in it for us. If we allow our brain to have all the control over us, then we will be forever lost, therefore, it's imperative that we learn to take the reins.

I must ask everyone the following question: "if you are riding a horse, is it not your responsibility for which direction you want the horse to follow? Is the horse going to go to the right. To the left, uphill or downhill? You got it. You and only you are responsible for which direction you want the horse to go. You have the power so you must take the reins. You must pull the reins towards the direction you want the horse to go.

Another example I would like to describe is the bicycle, and it's basically the same thing as riding a horse. We climb on our bikes; we grab the handles, and we stir in the direction we want the bicycle to go. It's a simple decision because this action will help us to control in which direction the bicycle will go. When we pull the handles to the right, the bicycle will go to the right, but if we pull to the left, then it's going to go to the left, and if we hold the handlebars in a straight position, then it's obvious that we will go straight…right?

There is so much information out there about our brain that I don't even know where to begin, but nevertheless, I am going to try to explain it, so bear with me. The human brain is complicated, and I'm not going to try and fully understand it or try to explain it all because it would take me a whole lifetime and beyond. Remember that whatever we are right now, whoever we are right now as a person is because of our brain.

Our brain controls every single cell in our bodies. It controls not only our mental state of mind, but it controls our physical bodies as well. All the mental and physical problems we encounter in life are the direct result of our brain in action. Everything is influenced by our brain in positive or negative ways.

Until a few years ago, scientists did not fully understand how the human brain worked, but now, they are working diligent on the study of the human brain. With each passing day they are getting closer and closer to unraveling the secrets of the human brain. The human brain is the most enigmatic and complicated machine in the universe. Nothing else even comes close to the complexity of the human brain. Not even the most powerful computers ever invented can compare. Everything starts with our brain. Our feelings, our emotions, our thoughts, and our ideas, are all there in our brain. Our thoughts and ideas make us who we are as a person today.

The human brain is constantly working. It's processing vast amounts of information because it has the capacity to process billions bits of information per second. At the same time, our brain is storing information in its database for future use. In fact, this is what my brain is doing right now. As I am attempting to explain how the human brain functions.

Again, the human brain is an amazing machine. It stores past and present information into the subconscious mind. Now! The subconscious mind is different from the conscious mind. The subconscious mind is the storage memory compartment, it's the hard drive. The conscious mind means that you are conscious, you are aware of what you are doing at any precise moment.

How does our brain collect the incoming information and where does it come from? Well, whether we realized it or not, our brain is constantly working, it's absorbing anywhere from hundreds to billions (depending on how active your brain is at any given moment) of incoming pieces of information from many different directions.

Our brain receives its information from our senses, through our eyesight, through our sense of smell, through our ears, by way of sound, through our taste, through our skin by physically touching an object with any part of the body. All these senses are constantly sending signals to our brain for interpretation and storage.

Every idea starts in our brain. Whoever or whatever we are as human beings is because of these ideas in our brain. We must understand that our ideas by themselves, will be of no consequence, but put these ideas into action and we will get either. Good results or bad results. To better understand how our brain works, we must understand that our brain is going to affect our nervous system, which in return, it's going to impact our health. For example, our physical problems are the direct result of our state of mind. In other words, our state of mind will determine if we will be successful or if we will be defected in achieving maximum health. All our diseases are influenced by our mental state of mind.

Our negative thoughts and emotions will prevent us from reaching maximum health, therefore, it's important for us to understand that our brain controls everything, from our state of mind, our diseases, our negative or positive thoughts and emotions. We always need to be aware of our mental state of mind because our mental state of mind will create a bridge between our health and our diseases.

Knowing that our brain controls everything is the key which is going to bring us health or sickness, success or failure, happiness, or unhappiness. We need to learn to take total control of our brain, and we can accomplish such a task by controlling our thoughts and emotions through our mind, we must not let negative thoughts and emotions to enter our minds because they will create habit in our bodies.

Every single negative thought and emotion that we have has the potential to lower our resistance, preventing us from being able to fight diseases. Again, our negative thoughts and emotions will interfere with our immune system preventing us from reaching maximum health. When our immune system is weak, we will not have the power or the strength to fight back as it was meant to do.

It would be amazing if everyone in this world would take the time to get to know how their brain works. If we want to accomplish total happiness, and if we want to accomplish maximum health, then, we must learn to control the power within our brain because understanding our brain and controlling its power will allow us to accomplish some amazing things. For example, it will allow us to reach maximum health, and at the same time, it will allow us to reach maximum happiness.

The Human Brain Part 1

Most animals on the face of the planet have a brain, but none compares to the human brain. The human brain is nothing less than a miracle, it is unique, and it gives us the power to think, it gives the power to speak, and it gives us the power to solve problems. Our brain can also store images in our subconscious mind. The human brain is truly an amazing human organ.

As I mentioned earlier, our brains control the conscious and unconscious through our five senses: hearing, vision, taste, touch, and smell. Our brain controls our body temperature. It controls our breathing, our blood pressure, our heart rate, and it controls our feelings and our emotions. The human brain controls our entire bodies by sending electrical currents throughout the nervous system. Scientists call it, "neuroscience or neurobiology." The human brain uses electrical currents called "neurons" or specialized cells. But what are neurons? Neuro refers to neurons. Neurons are nerve cells in our brain. Our cells are the building blocks of our brain and our nervous system.

Neurons are very much like other cells in the human body. The only difference is that neurons are specialized cells that transmits information throughout the human body. It receives, processes, and sends information through electrical chemical signals.

Scientist believed that the average human brain contains one hundred billion neurons, however, Dr. Suzana Herculano-Houzel concluded that there are actually eighty-six billions neurons in the human brain...not as many neurons as scientist previously thought, but nevertheless, eighty six billion neurons is a tremendous amount of neurons. Anyway, these electrical currents sends signals throughout the nervous system. These electrical currents are distributed through our five senses to communicate with the brain. I will address the human brain throughout several chapters within this book.

All you really need to know for now is that our brain has complete control over the entire human body, however, the body does nothing until it receives a signal from our brain. The brain is the hard drive where all information is stored. Any information stored in our brain sits there waiting for someone to push a button and allow that information to be distributed via electrical currents to every parts of the body. It's such a beautiful thing that I wish I could see it in action.

As I mentioned before, our miracle brain has the capacity to process billions bits of information per second. It's an unimaginable task. It's unfortunate that most of us are only able to process a small amount of information. Is there a good reason as to why we are limiting our brain potential? Yes, there is...and it has to do with the fact that we do not stimulate our brains enough. We do not feed our brains enough information daily and that is why our brains sometimes lapses into a mental dormant state. It is obvious that our brain will remain in a sleep mode, however, we have the capacity to wake up our brain anytime we want to by simply proving or stimulating it with new information. Furthermore, if we want our brain to stay healthy and sharp, then we must provide our brain with new information.

The human brain can perform beyond all expectations, in other words, it has no limitation in terms of what it can accomplish. But again, we must continue to feed our brains with new information.

There are an abundance of things that we can do to help us stimulate our brain, however, these things must be of the healthy type. For example, feelings of enjoyment, pleasure, tenderness, affection, sympathy, imagination, and feelings of inner peace will help us to stimulate our brain. We must never, or under any circumstances feed our brain with negative thoughts, negative feelings, or negative emotions because this will not only have a negative impact on our brain, but on our bodies as well. Negative feelings and emotions will suffocate our brain, preventing it from thinking clearly.

The Human Brain Part 2

There comes a time when our brain must be awakened from a dormant state of mind. There's no better time than the present time to unleash the power that we possess within ourselves. But how can we accomplish such a task? Well, it's actually very simple, we can start by putting some of our knowledge into action. Knowledge which has been dormant for too long. It's time for us to awake from the illusions that we have created for ourselves and others. Now is the time to reach out and go further than we ever have before. Now is the time to let go of the past. Now is the time to eliminate our old beliefs and replace them with new beliefs. Now is the time to get rid of our selfishness. Now is the time to get rid of the illusions that we have been confined for too long. Our erroneous illusions will limit our abilities, but they will prevent us from reaching our true potential as well.

The human brain is an amazing tool that we can put into action to help us accomplish anything that we desire. By using our knowledge, and imagination we can change our lives and the lives of our loved ones forever, but only if we use our most precious gift: our minds. We are human beings; therefore, we are going to make tons of mistakes within our lifetimes, but at the same time, we are undeniably, mentally, and physically strong to also make good sound decisions. Again, we are capable individuals. We can accomplish most of our goals, but only if we learn to awaken the power within our minds, and of course, we must have the desire to make these changes as well. It's important that we focus our energy on our positive thoughts rather than the negative ones. We must look at the bright side of our past accomplishments instead of our past failures. Remember that we must put our knowledge into action if we want to accomplish our goals and dreams. We must use the knowledge that we have in order to acquire the things that we want, whether they are materialistic things or spiritual.

Our new acquired knowledge will gain power and momentum, but only if we don't quit at the first signs of trouble. We can become a dynamic force for the good of humanity, but only if we put our knowledge into action. Our knowledge will help us in solving our problems, furthermore, our knowledge will help us in perfecting our skills. We must be ready to expand our knowledge and expand our awareness. We must be ready and willing to receive new wisdom and knowledge from others. Remember that our new knowledge must be used wisely and directed towards good deeds for other people and not just for ourselves.

Our Plasticity Brain

Up until a couple of years ago, I never heard of the word "plasticity" and I never really gave it much thought until now. I finally had the opportunity to find out what plasticity meant. Brain plasticity, also known as neuroplasticity, is a term that refers to the brain's ability to change and to constantly adapt to new information and new situations. I'm not suggesting that our brain is made of plastic, even though plastic can bend and adjust for a better fit. Plasticity simply means that our brains can adapt to changes very rapidly.

Our brain's plasticity can be a good thing most of the time, however, there will be some brain plasticity or changes that will have negative effects on our brain, for example, it might influence our behavior in a negative way, so we must be careful, we must be aware that plasticity changes to our brain can influence our good thoughts and bad thoughts as well.

Up until about fifty or sixty years ago, many researchers believe that the human brain could only change and adapt to new knowledge until the age of childhood, they believe that by adulthood the human brain was mostly permanent. But nowadays, researchers have demonstrated that our brain continues to grow, because it continues to create new neural pathways. Our brain can alter existing neural pathways and create new ones, it's able to adapt to new knowledge, new experiences, new information and it's able to create new memories as well.

I really gave it a lot of thought about our brain "plasticity" and I came up with the conclusion that our brain continues to grow as we get older. It's only logical to think that our brain keeps changing, it never stops learning. It does not surprise me that our brain keeps evolving because most of what I have learned, I learn as an adult. By the time I finish this book I will be sixty-two years old and I am still learning more things now than ever before.

Again, it doesn't matter how old we are, we will keep on learning. In fact, I believe that we were put on this earth to learn and develop into superior beings. Sure, as we age everything slows down, but it doesn't mean that we are unable to learn new things, we just learn at a much slower pace, but it's only because at a certain age we stop feeding our brain new information, we also stop feeding our bodies the right foods and as a consequence, we are starving our bodies from getting the right vitamins, nutrients, and minerals which it needs in order to stay healthy and strong.

Our brain is the "miracle Brain." The human brain can rewire itself after someone had brain damage from a stroke, in other words, it will be able to regain functionality. I can only imagine if we were to help our brain by inducing more blood flow to the brain by way of physical exercise and eating healthy foods. You see, the food that we consume turns into energy and this energy keeps our bodies strong and healthy. All this energy is then distributed throughout the body, including the brain. By feeding our bodies the right foods, we will be feeding our brain the fuel or energy that it needs to perform its duties at a high level. Furthermore, we must understand that our brain will not work properly when it's lacking the essentials. Brain food. That is right! Our brain needs fuel constantly, just like our bodies need food and exercise to maintain its good physical condition.

We must never separate our brain from our bodies. We exercise because we want our bodies to be in good physical condition, but most of the time we neglect to exercise our brain. We must remember that our brain needs exercise as well. We can expand our brain abilities by doing physical exercises and by feeding our brain with new information on a day by day basis.

Feeding our brain with new knowledge will help us to expand our communication network. It will improve our memory, our reasoning, our way of thinking and it will improve our learning abilities. Again, we must harness the power of our brain on a consistent basis by exercising our physical bodies and by feeding our brain new information. It's important to remember that when we exercise our physical bodies, the blood will flow to the brain's frontal cortex. The frontal cortex controls all our functions.

Again, we need to make sure that we feed our bodies the essential vitamin, minerals, and nutrients which it needs because whatever is good for the body, it's also good for the brain. Remember that if we fail to feed our bodies with the necessary ingredients which it needs in order to survive, then our bodies will grow weaker until they can't perform no more, and eventually, they will die. The same principal applies when it comes to our brain, when our brain doesn't get the fuel which it needs, then our brain too, will grow weaker and eventually will die, just like our bodies.

A word of cautious: Physical activities will race our levels of free radicals. These radicals can damage our brain cells, so we must be careful and exercise with moderation. Free radicals are atoms or molecules with an unpaired electron which makes them very unstable. You see, these free radicals are looking for extra electrons to steal, so that they can become stable.

We must reinvent ourselves by taking advantage of our brain plasticity. In other words, our brain has the tremendous ability to continually reinforce itself. It's important to remember that there will be a high price that we must pay for neglecting our brains by not feeding them the right foods, the right vitamins, and the right nutrients, furthermore, we also need to feed our bodies antioxidants which we can get from fruits, nuts, vegetables or plant-based foods. Our bodies have their own antioxidant defenses to keep free radicals in check, however, occasionally they need our help.

When we neglect to feed our bodies with the proper vitamins, minerals, nutrients, and antioxidants which it needs in order to stay healthy, our brain power will start to diminish, it will malfunction, and it will send us into a state of depression. Our memory and intelligence will start to decline as we age, we will start to develop dementia and eventually develop Alzheimer's, therefore, is important that we start challenging our brain right now, rather than tomorrow. We have the power within our brain to change who we are.

Our Brain Continues to Learn as We Get Older

Knowing how our brain works is one of my favorite subjects because I think that it's important that we know how our brain works. It's an exciting topic. After researching and studying the human brain for most of my life, I have concluded that our brain is an amazing miracle organ, and contrary to many old beliefs that our brain stays the same and that it doesn't keep learning as we grow older, the true reality is that our brain continues to learn. Not in the sense of getting physically bigger and expanding in mass, but rather, our brain keeps learning throughout our entire lives. Our brain never stops learning and there's plenty of evidence that shows it. It's only logical to think that our brain will keep on evolving, learning, and gathering information throughout our lifetime.

If we pay attention to a child, right from the beginning of their existence, we will notice that many changes will start to emerge, for example, the child will start to develop his or her own mentality, they will start to develop their own characters. Babies are very eager to learn, they will start to explore their surroundings as soon as they are born, they start to move their arms and legs, they will look around and listen for noises. Babies want to learn, they want to see, they want to hear, and they even want to talk. Sure, we don't quite know what they are saying, but nevertheless, they are talking, and it's called baby talk. Babies have a tremendous ability to learn and they learn very quickly. They are continually producing new brain cells, and yes, even adults can grow new brain cells continually.

The human brain has the capacity to continue to grow and evolve, even at the age of one hundred-years old and beyond. Just because we are getting older doesn't mean that our brain is not capable of learning new things every single day of our lives. We must continue to develop our brain well into old age because the day we stop trying to learn new things it will be the day that we are no longer here on this earth. Remember that our brain is always changing and is always willing to learn new things every day.

Neurotransmitters

Neurotransmitters are endogenous chemical messengers which are produced by the body. They are responsible for sending signals or information from neuron to neuron by way of electrical signals or chemical signals. Neurotransmitters are responsible for sending communication from one nerve cell to another or one nerve cell to various organs throughout the body.

According to new discoveries by scientists, neurotransmitters in our brains are responsible for who we are and who we will become in the future. Remember that our brain can be influenced by the foods that we eat so we must be careful about what we choose to put in our bodies. Our thoughts and our behaviors are affected substantially by those foods. Neurotransmitters are the highways that carries our thoughts and feelings throughout our bodies, including our brains.

Neurotransmitters are built by eating certain types of foods, for example, when we eat protein, (which is in every cell in our bodies) meat, dairy products, nuts, grains, and beans. Our bodies will break down these foods and convert them into different amino acids, such as, tryptophan, tyrosine, and phenylalanine. These amino acids will affect cognition and our moods in many ways. Tyrosine produces neurotransmitters, norepinephrine, and dopamine. These amino acids are important because they will help us to stay alert.

Chapter Two

The Power of the Mind Part 1

The mind is perhaps the greatest power in the universe, but we need to learn how to use it. When we know how to use the power and the energy in our mind and when we learn to control it, it will bring us peace, joy, calmness, and happiness. It will also bring us the satisfaction of achievement. We must know that there is a tremendous amount of power and energy hidden in our brains. It is there. Dormant, waiting to be released, waiting to be put into action, waiting for us to tap into it.

Knowing that we have all this power and energy in our brains, and we don't use it, it makes me shake from my head all the way down to my toes. Perhaps I should mention it again just in case you were not aware of it. There will be consequences for all those people who fail to tap into their brain power.

By using our brain power and energy, we can accomplish what we desire the most, which I am assuming is happiness. How do we accomplish happiness? Well, it depends on what your desires are. You must ask yourself, *what makes me happy?* Is it money, fame, or both? Perhaps it is something else. Maybe you would like to attain a sense of peace? Maybe your desire is to live a healthier life, free of diseases, or maybe you want to start a new career? Perhaps, you wish that all your family and friends could live in peace and harmony. Loving each other and supporting each other?

What would you like to accomplish in life? It is all about what you want. It is all about knowing the things that will make you happy. It is actually a simple process. You must do some soul searching to figure it out. Once you figure out exactly what makes you happy, then you need to work on it. Nothing is going to happen by just wishing for something good to happen. Nothing will move if you do not move. Remember that nobody else is going to accomplish your goals or your desires for you because everyone else is busy trying to accomplish their own goals and desires. You are in control of your mind. You are in control of fulfilling your own wishes and your desires.

We all know that we do not want to be miserable our entire lives. Nobody wants that. I am almost one hundred percent sure of that. Everyone wants to be happy, right? Who wants to be miserable? In fact, I have never heard of anyone in my entire life saying to themselves that they wanted to be miserable or unhappy. Okay, so if we do not want to be miserable and unhappy then we must not waste any more time. We must not waste our existence and energy on meaningless and unproductive tasks that have no merit.

If you want to be happy then you must make a change and you must make a change right now!!! Just remember that it is never too late to make a change and it does not matter if you are one-hundred years old because your mind will stay young well into the later years of your life. The mind does not die, it simply slows down, but not because it is old, but because people stop using their mind after their fifties and sixties. They stop using their mind and that is not a good idea. You see. When you are getting older, it is the right time to start teaching our mind new things.

We must not let our minds go into a sleep mode, we must re-train or teach our minds new ideas. We must keep on stimulating our minds so that our minds can stay healthy and young. Our minds were created to think and to be creative and if this does not happen because we got mentally lazy in our old age, our brain will eventually go dormant. Now, are you beginning to understand that we must keep our minds occupied? It is all up to us to not let our mind go into a dormant state of mind. We must awake our mind and not let it go into a winter long sleep.

It is for us to decide if we will let our mind go dormant or not...it is after us to decide how far we can go and how much we will accomplish in the future. We can start right now, but we must take it slowly we must take it one step at a time, we must also be consistent, we must do it daily. If we practice while we are still young, we will be able to keep our mind younger for many years to come. Remember that our brain does not question our orders...it will obey and follow those orders without
any hesitation. Remember that every thought and action starts within our mind and therefore our body is not going to move unless commanded by our mind to do so.

The Power of the Mind Part 2

Our brain is full of energy, and it's from there that we extract that energy that we required in order to do our thinking. It's similar to having solar panels on the roof of our houses, the panels collect the energy from the sun during sunny days, afterwards, that energy is available for us to use whenever we need it. Similarly, our brain collects its energy from the foods that we eat daily. All this energy is then distributed throughout our bodies, including our brain. Again, it's where we draw our energy to do our thinking.

I am sure that everyone on the face of this planet have done plenty of thinking throughout their lifetime. However, not all that thinking was correct. When we waste our precious energy on the wrong kind of thinking, we are wasting precious energy that we can instead use to accomplish more meaningful things. Things that will bring happiness to our hearts.

It's especially important for us to stimulate our mind so that it can stay sharp at all times. It's also important that whatever we are thinking is correct because if is not, then we need to retrain our mind to think accurately.

We must remember that our minds works through the power of autosuggestion. Therefore, our thoughts must be directed towards constructive thoughts, rather than destructive ones. There's no denying that our mind possess the power over every cell of our bodies, therefore, we must make sure that we have complete control over our minds and our actions, and we can accomplish this task by sending signals to our brain. However, those signals must be accurate, they must be constructive signals and not destructive ones.

I want you to imagine how wonderful it will be if you were able to achieve everything that you ever desire. Now, I want you to imagine that you have already accomplished those things. How do you feel now? You probably feel a sense of happiness and a sense of achievement, right? You probably feel good all over. Okay, so that was just pretending, now! Let us get back to reality. How are we going to accomplish all the things that we really want right now? Well, it's easy and not so easy at the same time. In order to accomplish what we want, we need to take control over our minds, in other words, we must never let our minds control us. It's important that we never give up until we have achieved what we want. Does this make sense? It does to me. Everything is possible, without a doubt.

I know for a fact that from time to time we are going to doubt ourselves and our abilities to perform at a high level, but it will be okay because it's perfectly normal, however, we must not panic or stress over it for too long. The important thing here is to keep trying until we can become experts at using those abilities. Remember that we will become experts, but only if we never give up. We need to keep in mind that our minds have been programmed for thousands of years to think in a limited way, therefore, it's going to take some time to retrain our brains.

We must take our time to retrain our minds and to do things right the first time. It's important that we don't set limitations for ourselves because when we set limitations, then we are going to prevent ourselves from achieving our goals. We need to remind ourselves that we are in charge and that whatever our desire is, it must be carried out. We must use the power of suggestion to send signals to our brain because our thoughts are more than just thoughts, our thoughts are who we are, therefore, we need to make sure that our thoughts are aligned with who we really are.

Our lives can be what we want them to be, we can make our lives simple, or we can make them complicated. I guess it depends on how well we know ourselves, and how prepare we are to take control over our affairs. There will be many choices that we must make in the future which is going to impact our lives and the lives of those who we love, therefore, we need to make sure that those choices that we are about to make are carefully thought out before we act. We must remember that the choices that we make now will be responsible for our future accomplishments or our future misfortunes.

Life is not that complicated. It only seems that way, but it's because we make it complicated. Furthermore, there's a perfectly good explanation as to why our lives are complicated and it's because our thoughts are not the right thoughts and our actions are not the right actions. It takes a great deal of energy and self-control to decide which thoughts and actions are the right ones, but nevertheless, we must take the time to examine them because the decisions that we make right now will impact our entire future, the outcome can be a negative or a positive one. Before we make any decisions, we must make sure that they are the right decisions.

We hold the key to our future. We are one hundred percent responsible for controlling our thoughts and our actions, whether we like or not. Remember that we never want someone else to hold all the power and control over our lives.

We should never be afraid to use the power of our minds, furthermore, we must never let the unknown prevent us from moving forward. Remember that we will be okay because we are more than capable, we will be successful if we don't give up at the first sign of trouble. Remember that we will accomplish most of our dreams and goals, but only if we practice on a consistent basis. It's important to remember that if we never give up, eventually, we will be victorious and we will be rewarded handsomely for our hard work and dedication.

There are a couple of things that I like to practice every single day which helps me to overcome any difficult situation that might arise during the day and that is to: Simplify my life, in other words, I don't make it any more complicated than what already is. Another thing that like to practice is quite simple as well, and that is to: Do one thing at a time and do it right. If we want to achieve success and reach happiness, we must try to simplify our life by not overreacting and not over worrying about any difficult situations that might arise, especially, situations which are out of our control.

You see, what we are really trying to accomplish here is happiness. We must learn to relax because when we learn to relax. We will be able to make better decisions. Thinking with a clear mind is the key which is going to put us over the top. The right approach to solving our problems lies in our ability to tackle them with an open and relaxed mind. Remember that we can only control our own minds and no one else. No human being can control another human being's mind unless he or she chooses to do so. It's God's given right to mankind, to be able to control one's own mind. No amount of force will persuade another human being to become a slave.

Chapter Three

Searching for Knowledge

For those people who don't know how the human brain works, you must know that it's a well-known fact that from the time of birth, our minds have been searching or reaching out for knowledge. We learned as much as we could as we were growing up, but now we must elevate our knowledge and our skills to a higher level because what we know now is just enough to support us today, but it won't be enough to support us in the future. Our future will be more challenging than ever before because of the new technologies coming out every single year, so, we must learn new things to keep abreast with the new world. By learning and adjusting to new technology, we will be able to support a new way of life on this planet. We have already seen some of these new technological advances in action, for example, we have solar energy panels for our homes, and new energy sources for our cars. But we must continue to improve our solar panel's efficiency and we must continue to improve the life expectancy of our car batteries. Flying cars? Yes, they are coming and perhaps, sooner than we think. Maybe in the next three to five years.

We must keep searching for new ways to improve space exploration by creating new technologies which are going to help us build bigger and faster spaceships that will take us millions of miles into outer space in little time. Anything is possible, but only if we join forces and put our heads together so that we can work for a single common cause. There are no limitations to what we can accomplish. Together as one, we can thrive.

There will be much more knowledge to learn. There will be new skills for us to learn now and in the future. The universe is vast. Therefore, we must increase our wealth of knowledge. We can accomplish this task by putting our imaginations into action. We must remember that our time here on earth is limited so we must not waste our limited and precious time here on Earth on meaningless tasks.

It's important to harvest our imagination so that it doesn't fall into stagnation. We must never fall back and get lost in our ignorance. We can accomplish anything that we want, but only if we use our intelligence and imagination. Humanity would be better served if we use intellect and skills, rather than force to accomplish our goals. We have tremendous abilities and talent that we must continue to cultivate.

We must remember that a man without knowledge is a man who lives in darkness. Moreover, people who have the knowledge will continue to soar, and they will continue to keep their hopes alive. We must remember that knowledge is power. Therefore, I welcome new knowledge into my life every single day of my life. I'm never going to feel satisfied or content with what I know. I will always want to learn more. I do not want to be a man who was afraid of learning or trying new things. I would like to be a man who tried everything. I do not want to become a man who failed to learn much of anything in life. Without knowledge, ignorance will start to creep in, it will get closer and closer and eventually is going to take over our thoughts leading us into darkness. Without knowledge, we will never be able to advance to the next level of super thinkers.

There are several sources from which one can accumulate vast amounts of knowledge. One way from which we can gather knowledge is through direct experiences. Another way is through the teaching from others, through verbal conversations. We can also use our imagination whenever possible to acquire more knowledge. Using our imagination will allow us to put ourselves in good situations from which we can learn and create new knowledge and new opportunities. Another way of gathering knowledge is by reading as many books as possible.

We can acquire new knowledge by never surrendering ourselves to laziness, and by never giving up on ourselves. My suggestion to those who would like to better themselves and their families, is to *attain new knowledge*. We must not only learn it, but we must also master it and put it into action daily. We must acquire and expand our knowledge to the fullest, but we can only accomplish this task by asking questions and searching for answers. The day we stop asking questions or looking for answers, is the day that we stop learning. It's important not to fall back into stagnation ever again.

We all know that if we want to achieve success in our lives, we must be willing to change our way of thinking and our way of doing things. We must let ourselves be coachable by others. We must learn to listen to what other people have to say in order to gain new knowledge. We can also learn many new things by observing others because they are doing things differently than we are or they are doing things that we never did before. So, we must learn from them.

It's important to pay attention when other people are talking because listening to others will allow us to learn and gain new knowledge which is required, well, that is if we want to become successful. Again, we shouldn't make decisions based on impulse. You see, in the past I made costly decisions which I later regretted, it cost me a lot of money, but it doesn't always have to be about money. Sometimes the price we pay when we don't listen to wisdom could affect us mentally and physically instead. There's never any assurance that we will be successful at what we do, but that shouldn't stop us from trying.

Remember that our goal in life should be to gain new knowledge, but at the same time, we must learn to use it because once we have mastered that knowledge, we will be able to achieve most of the things that we so desire. We must be willing to master our mind and our thoughts. It's important to become an expert of our own thoughts, because once we master them, we will be able to discover a whole new world full of wonderful surprises.

Accumulation of Knowledge is a Long Journey

Accumulation of knowledge is a long journey, in other words, it's a long-life process of hard work and dedication. We simply cannot rush knowledge to come to us all wrapped up in a gift box. Knowledge is not something we can acquire overnight, instead, knowledge must be learned in a slow and steady pace. It's only by taking one step at a time that we are going to reach the top of the mountain, but without getting exhausted. Furthermore, remember that reaching the top of the mountain is not our destination, it's only the beginning of our journey. The truth of the matter is that we are never going to achieve perfection by gaining more knowledge...no one can. I know that for a fact, so I will not be overly worried about achieving perfection. I just want to do the best I can with what I currently know.

Only a few people have ever come close to achieving perfection, but it requires a whole lifetime of hard work and dedication. It requires a whole lifetime of commitment and an accumulation of knowledge. One thing that I know for sure is that we must never stop learning, we must never give up, we must never surrender to mental laziness. We must never stop the learning process.

Most people are probably asking themselves, *'Why do I have to put myself in such a difficult situation? Is it necessary for me to go through all this trouble when I know deep inside that reaching perfection is an impossible task?'* It's not just about reaching perfection. It's about expanding our knowledge so that we can become better human beings. When we become a better person. We will be able to help others become better human beings as well. Furthermore, it's about knowing. It's about expanding our vision. It's about getting to know ourselves. Remember that knowledge will allow us to stay in control of every situation. Knowing ourselves and possessing the necessary knowledge will help us solve most of our problems. Knowledge is the key that will open the doors to happiness.

Remember, the more we know, the greater our confidence will be. We must familiarize ourselves with how our thoughts are processed and how they came to be.

We must understand that we will not be able to complete our long-life journey without first, knowing how to control our thoughts and actions. When our thoughts become crystal clear like a fine well-cut diamond and if we learn to master them. It's only then that we will be able to accomplish what we want.

We have the choice to make our journey exciting and fun or we can make our journey a painful experience. It's up to us on how we decide to handle it. Remember that we control our own destiny and that whoever we are as a person is the direct result of our own doing. We have no one else to blame but ourselves when we put ourselves in difficult situations.

I will try to guide you as much as I possibly can as we embark together on this long journey. Throughout this book, there will be an enormous amount of information and knowledge that you will be able to put into action for the long journey. I know that I'm going to repeat myself several times in this book, however, it's only by repetition that we will learn new things. We must remind ourselves that we need to learn something new every single day. It's a constant reminder on your part, it's a daily ritual that we must go through, but remember that at the end, all will be worth it because we will learn to master our thoughts and it's because we have accumulated enormous amounts of knowledge.

It's important to remember that whatever we do in life, whether, we are trying to expand our knowledge, or we are trying to get physically fit, we are not going to accomplish it by practicing it once in a while. We are not going to be physically fit if we only workout occasionally. we must be consistent, in other words, we must make it a daily routine because it's only by repetition that we will get the results that we want. Again, remember to practice, practice, and practice some more.

Using Our Knowledge to Help Others

Amazingly enough, most of us do not realize that we possess some tremendous abilities, for example, we possess the ability to help other people that are less fortunate, but how can we help others? We can help others by listening, we can help others, perhaps, not by giving them money, but by showing them the way, by showing them how to survive in any difficult situations, by giving them the importance, by giving them the acceptance, by given them the recognition and by given them the appreciation which they deserve, furthermore, this help should only be given to those people who actually want to be helped. What do I mean by this is that they must be willing to accept our help. When people work hard and they have done their job the right way, they deserve to be acknowledged.

Don't get me wrong, everybody needs help at one time or another, but some people don't know how to appreciate that help when they get it, instead, they think they deserve it, they think that they should be appreciated despite not working hard or doing a good job, they think they are entitled to everything. We should always help those people who deserve to be helped. There are many ways in which we can help others. We can help others by teaching them to like themselves, we can help them by teaching them that life can be hard, but at the same time, life can be beautiful, rewarding and wonderful when they learn to use their imagination and put it to work, these are only a few of the many ways in which we can help others in need. We must practice our good human relations with our families, friends and outside our homes, for example, on the streets with complete strangers, and at work.

We can use our knowledge to help ourselves and at the same time, we can reach out and help others in need. Helping others will give us a tremendous amount of satisfaction and it will bring us bigger rewards in the future, especially if we can make someone smile, even if it's only for a moment. We will feel a tremendous satisfaction knowing that we have made a difference in someone's lives. It's important to remember that the human mind has no limitations. The only limitations that we have are the ones that we place upon ourselves. Together, we can expand our awareness, creating a formidable team.

We must conduct ourselves with vision, passion, motivation, and most importantly, dedication. We have the ability and the power of our minds to be valued creators for ourselves and for others. Every person on the face of our planet has the same opportunity to help others. When we have the knowledge, we can do greater good for humanity. We must not let all that energy and power inside us go to waste. We must use it. We must put it to work for the good of humanity.

We must never forget about our courage, our brain power, and our abilities, and we must remember to be proud of ourselves for what we have accomplished so far. We must always hope for a better tomorrow because there will be new opportunities and new challenges coming our way. We must take advantage of every opportunity because we do not know how many more opportunities we might have left.

There will be plenty of new challenges in our future that we must learn to overcome but knowing that we can use our knowledge to our advantage is going to make those challenges that much easier to defect. We must also remember that any new changes we make in our lives will lead us to a better life, not only economically, but physically, and spiritually as well.

Furthermore, we must remember that any new changes we make to our lives or any new challenges that we might encounter is going to lead us to new knowledge and with new knowledge comes more knowledge, therefore, we must not ignore this new knowledge, we must always welcome all this new knowledge with open arms because new knowledge is going to make us stronger in every way.

Chapter Four

Searching for Happiness Part 1

How do we find that elusive happiness that we have been looking for so long? Happiness is the purpose of conscious life. Therefore, human consciousness is too valuable to fall into the death cycle of nature. Human life is supreme, and it must never die. We must not let the years take away the feelings of joy and love, for if we do, we are going to be left with emptiness within ourselves.

It's a fast and stressful world, where everything needs to be done fast, especially at work. Our jobs require us to do everything fast and accurate and consequently our lives become full of stressful situations. But somehow, we need to find time for relaxation, and I think that the only way to accomplish such a task is by re-structuring our lives and changing the way we think. Perhaps, we can start by working for a different company or switching careers or working part time if possible, there are a lot of changes that we can make to help us find happiness so that our lives will not be in disarray.

Is there anything else we can do to help us find happiness? Yes, there are plenty of things that we can do, for example, we can use some of our precious energy and redirect it towards finding happiness. By investing our time and energy, we will, eventually, find that elusive happiness that we have searching for so long. Remember that the true purpose of life is to be happy. In order to find happiness we need to start by making little changes to our lives, afterwards, we can use most of our time and energy on making sure that our dreams become a reality, whatever our dreams might be, we must not let them die. We must find true happiness even if it's partial happiness. We should make it our number one priority because when we are happy, our entire family will be happy as well, at least I hope so.

What about you, are you happy or are you miserable and unhappy? I think most of us at some point in our lives asked ourselves the same question before, I know I have. As you know, nothing we do in this life comes easy. We all must work hard for what we want, whether it's money, a career, or our own happiness.

Finding happiness is like everything else in life. We must work hard every single day in order to find it. If for some reason one cannot find total happiness, at the very least we can accomplish some degree of happiness. Nothing will come easy as we must put a lot of effort into it. Imagine if everything was effortlessly easy to accomplish, then life would probably be boring plus the fact that we wouldn't learn much of anything. Again, the whole purpose of life is to find happiness, to learn and grow as human beings and if along the way we make mistakes then so be it, we will learn from our mistakes, hopefully?

Let me ask you a question. Are you ready to find happiness? Are you ready to live a better life, a healthier life, a more fulfilling life, a life full of happiness, a life full of calmness and peace? We can achieve all this and much more, but only if this is what we really want, only if we have a strong desire to find happiness. Remember that the whole purpose of life is to be happy. However, we must make it happen ourselves. No one else is going to make it happen for us. People have their own lives to live and worry about, so it's our responsibility to try and find happiness for ourselves.

I know that as you are reading this chapter, you are wondering or better yet, you are asking yourself, how can I find happiness when all I have ever known is a life of misery, unhappiness, regrets, fear and worries? I know that at this moment in time it might seem like an impossible task for most people but believe me when I say to you that everything is possible. Remember that the best time to search for happiness is when all our thoughts are in order and there's no better time than now. I always tell myself, "If not now, then when?" Anyone can find or achieve happiness, but only if we are willing to try.

Always remember that happiness is just around the corner and if we really try to find it, we will find it, eventually. Most often than not we are not willing to find happiness, either because we don't know how, or we are afraid of failing and it's because in our minds all we can see is failure, and therefore, we will fail.

Remember that we are who we think we are. If you think you are a failure, then most likely, you are going to be a failure, on the other hand, if you think you are going to be successful, then most likely, you will be successful. We must never think about defects because once we do, we are going to lose ourselves, rather we should always think about being successful and happy all the time.

Again, we must never and under any circumstances think about defeat because when we think about defeat, then we are going to be defected quite easily. When we doubt ourselves, or we have nothing but doubt in our minds, we are already defected. Rather than thinking about defeats, we must think about winning instead of thinking about negative thoughts, we must think about positive thoughts. Here is what we should be thinking instead. We should be thinking about the things that we want and not the things that we don't want.

Remember that whatever we think about most, is what we will get in return. For example, if we think about getting sick, then we are going to get sick, but on the other hand if we think of ourselves as healthy and strong then we are going to feel healthy and strong. We must understand that it's the power of suggestion in action here. It's the law of attraction in action that will trigger our desire to be happy or unhappy because that is what we are thinking about the most. Furthermore, I must remind everyone that by simply wishing for something good to happen is not going to be enough. We are not going to get what we want out of nothing; we must help our wishes become reality by giving them a little help, in other words, we must go get what we want. We must use every available resource that we have in our arsenal to accomplish what we want. We could make it happen, but it's not by standing still, instead it's by putting our bodies in motion that we are going to accomplish what we want.

It's important to always think about the things that will make us happy, for example, positive and fulfilling things, calmness, peace, and positive energy instead of chaos, and negative energy. Positive energy will heal our souls and bodies, but negative energy will destroy them.

Searching for Happiness Part 2

Everyone is looking for something that is going to bring joy to their hearts, am I correct? Not a single person I ever knew, in my entire life, told me that they are looking for something that is going to make them miserable.

Some people know exactly what makes them happy, but for the rest of the population that is not always the case, maybe it's because they haven't figured out what makes them happy yet. Or perhaps, they simply haven't taken the time to think about it…until now.

Again, the true purpose of life is to find happiness, but unfortunately most people have no clue as to how to find that elusive happiness or how to achieve it. It has been a plague for humanity for thousands of years, so it must be reversed by those who wish to find happiness.

Now, as for those people who are wondering if there's the possibility of ever finding happiness, well, there are good news for them, finding happiness is not really that difficult, it's a matter of wanting to be happy, it's a matter of choice. It's a personal choice, and therefore, we cannot expect others to make that choice for us because they are too busy trying to find their own happiness. If we want to find happiness, we must make the choice to be happy on our own.

There are three important factors which must take place in order for us to achieve happiness. The first factor which needs to take place is a strong desire to be happy. The second factor is that: We must put some type of effort on our part. The third factor and perhaps the most important of them all, is that: we must remind ourselves every single day that we want to be happy because we deserve to be happy.

There's no special time of the day to remind ourselves that we want to be happy because any time and everywhere is a good time, however, the most important time of the day is in the morning, right after we wake up because our minds are in a state of calm and this in turn will set the tone for us for the rest of the day. It's important to remind ourselves that we want to be happy every single day and without hesitation. It' also important that we add this routines to the rest of our daily routines that we do on a day by day basis, for example, taking a shower, eating breakfast, or drinking our coffee. I have several daily routines that I do throughout the day. Adding one more routine to our daily lives is going to make all the difference in the world because our happiness should be our number one priority and it should be the number one routine for everyone and for many years to come.

Furthermore, what will happen if we fail to eat our breakfast and drink our coffee every morning? Well, most likely our minds and bodies will not function properly throughout the day, right? It's important to eat our breakfast and drink our coffee every single morning, but it's also important to remind ourselves that we deserved to be happy. Again, the best time to do ritual is when we are eating breakfast or drinking our coffee.

The following three things are key ingredients for a happy life, first, we must have the desire, then we must make the effort and do everything within our power to be happy, and finally, we must make it a daily routine. If we are missing any of these key ingredients from our lives, chances are that we are not going to find happiness.

There are two types of people in the world, those who know what makes them happy and those who don't. I think it's fair to say that at least fifty percent of the world population are not aware of the things that will make them happy. I also think that it's because they have not really taken the time to figure it out.

As for the rest of the population, they know what they want out of life, they know what makes them happy and they also know how to find happiness. The people who know how to find happiness are the ones that we should be imitating because they are the ones who are going to teach us how to find it.

Most of us are wondering who these people are and how they will help us? Well, the people I am talking about have the secret. They know what makes them happy. They know how to achieve a life full of happiness. The people I am talking about are not scientists, they are not doctors, and they are not necessarily rich. The people I am talking about are ordinary people...happy people who know that happiness comes from within. No matter what life throws at them they will not bend, they will stay true to themselves.

I personally have not met a whole lot of people with these qualities, however, I have met a few of these people before, and I must admit that you can tell right away that they are honest and happy people. I know most of you are probably wondering, but how can I tell who these people are? Well, believe me when I tell you that I know, I instantly know because I can see it in their face, I can see it in the way they walk, I can see it in the way they talk because their talk is gentle, calm, and peaceful, it seems to me that they have a halo around their bodies, they look so in peace and they act accordingly, also, it seems to me that nothing rattle their cages. When I see people who are happy, I think to myself, what a great honor to meet them because their happiness is contagious.

I learned many things from people who are happy just by observing how they conduct themselves. Sometimes we do not have to ask them anything to figure out that they are happy people. These are the type of people that we should be associating ourselves with because we can learn from them, we can learn how to be happy ourselves. Our entire life will change forever if we associate ourselves with happy people. We will instantly feel good about ourselves. We will feel a big change happening within ourselves when we talk to them.

We can all learn a thing or two from happy people, however, we must be willing to learn, we must always keep an open mind, and finally, we must be coachable. My advice to anyone who is looking for happiness is that we must take every opportunity to talk to as many happy people as possible because it's not often that we will have such an opportunity to meet genuine and happy people who will make us feel good about ourselves. Please try not to miss such an opportunity.

We can find happiness in many ways and in many places, we just need know where to look, for example, we can find happiness through other people, by talking to them by listening to them and by imitating them, but the most important thing to remember is that happiness comes within and that we don't always need to rely on other people in order to find happiness. We can find that elusive happiness that we have been looking for so long, but in order to find it, we must be willing to change our way of thinking, we need to find what makes us happy and eventually we will find it. Remember that it is only a matter of wanting to be happy, it is about having that burning desire to be happy. Finding out what makes us happy it's not that complicated, but we make it complicated, it should be a simple process.

Once again, if we want to accomplish happiness, then we must wake up every morning and we must decide right away if we want to be happy or miserable for the entire day. Remember that we only have two choices, so which one would you choose? It does not take a genius to figure this one out. Happiness is the logical choice to make. Remember that life is all about choices, so what type of choices are you going to make? Good choices or bad choices?

Sometimes we look for happiness in all the wrong places because we are so preoccupied with our thoughts that we fail to see that happiness is right in front of us, for example, the miracle of a smile from a child, especially or even a smile from a complete stranger can brighten our day. I do not know about other people, but for me, one thing is for sure, a smile from a child always brings happiness into my life. It gives me great joy. Whenever I encounter a happy person, whether it is an adult or a child it makes me forget about my own problems because their smile is the best medicine that anyone can take to cure their sadness.

We must remind ourselves to smile more often. In fact, we should smile every single day, every minute of every day. When we finally learn to smile on a consistent basis, everything we do in life will be that much more enjoyable. We should smile in the presence of our family, friends and yes, we can even smile in the presence of strangers. Smiles are powerful and contagious. Sometimes a smile does not have to come from someone else, it could be your very own inner smile. We all have an abundance of different feelings that will make us feel bad about ourselves, but this is what I do when I'm not feeling myself, when I'm feeling lonely, sad, when things are not going my way or when I'm frustrated. I think to myself. I need to smile more, and I do, on the inside, and that makes me feel good all over again. It is the best medicine for the soul. Always remember that happiness resides within us.

The Secret to Finding Happiness

It's not really a secret, per say, The secret to our happiness rests in our ability to know what makes us happy, however, when we don't have a clue as to what makes us happy, most likely we are going to be searching forever for those things which are going to help us to find happiness.

Another one of the secrets to finding happiness lies in our ability to enjoy, not only the big things that life has to offer us, but the little things as well. Life has a lot to offer us, so it's important that we use our time wisely, we must not waste our days on unproductive activities that will prevent us from finding happiness. We must remember that life is too short and too precious to be wasted on meaningless tasks.

We must not outrun ourselves, for if we do, we are going to end up regretting it for the rest of our lives. We do not want our lives to end up unfulfilled and full of regrets. Our current lifestyle is too fast and therefore, is of great importance that we remind ourselves to slow down a bit so that we can enjoy life to its fullest. Slowing down will allow us to find the time and to enjoy the things that make us happy the most, because as I said before, the real purpose in life is to find happiness. Remember that if we learn to slow down, we are going to be able to enjoy life to its fullest.

Can we really find joy in everything that we do? Realistically, yes we can, but it all depends on our state of mind, if our state of mind is low and in despair, then we will not find peace, joy and happiness, however, if we tune our minds into a higher frequency, then and only then, we will be able to enjoy all the little things as much as the bigger things that life has to offer us.

We must learn to find the value in everything. We must also leave something to be desired because it's the key to not dying of boredom. When we have everything that we desire, then there will be no more joy, there will be no more hope and our spirits will begin to die. It's important to keep our curiosity, our desires, and our hopes alive well into our old age.

Chapter Five

Our Feelings and Emotions Part 1

Most people don't know what the difference is between our feelings and emotions. In this chapter I will briefly attempt to describe the difference between the two. This is a complex topic so I will keep it short. It's not going to be an easy task; however, I will do my best. Scientists do not fully agree on what the difference is between our feelings and our emotions. Our feelings and emotions are interchangeable, in other words, they are closely related, but the big difference between the two is that our emotions are temporary, while our feelings are a manifestation of our emotions and it's because they are in a mental association with each other, in other words, our feelings is a reactions from our emotions. It's like a circle of confusion, but nevertheless, it leads me to believe that our emotions happen first.

We know now that our feelings will arise because of our emotions. For example, feelings of isolation, embarrassment, attraction, sadness, and grief will stay with us forever. Our feelings are the function or the power of perceiving by touch. It's a physical sensation. Physical sensations are not connected with sight, hearing, taste, or smell. Our emotions are felt inside our brain, and our feelings are based on our conclusions, judgments, opinions, and experiences. Feelings are the primary motives of human behavior.

Our feelings will develop from the information gathered by our brain. Our feelings can turn into action and it's there that we must be careful because we have good feelings, but we also have bad feelings. Our feelings must be understood because they define who we are as human beings. There's no denying that we are what we think. For example, when we think healthy thoughts, good things are bound to happen, however, when we think unhealthy thoughts, bad things are bound to happen as well. Bad feelings, who needs them? *Anyone*? I'm sure that I don't need them in my life, therefore, I will be tremendously happy to get rid of them forever. Bad feelings we want to get rid of.

Good feelings we want to keep around forever because good feelings will make us feel good.

Can we "feel" feelings? It's obvious that the human body, indeed, does feel our feelings. "We feel our feelings" when we feel disappointment, when we feel sad, when we feel anger, when we feel distress or when we feel panic attacks or anxiety. So yes, we can feel our feelings throughout our entire bodies. Most of us do not understand how our feelings work because we are lacking the knowledge and experience necessary to understand how our feelings evolve inside our brain. An important question suddenly crossed my mind; do we focus our energy on our feelings or on our behaviors, or both? It would be wise to focus our energy on our feelings first and then on our behaviors because if we know what we are feeling at any given time, then we will be able to control our behaviors.

If we try to figure out our behaviors first without having a good understanding of how we are feeling on the inside, then how are we supposed to know why we are behaving the way we are? how can we know if we are making the right decisions? Does this make sense? It does to me and perhaps I could be wrong. But it makes sense to me because our behaviors reflect our true feelings.

Sometimes we act accordingly to how we are feeling and that is not always such a good idea. We should never make any important decisions when we are experiencing negative feelings and emotions that we might regret later. We should only make important decisions when we have our feelings and emotions under control. I'm sure that most people have the capacity to keep their feelings and emotions under control, however, some people do not. I know I do. Most often than not we think about what we are about to do, but other times… not so much. Sometimes we get carried away and we act solely on impulse not knowing if we are making the right decision or not. We must remember that our behaviors come from the manifestation of our own feelings.

Let us go on a mission together and try to eradicate any negative feelings and emotions from our minds. Those negative feelings and emotions of anger and hate which have the potential to turn into anxiety.

As for our good feelings and emotions, the ones that will make us feel good all over again, for example, feelings that makes us feel as if we are worthy, the ones that make us fall in love, the ones that make us feel happy and content, the ones that make us feel warmth on the inside, the ones that makes us feel confident, important, satisfied, alive, wonderful, peaceful, comfortable, relax, loving, and warm. Those are the ones that we need to nourish, embrace, and hold on forever because those are the ones that will make our lives worth living for.

On an average day, we make hundreds of decisions which will affect our lives and the lives of those who we love, therefore, we are the ones that must decide if the decisions that we are about to make are good or bad decisions. It's at this time, when our brain is processing our feelings and emotions, but at the same time, we must decide whether we should put those feelings and emotions into action.

We must always question our motives for doing whatever we are about to do. We must ask ourselves if we are helping or hurting ourselves. We must make sure that we are not hurting others in the process as well. Whenever we decide to do something, we need to make sure that it's a decision which has been carefully thought out because if those decisions are wrong, then we might regret it later on, and perhaps for the rest of our lives. We do not want that burden in our consciousness. We must take control over our feelings and emotions, so that we can make the right choices in life. We must never forget that we are the ones who should be in total control and not our feelings and emotions. Our feelings and our emotions are not in control, we are.

Furthermore, we should never let our feelings and our emotions dictate what our actions should be. For example, most often than not, we go to the grocery store when we are feeling hungry, and therefore, our tendency is to buy food that we end up not eating. Maybe we will, but if we end up not eating that food, then most likely, it will end up being thrown away, and to me, that will be a waste of my money. We must never decide to buy or do things based on first impulse. For example, buying a new pair of shoes, a new jacket, or even a brand-new car, we must first ask ourselves, do I really need these things right now?

As human beings we normally buy things that we don't need. Furthermore, sometimes we do things without even thinking about it, and it's because that is our brain in action. I will attempt to explain how our human brains work in a different chapter.

Our Feelings and Emotions Part 2

We know now that our feelings and emotions are closely related, however, we must understand what the difference is between the two. Knowing the difference between our feelings and emotions is critical to our happiness because it's going to allow us to change our lives forever. Our emotions are physical and instinctive. Their purpose is to respond to specific stimuli. For example, when I'm walking alone in the middle of the forest when suddenly I'm face to face with a mountain lion, most likely, I'm going to be paralyzed by fear.

Human emotions can be measured by blood flow, brain activity, facial expressions, and stance. Our emotions can sometimes be intense, but they can also be brief. We need to understand that our emotions will affect our relationships with others in a good way, but they can also affect our relationships in a negative way, therefore, we need to keep our emotions under control. One important thing to remember is that our actions are initiated by our emotions. I believe that our emotional intelligence is more important than our IQ.

As I mention in the previous chapter, our feelings and emotions are somehow related to one other, they affect each other, either directly or indirectly, however, they are not the same. Our thoughts will normally trigger a feeling and a feeling will trigger a thought, so most of the time, our feelings are the direct result of our thoughts.

One thing that we know for sure is that our thoughts, feelings, and emotions will influence our behaviors. Furthermore, we must remind ourselves that we have negative and positive feelings, and we also have negative and positive thoughts, and depending on what type of feelings we are experiencing, whether those feelings are good or bad, they will influence our behavior. It's much easier to share our thoughts with someone than to share our feelings, normally, we share our thoughts with someone else, but we have a hard time sharing our true feelings. I hope that this shines a little bit of clarity, and I hope that this was enough for everyone who needed to understand what the difference was between our feelings and emotions.

We all have experienced some type of negative feelings in the past, for example, anxiety, fear, anger, and even depression. These types of negative feelings are normal among human beings. They are part of our daily lives. However, it doesn't mean that we must live with them twenty-four hours a day. These types of negative feelings will drain the energy from our minds and bodies completely leaving us feeling weak and sometimes in a depressive state of mind. These negative feelings can end up hurting us in many ways. But, from now on, there will be no more need to worry about them in excess. Because throughout this book, I will be talking about how we can overcome all those negative thoughts, feelings, and emotions which we might have inside us. All our negative feelings and emotions of anger, despair and rage will become almost extinct. They will become a thing of the past once we learn how to get rid of them, or how to keep them in check forever.

It's important for us to remember that we are never going to be able to completely get rid of every negative feelings and emotions that we experience because it's part of being human, they are part of who we are, they are part of the learning process, they are part of our lives and there's no way to get around them, however, we will be able to get rid of most negative feelings and emotions. But not all of them. Well, it all depends on the person. Some people will be able to eradicate most of them, but it will take a tremendous amount of self-control on their part.

Just so there's no misunderstanding on our part, we will be able to eradicate most of our old negative feelings and emotions and that is a fact, however, we will eventually acquire new ones, and whether they are feelings and emotions directed towards ourselves or others, the fact of the matter is that we will be vulnerable to new negative feelings and emotions. Again, we will be vulnerable to new negative thoughts and emotions, but if we stay on top of them, we will be able to eradicate them from our lives once again. So, remember that if we keep them in check, then we will be alright.

Now that we all understand that having negative feelings and emotions is part of being human. We can prepare ourselves for the battle. We will be able to defeat them a lot easier. We need to have those negative feelings and emotions because they will remind us that we are not perfect. What we need to understand here is that. We have the power to minimize our negative feelings and emotions by simply...and here it is...this is the secret... by simply turning the OFF switch. Yes! We need to have an off switch that we can turn off whenever we find ourselves experiencing any type of negative feelings or emotions. We already have an automatic internal switch ON, and it stay on twenty-four hour a day. It's our survival switch. It's what makes us stay safe in times of danger.

Now, let us talk about our OFF switch. It's obvious that our off switch is the most important of the two switches because the OFF switch is the one which is going to allow us to turn off our negative feelings and emotions. I know that it sounds ridiculous. I know that it sounds too simple, too good to be true, but that is what makes it work because it's effortlessly simple.

The OFF switch is an amazing tool that we can use whenever we are in distress. Everyone must trust me on this one; I know that it works because I use it all the time, in fact, I use it so much that it has become an automatic daily routine for me, it helps me to keep my negative feelings and emotions in check.

Remember that we have the option to turn OFF our switch immediately, right after we find ourselves experiencing some type of negative feelings or negative emotions. We must turn that switch OFF before we fall into the grasp of depression, fear, anger or even anxiety. We must turn OFF our switch and concentrate on re-directing our energy towards positive feelings and emotions rather than doing the opposite.

Our Feelings and Emotions Part 3

We already learned what the difference is between our feelings and emotion earlier in the chapter. However, I was thinking about our human emotions and I arrive at the conclusion that our human emotions come first, before our feelings and I will try to further explain why, you see, in nineteen ninety four my wife and I went on a cruise to the Caribbean, we already had the airline tickets to fly from California to Florida, but I was afraid of flying because of my anxiety, so instead I took the bus, and by the way, It took me seventy four hours to finally get to my destination, however something happened along the way, about two days into the trip, on one of the regular bus stops, I got out and decided to call my wife to let her know that I was doing good, by the way, she was still in San Jose, Ca. She was going to fly and meet me in Miami, anyway, as I was talking to her and for some unexplained reason, I got very emotional, I got teary eyes, I felt such an emotion running through my entire body that I could not swallow or talk, so if that is not an emotion, then I don't know what else and emotion could possibly be? You see, the fact that I was away from my family for more than two days and unable to talk to them and see them caused me to have an unexpected emotional response as soon as I heard my wife's voice.

We are all very different and unique people, we all have different personalities, each and one of us is unique in our own way, each one of us learns to cope with our own difficult situations in different ways, however we are all similar when it comes to our emotions, especially if it's a good feeling type of emotion. I have my own way of dealing with my emotions, for instant, I try to control my emotions by staying busy.

One of the ways in which I get rid of my stress, a difficult situation or my negative thoughts is by reading a book or by simply working on my book, furthermore, reading and writing will prevent me from going insane, and is something that I must do daily so that I can keep my sanity and my emotions in check. You see, when sadness invades my mind, or I feel a sense of hopelessness the best remedy for me is to pick up a book and read, and if I'm not reading, than writing will have the same effect on me as reading a good book. Reading a book or writing, along with photography is the food which feeds my soul, it's the best remedy for me because it makes me feel in a complete state of relaxation, it makes me feel alive again, it makes me feel at peace and it makes me feel like that I can accomplish many wonderful things.

Again, reading, writing and photography is one way for me to get rid of my negative thoughts, feelings, and emotions, as well as my fears, and anger. Yes, I do have all those thoughts, feelings, and emotions inside me, and so does everyone else, it's what makes us human. We must not be afraid of letting our guard down, we must learn to share our true feelings with others, but these feelings must be feelings of love, feelings of caring, feelings of compassion and feelings of understanding for others. We must never show our feelings of anger and hate towards others because they will eventually come back to us. Those feelings of anger and hate must be eradicated from our hearts forever.

Sometimes we worry in excess about everything. Not knowing, or not realizing that we cannot solve all the problems of the world by ourselves, especially because they are problems beyond our control, but nevertheless, we must try to do the best we can with what we have at the time, but without making our bodies sick. We don't need to torture ourselves and our family when trying to solve our problems or trying to solve someone else's problems. What we need to do here is...to try and control our emotions because when our emotions are in complete control. We can accomplish so much more than when our emotions are out of control. We must learn not to overreact when faced with a dilemma or some type of aggression from others. Our negative emotions must always be in check.

Our negative feelings and emotions will rob our bodies of precious energy which we need to fight off diseases. When we overload our nervous system, we will put our entire bodies under tremendous stress. Furthermore, when our feelings and emotions are not under control, they will affect our thinking, thereby making us acceptable to diseases which will make us sick or even kill us.

When our brain is healthy and our feelings, and emotions are under control, our bodies will respond by regulating all bodily functions, it will be ready to fight for us when needed. When we have good coping skills, our stress levels will be low, along with exercise, good nutrition, and plenty of sleep, our bodies will be ready to fight back against any diseases. We must focus our energy on future goals, rather than wasting it on negative thoughts and emotions.

It's always easier for someone to give up on their dreams and goals than to try to conquer their negative feelings and emotions. It's easier to focus on our past failures than to focus on our future goals because we don't know any better. We know what we know and that is it, but we must leave behind our old way of thinking and find new and exciting ways of doing things so that we can come up with new results, instead of the same old results. Sometimes we get stuck in a pool of quick sands and we don't know how to get out of it, so we stay there, and we stay there because we become too comfortable being there, we don't want to move because we are afraid that if we move, we might sink even further.

You see, if we focus on our failures most of the time, then our minds will help us in creating a way to make it happen because it's a human tendency to take the easy way out, it's the path of less resistance. From now on, we must take control of any negative feelings, thoughts, and emotions which we might have, we must take control of every situation, we must take total control of our lives because it's the only way in which we will excel and be successful in life.

It's not that complicated, but it will take some effort on our part. It will take perseverance, constant dedication, and reminder on our part. It's a learning process that everyone must go through. Once we learn to take control of our negative feelings, thoughts, and emotions, we undoubtedly going to feel like a brand-new person. We will become a new generation of super humans, and our old personalities will be no more.

In life, we have choices. We can choose positive and productive thinking or negative and unproductive thinking instead, which one do you rather choose? I know I would most definitely pick positive thinking one hundred percent of the time. Not that it will be easy, but then again. Nothing is ever easy in this life. We must work hard for everything that we want because nothing is given to us for free. Positive thinking is an ability that must be developed over time, it's not enough to think positive part of the time, it's a full-time job rather, therefore, we must treat it like a full-time job.

We must focus our energy on what is most important to us. We must focus on what we want and not on what we don't want, in other words, we must focus on the positive aspects of change versus the negative. We must learn to take control of every situation. We must take control of our thoughts today so that we can become motivated and start pursuing our goals. I know that it's not an easy thing getting motivated, but here is a good piece of advice for everyone. You must take a few minutes every single day so that you can learn to relax. You must close your eyes and think about nothing but relaxation, let everything negative in your life go. Feel the peace and calmness within yourself.

Now! Take nice and long breaths of fresh air into your lungs and at the same time think about yourself being at the beach on a not so hot and not so cold day. You are lying down on the warm white sands and you feel a gentle breeze going through your entire body. Oh, you feel so at peace, it's an amazing feeling. You must remind yourself to do these steps. If not every day, at least try and do it two or three times a week. Good luck to everyone.

Chapter Six

Getting to Know Our True Inner-Selves

Every chapter in this book is important because I talk about how we can acquire tremendous amounts of knowledge…knowledge that we didn't know we had before. Knowledge which is hidden within us. I will talk about a variety of ways which is going to allow us to find true happiness, but most importantly, I will talk about how we will be able to discover our true selves once again. Getting to know our true selves is the key which is going to open the doors and allow us to gain new knowledge and find true happiness.

The doors to our happiness have been closed for too long, but that was then, now we are going to learn to unlock the doors which have been closed for too long. If we want to find true happiness, then we must get to know ourselves first, in other words, we need to know who we are on the inside. We need to know what makes us happy or unhappy.

First, what is our inner self? Our inner selves is best described as our soul. Our inner self is a state of consciousness, in other words, it means that we are self-aware individuals of who we are. Moreover, it means that we are aware of everything that we are doing. Our inner self is linked to our personal values, for example, our thoughts, our beliefs, and our goals. Knowing our inner self is being aware of who we are as a person and what we stand for, not on the outside, but on the inside. Furthermore, to know oneself is to know what our expectations and our beliefs are. "I'm aware of who I am. I'm aware of what my values are and I'm aware of what I represent." What about you? Are you aware of who you are? Do you have a high level of self-awareness? Knowing our inner self is not something we can acquire in a day or two. It requires a life-long of search, dedication, and patience.

Our beliefs are what makes us who we are, however, it doesn't necessarily mean that we are the person that we were meant to be or the person that we want to become. Finding out our true-inner selves. Our identity and our true personality is something that we need to discover for ourselves over time and without any interference from others.

We all have different identities, for example, we can be a husband, a father, a son, or a friend. Each of these identities are extensions of who we are but none of these extensions will describe who we really are on the inside. If we want to discover our true selves, our true- identities, then we must become self-aware of who we want to be in the future. We must develop our own true personality and without being influenced by outside forces. It's important that we don't get cut up in the excitement or get cut up in what other people might say about us because some people will say things which are untrue.

Most people are afraid to speak the truth and it's because they haven't found their true selves or their true identity yet. The main reasons as to why people behave badly is because they are looking for attention and recognition from others, but whatever the case might be, it will make more sense to speak with the truth.

We must be careful. We must use our own judgment when trying to determine if people are telling us the truth. We must keep in mind that honest people will speak with the truth, (well, most of the time) and they will back it up one hundred percent. We must listen to our inner-self because our inner-self knows what is best for us. Our inner self will never let us down. Our inner self is the only person that we can always trust.

Again, knowing our true inner self comes from having the self-awareness of everything that we are doing. Everything that is happening within ourselves and our surroundings, in other words, our inner self is always aware of everything that we are doing at any given moment. To know oneself is to know what our goals, values, expectations, and beliefs are. Most often than not "I'm aware of who I am." I'm aware of what my values are and I'm aware of what I represent." It would be such an amazing accomplishment, if everyone had the awareness of who they really are, however, few people have that level of self-awareness. What about you? Do you have a high level of self-awareness of who you truly are? Finding out who we truly are as a person is not something we can acquire in a day or two, it requires time, search, dedication, knowledge, and patience.

We have many identities but none of them is going to describe who we really are on the inside until we find out our real identity, the one that will define our true personality.

One of the first things that we need to do, if, we want to accomplish our goals is to believe in ourselves, regardless of what is happening with our surroundings.

Again, this chapter is about finding out who we really are as a person. It's about getting to know our true selves, it's about continuing our education beyond the High School years, it's about finding our true identity and it's about finding harmony within ourselves and the universe.

Knowing our true-inner-selves is perhaps, one of the most important things that any human being can ever accomplish in their lifetime. As you may know by now, from the time of our infancy, we start to develop our own identity, but somewhere along the way, we lost it and once that happens it's almost impossible to find ourselves again. But why do we lose our identity? Well, the answer to that question is amazingly simple. We lose our identity or we lose our true selves because we use most of our time and energy on meaningless tasks or on helping other people, but don't get me wrong, helping others is a good thing, however, when this happens, we stop thinking about ourselves. We passed on the opportunity to get to know ourselves further, we forget who we are as a person, basically, we stop loving ourselves, we forget about our own needs because we put other people's needs before ours.

When we are first born, we come into this world with nothing more than our whole future in front of us. We are not born rich, well, it's true for most people, however, some people are born rich, but it's only money and not wisdom, but nevertheless, we come into this world with nothing. The real fun begins later in life or as we grow up. It's at this time when we will be able to grow in wisdom, and discover new things that we are, either going to like or dislike. Furthermore, as we continue to learn new things, we will acquire new wisdom. We will learn many valuable lessons such as learning the value of money and what it can buy. We will slowly gain valuable knowledge which is going to help us to better understand ourselves and help us to discover who we really are.

Is there a time when we stop learning? Well, yes and no, and "I will explain why." Our first eighteen years of our existence are some of the most important and exciting years of our lives. It is a time when we go to school. It is a time when we try to learn as much as possible, it is a time when we start to further develop our own identity, it is a time when we begin to figure out what type of person we will become in the future, it is a time when we begin to know what we want to do for the rest of our lives, it is a time when we will find out what we like or dislike, it is a time when we are trying to figure out what our values are, it is a time when we start to develop our own true character and finally, it is a time when we will learn some valuable knowledge.

After we are done with High School, our lives become more complicated because some of us will move on to college. Others will find a job and the rest of us will find the love of our lives and get married. In a perfect world, and if I had the opportunity, I would choose to go to college first, then I would try to find the love of my life, then I would get married and eventually have kids.

After high school we think that we have our future all figure out but unfortunately life doesn't always take us in the direction that we had planned because as we begin our new life, things will get a lot more complicated and as a consequence, we will start losing track of some of the most important things in our lives, we will slowly star to lose our true selves, or our true identity

Again, after the High School years, we start to lose our true selves. We lose our identity and eventually we lose our way. We lose our way and our identity because of several reasons: For example, we become enamored with money, power and sometimes even fame. Our desire to acquire riches becomes overpowering, all we can think about is making as much money as possible and consequently, we will end up losing our way. When our thoughts are only directed towards our jobs, making other people happy and making money, and because of that, our lives will eventually become stale and boring.

It's a fact of life that most of us will never be satisfied with what we have. We always want more and that can be a good thing, however, we must never lose sight of the most important things in our lives, the things that will make us happy. For example, we must never stop the learning process because we need to continue to explore new things. We need to continue to educate ourselves. We need to continue our self-exploration so that we can continue to discover our true identities.

Rediscovering my true self is one of the greatest things that ever happened to me because there's no greater feeling or joy in the world than to be able to feel alive again. I rediscovered my passion for life again. I rediscovered that I could become a better man, a better husband, a better father, a better friend, and a better son. By becoming a better man, I will be able to make a difference in our society. By becoming a better man, I will be able to make our world a better place.

I can also become a better man by sharing some of my knowledge with others.

It's been a long time since I rediscovered my true and sincere love toward my fellow man and woman; in fact, I always had this burning desire to show other people my true love for them. It's unfortunately that sometimes we lose our way and we end up losing the desire to show others our love for them, furthermore, sometimes we are too preoccupied with our own thoughts that we forget to show our love true for humanity. We must never fall into despair but if we do, we must remember that we are very capable of rediscovering our true selves once again.

I have lost my true self or my identity many times before and I'm sure it won't be the last one, but I know that I can always make a comeback, because I'm a very determined and capable individual.

When we are in tune with ourselves and the universe, we will discover a whole new world never envisioned before. We will discover that there's no greater value in the world than to know that there is hope for humanity. We need to remember never to lose our hope no matter how bad things might get because without hope our lives will have no meaning. When we are in tune with ourselves and the universe, we will no longer need to live our lives in fear of the unknown. We will never have to feel alone in this world again, we are never going to feel hopelessly and unable to reach our goals, no longer we will feel unable to help others in achieving their own goals either.

I rediscover that we can all be value creators by contributing to society in many ways. I rediscover that we can contribute in small ways and we can contribute in big ways, I rediscover that we can achieve and experience our full potential through the integration of our minds. I rediscovered that we could use our human abilities to help ourselves and to help others less fortunate. I also, rediscover that nothing can stop us from achieving our goals, well, that is if we are willing to combine our knowledge and work as a team. We will accomplish bigger, and better things when we work together and not against each other.

I'm also thankful for being able to rediscover the inner child inside me, the child that was hidden for too long. Why is it so important for us to rediscover our inner child again? Well, because as adults we forget to have fun. We forget that we need to let our inner child come out, play, and have fun. Let's not forget that as adults, we must try to be happy, after all, the whole purpose of life is to find happiness.

I honestly think that I'm in a good place right now because I learn to know myself well, however, I'm not going to say that I am a perfect human being because there are times when I feel that I'm going backwards instead of moving forward, but I also know that I will rebound right back because I'm consciously aware of my situation, I know that I will be able to overcome most of my challenges that life throws at me.

How about you? How well do you know yourself, and why is it important to get to know yourself? Are you in touch with your inner wisdom? Do you know what kind of values and beliefs you possess? Are you honest with yourself and others? What about love? Are you capable of loving yourself and others as well? Are you in total control of your thoughts, values and beliefs or they are in a constant spiral and disarray? Are your thoughts, values, and beliefs resistance to social pressure? What are some of the things that matters the most to you? What are some of the things that will make you feel alive? Oh boy! These are a lot of questions, but believe me, there are more questions that you need to ask yourself in order to get to know yourself.

Asking yourself these questions is necessary because it will help you to understand who you really are as a person, now and in the future. Furthermore, there is one other important question that you must ask yourself, "Do I have confidence in my abilities?" You must know that building your self-confidence is going to take time because it's a long process. When you don't have confidence in yourself, other people are going to notice, and in turn, they will not have confidence in you either. You need to always know what you want out of life. You must always have confidence in yourself and you must always be assertive in everything that you do.

You must always have confidence in your abilities, especially when making important decisions that will impact your entire life. Yes, you will learn to have confidence in your abilities, In fact, if you must make this your number one priority, and you must have confidence in yourself and your abilities, it's only then that you will be successful in everything that you do in the future. Remember that you need to think as yourself as a well-rounded and confident individual who knows what it wants out of life.

Furthermore, you must ask yourself, "What are some of the things that makes me feel happy or upset?" I believe that most people have a good idea of some of the things which makes them happy or unhappy, but just in case you are not aware, I want you to know that you must take the time to figure out what those things are…the ones that make you, either feel good or feel bad on the inside. After you find out what makes you happy or miserable, you must, and I will repeat it again, you must stop doing those things which is going to make your life miserable and instead, you need to do more of the things that will make you feel happy.

What about your job, do you enjoy what you are doing? If you like what you are doing and if you are happy then there is nothing more for you to do, other than to continue doing what you are doing. Now! If you don't like your current job and you are miserable doing what you are doing right now, then it's time for you to make a change. It's time for you to redefine your career. Remember that you deserve to be happy instead of miserable.

Sometimes staying in your current job might be the only choice you have at this time and if that is the case, why not try to enjoy it anyway. Remember that time is precious, and it must not be wasted on something that you don't enjoy doing. At the very least, you can try to enjoy your job a little bit more until you can find another job or maybe you can switch careers, if possible. Always remember that you have other options and that nothing is written on stone. You don't have to be stuck in one place forever, also, remember that any changes you make to your way of life it's always going to be a good thing. Always thrive to do the things that you really love to do rather than the ones that you dislike.

You must believe in yourself, and you must constantly remind yourself that you will accomplish anything that you want. Always tell yourself: Yes, I can because I'm a capable individual. I can accomplish anything that I want and much more if that is my desire. Remember that everything begins with a desire and anything that you desire will become a reality, but you must try your best to make a reality. Keep in mind that everything in this life requires some type of effort because without it, not much is going to be accomplished, unless it's by mere coincidence or a stroke of good luck.

Have you ever thought about how you want people to perceive you as, and why is it important for you? Often people will have a perception of who you are as a person by the way you act. Your actions are always going to speak louder than your words because your words are just words, but your actions will live up to your words. Your actions will be more revealing of your true character because it will take a lot more effort on your part to start something and finish it, than to say things or make promises that have no merit. Always let your actions speak for themselves, rather than your words. Remember that you have the right to fight for what you want. You have the right to fight for what you stand for and you have the right to fight for your beliefs, but you must remember to always conduct yourself with honesty.

What is most important to you, having plenty of money? Being surrounded by family and friends that you love? Being healthy? Or perhaps all these things are equally important to you and that is perfectly fine. It's not about being selfish, instead, it's about being happy. Having plenty of money is important to everybody; however, it's not the most important thing in this world. Sure, it's nice to have money because it gives us more freedom but believe me when I say that I rather have less money and more love from my family. My friends and other people. Why? Because it makes me feel good on the inside and it makes me feel happy when the people that I love are happy as well.

Having my health is also more important to me than having tons of money, but why is that? Well, because when sickness strikes our bodies, the last thing we will think about is money, because in that precise moment in time. Money becomes secondary and all we want is to be healthy once again.

Knowing who we are as a person and knowing what we want out of life is going to bring us many big rewards because when we express who we really are and we know what we really want, we will be able to accomplish a lot more. We will feel much happier and content when we feel a sense of belonging, when are able to make better decisions for ourselves, when we have better self-control, when have more patience, when we have more tolerance and understanding for other people's needs.

We must always try to be the person that we were meant to be and not the person that everyone else wants us to be. We should always try to be a happy person. A person with no inner conflicts, a person that knows what they want and knows themselves very well. When we get to truly know ourselves, we will feel more alive than ever before, also, our life will be more rewarding.

Our values that we have right now will play an important role in our success or in our failures. If we are not sure what our values are, then we need to start re-evaluating those values and without further delay because there's no better time than present to change those values. We must decide what our values will be now and, in the future, and I'm hoping that we will make a wise decision and choose some good values. Now! When I say good values, I meant uncompromised values, with a solid reputation of trustworthiness and honesty.

We must remind ourselves that, it's not the person who has the most money; the most brain power, the most skills and the most fun out of life who will be the happiest or the most successful person on the face of the planet, rather, it's a combination of those things that will make us happy. Furthermore, the person who learns to develop their own personalities are the ones who will be the most successful, in dealing with others. If we want to be successful at dealing with other people or dealing with difficult situations, we need to understand ourselves better. Understanding who we are and knowing ourselves better is going to also help us to understand other people better.

When we finally know ourselves, we will be able to make better decisions. We intuitively will know which things make us happy or unhappy the most. Every single day that passes by, I remind myself that I need to do the things that will make me happy and not the things which are going to make me unhappy.

We need to remind ourselves that it's not enough knowing what things will make us happy, we must go out and do those things because we don't want to be self-satisfied with what we have accomplished thus far.

I know myself very well and I also know what things I should be doing in order to find true happiness, but sometimes no matter how hard I try, I come up short. However, I always try to do my best. There's two things which are especially important in my life, and that is family and almost nothing else will come first because without the love. The support from our families and friends, we will be nothing more than an empty soul and the second is: piece of mind, but why is it so important to have piece of mind? Well, because having some piece of mind is going to help me to relax and that in turn is going to allow me to concentrate and think clearly, in other words, it's going to allow me to do the things that I need to do… the things that will make me happy.

It's of great importance that we learn to know ourselves and know exactly what is going to make us happy and bring joy to our hearts, because it's only then that we will be able to move more rapidly towards achieving our goals. We must never forget about the things that will make us happy, whether it's a good paying job that we love to do or having a loving family that loves us, or perhaps both. Remember that we can accomplish anything that we want; however, we must do our best to accomplish it.

Always be prepared for the unexpected and never be afraid to turn the corner because we never know what we will find around that corner. Remember that in order to find the answers we are looking for, we must ask ourselves the following questions: Who, why, what, when, where, and how. Asking ourselves these questions is going to help us find the answers we are looking for.

We need to consistently ask ourselves as many questions as possible whenever we are about to do a task, and it doesn't matter what task it is. Asking ourselves as many questions as possible is going to prevent us from making costly mistakes. Consistency is going to allow us to do a better job and is going to help us to better understand ourselves.

Moving on, we must understand one important factor when we are searching for our happiness and that is that we are never going to find total happiness. We will come close but we cannot be happy all the time and there is a perfectly good explanation as to why we can't always be one hundred percent happy and it's because from time to time, we will forget to do the things that will make us happy and bring joy to our hearts. I know for a fact that when we do our absolute best, we will be able to accomplish, if not total happiness, at the very least, we will find some happiness. Furthermore, we cannot be happy all the time unless... we learn to love and know ourselves first. Learning to love and know ourselves is undoubtedly the most important factor when trying to achieve total happiness.

I believe that the number one reason as to why people can't find peace and happiness is because they are not happy with their current jobs. It's an obstacle which is preventing them from finding that elusive happiness which is missing from their lives. But why is that? Well, it's actually very simple, we spend the majority of our precious time doing our jobs and at the end of the day there isn't much time left for anything else and on top of that, we are miserable doing a job that we don't enjoy. It's important to remember that when we don't like our jobs, our happiness is going to suffer tremendously and it's at this time in our lives that we must make a decision, but we must make it fast, we must decide if are going to continue and stay where we are, in other words, we can stay where we are and continue to be miserable and self-complacent or we can do something about our current situation.

One of the things that will make us happy is knowing that we are financially secure for the rest of our lives, but unfortunately, that is not always the case for most people. In fact, seventy percent of the world population lives in poverty. If having a good paying job is important to you. A job that you really love to do, a job that you are crazy about, a job that when waking up in the morning will make your face light up of joy, then you must keep on doing what you are doing, however, if you are not happy with your current job, then you must retrain yourself. You must try harder and find the job that you always wanted, a job that it' going to make you happy for the rest of your life. If we want to better ourselves, then it's important that we make a few sacrifices along the way, in other words, we need to switch careers. Never forget that switching careers is going to open new doors to a better future for us. We must keep in mind that not too many people on the planet is able to have a good paying job… a job they are crazy about.

One thing that we must never do is to fall into despair because there's always a solution for everything. For example, if we don't like our current jobs, then we need re-train ourselves. We must make the time, go to school, and learn a new career. I know it's easier said than done, but nevertheless, it must be done. We must make time; we must make the sacrifice because nobody else is going to do it for us, we are the ones who need to decide if we want those changes in our lives. Millions of people around the world are retraining themselves. So why not us, why not now?

Again, we must find something that we love to do, something which is going to make us, and our family happy, but in order to accomplish that is by knowing exactly what we want to do for the rest of our lives. Perhaps we want to be a professional athlete, a scientist, a biologist, an artist, a photographer, a musician, an electrician, or an engineer? There are plenty of short careers that we can learn in little time. These short careers are probably our best option because it only requires anywhere from six months to a year, but honestly, six months to a year is not an exceptionally long time compared to the rest of our lives. It's all going to be worth it because at the end, when we are all done. We will feel much better about ourselves; we will feel happier, we will feel satisfied and we will feel content with ourselves because we are finally going to do a job that we really love to do.

Imagine how happy we will feel knowing that we are finally getting to know ourselves. We are finally going to do the things that will make us happy. We must stop wasting the little precious time that we have. We must stop procrastinating or make excuses for ourselves and just go out and do it. Now! I'm going to give you a few examples of the different types of short careers that are available out there. For example, air conditioning repair, Appliance Repair, Plumbing, Carpet Installation, Sales and Computer Repair. All these jobs can be very lucrative jobs. We must decide for ourselves what is going to take for us to finally be happy.

The main reason as to why many people are so unhappy with their current life situation is because most of them have no clue what type of work they want to do. They don't know what will make them happy and it's because they haven't taken the time to sit down and evaluate their situation.

Learning to Love Ourselves

Really? Do we really need to learn to love ourselves? Isn't that being selfish on our part? No is not! And I will explain why. Most people probably think that loving ourselves is a selfish act on our part, but we couldn't be more wrong because if we think about it for a moment, we will find out that loving ourselves first is the key which is going to open the doors and enable us to love other people as well. Now! The question is: Are we going to love ourselves enough? And if so, are we going to be able to love others as much as we love ourselves? That is why it's so important for us to know how much we love ourselves and why? It's obvious to me that most of the time we don't love ourselves enough and I'm sure that it's because we don't fully understand ourselves very well. We don't know who we really are, we don't know what we like or dislike, in other words, we don't know what makes us happy, and it's because our state of mind is not on a high level of self-awareness.

It's obvious that if we don't know how to love ourselves, then we won't be able to love others in return, but on the other hand, if we truly love ourselves enough, then we will have the capacity to love others with the same amount of love that we have for ourselves. Learning to love ourselves first is a must if we are ever going to learn to love others.

Jesus once said that we must love our neighbors as we love ourselves, wow! Those words are powerful, and they make sense to me, but just so we are all on the same page, Jesus never actually said love yourself first. He said love others as you love yourself, he assumed that we already love ourselves. We are always looking for something new and exciting to do, something which is going to make us happy, but unfortunately, most of us don't know that happiness comes from within and if we are ever going to find true happiness, we will have to learn to love ourselves first. Believe me when I say that loving ourselves first, it's not a sin; as a matter of fact, when we love ourselves first, we will be well prepared to show our love for others. We must learn to love ourselves first, then, and only then, we will be able to show others our true love for them.

We should not feel bad about loving ourselves first because it's not about being selfish. It's not about being arrogant or self-centered, instead, it's about feeling good on the inside. It's about knowing ourselves. It's about finding true happiness. It's about living in harmony within ourselves and the universe.

We must remember that there's only one purpose in life and that is to find happiness, therefore, we must do everything in our power to find it, but we must accomplish it without being selfish on our part. We must never overstep our boundaries and make other people suffer in our quest to find our very own happiness because that would be wrong. It will be selfish and unproductive on our part. We must learn to love ourselves. We must always be proud of ourselves. We must be proud of everything we do. We must be proud of everything that we have accomplished in our life. Furthermore, we must lift our heads up high when we walk because other people will notice, they will notice that we love ourselves, they will notice that we love life itself, they will notice that we are proud individuals and they will notice that we are in total control of our life.

Helping and loving others will help us to love ourselves even more. I know I feel a tremendous amount of joy when I'm able to help others to help themselves because it makes me feel good and warm on the inside. Sharing whatever I have (as far as monetary value) or sharing some of my knowledge will bring me great satisfaction, plus the fact that it makes me feel as if I have accomplished something meaningful in my life. Try it, I can assure that you will like it, and at the same time, it's going to make you feel that you truly have a purpose in life. Helping others will lift our spirits up tremendously because when we do something good for someone else, our spirits will feel in peace and harmony with the universe, and that is when we will finally know that we are indeed capable of loving ourselves and love others as well.

Another thing which we can do to help us love ourselves is to (and it's my personal opinion) keep our bodies in good physical condition because believe it or not, it will to allow us to feel good about ourselves and that in turn is going to allow us to love ourselves a little bit more. Really? How is keeping our bodies in good physical conditions is going to help us to love ourselves? Well, because when we are physically healthy, we will feel better about ourselves. We need to give our bodies the exercise which it needs, well, that is if we want to feel good overall. Not only do we need to feel good on the inside, but we need to feel good on the outside as well. If we want our bodies to feel good and stay physically strong for many years to come, we need to exercise on a consistent basis.

Never forget what happens when we are not physically fit. We tend to drag our feet all day long and it's because we are feeling tired, especially at the end of the day, when there is no energy left in our bodies to do other tasks. When we don't exercise and we don't take a shower to help us re-energize our bodies, we will be feeling miserable throughout the day and that is not going to help us to love ourselves.

It's not in our best interest to feel lethargic all day long, and I'm sure that we all feel that way from time to time. Normally I don't feel good about myself when I'm feeling tired and unable to do much of anything. I guess I'm a clean freak because I also don't feel relaxed when my car isn't washed or clean on the inside. My philosophy is that I must feel good in order to be able to love myself. Remember that when we feel good and we look good, then we will be able to love ourselves even more. Personally, I feel good after I'm done exercising, sure, I will feel tired afterwards, but you know what? After taking a shower, getting dressed and combing my hair I will feel relaxed and rejuvenated, in other words, I will feel as if I was worth a million dollars. I know for a fact that it takes a lot of self-discipline to do the things that we need to do in order to keep us healthy and strong but we must remember that there will be no rewards without pain, in other words, if we risk little our rewards will be little. We must try everything in our power to find true love within ourselves, but we can only accomplish it by doing the things that will make us happy instead of miserable.

There are plenty of things that we can do that will help us to feel good throughout the day. For instance, when we wake up in the morning, we need to tell ourselves, "Today I decided to love myself and love others as well. Today is going to be a beautiful day full of excitement, even though it's gloomy, cloudy and rainy outside." We must make it a habit to remind ourselves that we deserve to be happy every single day of our lives. Furthermore, it's important for us to remind ourselves to be grateful for all the things that we currently have. We also need to get excited about what the future is going to bring us. We must do our best to stay upbeat and positive, no matter what happens in our lives because staying positive throughout the day will prevent us from feeling down and depressed. We don't want to be in a negative mode. We don't want to be upset and we don't want to be in a depressed state of mind because if we do, then we won't be able to be productive and we won't be able to love ourselves because of the way we are feeling.

I must remind everyone to stay calm and positive throughout the day and don't try to do too many things at one time because doing so will wear us down mentally and physically and it's something that we are not going to enjoy. Nobody likes to be unhappy, not even for a moment.

We must try to accomplish as many tasks as possible but without getting frustrated and without getting overwhelmed. I done exactly that in the past, and as a consequence, I develop a tremendous amount of anxiety, so I decided to write myself a daily list of things to do and I did that for many years, but I must admit that I'm no longer writing myself such list because I became really good at it that I don't need to do it anymore. Nowadays everything becomes natural for me because I have learned to trust myself. I have learned to trust my instincts and my instincts will tell me what to do, when to do it, and how fast I should do it.

The list of things to do which I wrote for myself worked wonderfully for me because it allow my mind to be in a state of calmness most of the time. It was an amazing experience. A list of things to do can also do wonders for you too. Again, I'm no longer have the need to write myself a list of things to do because I'm always aware of what I need to do on a day-by-day basis. Only occasionally do I need to write a list of the things that I want to accomplish throughout the day. Furthermore, I write a list of things which I want to accomplish in the not so far future, but that is only because I don't want to forget.

Before I implemented my list of things to do, my life was chaotic and full of frustration and anxiety, but nowadays, I no longer get frustrated' I no longer have that anxiety which I use to have. Making a list of things to do is one of the best things that we can do because it's going to help us alleviate some or most of our stresses. We must use this system until we can regain our confidence or until we learn to trust ourselves to do the right thing at the right time.

My advice to everyone who is willing to make a list of things to do is to remember that if you don't accomplish everything on your list, then so what? Who cares? Remember that tomorrow is going to be a brand-new day which is going to allow us to start fresh and perhaps we will finish doing the things that we didn't finish the previous day.

Writing ourselves a list of things to do is important because it will give us the power to remain calm; it will allow us to breathe in slowly throughout the day. If we can accomplish such a task, then we won't have to stress ourselves so much and we will be able to love ourselves that much more.

Finding Harmony Within Ourselves

What is harmony and how do find it? Harmony is a state of mind in which we are in tune within ourselves and the universe. In other words, the mind, body, and soul must be in total balance. We must be conscious of everything that we do and not just on the inside but on the outside as well. When we are in total harmony within ourselves and the universe, we will find peace and happiness. It sounds easy, doesn't it? But really, how do we find harmony within ourselves? Finding harmony within ourselves is a difficult thing to accomplish by most people because it require a tremendous amount of self-discipline on our part.

Everyone know that life can be chaotic most of the time, but if we are to find peace and harmony in our lives then we must learn to simplify our lives. Believe it or not, simplifying our lives is going to help us to create an inner and outer well-being that will give our lives harmony and balance.

It's not an easy thing finding harmony and peace within ourselves, but why is that? Well, as human beings, we are notorious for worrying too much. We are forever worrying about everything. We worry about the past, the present and the future. Furthermore, we are constantly overstressing burning out our minds and bodies to the point of exhaustion. Furthermore, we must remind ourselves constantly not to live our lives in the past and stop thinking too far into the future because doing so is going to drain most of our precious energy, instead, we should be using that energy on living our lives in the present time. We must remind ourselves that we gain nothing (well, maybe stress, and anxiety) when we worry about the past or the future.

Life has many uncertainties, but we must not waste our precious energy worrying about those things, instead, we need to use our energy on more meaningful things, for example, on finding peace, harmony, and happiness within ourselves and the universe.

The first thing that we need to do if we want to find peace, harmony, and happiness, within ourselves is to get rid of our worries. Getting rid of our worries it's going to help us to think clearly and accurately because that is when we will be at our best. That is when we will be able to make good sound decisions. Again, we must stop worrying so much about life difficulties and unforeseen events or we will lose ourselves forever. You see, once we find that elusive harmony which has been missing from our lives for so long, we are going to discover an amazing and wonderful inner peace. Once we accomplish inner peace, we are going to be able to discover new and exciting things. For example, we will be able to do the things that will make us happy instead of miserable. Things that will stimulate our senses, things that will bring joy to our hearts.

I cannot emphasize enough about how important it is for everyone, (including me) to start making changes to their current way of life, and yes, we must start making those changes as soon as possible. We must not wait till tomorrow; we need to start right now before it's too late. Again, we possess a tremendous ability to change our way of life if we so desire. We must believe in ourselves. We must believe in our abilities and we must put those abilities to work for us and not against us. We must learn to cope with adversity, and at the same time, we must not overreact to adversity.

There are three important factors that we must keep in mind when we are trying to accomplish harmony, happiness, and peace within ourselves: First, we must have the desire. Secondly, we must set goals for ourselves. Thirdly, we must follow with action. Most people have the desire to make a change in their lives, but they don't know how to do it. They start something, but they never finish it, they give up when things get difficult. Remember that giving up is easier than to keep moving forward because it's the path of least resistance.

Again, we must have the burning desire and the passion to pursue our dreams and our goals because without the desire and the passion there will be no success. Sometimes having the desire and the passion is not enough, we also need to follow through with action on our part, we shouldn't quit until we accomplish what we want. We must never give up just because we encounter a bump on the road. Success will become easier when we have faith in ourselves and our abilities. Furthermore, we need to have faith and trust in other people as well but remember that we must be careful who we trust, not everyone is to be trusted.

Whether we realized or not, it seems to me that we are forever searching for something that we can do to make our lives more meaningful and satisfying, but for some unexplained reason we can't seem to find it. What is the number one reason as to why we can't seem to find happiness? Well, maybe we have been looking in all the wrong places? We must start looking in the right places for those things that will make our lives more meaningful and that place is inside ourselves.

In life, we only have two choices, we can continue to pursue a life of pleasurable things that will bring us temporary joy, or we can pursue a life of harmony. Peace, and happiness.

Again, remember that we are forever searching for happiness, but if are ever going to find it, then we must find harmony with oneself and the universe first. Know that once we find harmony within ourselves, we will be able to put our thoughts in order because we will be less anxious and less stressed when things go wrong. Remember that we must create positive images of ourselves instead of negative images. Positive images will help us when in need of solving difficult situations. Positive images will help us build and boost our confidence. Negative images will destroy our confidence and our abilities.

We must not let our unhealthy emotions such as: rage. Anger, depression, or anxiety enter our minds, instead, we should learn to distract ourselves with suitable distractions from anxious moments. For example, by redirecting our attention and energy tours rational thoughts and beliefs, instead of irrational ones. Remember that we need to replace our damaging thoughts and beliefs with images of total relaxation if we want to find harmony and happiness.

Oh! Just one more thing...don't make too many unrealistic demands for yourself. Instead, start with one or two and once you accomplish those demands, you will be able to move to other more demanding goals with a lot more confidence. For those people who want to be successful in life or want to be successful at anything, you must give up your unrealistic demands and create a more realistic one at first. We must learn to deal with our demands one at a time because it's going to help us to build our confidence. Changing our demands to preferences it's a wiser decision on our part because it's going to be more manageable and realistic.

Do One Thing at a Time and Do it Right

I have a simple philosophy as far as doing certain tasks, and that is to do one thing at a time and do it right the first time, and it shouldn't matter if we are getting paid for doing it or not, maybe we are just helping a family member or helping a friend for free, regardless, we must try our best to do a good job and without cutting corners. When a family member or a friend asks for our help whether they are going to paint their house or any other help they might need, we are not going to do a croppy or messy job just because it's not our house? Absolutely not! We must be willing to put our best effort into it and do a good job. We must never go through the motions and pretend we are doing a good job.

I believe that most people want to do things right the first time, at least most of the time, however, not everyone is going to be successful because some people might be thinking that whatever they are doing, they are doing it right, but the reality is that they are doing all wrong. How can we avoid doing the wrong thing and how do we know if we are doing the right thing? First, we need to make sure that we are not cutting corners, especially, when we get paid a certain amount of money for doing a specific job. What this really means is that we must stop doing whatever is the most convenient for us. The most practical for us, we must stop rushing ourselves to finish a job in little or no time. We must commit ourselves to finishing our jobs in a timely manner and we must do it the right way.

Nowadays! We live in a fast-paced world where everything we do must be done fast. But why is it that we must always have to do everything fast? Well, the number one reason is…money. Everyone wants to make lots of money in as little time as possible. As individuals, sometimes we want to do the job right the first time, however, sometimes there external forces (companies or corporations) who will prevent us from doing a good job or the right job and for good reason, they are in the business of making as much money as possible and as a consequence the quality of their work or the quality of their services diminish tremendously.

We know now that money is the number one reason as to why people don't always do their job the right way, however, it's not the only reason, there are several other reasons, or excuses, as to why we don't always do our jobs the right way and on time. What we need to understand is that when we fail to do our jobs right the first time, we will delay the inevitable and that is to come back and finish the job and that in itself is a waste of time on our part.

When we do a job right the first time, we will not only be saving precious time and energy, furthermore, we will be saving ourselves the inconvenience and the disruption of other people's lives. Furthermore, it is my understanding that some people's intentions are to do the job right the first time, however, sometimes the pressure from their peers to finish the job as quickly as they can and this creates a tremendous burden on the person doing the job. Furthermore, some companies encourage their workers to take "short cuts."

Most often than not, companies and private businesses will overcharge customers to do a certain job, because as I said before, people want to make as much money in as little time as possible. Normally, I would like to get my money's worth, but unfortunately, that is not always the case, in fact, sometimes I end up getting shorthanded. For example, we just finished installing a brand-new water heater. The water heater was leaking at the bottom (good thing we caught it on time). Anyway, it seems as if it took forever to finish the job because the person doing it had to come back several times. You see, the work was not done right the first time. I believe the person doing the installation and for some unexplained reasons was taking "short cuts." Don't get me wrong, the guy seemed to know what he was doing as far as knowing his stuff, however, he failed to keep up with the new codes from our city and consequently he had to come back several times. The person doing the work had to come back one last time, however, this time around it wasn't his fault, he had to wait for us to hire a handyman person to come and install sheetrock behind the water heater, and then, he had to come back one last time to install brackets on the pipes and attach them to the wall and it was because he failed to attach them to the wall in the first place.

By the way, there were about six different people involved with this job. The first person who came to our house on the first day was the one that gave us the original estimate, then, on the second day a different person showed up to do the job, then there was the coordinator, the one that takes care of the city permits and coordinates that everything is done up to code, then, there were two other guys who show up later to finish the job. These two men had the responsibility of containing a small area due to black mold behind the water heater. The main reason as to why there were too many people involved is because the company, we hired sub-contracts the jobs to different people.

I used to have my own sign company, but I must admit that everything I did was done right and on time. I always made sure that I learned everything that there was to be learned about every job. I was knowledgeable about every single job that I was doing, so it allowed me to do my job right the first time. Having the knowledge allows me to be successful and at the same time, it allows me to keep my customers happy. By the way, in eight years of servicing my customers, I only had two complaints and it wasn't because of the work we did, instead, it was because some of the transformers which we use in the process were defective by the manufacturer.

I personally took care of every little detail of every job. I was the salesperson. The coordinator and even though I subcontracted the jobs to a different company, I always made sure that I hire the right people for the job. About the only two things that I did not personally take care of was making the signs and installing them, however I was there through the whole process.

When we have the knowledge; when we take the time to do the job right, when we provide people with a fair price and when we know exactly how long is going to take to finish the job, then we will be able to deliver the best possible service to our customers. It's a win-win situation. Even after I closed my business. After five years, people were still calling me to go and fix their signs. I was always proud of what I did, maybe because my pride is bigger than myself.

My advice to all those people who want to improve the way they do things is to: never try to do more than one thing at a time because we can only do one thing at a time. When we insist on doing more than one thing at a time, (or as they say, multitasking) we will drive ourselves crazy and on top of that, we will eventually develop anxiety, trust me, I know. The trick here is that we only do one thing at a time and we must do it right the first time, even if it takes us longer than originally estimated. We must take our time. We must be creators of good things, not bad things. We need to always make some good sound decisions because we are creating our own future.

It's important to remember that it makes absolutely no sense to do a slappy job. Whether it's a work-related project or a personal project, we must try our best to always do the best possible job and without thinking only about the money that we are about to make. We must think of ourselves as individuals with honor first. Once again, we must take the necessary time to do a good job because you are (somehow) going be rewarded in the future, so, don't be in a rush to finish a job too quickly, especially, if you are going to end up doing a lousy job at the end, and all because we were in such a rush to get it done. It will be a waste of time and energy, furthermore, it will be unproductive. It's always best not to start a project if we are going to rush through the process and end with a sub-par project or even worse, not being able to finish the job. We must care enough about what we are doing in order to do a good job. We must do our homework, we must learn everything that we need to know beforehand about the projects that we are about to do, well, that is if we want our projects to be done the right way.

If we want to learn new skills, then it's okay to go ahead and practice those skills, however, we must never practice those skills at the expense of other people's money.

Chapter Seven

The Conscious Mind

What is the role of the conscious mind? First and foremost, the conscious mind is different from the subconscious mind. The subconcious mind is a storage compartment where our thoughts, memories and feelings are stored, whereas the conscious mind has no memory. The conscious mind is only capable of processing one thought at a time. The conscious mind basically gathers information from our surroundings through our six sensors, smell, sound, sight, taste, tough and feeling.

The conscious mind is responsible for logic and reasoning.
But what does it really mean? Well, it means that as human beings we are conscious of everything that we are doing. It means that we possess the ability to think in a rational manner, it means that we possess the ability to process tons of information by ways of logic and reasoning. Again, to be conscious means that we are aware of everything that we are doing at any given moment, also, it means that we are responsible for our actions.

Our conscious mind can absorb billions bits of information per second which is then transferred and stored into our subconscious mind for future use. Our conscious primary job is to help us decide what's right from wrong, in other words, it means that we are aware of everything that we are doing. Our conscious mind has the power to analyze all our surroundings for possible danger. The conscious mind is fully aware of everything that is happening with our lives, whereas the subconscious mind is the part which is not fully aware because it doesn't have the capability to think. It's not in complete awareness of what is going on. Remember that the subconscious mind's job is to store information for future use and that is it.

Furthermore, the conscious mind means that we are human beings with the capacity to think and feel, thereby creating awareness of oneself as thinking human beings. It's the state of being conscious or being aware of our thoughts and feelings. Furthermore, the conscious mind is aware of external objects as well. The conscious mind give us the ability to experience or to feel whenever we are awake. Again, the conscious mind is responsible for critical thinking.

The Subconscious Mind

What is the subconscious mind? As I mention earlier, the subconscious mind is a storage compartment where our past experiences and ideas are recorded, and it doesn't matter if those experiences and ideas are correct or incorrect. Happy or unhappy. Everything that we ever experienced in the past. Our ideas, our feelings, our emotions, and our actions are recorded in our subconscious mind whether we are aware of it or not, whether we like or not. These ideas and experiences will stay in our subconscious mind for the rest of our lives. They will not change

Unless of course, we decide to replace them with new ideas and new experiences. The important thing here is that those ideas and experiences from our past are ready to be put into action by us, they are ready for interpretation, however, we must be careful how we put them into use because if we use them the wrong way, then the results can be devastating.

Again, the subconscious mind responsibility is to store information in its database. We need to keep in mind that our subconscious mind does not discriminate. In other words, it doesn't reject any information acquired through our six senses; it simply obeys. Its job is to store information and that is it. Our subconscious mind does not have the power to think or to reason. That job belongs to the conscious mind.

The subconscious mind has basically one function and that is to stored information in its memory bank. Our subconscious mind defines who we are, it holds our beliefs. Our values and our attitudes. The subconscious mind and the computer stores information for future use, however, there is a difference between the two, the subconscious mind has absolutely no control as to how we use that information. It doesn't think, it simply obeys. Furthermore, the subconscious mind does not guarantee any degree of success or failure. It's after us to determine how we will use that information. Everything that we ever experience in the past is stored in our subconscious mind.

We know that both, the subconscious mind, and the modern computer is a place where information is stored. The computer programmer enters information into the hard drive. It is information that will sit in there and wait for someone to extract it and put it into use. Now! when we are finally ready to put that information into action then we extract that information from our computers and we expect that information to be accurate, whereas the subconscious mind doesn't know what is right from wrong, that job belong to us, we are the ones that must decide for what's right or wrong.

The information inside our subconscious mind (and it's obvious) doesn't come from a computer programmer, it comes from different sources. In other words, it's an accumulation of information from our past experiences.

There's only one similarity between the subconscious mind and the computer, and that is that if we don't like the current information in the computer program, then we have the option to change it from inaccurate to accurate information. The same principal must be applied to our subconscious mind. If we don't like the information store in our memory bank or our subconscious mind, then we have the option to update that information. It's important to remember that we are consciously making decisions that will impact our lives in the future. Therefore, we must be careful how we use the information which is stored in our subconscious mind.

The subconscious mind gathers its information from our conscious mind through our six senses, afterwards, that information is processed through our conscious mind and finally, that information is recorded into our subconscious mind.

Again, both, the computer, and the subconscious mind will not reject any information that we put into them. They don't know how to distinguish between right from wrong, good or bad, they don't care either way, they simply store the information given to them and that is it. It's important to remember that it's not their job to determine if that information will hurt or benefit us when put it into use. We must understand that both the subconscious mind and the hard drive in the computer were not designed for deciding what is right or wrong. They simply perform their tasks, which is to store information. They cannot reject any information and they can't select what's best for us. Therefore, the responsibility falls onto us. It's totally up to us to decide what is best for us.

Our subconscious mind lives deep within our brain and everything that we are right now is because of our brain. I would not exist if I didn't have a brain. Everything starts in our brain and everything that we are right now is because of our brain. It's just that simple.

Again, our subconscious mind has been programmed with tons of information from our past experiences. Everything that we have done and experienced in our lives is stored in our memory bank, it's there, waiting to be extracted and put into action.

The action of our subconscious mind is reflective in nature and is not governed by reason or thinking, thereby, our subconscious mind has little or no conscious perception on the part of the individual, however, our conscious mind is aware of oneself as a thinking being. Our conscious mind has the awareness of things and it has the awareness of our surroundings, furthermore, our conscious mind can feel and think. It makes sense to me: that our conscious mind is synonymous with being aware not only of oneself but being aware of our surroundings as well. Being aware of what we are thinking and being aware of our past experiences. Our consciousness encompasses all the phenomena that we are conscious of awareness, experiences, including our thoughts, our feelings, our anger, our stress, our images, our dreams, and our body sensations.

Some people suggest that our subconscious mind is nothing, but pure knowledge and I must agree with them because it makes a lot of sense. It's an accumulation of past experiences and events that get recorded in our subconscious minds and I'm a firm believer that this knowledge can be used to our advantage in the form of auto-suggestion and affirmation to harness the power of the subconscious mind to influence our lives and the outcomes.

Furthermore, we can harness this knowledge of the subconscious mind to perhaps cure or heal our bodies from sicknesses and diseases. Off course, there will be skepticism about these claims, but it doesn't surprise me at all because some people will criticize and question everything, but that's only because they don't know any better. It's obvious that our thoughts and feelings can be controlled by us, but only if we have self-discipline, the desire and the determination to do so.

One final thought, our subconscious mind experiences are forever changing. For example, in one instant, we might be focused on watching television, but our consciousness might then shift from watching television to a past memory of a loved relative. Furthermore, our consciousness might shift yet again, from watching television to remembering other past events in our lives. Anything we see, smell, hear, taste, or feel will trigger those memories; it's an ever-changing stream of thoughts and ideas that will change dramatically from one minute to the next. We must never forget that our consciousness is a memory bank, it's where all our information is stored, and it's from there that we are constantly withdrawing information. Our past thoughts and actions are all there. I believe that our consciousness will not be lost forever. It's unthinkable to me that once we die that everything will end. Our existence should not end this way. I cannot bring myself to accept it and I will never accept that all our experiences throughout our lives will end upon our deaths, it makes no sense whatsoever. Life is too precious and too valuable for me and that is why I refuse to think about the idea that everything will end at our death.

The Power of Autosuggestion

What is autosuggestion and how does it work? Autosuggestion is simply a mental act on our part to influence one's thoughts attitudes, and behaviors. Whether we realize it or not, we have been using the power of autosuggestion our entire lives and is something that we do naturally. We can either use the power of autosuggestion to help us accomplish our goals and desires, but unfortunately, most often than not, we use the power of autosuggestion in a negative way, in other words, we use it unconsciously to prevent us from achieving our goals and dreams. Again, the power of auto suggestion will help us in many ways, but it can also work against us if we are not careful. Sometimes we use the power of autosuggestion to tell ourselves that life sucks and when that happens, then guess what? Life is going to suck indeed.

We are forever blaming other people for our own problems. Our lack of knowledge and ignorance. We bring ourselves down to a state of desolation by always thinking in a negative way. Often, we think the worst about other people instead of thinking about the good things in them. It's important for us to always think in a healthy and positive way no matter how difficult life might be, but the good news is that we can use autosuggestion to help us change the way we think.

We should always use the power of autosuggestion to reassure ourselves that we can accomplish anything that we want. We can use the power of autosuggestion to help us relax and to breathe in slowly whenever we find ourselves in a difficult situation, and we can use it to help us regain our concentration and redirect our energy into thinking happy thoughts instead of unhappy ones. Furthermore, we can use the power of autosuggestion to help us smile more often or use it to help us change our bad moods into good moods. We can use the power of autosuggestion to help us boost our self-confidence at work, at home or on the road and we can use it anytime and anywhere.

Auto suggestion is a powerful weapon that we can all use to help us change our lives forever and not only our lives, but the lives of everyone else on the planet. Imagine how much more powerful we can become when we finally learn to use the power of autosuggestion. We should be using the power of autosuggestion to do the things which are going to make us stronger, happier, and content. By suggesting to ourselves good and pleasured thoughts instead of unpleasant and negative ones, we will be able to change our lives forever. Together we can change the future of humanity and perhaps we can heal ourselves from diseases as well.

Remember that if in our minds we think of ourselves as healthy, then we will be healthy, but if we think of ourselves as being sick, then we are going to be sick. Our bodies are simply following our autosuggestions, in other words, our bodies are reacting accordingly to our wishes. It's the power of autosuggestion in action. Our state of mind and our thoughts are responsible for making our bodies, either healthy or sick. The best time to test our auto suggestion abilities, is when we are feeling sick, and we start by sending our bodies a direct order to start healing themselves and they will obey. It's mind over sickness. Again, it's all about the power of autosuggestion. Whatever we are thinking right now is exactly what we will become so we must always be careful what we are wishing for because it might come true. Furthermore, we need to remind ourselves to always think of ourselves as healthy individuals and in good physical condition.

We need to be careful how we think because our negative thoughts and our beliefs will become true. Auto suggesting or self-talk can affect our lives in a constructive way, or it can affect our lives in a destructive way. When we are not paying attention to our thoughts and we let them run wild, we can find ourselves in big trouble without even realizing it.

We must always remember that our thoughts and ideas are being recorded into our subconscious minds and that we must never autosuggest to ourselves any destructive ideas or self-talk ourselves into a negative state of mind. Again, we can stop our bad habits using the power of autosuggestion any time. Anywhere, day or night. We have been exposed to countless negative and destructive thoughts and ideas in the past and consequently those thoughts and ideas are forever encrusted into our subconscious mind, but now, it's time for us to delete all negative self-talk from our database or from our subconscious minds.

All that we really need to do is change our way of thinking by replacing our negative self-talk with positive self-talk. We can also replace our old habits with new habits, and old thoughts with new thoughts, it's that simple. Good thoughts and good ideas equal good vibrations and good vibrations is the key to living a longer and happier life. We don't need destructive thoughts or destructive ideas in our life.

We must always think of ourselves as happy people which in turn is going to help us become the person that we were meant to be... a happy person. We must get rid of our junk information store in our subconscious minds and replace it with accurate information. Remember that using our imagination and the power of autosuggestion is going to take us to new heights, so we must get creative, and we must get motivated, so that we can find new confidence and self-steam in ourselves.

We must learn to love ourselves and not let others dictate our life, unless of course, we want others to run our lives for us. Remember to only ask for advice from others if you really need to do so. Sometimes it's good to hear what others have to say about us to realize if we are doing something wrong.

Remember that some people will be successful at everything they do, but others are totally the opposite. Those people who are successful are doing things the right way, but those people who are not successful are doing things the wrong way, either way, we can learn from both, we can learn from successful people and we can learn from unsuccessful people. We must be aggressive in our search for happiness, but at the same time, we must always be in total control and we must remind ourselves to always stay humble and we can accomplish it using the power of auto suggestion

Again, we must think of ourselves as being healthy instead of sick. We must think of ourselves as individuals who have no limitations, someone who is successful, young, healthy, and fortunate. We must leave those feelings of failure and rejection behind and think of ourselves as a superior and not as an inferior human being, but at the same time, we must remember to stay humble. We must use the power of autosuggestion to tell ourselves that we are worth a lot more than what we thought we were worth; we must not limit ourselves in any way. Remember that we have the power to do and change anything that we desire. Also, remember to smile more often because it's going to give us that feeling of peace and warmness. We must use the power of our imagination and the power of autosuggestion because these two things are some of the most powerful tools that we possess which can be used to help us improve our life tremendously. We can help ourselves in many ways when we use the power of autosuggestion. I can talk forever about the power of autosuggestion, however, the space in my book is limited, but not to worry because I think that you are on your way to a better life with what you have learned so far. Just remember that now you have the power of auto suggestion, the power of imagination and you also have the knowledge and the skills which can be used to in order to become successful at anything that you do.

The Best Medicine for the Soul

Okay, so what is "the best medicine for the soul" Well, there's actually more than one, but there's two that immediately comes to mind is laughter and music. Meditation, and autosuggestion is also a good medicine for the soul. As you can see, I wasn't talking about prescribed drugs from a doctor, instead, I was talking about the type of medicine which our souls need for those occasions when we are feeling lonely, depressed, unloved or unwanted. We all know that whenever we don't hear those uplifting and kind words, (especially from the people that we love) which are going to make us feel good when we are feeling down, than we might end up in a state of depression and loneliness as a result.

The best thing about this medicine is that it doesn't cost anything as far as monetary value, it's free, enjoyable and it's easy to use. Plus, the best part about these medicine is that there's no negative side effects. This is the only medicine that we can take for those days when we are feeling the blues. For those days when we are having feelings of unhappiness, feelings of unworthiness or feelings of depression. We don't need to intake drugs for this type of ailments, except maybe for depression, but even then, I wouldn't take any drugs for that ailment either, I rather look for other avenues.

Moreover, what will happen if no one tells us those uplifting and kind words that we want to hear? Are we going to feel as if our life is over or that our life is not worth living for? Of course not, on the contrary, we must try to wake up from that state of mind in which we find ourselves. What we really need to do is to stop feeling sorry for ourselves. We must try to get ourselves out of that state of mind. We must pick ourselves up and stop following the path that will take us in the wrong direction.

But how are we going to get ourselves out of such a situation? Well, we can set aside a few minutes every single day for laughter, listen to music and meditation. Laughter music, meditation, along with autosuggestion is perhaps the best four medicines that we can take for our broken spirits. Sometimes the best medicine we can take when we are feeling down is to talk to our friends, but not just any friend, but they must be true friends who are willing to listen. Friends that will stay by our side, true friends that will always be there for us, true friends that will tell us the truth. Real friends will make us laugh when we are feeling down. We must surround ourselves with happy and optimistic family and friends instead of surrounding ourselves with unhappy and toxic people.

So, laughter is a good medicine for the soul, so we should laugh more often because laughing has the power to make us feel good once again. Every time we smile or laugh, we are going to immediately feel a sense of relief and happiness, so why not use it more often? We must remember that when we laugh more often, we are going to improve our overall health. Our laughter is a powerful medicine, not only for the soul, but for our physical bodies as well. Laughter is going to improve our immune system. It's going to boost our moods and it's going to diminish our physical and emotional pain.

Furthermore, laughing more often is going to protect us from the damaging effects of stress. We must remember to laugh more often like when we were children because as adults, we sometimes forget to laugh and have fun. We should learn from our children, they laugh constantly, so we should do the same, well, that is if we want to improve our overall health and happiness. Children laugh hundreds of times per day, and it's amazing that we don't learn to laugh from them more often.

We must look for as many opportunities as possible to find ways for us to laugh more often. Let's not forget that when we laugh or smile more often, we will be much happier, plus the fact that happy people will be more productive in everything they do. Laughing more often will allow us to live longer, in other words, we will be adding, perhaps, many years to our lives because laughing will reenergize our souls and bodies with new energy.

So, laughing is good for our health and everyone around us because it will improve our relationship with friends, family, and yes, even with complete strangers.

It's obvious that laughter has a lot of good benefits, and one of those benefits is that laughter is a powerful stress reliever. Good humor and laughter will give us new hope and it will put our bodies in a complete relaxation mode. Laughing will boost our immune system by releasing endorphins which are the body's natural feel good chemicals. Laughter will protect our hearts by improving the function of blood vessels and increasing the blood flow through the entire body.

Did you know that music is also a good source of medicine for our souls? Indeed, music possesses therapeutic healing and calming effects on people. Music has always been considered as the soul of our bodies, so listening to some pleasurable and pleasant tunes is going to allow our minds and bodies to reach a state of complete relaxation.

Music is a very potent medicine. It is one of the best medicines for relaxing our souls. Music will help to fight many psychiatric issues and many medical problems that we might be experiencing. Again, there's other types of natural medicine for the soul. For example, the sound of waves at the beach. The sound of gentle water flowing down a river, the sound of the rain hitting the roof of our houses has the same effect on the soul.

There are countless sources of natural medicine out there that will do wonders for our souls. For example, helping other people who are less fortunate because we all know that giving is caring and giving something or helping others will bring us great satisfaction peace and happiness. When we help other people, we are going to feel good about ourselves because we know that we did something good for someone else, other than ourselves. We can help other people in many ways, for example, money, or by listening to them. We can help them by saying kind words, we can help them by encouraging them to do better, we can help them by offering them the healing power of laughter or a smile, we can show them our true love, we can show them some compassion and we can show them that we are willing to help them by listening to their afflictions. We must remember that whenever we don't laugh enough and listen to music that we are wasting another beautiful day.

Chapter Eight

Judging Others

We must not be so fast to judge other people because we don't actually know them. We think we know them, but in reality, we don't know them, we don't know what they are going through, we don't know their afflictions, we don't know what they are thinking about, and we don't know how they are feeling on the inside. My philosophy is to never rush into judging other people. After all, who am I to judge them? Again, we must never judge others so harshly when we don't even know them. Remember that everyone deserves the benefit of the doubt.

People are always going to do things according to their own needs and their needs are probably not the same needs you and I have. People will do the things they need to do in their own way, and perhaps it's not the right way, but it's their way of doing things and not our way. We must keep in mind that we all have different ways of doing things. However, it doesn't mean that we are doing them the right way. Perhaps we can teach others how to do some things the right way, but only if we are doing those same things the right way ourselves. We must keep in mind that other people know what they know and that is it, therefore, they will continue to do things their own way until someone else teaches them a better way.

There's always, and in most cases, a better way to do things. Again, the way people do things is probably not the way you and I do those same things, sure, there's a lot of different ways to accomplish the same results, but other people's way is perhaps the only way they know how, it's thereby that we should never judge others without knowing them. Even if we know people, I don't think we have the right to judge them. we can only suggest to others, but we cannot judge them.

Sometimes we find ourselves judging other people because of their irrational behaviors, but we must remember that our judgments are based on how we think people should and shouldn't behave or how people should do things. We are constantly judging others, for example, we judge them for the clothing they are wearing. For the cars they drive, for the way they speak and for the way they eat or for what they eat. It's a never-ending story, but why do we do it? Maybe we judge other people because we are insecure about ourselves, because we are living an unhappy life full of regrets, or because we are scared and lonely, and therefore, we start judging others, thinking that perhaps it's going to alleviate how we feel about ourselves.

As I mentioned before throughout this book. When we don't know ourselves; when we don't know who we are as a person, when we don't know what we want out of life and when we don't know what makes us happy, then the only thing left for us to do is to start judging and blaming other people for our misfortunes. It's important to remember that judging other people is not going to alleviate how we feel about ourselves.

So, are we ever going to be able to stop judging other people and how can we stop ourselves from being so judgmental towards others? Well, I cannot emphasize enough about how important it is to remind ourselves that we must stop judging other people. One way we can stop judging others is by judging ourselves first. I know we are imperfect human beings, but for crying out loud let's stop the madness. Let's all grow up and become happy and decent humans beings together and become the person that we were meant to be. Remember that judging other people does not define who they are, it defines who we are instead. We can't spend the rest of our lives judging everyone for everything that they do. Now! Is there a good time in which we can judge another person's behaviors and actions? I would assume that it's never a good time to judge other people because our job is not to judge them, that job belongs to God. We must stop judging others because as Jesus Crist once said: "In the same way you judge others, you will be judged." Again, remember that we can only make suggestions to others. We must never impose our will upon others.

Chapter Nine

Positive and Accurate Thoughts

First of all, it's important for us to understand that our thoughts are a direct link to our feelings and to our behaviors. Our behavior is the direct result of how we are feeling at any given moment and it's because of our thoughts; our feelings and behaviors influence each other, one cannot live without the other, so when we have positive and accurate thoughts, we will have good feelings and as a result our behaviors will be in line with what we are feeling. We must have positive and accurate thoughts in order to find happiness. We also need to have accurate thoughts in order to be successful in accomplishing our goals. The difference between having a high rate of success and failure is to have accurate thoughts. Accurate thoughts will allow us to know what to do in every situation. One of the most important things that we need to remember is that we have the power of decision making on our side. Everything that will happen to us in the future will be because of our decision making, it is therefore, that we must decide wisely.

We must keep in mind that we are responsible for our own actions, therefore, it's important that we take full responsibility for everything that we do with our lives. By having our thoughts. Our feelings and our behaviors under complete control, we will be able to control the outcome of our actions. We must keep in mind that knowledge is power and that those who have the knowledge and know how to use it will have the power to change their lives forever.

We need to make sure that we have accurate thoughts and accurate information before making decisions because whatever we decide to do next could potentially ruin or improve our lives. It could impact our entire lives in a positive way, or it could impact our lives in a negative way as well.

From this day on, we must be our own true selves. We must not allow anyone else to make important decisions for us, we must not allow anyone else to do the thinking for us, we must do our own thinking because we are capable individuals with the capacity to think for ourselves, we are independent thinkers, so therefore, we don't need outside forces to influence our lives in a negative way. I can never emphasize enough that if we want something done right, we must do it ourselves, nobody else is going to do it like we do it.

I'm not suggesting that we shouldn't listen to other people because sometimes it's a good idea to listen to others, especially if they are knowledgeable individuals who know how to be successful. Again, we need to listen to other people first because by listening to them we might be able to acquire new knowledge, which we can apply to our decision making in the future, but we must only apply that knowledge if it's the correct knowledge. It's always a good idea to listen to other people and see what they have to say, however, we must remember that we don't have to do everything they're suggesting. We simply need to listen because we might be able to incorporate some of their knowledge and ideas into ours. We all know that people won't always tell us the truth. Therefore, we should approach everything with an open mind, but with caution at the same time. It's only then that we will be able to go further than ever before.

We must never forget that we need to learn and follow the chain of accurate thought because it's the only way that we are going to be able to reach the best possible solutions to our problems. We must never look for the truth or the answers somewhere else, instead, we must try to find them inside ourselves first, however, If we don't find the answers that we are looking for within ourselves, then we can look somewhere else. No matter what we do in life, we must remember that we don't always know everything, in fact, we must never pretend to know everything either. Furthermore, we must never pretend to know other people when we don't actually know ourselves. We must learn to know ourselves first and then we can work on understanding others. We have the power and the knowledge hiding within ourselves so it's time for us to start using it the right way. We must become the masters of our own domains, but we can accomplish such a task by understand everything which is happening with our surroundings.

We must practice patience every single day of our live, but without We must getting discouraged when things don't work out the way we wanted. We need to remind ourselves whenever we are attempting to accomplish our goals that we will have success because we have failed before, but this time around we will be victorious because we know what to do now. If we want things to be done the right way then we need to have a good understanding of how things should be done, also, we need to be in the right state of mind. It's only through accurate thoughts. Reflections and meditation that we will, eventually, learn to master our thoughts. Our feelings, our actions, and our behaviors.

From time to time we will be reminded of our past failures and that is a good thing because it's going to make us stronger in the long run, but only if we learn not to make the same mistakes over and over. Remember that most of our past failures can be corrected, however, there are some mistakes or failures that we can't go back and correct, for example, let's assume that one day you get drunk to the point where you can no longer drive safely but you went ahead and drove anyway. Now! You find yourself driving at very high speed on the freeway when suddenly you lose control of the car, the car flips over several times but luckily enough you survive, except for the fact that one of your legs was badly damaged so you won't be able to walk normally again. You will walk with a limp for the rest of your life.

In this situation you were lucky but what about the next time? Are you going to be just as lucky? Are you going to learn anything from that unfortunate episode? I sure hope so. This is a good example of something that could have been prevented by simply making the right choice not to drive while you were under the influence of alcohol. This costly mistake will become a permanent reminder of your irrational decision for the rest of your life.

Affirmative Thoughts

It's important for us to start our day with a positive attitude and affirmative thoughts. It's also important to start our day with a big smile on our faces because it's going to brighten our entire day. One of the things that we can do to help us in accomplishing such things is by thinking of happy places, for example, an exotic island or any other happy place where we rather be right now. Now! If throughout the day we start to get those negative thoughts or unhappy thoughts in our head, then, we need to immediately redirect those unhappy thoughts to happy thoughts. Everything that we do in life requires some type of effort on our part, so it's going to take plenty of self-determination and consistency on our part. We need to constantly remind ourselves that affirmative thoughts are more powerful than negative thoughts and that happy and affirmative thoughts will lift our spirits up. Unhappy thoughts will bring our spirit down, happy thoughts is only going to add value to our lives, happy thoughts will allow us to overcome most of our obstacles that we might encounter throughout our lives. Happy thoughts are not going to allow us to quit when things go wrong. Affirmative thoughts will give us more energy than negative thoughts. Remember that negative thoughts will zap most of our energy out of our bodies.

When we change our negative thoughts to happy thoughts or when we change our negative thoughts to affirmative thoughts. We will change ourselves from being an unhappy person to a happy person. When we change our negative thoughts to affirmative thoughts, we will be able to change the entire world. We must remind ourselves that it's always easier to think negative thoughts than positive and affirmative thoughts. It's always easier to sit down and do nothing than to go out there and do something which is going to lift our spirits up and make us happy. As human beings, we are not born with negative thoughts inside our minds, instead, is something that we learn as we grow up and it has to do with the fact that we tend to pay more attention to our negative thoughts and negative feelings than our positive and affirmative thoughts. We need to redirect our negative thoughts, emotions, feelings, anger, sadness, and disappointments towards feelings of happiness, joy, and contentment.

We must do our absolute best to stay positive every single day of our lives. We must try to think about the things that will make us happy and not so much about the things which are going to make us miserable and unhappy. We must think about the good news and not the bad news because the good news will stay with us for a short time, but the bad news will stay with us for a long time. For example, when we think of a happy place that we want to be instead of being stuck at work, and by the way, normally this happens in the mornings, however, by midday we forget about our happy place because our minds are preoccupied with our tasks from work. You see, it's all about our plasticity brain and what this means is that our plasticity brain will adapt to changes in an instant. It's designed to change and to adapt constantly to new circumstances, new thoughts, and new ideas in a blink of an eye. Now! When something bad happens, for instance, a violent crime, or a terrible fire like in Paradise Ca it will stay with us for an exceptionally long time.

What all this means is that bad news are somehow more addictive than good news, however, there are occasions when good news are more powerful than bad news, for example, when someone wins, perhaps millions of dollars in the state lottery. It's something that will stay with us for a long time and it has to do with the fact that it's such a wonderful feeling to experience that we don't want to end it. In other words, it's something that we don't ever want to forget. Now you see how a positive feeling or emotion can have in our lives. This emotions will teach us that we must stay positive at all time because staying positive and affirmative will bring us more joy, instead of stress and unhappiness. We must never choose to suffer. We must never choose to be in pain, but if we are indeed suffering is because we choose to be in that situation. It's all about what we are thinking about the most that we will feel the most. If we think about being in pain, then we will be in pain, but if we think about happy feelings, then we will experience happy feelings. The choice is ours to make.

How can we get rid of our mental pain and our affliction? Well, here are a few things which we can do to help us accomplish healthier thoughts. Again, meditation is an amazing tool that we can all use. Meditation is going to help us to re-energize our minds and bodies by simply eliminating most of the harmful chemicals in our bodies that we consume through the food that we eat daily. These harmful chemicals will put a tremendous amount of stress and anxiety on our bodies and in our minds. As I mentioned before, meditation is the best medicine for our souls. The beauty of using meditation is that we can use it anywhere and anytime, day or night, rain, or shine. Meditation will help us to rewire our brains. Meditation will help us to go from non-affirmative thoughts to affirmative thoughts in a short amount of time. Meditation is going to help us to clear our minds from unnecessary debris and junk. Meditation will help us to turn our negative thoughts into positive and affirmative thoughts.

Here are a few more examples of positive thoughts or affirmative thoughts that we must practice on a daily basis, for example, "I will not go through life stumbling and falling, but if I do stumble and fall from time to time, I know that I will be able to get right back up," "I will not go down in defeat because I know the truth about myself and the things that I can accomplish," "I know that I'm capable of achieving many wonderful things," "I also know that I can overcome most of my weaknesses because I have an advantage over them," "I will defect my weaknesses, they will not defeat me."

Words of Encouragement

I have learned many valuable lessons throughout the years of my life. I also acquired valuable information and knowledge which is going to help me in overcoming most of my weaknesses. I have learned to accept responsibility for my actions, so therefore, I will not fool myself deliberately by denying myself from accomplishing my goals and to become a better man. I will not, unnecessary, punish myself when things go wrong. I will never quit; I will never stop trying in becoming the person that I was meant to be. I will master and learn to overcome difficult obstacles. I will adapt myself to new environments and new situations. I will learn by not criticizing others. I will turn my weaknesses into my greatest strength. I will learn from my previous mistakes and I will learn from the times that I was pushed around. Humiliated and defeated by others.

Remember that victory does not come easy. Victory will only be accomplished by those individuals who learn to control their thoughts. Their knowledge will be their strength because they will be able to apply that knowledge to their advantage. Victory will come to those people who have the courage to go get what they want. Victory will come to those people who have the determination to win, victory will come to those people who have the desire, the control, the calmness, the focus, the self-confidence, and accurate thoughts.

Negative Thoughts

Negative thoughts are part of everyone's daily lives. It's something that we can't avoid because it's in our nature. We are programmed to search for problems to fix, but when we try to fix them, our lives become full of stress and anxiety. Our negative thoughts will interfere with our mental state of mind. They will interfere with our health and our ability to live a normal life. Our negative thoughts can be crippling. They are destructive at times and they will fog our brain, preventing us from thinking clearly and rationally. Most of our negative thoughts must be vanish from our minds whenever possible because if these negative thoughts are put into action, they will cause a tremendous amount of damage to our health, and to our pocketbook as well. Destructive thoughts are perhaps the longest ongoing plague in human history. It's a plague that we must keep under control at all time.

We are human beings; therefore, we are going to have negative thoughts from time to time because they are part of our lives. In other words, they are part of our DNA. Okay, so how can we eliminate our destructive thoughts completely from our mind? It's obvious that we won't be able to completely get rid of every negative thought which crosses our minds, however, we are very capable of eliminating most of them, but the only way that we are going to be able to get rid of them is by taking total control of our thoughts. Controlling our thoughts and emotions is the key to making good decisions. Again, it's our right as human beings to have negative thoughts, but we also have the right to make the right choices at the right time. The one thing that will help us in overcoming most of our negative thoughts and that is by learn to overcome our negative thoughts and we can accomplish this task by not filtering out our positive thoughts because if we do, then all we are left with is our negative thoughts and the more we think about them, the less time we will have to think about our positive thoughts.

Why do we have so many negative thoughts? Well, because we just can't help ourselves. Our brain is programmed this way. It's designed to ask as many questions as possible, but when we don't find the answers we are looking for, then our brain quickly jumps into the wrong conclusions. We must have the discipline to train ourselves or better yet, we must train our negative part of our brain to not jump into any negative conclusion until we have all the facts first. Most of the time, our brain will take us to places we don't want to go. It will try and take us into a negative place by distorting the facts, but now we know better. Remember that it will take a lot of self-discipline on our side to eventually become good at stopping our wandering mind from jumping into the wrong conclusions. Not all our thoughts will be of the negative type. Some of them will be positive thoughts that will make us feel good on the inside. However, our negative thoughts are the ones that will make us feel bad about ourselves. They are the ones that will make our life miserable. It's therefore that we must try to do our best not to let our negative thoughts influence our life in a damaging or negative way. Another way of getting rid of our negative thoughts is by welcoming them but wait a minute! I thought we were trying to get rid of them! But now I'm saying that we should welcome them in. How is that possible, why should we welcome them? Well, because if we don't let them in, they will hang around for a long time. You see, we must let them in, however, once they are in, we need to release them by letting them pass by but without giving them any further attention, but on the other hand, if we feed our negative thoughts with our attention, they will be lingering around for a long time until we no longer feed them with our attention. When we become aware of this situation, we will finally step back and observe our negative thoughts from afar. Our negative thoughts will still be there. They will be in the back of our minds, but we don't need to give them any more attention than we need to.

Our future success is going to depend entirely on whether we have good positive thoughts or not, furthermore, our future success is going to depend on whether we make the right choices on a day by day basis. We need to keep in mind that if we make the wrong choices, then we will pay the price for having made the wrong choices, but on the other hand, if we make the right choices, we will be compensated handsomely.

We can no longer afford to keep making the same old mistakes and expect to get different results. We must be in total control of ourselves, and we can accomplish this task by controlling our thoughts, and in return, we will be able to control every possible bad situation. I know that it's not an easy thing to do, but nevertheless, it can be accomplished by constantly reminding ourselves that we must make the right choices every single time. Furthermore, we must remind ourselves never to make any impulsive decisions without first going through the thinking process.

Our destructive thoughts are a plague which needs a cure and treatment. They need therapy and if we give our negative thoughts the right therapy, then we will finally achieve happiness. For those who have the knowledge and understand how to use the power of the mind, know that success will come to them more rapidly. We must accept the positive thoughts and reject the negative and damaging thoughts.

We must not waste our precious energy on negative thoughts, instead, we must learn to concentrate that energy and use it towards positive thoughts. Most people don't realize that it takes a lot more energy to think about negative thoughts than it takes to think about positive thoughts, does this make sense? What would you rather do, use your precious energy to hold on to your negative thoughts and negative ideas or do you rather use less energy on your positive and affirmative thoughts? It's true that our negative thoughts will drain our bodies of precious physical and emotional energy more rapidly than our positive thoughts, so why do it?

We must follow our instincts when we are trying to change our negative thoughts to positive thoughts. We must ask ourselves if whatever we are thinking at any given moment makes sense or not. Our inner self is going to guide us through difficult times like this, so therefore, we must listen to it

We must keep in mind that we will encounter resistance on our part wherever we are trying to get rid of our negative thoughts and this is completely normal because we are, as I said before, programmed with old ideas and old thoughts, but knowing that we can change those old ideas and old thoughts for new ones is going to give us the strength and the power that we need in order to defect our negative thoughts. It's all about reprogramming our minds with new and fresh information.

There's one thing that we must never do and that is to never give up when things don't go our way. We need to constantly remind ourselves that if at first, we don't succeed then we will keep trying until we can accomplish our goals. We must stay positive throughout the entire process. Another thing that we must do is to never worry in excess because we will be sending negative vibrations and negative energy throughout our entire bodies.

The responsibility of knowing what's right and what's wrong falls on our shoulders. We must decide for ourselves if something is true or false. Remember that everything that we are thinking about will become part of us. It's what defines who we are, whether it is right or wrong.

We need to take our minds into a new level of thinking never-before experienced by us. We must always believe in ourselves and at the same time believe that we will accomplish most of our goals. We must believe in "infinity intelligence" because we have the capacity to be the creators of many good things. We are all creators of good and positive thoughts. We are all creators of good vibrations. We are all important human beings to society and to God. We are all important pieces of the big puzzle that God created, so we must never let others tell us any different.

We mustn't forget that we are constantly bombarded with an array of negative thoughts throughout the day, there's no way to avoid them, however, with a little discipline on our part, we will be able to get rid of them as soon as they appear inside our minds. Never forget that time is our best friend and that it's only with time that we will be able to master the art of self-control and learn to deal with our emotions and keep our negative thoughts under control.

Furthermore, we are constantly confronted with many difficult or dangerous situations but knowing how to deal with them is the key that is going to allow us to finally be successful.

It seems to me that there's always more questions than answers about everything, but that is how the human brain works. We must remember that our brain is capable of processing millions bits of information at blazing speeds, so we must take advantage of this superhuman computer and put it into good use. There's one important factor that we must keep in mind before making any decisions and that is to go through the thinking process of elimination so that we can make the right choices in life.

We have the power to change the outcome of every situation that we might encounter in the future. However, we must remind ourselves that we need to make the right decisions every single time in order to minimize making too costly mistakes. We are the only ones that can control the outcome. Don't get me wrong, having negative thoughts is a big part of our lives but it's how we deal with difficult situations that will define who we are as a person.

Having negative thoughts from time to time is a good thing because it's going to help us to learn and grow. It's going to help us build our own true character. Remember that without negative thoughts, we wouldn't be able to learn much of anything. It's what makes us human and it's part of the evolution process. It's not about having negative thoughts in our minds, instead, it's about how we cope with those negative thoughts that will define us.

Organizing Our Thoughts

The human minds is a powerful weapon that we can use to help us organize our thoughts. We have the power and the ability to seize control of our own thoughts. We also have the power to break away from our unconscious way of thinking.

It's important that we break away from our negative way of thinking and we can start by getting rid of our negative thoughts, but the only way that we will be able to accomplish such a task is by changing the way we think. In other words, we need to organize our thoughts, we need to make sure that our thoughts are crystal clear because if they are in a state of confusion, then our lives will be in disarray.

It's important that we learn to organize our thoughts daily and on consistent basis, because it's only then that we are going to find out that most of our erroneous thoughts can be replaced with more accurate thoughts. Remember that if we have our thoughts in order, we will be able to eliminate most of our afflictions, our unhappiness, and our sufferings. By simply paying attention to our thoughts our lives will change forever. It does make sense, doesn't it? It's not that difficult. We can take a few minutes every single day to organize our thoughts and If we learn to do this on a day by day basis, our days will be much brighter.

One important thing to remember is that we are going to experience good and healthy thoughts throughout the day, but we going to experience negative thoughts as well. It's inevitable, it's a fact of life, but what really matters here is that we need to organize our thoughts by simply replacing our negative thoughts with positive and pleasant ones. We must remember that our negative thoughts will create chaos in our lives because they are destructive thoughts, so it's important that we get rid of them as soon as possible. Remember that we have choices and that we can either choose to be happy or we can choose to be miserable. We can choose to keep our negative and destructive thoughts, or we can choose to keep our good and happy thoughts. We always want to keep our thoughts well under control… it's actually quite a simple task that we need to perform daily. Well, that is if we want to live a more satisfying and happier life.

Remember that our lives are already complicated enough, so we don't need to complicate our lives more than we need too. If we keep our negative thoughts under control, then they will become harmless. Now is the time to break away from our current cycle of negative thinking. It's not going to be easy getting rid of those damaging thoughts at first, but with a little practice and patience on our behalf, we will be able to succeed.

Another thing we can do to help us get rid of our negative thoughts is by examining our past experiences and then make the necessary changes. Remember that everything we do begins with a thought and without a thought nothing will exist. We must focus our attention on the positive side of things rather than the negative side of things. We have the power of our minds; we have the knowledge and the ability to help us redirect our energy towards healthy thoughts.

In order to survive as human beings, we need to stop being selfish. We need to put aside our survival of the fittest mentality and join forces so that we can become a powerful single force. We can overcome and solve most of our problems much faster as a team than doing it by ourselves. We must pass on some of our knowledge to those who are willing to learn, however, they must be coachable, it's the only way that we are going to be able to become a formidable force.

Remember that our thoughts controls our thinking, our feelings, and our behaviors so when we learn to control our thoughts, we will be able to control our thinking, our feelings, and our behavior. Our healthy thoughts will put us in total control of our actions, but on the other hand, our unhealthy thoughts will cause panic and will make us lose control of ourselves and when we lose control of ourselves, we will cope poorly in the face of adversity. Our healthy thoughts are based on realistic fear. Our unhealthy thoughts are based on unrealistic fears.

I believe that if we want to achieve a healthier life and achieve complete happiness, then we need to do a better job of controlling our negative thoughts. The root of our problems resides within our own thoughts. Most of our troubles that we encounter throughout our lives is because of our unhealthy thoughts, including our physical problems, therefore, we must eradicate of our unhealthy thoughts forever.

Letting Go of Our Negative Thoughts

Negative thoughts are like a plague, it's something that we experience on a daily basis and no one is immune from having those negative thoughts. Our thoughts of anger and hate towards others will be very damaging to our health, so therefore, we must learn to let go of those negative thoughts and negative feelings.

We must understand that our thoughts are always in action, we are forever thinking about something or someone, our thinking process is always in action and this is the time when we must be careful how we process our thoughts because our thoughts are immensely powerful. We can either use our positive thoughts to accomplish a lot of good things for ourselves and for others or we can use our we can use them to inflict ourselves and others a tremendous amount of emotional and physical damage.

I'm not by any means free from having negative thoughts from time to time, however, when those negative thoughts invade my mind, almost instantly, I send them into outer space. I don't let those negative thoughts hang around for too long because they are not my friends, sure, they want to be my friend, however, I will not allow that to happen because they are not good for my health. In fact, they are worthless and not only for me but for everyone else as well. Anyone can dispose of their negative thoughts by doing the same thing that I always do and that is to put them in spaceship and send them out into space. It sounds hilarious, but that is what makes it fun, I rather have fun and experience good feelings than no fun and full of depressing feelings.

You see, we can turn our negative thoughts into positive thoughts any time we so desire by simply converting our negative energy into positive energy. Positive energy is going to allow us to focus on replacing our negative thoughts into positive thoughts. Getting rid of unwanted negative thoughts is going to be a challenge for most people at first, but we must remember that everything that we do in life is a challenge as well. Remember that we were created to challenge ourselves every single day and we can start by letting go of that negative energy and those negative beliefs. We must not have feelings of despair, feelings of loneliness, feelings of anger and feelings of failures.

Letting Go of Our Past Failures

I strongly believe that when we fail at something is because we are lacking the knowledge. We are lacking the necessary education and we are lacking the experience. Without the knowledge, the education, and the experience, we are not going to be successful in accomplishing our goals. Remember that knowledge is going to help us to make good sound decisions, it's therefore, that we need to educate ourselves first.

When we fail at something is because we are lacking the understanding of how things work, so before we embark on a journey. We need to know our destination first. We need to know in which direction we are heading. We also need to know how we are going to get there and when.

Knowledge is a powerful weapon which is going to help us solve our problems much faster, however, the real power is knowing how and when to use it. Remember that our ignorance or lack of knowledge will prevent us from achieving our goals, in other words, our ignorance will become our worst enemy. Ignorance can and will rob us of our happiness if we are not careful. Ignorance can and will be expensive, meaning that it will cost us a lot of money and grief in the long run. Let's recap. When we fail at something it's because we lack the knowledge, the education, the experience and the know-how. Moreover, when we fail, we fail because our ignorance is greater than our knowledge.

Okay, so how can we improve our lives, and how are we going to get rid of our past failures? Well, we can start by allowing ourselves to let go of our past failure. You see, by letting go of our past failures, we will be able to move forward with new confidence. We don't need all that extra baggage from the past, therefore, it's important for us to let go of our past failures or mistakes so that we can move forward. The only thing that we need to take with us from the past and into the future is the desire and the determination to succeed and to become a better person.

We need to keep in mind that we are going to make mistakes as we embark on our journey towards finding happiness and accomplishing our goals, however, we need to remind ourselves that it will be okay. As long as we minimize the bigger mistakes or the costly mistakes then we should be on the right path. Remember that without learning from our past mistakes and failures there will be no success. Learning and failing is part of being human, so we must embrace those mistakes, but at the same time we must learn from them. It's the only way that we will continue to learn and grow. It's the only way that we will achieve our goals and it's the only way that we will achieve more valuable knowledge. Our past failures will teach us how to be successful in the future, so don't get upset when you fail. Learn to let go of your past failures and anger, and you will find happiness much quicker. Remember to allow yourself to let go of the past because the past is long gone, plus the fact that you gain nothing by holding on to old failures, thoughts, and feelings of failure.

Sometimes the price we must paid for our failures is too high, that's why it's vital that we learn from our previous failures because when we fail to learn from our failures or mistakes, we are going to be at the mercy of those who have the knowledge and believe me when I say that they will put that knowledge into action and use it against us.

For those of us who fail to learn from our mistakes and fail to gain new knowledge will be left behind in a cloud of dust. We will be left behind in the hot sands of the desert; we will be lost forever and feeling alone. Is that what we really want out of life? of course not! that is not what we want, because we deserved better than that.

We mustn't forget that failure is not permanent. It's only a temporary defect, however, if we insist on holding on to our past failures, they will become permanent. Failures are a blessing because they will teach us some much needed and valuable lessons. Sometimes we will pity ourselves because in our own minds we feel that we are total failures and that is a good enough reason why we shouldn't hold on to our thoughts of failures for too long because if we do, than they will become permanent failures and as a consequence, it will be devastating for our health.

Instead of holding on to our thought of failures, we should be working on getting rid of those negative thoughts of failures forever. Again, it's important for us to continue to move forward but without holding on to our feelings of failure. We must keep moving forward because there will be better things coming our way soon, however, we need to be ready for them with open arms or we will miss out on experiencing some wonderful new experiences.

Remember that our failures don't need to be permanent. They can be corrected most of the time by turning them into positive experiences. Most of our failures are short-term challenges and only rarely those failures suggest a lack of competence on our part. We need to challenge ourselves daily by working harder on discovering our true potential.

Remember that we must learn to let go of our past failures or mistakes, but at the same time, we need to embrace our failures or past mistakes and learn from them. Never forget that if we never fail, then we are never going to be successful. We must view our failures as a steppingstone for future success. Our failures will bring us closer to our goals, as our failures can spur new ideas.

Chapter Ten

Our Hidden Talents

We are born with many hidden talents, but most often than not we have no clue what they are because we have not taking the time to figure out what those talents are. The number one reason as to why we neglect our hidden talents is because we are too preoccupied with our jobs and our busy daily lives. Other times we know exactly what we want to do with our lives, but we are stuck in rut and we don't know how to get out of it or we don't have the energy to keep moving forward and so we abandon that idea of doing something special with our lives.

We know now that we have many hidden talents when we are born, however, as years go by, we will discover or develop new talents that we didn't know we had when we were born and it doesn't matter how old we are because we will continue to discover new hidden talents within ourselves. One thing to keep in mind is that most of our talents are dormant, but only until we decide to wake them up. It's obvious that we have many hidden talents within ourselves, however, it's up to us to find out what they are and it's up to us to further develop them and put them into action.

Most of these hidden talents are hidden talents that God gave us when we were born, but sometimes I wonder where these hidden talents are. Are they hidden deep inside our brains? Yes, our hidden talents are hidden inside our brains. They are all there waiting for us to be discovered and put into action.

We know that our hidden talents are inside our brain, but how are we going to recognize them? Well, I'm not really talking about our hidden athletic abilities, or the incredible gift that allows us to sing or play music, although those are some incredible talents in themselves. Rather, I'm talking about our other hidden talents, the ones that we normally don't think about. The hidden talents which I'm talking about is the power of our minds, the power of logic, the power of self-awareness, the power of visualization, the power of imagination, the power to adapt to new circumstances and new concepts, the power of believing in ourselves, the power self-confidence, the power of innovation and finally, the power of intuition. We have a tremendous ability to solve most of our problems. We have the capacity to come up with new ideas and we have a tremendous amount of creativity. As you can see, we have many hidden talents inside ourselves waiting to be unleashed. We must never forget that we were born to be creators and inventors of many wonderful things.

Chapter Eleven

What to Do with Stressful Situations

Most people's lives are full of stressful situations, including myself, because it's all that we ever known. It's what we grew up with, but there's a perfectly good explanation as to why our lives are full of stressful situations. You see, most people are not aware that they are living their lives in a stressful situation. They don't have a clue that they are unconsciously putting themselves into those types of situations and it's because they created those situations for themselves. I know for a fact that nobody wants to be in those types of stressful situations, but sometimes we can't avoid them because sometimes things will get out of control or they are situations created by someone else, and therefore, we don't have any control over them.

Life is already complicated enough that we don't need to add more stress to our daily lives if we don't need to. Anyway, what can we do to solve our stressful situations? Well, this is what I normally do when I encounter myself in a difficult or stressful situation and it's actually a very simple solution, for example, whenever I find myself trying to convince someone about something that they did wrong, and by the way, I know in my heart that I am one hundred percent correct, they simply refuse to listen or they don't want to listen because they are too stubborn. They don't understand that I'm simply trying to help in turning a bad situation into a good situation. Perhaps In their own mind, they understand what I'm trying to do here, but for some unexplained reason, they still refuse to listen. What can I do in situations where the people I'm trying to help don't want to be rescued? Well, my only choice is to walk away and it doesn't mean that I'm giving up on them, but at that time, the best thing for me to do is to walk away because I know deep inside me that I'm not going to win that argument, no matter what I say or do to try and convince those people that they are wrong.

Sometimes people don't have the ability to use the power of reasoning or just plain and simple, they don't want to know the truth. They won't listen to reason, they don't have the mental ability to understand the gravity of the situation and therefore, it will be fruitless on my part to stay and try to win that battle, so the best option for me is to retrieve and walk away, it's that simple.

Walking away does not mean that I am a loser or that I have given up, on the contrary, I'm walking away because at that precise moment I have to be the bigger man. I'm the one in control. I'm the one that has the knowledge and I know that walking away is the best solution for everyone in any kind of difficult situation, and I'm also aware that I will survive to fight another day.

I know that walking away from a difficult situation is not an easy thing to do, especially if we know that we are in the right. Most often than not, people will think to themselves that they are also right when indeed, they are wrong. Sometimes people think that they know everything, but it's only because they are accustomed to doing things their own way, and therefore, they are not willing to change their ways because they must have it their own way or nothing. It's a sad reality, when we don't realize that we are only hurting ourselves by not listening to the truth.

Sometimes we need to leave our pride behind and come to the realization that we cannot be right all the time and we cannot win all the time either. For me is not always about winning, instead, it's about being right and if at any time I'm wrong, then I want people to let me know so that I can correct myself. We need to learn to avoid stressful situations whenever possible, because as I will mention numeral times in this book, stress can inflict a tremendous amount of damage to our wellbeing.

We must learn to let go of any stress that we might currently have and at the same time avoid future stressful situations at any cost. We also need to let go of negative thoughts, negative feelings, and negative emotions because all that negatively will bring us more of the same. It's a vicious cycle that will never end. We must remember that our feelings of worry, anger and hostility will eventually lead to anxiety and anxiety will lead to depression. Remember that good thoughts produce more good thoughts, but bad thoughts produce more bad thoughts.

We all know what stress is, and how damaging it can be for our bodies and for our state of mind. Stress weakens our immune system by attacking our physical bodies, in other words, stress will sap most of our mental and physical energy, so therefore, we must always be on the alert because It will leave us with little energy left to combat or fight diseases. Furthermore, stress is already a disease, it's a silent killer and it will sneak up on us without even knowing it, so always be aware.

If we get too concerned about certain stressful situations or events, then those concerns will turn into worry and worry will turn into stress. Stress will cause us to be fatigued and unable to concentrate during the day. It will clog our minds with all kinds of negative and irrational thoughts, but if that wasn't bad enough, stress will prevent us from falling asleep at night as well. When we encounter any type of stressful situations during the day, our cortisol levels will get elevated in response and that is not a good thing for our minds and for our bodies. Stress is a silent killer and will kill us if we don't do something about it. Now! How can we avoid getting stressed out when all we ever know for most of our entire life is stress? Well, the first thing that we need to do is to be aware of the situation and then we can decide if we want to tackle that situation or not.

Our survival depends totally on our ability to know how we will handle ourselves when we are presented with any difficult situation. How would you respond to a difficult or stressful situation or stressful events? And may I mention that it doesn't matter if those stressful situations or events were part of our own doing or they were created by outside forces that we had nothing to with, again, how would you react? How would you handle it?

The solution to our stressful situations can be an extremely easy solution or it can be an extremely complicated one, it all depends on ourselves or on how we choose to handle them. There's actually a very simple solution to solving any stressful situation and it has to do with the fact that we need to learn to deal with our stressful situations one at a time and on a day-by-day basis. It's also very important that we learn to identify each situation as a low, medium or high stress situation and then we will be able to mount an effective plan of action to resolve it. It's vital that we learn to deal with one stressful situation at a time because if we try to deal with all of our stressful situations at the time, then we will be defeated and as a consequence our mental and physical energy will be drained out of our bodies so we must be careful how we handle them.

Remember that there's nothing you and I can do in a situation where we had absolutely nothing to do with. We must try not to worry about it too much because there's absolutely nothing that you and I could have done to prevent such a situation from happening, so again, why worry about it? We would only make our lives more stressful than what they already are. There are certain events, for example, earthquakes, tornados, tsunamis, title waves and asteroids which are events that we have nothing to do with, so therefore, we mustn't worry about them too much or we will drive ourselves insane. We shouldn't worry too much about stressful events that might never happen anyway, instead, we should be focusing our precious energy on preventing our imaginations from wondering about those stressful events. We should be using our imagination and our energy on more pleasant events, for example, searching for a happier life with our loved ones.

Excessive Worry Can Kill Us

Often, we worry unnecessarily, but why do we worry so much when we know that worrying excessively will destroy our ability to concentrate and if we are not careful, our minds will become foggy and eventually they will shut down completely, in other words, we will lose our ability to think clearly and rationally. Furthermore, we will lose some of the power which enables us to make good sound decisions. Again, our minds and bodies will shut down if we are not careful, therefore, we must avoid putting ourselves in difficult situations whenever possible.

We are human beings who worry about anything and everything. We worry about the past and we worry about the future, but we don't realize that we gain nothing by worrying. We must not worry too much about what tomorrow will bring because tomorrow is not here yet so why worry about it? I'm not saying to completely ignore the future because the future is an important part of our lives. We should worry a little; however, we don't need to worry excessively to the point where we will make our lives more difficult than they already are. We should concentrate most of our energy on dealing with the present, in fact, we should all concentrate on doing the things that matter the most right now.

I cannot emphasize enough about learning to think clearly because when we do, we are going to be able to accomplish that much more.

When we learn to let go of our worries, we are going to find what we have been looking for: our happiness. We will be much happier when we learn to let go of our worries. If we can manage to get rid of our worries, we will be able to release our negative energy, and replace it with a new kind of energy: a positive energy.

When we finally learn to let go of most of our worries, and when we learn to think clearly, our minds will finally be free from junk and debris that we have been accumulating for so many years, then and only then, we will be able to think clearly like it was meant to be. When we finally learn to think clearly. We will be able to discover a whole new world full of new and exciting surprises, a world full of new solutions to problems that we didn't know existed. Remember that when we worry too much our health and our sanity is going to suffer. We will develop stomach ulcers, heart disturbances, insomnia, headaches, and many other ailments.

It's true that when people go the doctor is because they are indeed sick. However, there are people who will go to the doctor because they think they are physically sick. When in fact, they are perfectly healthy, they don't realize that it's all in their minds. Sometimes we let our imagination run wild. We think that we have some type of sickness, however, our sickness is imaginary and eventually our imaginary sickness will become real.

There are plenty of things and events that will make us worry excessively, but if we are not careful, our worries will turn into fears and our fears will turn into anxiety. The sad reality is that most of our fears are just that... fears. Most fears are unfounded fears, meaning that those fears are imaginary. They are unfounded fears which are probably never going to materialize.

We must keep in mind that our fears and worries will turn into anxiety, and in return, our anxiety will turn into more worrying and so on, it's a vicious circle that is never going to end, unless we put a stop to it. That vicious cycle or chain of events must be broken now, before it's too late.

When we worry, we make ourselves so tense and nervous that our whole nervous system goes from normal to abnormal creating even more emotional distress in our bodies. Did you know that we don't get ulcers from the food that we eat? We get ulcers from what is eating us inside. We become sick from unnecessary and endless worry.

We are a nation of worrying people. We worry about everything, we worry about not having enough money, we worry about work, we worry about what type of food we are going to eat, we worry about our children, we worry about the past and we worry about the future. Most of our illnesses do not come from physical labor, but from our mental state of mind. By our mental melt down, by our worries, by our fears, by frustration and by unnecessary hatred. We are making ourselves sick and I ask myself if is worth it. What do we gain by worrying? Absolutely nothing.

The only thing that we gain by worrying is more fears, colds, heart abnormalities, high blood pressure, diabetes, frustrations and consequently, more anxiety. Now! Can we really find happiness? Can we reach our goals and be successful without worrying so much? Yes we can, we are capable of that and much more, we just need to let go of most of our worries, and we also need to clear our minds completely from junk and debris, we must bring our mind to a state of calmness, it's the only way for us to accomplish happiness because when our minds are in a state of calmness, we will be able to think clearly.

We must never retreat when faced with adversity, however, we must face it with calmness and that is when we are at our best. When we are in a calm state of mind, we will be able to cope with adversity much easier.

We must face our problems face to face, but with calmness and not by worrying about them excessively. We must tap into our inner source of power and vanish some of our worries forever. Remember doctors can only heal our bodies, not our minds. Only you and I can heal our own minds. Remember that when we heal our minds, our physical bodies will cure themselves. Furthermore, remember that a cheerful mental attitude will help our bodies to fight disease, so don't worry, be happy.

Excessive Hate and Anger Can Kill Us Too

Excessive anger and hate are two powerful emotions. They will kill us if they are not kept under control. Not only will they kill us, but they will affect our family as well. I asked myself, but how can my anger and hate have a negative effect on my entire family? Well, it's inevitable because our families are going to notice. They will notice when we consciously or unconsciously show our anger or hate towards other human being.

People are going to notice every time we show our emotions of anger and hate. We must remember that happiness is contagious and if we show people how happy we are, then they are going to follow because they also want some of that happiness that we are showing.

Always remember that when we show anger or hate, people will notice whether we are aware of it or not. Any good or bad action we take against someone else is going to have a negative or a positive affect our family members, our friends and the rest of the word.

When we show our anger or hate towards someone else. We are going to make everyone around us become angry and hateful as well, so in this situation people around us do not want to copy us because they don't want to be full of anger and hate. We don't want to create a domino effect, because once a piece starts to fall, the rest of the pieces will follow. We must learn to control our anger and hate because those emotions will have many negative consequences, so we must be careful how we show our emotions.

It's obvious that I'm not immune to having feeling of anger and hate towards someone else, however, as soon as those negative emotions invade my mind, I immediately revert back to feelings of love because feeling of anger and hate are not part of who I am, in other word, it's not in my nature any longer. There was a time when I didn't know how to control those negative emotions as well as I wanted, but not anymore. I'm not going to sit here and pretend that I don't feel the urge to get angry towards certain individuals, however, I immediately try to control my anger because I'm conscious that my hate and anger can be kept under control.

You see, when someone makes me angry or upset about something, I instantly go into a protective mode, I protect my mind and my body from the damaging effects of my anger. I'm able to accomplish this task by not holding on to it. I channel that anger from within my mind and immediately I let it go out into space. I learned many years ago that anger and hate is not in my best interest, so I learn to let those emotions go. I don't hold on to them and I also think that everyone can learn to do the same thing.

I must say that I have been practicing not to get angry for many years and it works for me, I think it has to do with the fact that I have been doing it for so long that it just becomes second nature for me. Again, it works well for me, but if anyone out there wants to accomplish the same results as I have, then they need to start practicing it on a day by day basis. We must practice, practice, and practice some more, until we no longer have the burning desire to hate anyone. Remember that practice makes perfect, well, almost perfect.

The truth is that nobody is immune to getting angry, in fact, everyone in this world is bound to get angry from time to time. Anger and hate are negative emotions that need to be kept under control. Anger and hate is a destroyer of all good things and it's something that no one wants in their lives. There's already plenty of that going around in this world that we don't need to add to it.

When we get angry or hate someone, we are not really hurting them in any way, instead we are hurting ourselves, furthermore, our enemies might not even know that we hate them or that we are angry at them. The reality is that no human being wants to be hated by others. We are all looking for approval from others. We all want to be praised and to be loved by others, even if we don't admit it. We must keep in mind that when we hate someone, we are not actually hurting them as much as we are hurting ourselves. When we hate someone, we are giving them the power over us.

Hating others doesn't make sense to me because I know that it's going to have a negative effect on my health. We have the potential to become mentally and physically ill when we have feelings of anger and hate towards others. Whenever I find myself in a bad situation where someone has done me wrong, my first instinct is to get even. It's only natural that I feel this way, after all, we are human beings. But you know what? I always try to refrain myself from causing others any irreversible damage because once we cross that line, there will be no going back. I know I must never act on impulse or on first reaction. We must control ourselves from causing physical or emotional damage to others. We must regain our composure and remain under control one hundred percent of the time.

I learned a long time ago that it's not my first choice to hurt others in any way or form, in fact, it's the last thing on my mind. Sure, it hurts when someone does you wrong, but I know deep inside me that the hurt will go away soon enough. It's only a matter of time because I know that time will heal all wounds.

We must learn to control ourselves, also, we must learn to control any bad situation that comes our way no matter how bad that situation might seem at the time. We must remember that we always have a choice, so we must choose wisely. We must not retaliate immediately. We must take a few minutes to reflect on what our next move will be and I can assure everyone that after a few minutes of reflection, we will come to a logical conclusion, which is not to retaliate, in fact, it's a great idea and besides, we will be better off not to retaliating.

We are intelligent human beings with a great capacity to understand. Capture and process complicated situations, so let's start acting like intelligent human beings that we are. Never forget that we are very capable of adjusting to any difficult situation that we might encounter now and in the future.

We are a planet of rational human beings. However, sometimes we fail to remember to use our most precious gift…the power of our minds. When we fail to use our minds, the results can be devastating. Remember that there will be a high price to pay when we choose to cause physical damage to others, so let's not act on pure impulse.

Always remember that we must not make any decisions when we are angry at someone. We must take the controls and stop ourselves whenever we feel the need to cause damage to those who have offended us. We must learn to trust ourselves. We must trust our instincts when dealing with anger, we must learn to take baby steps towards controlling our anger and we must remember to always stay tune, we must never get caught up in the heat of the moment, because one thing is for sure, we will regret it later if we act upon our anger and hate.

Again, we must remind ourselves that we gain nothing by being hateful. We must remind ourselves that we gain nothing by becoming angry, we must remind ourselves that nothing good can come out of it. We must follow our internal guidance. We must keep our focus when in anger, we must stop and think before reacting, and finally, we must remember to be the better man: Amen.

Anxiety is a Silent Killer

Many years ago, I was self-diagnosed with anxiety. I didn't know what anxiety was at that time, in fact, I didn't know that I had until one day something dramatic happened to me. You see, I was in a meeting on the second floor of a building in Fremont Ca. It was hot in the room and as a result I was feeling uncomfortable, but I decided to stay anyway. I did my best to stay calm, however, as time went on I started feeling uneasy and nervous, I felt like I was being cooked from the inside out, my heart started pounding extremely fast, going a hundred miles an hour, my entire body was sweating profoundly, I didn't know what was wrong with me at that time. Finally, I couldn't take it any longer, so I decided to get up and walk away from the meeting, but at the same time I couldn't come up with an excuse as to why I was leaving, however, I decided to go anyway, but before I walked out of the room, I decided to go to the bathroom to wash my face with cold water and as I was splashing water on my face I realized that nothing else matter at that moment in time, in other words, when you are sick, your high stress job doesn't matter. All your plans that you had for the future no longer matter. You start to see life from a different perspective.

After I was done washing my face I went outside to the parking lot where my car was parked, but before I left the meeting and as I was walking through the meeting room someone asked me if I was feeling okay and I responded that I had to go because something important came up. My intention was to go to my car. Get in it, close my eyes, and relax for about half an hour and that is exactly what I did.

Afterwards, I spent an extra half hour trying to declutter my mind of unnecessary junk. I was thinking about my life and how I got to the point of exhaustion. Everything was beginning to make sense to me, the big puzzle was beginning to take shape, all the pieces were coming together.

I realized that I was trying to do too many things at one time, too much too fast and that is a recipe for disaster. I was drinking a six pack of caffeinated sodas per day, and if that wasn't bad enough, I was drinking coffee and beer. I was smoking as well, plus the fact that I was not eating healthy foods and not sleeping much either. Can you imagine that? All the sodas. The coffee, the smoking, the beer, not sleeping enough and not eating healthy foods were some of the main contributors to my anxiety, along with the daily stressful situations, which by the way, those were situations that I put myself in. I created most of those stressful situations and have no one to blame but myself.

All my worries and my stressful situation contributed to my anxiety. All those things drove me to the point of exhaustion. They all had something to do with it. Anyway, after spending about an hour resting. Relaxing and trying to figure out what went wrong, I felt much better about myself. I started feeling an inner peace never experienced before, I was feeling relaxed and I was feeling much happier about the whole situation. I felt an inner peace invading my body because I finally knew what to do to help me make a change and improve my overall life. That was the turning point in my life so from that point on, I decided to completely turn my life around I started reading some amazing books on self-improvement and several books about anxiety.

Through these books, I found out that for the past ten or fifteen years I had this terrible thing call: anxiety. I didn't know what anxiety was until I started reading about it, in fact, I think not too many people knew what anxiety was at that time, however, most people do now know. Nowadays people are more aware of what anxiety can do to a human being. You see, the main reason as to why my life went into a deep spiral was because I was trying too hard to please everyone, in other words, I was trying to do too much, too fast, no wonder I became invaded by anxiety.

I decided that this was a good time for me to make a change to my way of life. I decided that from that moment on, I was going to become be a different man and a better human being. I promised myself that in the future, I wasn't going to try and do too many things at one time because in reality... all we can ever do is one thing at a time and no more, so from that day on I took one step at a time.

One of the things that helped me change my way of life was the fact that I decide to write myself a list of things to do for each day of the week. This list was going to help me by reminding me that I needed to take it slow and only do one thing at a time. This list was going to help improve my way of life, but at the same time I needed to make this list but without stressing about it.

I promise myself that I wasn't going to stress myself about not finishing all the things on the list for each day of the week because I decided that my health was more important than anything else in the world. I needed to remind myself that there was going to be a new tomorrow. Anyway, I wrote the most important things on the list first, and if I didn't finish everything on the list by the end of the day, I knew that everything was going to be okay. From that day on I was conscious of not making irrational decisions. I became responsible for my future actions.

By the way, that was not the end of my story about my anxiety, a few weeks later I decided to have another meeting, however, this time around, I decided that this meeting was going to be at my house because I thought that I would feel more at peace being in my own house, however, that wasn't the case, everything was going well for a while until something change, I started to get antsy and nervous again, I was not feeling at peace, something was wrong so I excuse myself and went outside for some fresh air. This time my anxiety wasn't as severe as the previous time, but it was happening again.

Anyway, I was outside relaxing and trying to figure out what was wrong with me when suddenly, one of my friends came out from the meeting and asked me if I was all right and I responded that I was feeling a little stressed, to which he replied, you know? "I've been watching you for the last few meetings and I noticed that you seemed okay, but only for the for first half an hour, but I also notice that after the first thirty minutes you start to feel a little uncomfortable. You don't look like yourself after a while" then he proceeded to tell me that I needed to spend roughly about fifteen minutes every day for myself and without any distraction, he then told me that I needed to meditate so that I can learn to relax, he also told me that if I do this every single day that it will help me with my stress and anxiety.

I decided to listen to him, and I did what he told me to do, but to my surprise, it did work. It was wonderful. It was an extremely rewarding experience for me. That was the trick. That was exactly what I was missing from my life: meditation. Some meditation and relaxation daily, even if is just for a few minutes, it will be enough to make us feel good all over again. Meditation is a good medicine for getting rid of our worries and anxiety. Meditation will remind us that we need to take it easy. I knew something about meditating and relaxation before my friend told me about it, but somehow, I forgot all about it. I got lost along the way. Sometimes we need to hear from someone else that we are doing something wrong in order to realize it. We need someone else to tell us what to do and how to do it.

But wait, it's not over yet, before these episodes which I had with my anxiety, I felt like an afraid little child, I was always worry about something, I was afraid of my surroundings, I was afraid to go out of my house because I thought that something bad was going to happen to me along the way, to put in a different prospective, I thought to myself that I was going to died. I was afraid of crossing bridges because I thought the bridge was going to collapse as I was crossing it. I was afraid of being surrounded by people, especially where there was big crowds of people. I was afraid of tight and enclose places. I was afraid of flying and to this day I'm still afraid of flying. I was afraid to go out and eat with my wife and the rest of my family because I thought that if I go out and eat with them I was going to choke on my own food, it felt like I couldn't breathe, It was an ongoing and terrifying experience for me for many years.

Flying is something that I have yet to conquer and I don't know if I'm ever going to be able to conquer my fear of flying, but nevertheless, I feel like I'm at least eighty percent cured from my anxiety. I have never taken or believed in drugs for my anxiety because I don't believe that it would help me, instead, I took control of my situation and started reading as many books as possible about what anxiety can do to us. Where it comes from and how we can get rid of it. Another thing I decided to do which help with my anxiety was to start drinking mangos-teen juice, which I had and continue to have faith in it.

The following four things will help us with our anxiety:
1. Don't try to do too many things at one time because it will only drive us crazy.
2. Reading lots of books about anxiety so that we can learn all that there is to know about the disease. Some of these books are amazing. They will show us how to keep it under control, or even better, they will show us how we can get rid of it forever. In my situation, I was able to control it about eighty to ninety percent. This means that I'm not one hundred percent cured; however, I will take those odds any day. Even fifty percent is better than 0%.
Imagine yourself without any anxiety whatsoever, imagine yourself being able to take control of your life and your own destiny, wouldn't that be amazing?
3. We must make some alone time for ourselves, at least fifteen minutes per day so that we can do meditation and relaxation.
4. Drinking some of that wonderful mangos teen juice, but let me remind you, that you must have faith in the juice because If you don't have faith in it, chances are that it's not going to work. Remember to have faith in everything that you do because if you have faith, then anything is possible.

More about anxiety, but not to worry I won't talk about my anxiety anymore. Rather, I'm going to talk about anxiety in general. People say that more is better, but in this case, more is not good. Not when it's about anxiety, in this case, less is much better. It's time for you to re-examine your life because when you are done, everything will become much clearer. Remember that there will be a high price to pay when you continue to live your life the way you are living it right now, especially for those who have high demanding jobs. It's unfortunately, but it's a way of life for many millions of people around the world. People drive themselves into the ground without even knowing it, because all they know is what they know and that is it. They work to the point of exhaustion; they get burned out from working too many hours per day and in some cases, they might even work eighty to a hundred hours per week because sometimes it's expected from their peers.

For most people, work is all they know. They live for their work; they dream for their work and they eat for their work. People get nervous at work. They get exhausted and they become irritated against their co-workers creating even more chaos and confusion among them. Who is responsible for our anxiety. Is it us, is it the company we work for, or is it a combination of both?

It's obvious that most companies have a lot to do with the development of anxiety for many people around the world because their working environment is not ideal for most people. There's a tremendous amount of pressure for people to finish their tasks as fast as possible and this in turn will create all kinds of worries, stress and anxiety among their employees, but companies are not all to blame for our troubles, we are also responsible for many of our afflictions. Regardless of whose fault it is, we must learn to take responsibility for ourselves and make a change in our life.

We must stop stressing ourselves to death because stress is going to damage our bodies and our minds. We need to learn to slow down because long lasting stresses from everyday events such as financial worries, will eventually wear our brain down. Stress is never a good thing, the only time that we should ever be stressed is when we are in a dangerous situation and it's because it's only a short-live stress. Short live stress is a good thing because it will trigger the "flight or fight syndrome" it's a signal that we were born with. It's the signal, which is going to save our lives, it's the signal that is going to save us from any imminent danger.

Chapter Twelve

Our World as We Know it Now

It's a beautiful and magical world. A world full of wonders, a world full of undiscovered treasures. A world full of breathtaking panoramic views from down below and from above as well. We have some beautiful and majestic mountains covered with white snow in the wintertime. We have beautiful rivers with fresh crystalline water running on its way to the oceans, we have beautiful oceans across the entire planet along with its countless white sand beaches, we have beautiful and breathtaking waterfalls throughout the planet, we have colorful hills and valleys, we have amazing assortment of colorful trees in the fall, and we have some amazing and colorful rainbows. We are surrounded by beauty and I can't help but asking myself the following question "where else in the entire universe we are going to find such a beauty?" Perhaps there's other planets within our solar system that are just as beautiful as our planet, but we don't know for sure, so we might as well enjoy the beauty of our planet. We must not take everything for granted and enjoy what we have right here in our backyard. Let's all enjoy and admire such a beauty with our own eyes.

It's unfortunately that sometimes we forget to enjoy all of the beautiful things that our world has to offer us, and it's because we are always too preoccupied with our negative thoughts. Most of us spend our lives worrying and stressing about insignificant little things that we forget to enjoy all the beautiful things that our world has to offer. Its beauty, contrast, and diversity. Oh! And let's not forget about our beautiful Grand Canyon, which took millions of years for Mother Nature to sculpt. We also have many beautiful lakes with turquoise and blue waters across the planet, and finally, we have many beautiful national parks with an abundance of wildlife.

What else can we possibly ask for? I know we always want to see more. We always want to explore more because we are human beings, and as such, we are never satisfied with what we have because it's in our nature. We always want to explore and learn more about our beautiful planet and that is a good thing, because we are a planet of explorers and we have an insatiable thirst to learn new things.

There's nothing wrong with wanting to explore and learn more about our beautiful planet and there's nothing wrong with wanting to learn more about our universe, however, we must not forget about our very own planet. We must try to enjoy the beautiful things within our planet every single day. Again, sometimes we are too preoccupied with our own problems and our daily routines that we forget that there's a wonderful and beautiful world out there for us to enjoy. We must learn to enjoy more of the things that we have rather than the things that we don't have. We must make time from our busy schedules for enjoyment, we must make time to enjoy some of the things that our planet has to offer us and we must enjoy those things with the people that we love.

The Ugly Side of Our World

We all know that our world is a beautiful place, but at the same time, it's a world full of stressful situations and anxiety. The true reality is that our world has nothing to do with our problems. The world is not to be blamed for our own doing. The world is not responsible for what happens to us. We are the ones to blame because we are in constant disarray, and it has to with the fact that we are constantly under tremendous pressure to succeed in everything that we do, we are constantly under pressure to perform and do our jobs well and in a timely manner. The pressure and stress from work can be overwhelming for most people, no wonder we are the way we are. No wonder we feel the way we feel.

Not only do we have the pressure to succeed and to perform at a high level at work, but we also have the pressures to succeed and perform at home. The pressure we feel to succeed and perform at home is not much different from what we experience at work. The pressure we feel to perform at home includes taking care of the kids and sometimes we must take care of other family members as well. We have pressure from our banks because we need to pay the mortgage loan, or else, we won't have a roof under our heads. We have the pressure to pay other bills in a timely manner, and we also have the pressure to put food on the table for our family every single day.

Furthermore, we have the pressure to clean and maintain our house. For example, Cleaning the dishes, dusting, mopping the floors, grocery shopping, putting gas in our cars, washing our cars, cleaning the pool, cutting the grass, trimming the bushes, putting the trash out on the curb for pick-up and checking the mail. We put a lot of pressure on ourselves and it's all very overwhelming. I'm sure that there are still plenty of other things that we need to take care of when we are at home, but I won't get into any more details because you probably get the idea by now, right?

We all have different needs, different things that we need to take care off. Some people have more things to do than others. What I'm trying to say is that: after doing all these things there isn't any time left on the day for other important things. For example, taking care of ourselves eating healthy foods and relaxing. There's not enough time left for us to sit down and watch a good movie. There's no time left for exercise and there's no time left on the day to go out and have a good time without having to worry about a million of things that we need to do on a day by day basis. Something must give. Perhaps our health will suffer, and our relationships with the people we love is going to suffer as well. Everything is going to suffer because sometimes we just don't know how to deal with all the different tasks and chores that we must do on a day-by-day basis. It doesn't mean that we are doing everything wrong; we just need to learn to organize our lives, but in order to accomplish such a task is by simplifying our lives, in other words, we need to decluttering our minds from unnecessary junk, in other words, we need to declutter our minds from negative thoughts, furthermore, we need to declutter our lives from materialistic junk as well. We need a fresh start, but the only way that we are going to accomplish it is by regaining total control of our lives.

We need to take control of every situation. We need to confront our problem head on or as people say: "we need to take the bull by the horns." However, we must do it without overstressing ourselves too much because that will be unproductive. I know for a fact that it's not going to be an easy thing to accomplish, but believe me, I've been there and done that. One thing that we must keep in mind is that our lives are never going to be perfect, however, we must always thrive to make our lives a little less complicated by simply getting rid of unnecessary junk that we have been accumulating throughout our lives.

Work Related Stress

First, I want to dedicate this chapter to my wife, Norma because I know firsthand what working long hours will do to a person. Working long hours will bring a tremendous amount of stress to everyone, but that's just the beginning, because when people work long hours their health and happiness will be compromised, and if that wasn't enough, their families will suffer as well. It's a heavy price millions of people around the world must pay for working to exhaustion. People will get burn-out from working long hours, I can see it in my wife and that's why I will support and encourage her with kind words to lift her spirit up.

Work related stress has been a problem for a long time, not only in the United States, but around the world as well, and It continues to grow at an alarming rate. Work-related stress will weaken our immune system. It will affect our overall health, not only physically but mentally as well. Furthermore, work related stress is going to affect our productivity and performance, but that's just the beginning, work related stress will cause many other symptoms or side effects, for example, sleep deprivation, insomnia, stomach ulcers, headaches, high blood pressure, depression, anxiety and coronary heart diseases, and consequently, we won't be able to concentrate on our work-related tasks. It's also possible that we might become overwhelmed by uncontrollable anger, and if that wasn't enough, we will compound our problems by overeating unhealthy foods which can lead to obesity, or start drinking more alcohol than usual and perhaps, we will start using drugs to help us fall asleep.

There are other reasons as to why people get burned out and become overwhelmed by stress from work, for example, long hours, heavy workload, job insecurity, conflicts with co-workers, including our bosses, low pay, and no opportunity for advancement. But is there anything that we can do to alleviate some of the work-related stress? Yes, there is, we all have the power to contribute in little ways and in big ways, and even though, there will be many things that will happen at work that will be beyond our control we can still try to focus our energy on the things that we can control.

If we learn to work as a team at work, then it's going to allow us to create a better working environment for everyone, for example, we can stop backstabbing and insulting our co-workers. We can change our bad behaviors by being civilized with one another.

In addition, we can try taking better care of our health by eating a balanced diet. We can also start meditating and exercise more often because that will relieve some of the work-related stress. As you can see, there are plenty of things that we can do to make everyone at work have a memorable and enjoyable experience. Finally, as a boss it's your responsibility to listen to what people have to say because in order for an employee to feel good about themselves, they need to be listened by their superiors, especially, when they come to them with any concerns or new ideas that is going to make the workplace more enjoyable for them, furthermore, when an employee feels as if he or she is part of the big picture, then they will be more productive and at the same time, they will be much healthier as a result. We must remember that somehow, we are all connected, in other words, we are all in this together.

Chapter Thirteen

The Power of True Love

As human beings, we are constantly craving the love, the attention, and the approval from the people that we love, but we also crave it from our friends and strangers. It's something that we have been looking from the very beginning of our existence. We want other people to like us and love us. We want them to give us the recognition that we are looking for and even though sometimes we don't deserve it, we still want it. In fact, we are forever cravings for a lot's of things but craving love from others is perhaps the biggest of them all. It's a human condition which nobody can deny. We all want to find love and it's because we know that if we are lucky enough to find it, then we are going to find happiness, at least most of the time.

Love is one of the most powerful human emotions that we can ever experience. However, there are other human emotions that we experience from time to time, for example, anger, rage, and hate, but I'm not going to talk about those right now because I will talk about them in a different chapter.

We need to understand that love has different degrees of intensity. It's something that some people might not be aware of. We all have the capacity to love someone, but do we really know to what degree of intensity we love them? It's something that we normally don't think about often, but it's important that we know how much we love someone because it's the only way that we are going to take our love for someone to a higher degree of intensity.

If you are not sure about the degree of intensity of love that you feel for that special person in your life, then you need do some soul search, well, that is if you want to find out, and If you discover that the degree of intensity is not what you expected. If you discover that it was too low, then you have the choice to elevate that special love to a higher level. You see, you must take that level of intensity and raise it to a higher-level. If you raise your degree of love that you feel for that special person in your life, it will mean that you really care and love that person.

It's important for us to remember that when we truly love someone, we should give them, not twenty-five or fifty percent of our love, we should be in it one hundred percent of the time and nothing less. The love that we feel for that special person is like a ten-speed bicycle, in other words, a bicycle has up to ten different speeds, and so is love. The intensity of our love can be anywhere from 1-10 so we must keep that in mind when we tell someone that we love them. We must ask ourselves the following question: "What is the degree of intensity of love that I feel for that special person in my life?

Furthermore, we must ask ourselves another question "what is the degree of love that we feel for our spouses. Our parents, our brothers and sisters, our nephews and nieces, our uncles and aunts, our friends, and even people that we don't even know?" "What about God?' "What is the degree of intensity of love that we feel for God?" These are especially important questions that we must ask ourselves because it's the only way that we are going to be able to raise our degree of happiness.

I promise that I will talk more about what true love is, but before I continue, I have a couple more things which I need to talk about. First, we need to be aware that there's different types of love, for example, the love we feel for materialistic things. Like a new car or a new house and if you recently bought a brand-new car, you probably brought that car because you like it, and if you like it, that would only mean that you love that car, right? Furthermore, when people ask you if you love your new car, your answer will probably be the following: "Oh! I love my new car" however, you must remember that this type of love is purely materialistic.

Secondly, there's the romantic kind of love that we feel for someone, in other words, it's the kind of love that we feel for a man or a woman.
When we discover someone who we are attractive to or someone who we are falling in love with as of right now, we are going to feel a tingling sensation on the inside.

There's other types of love that we feel for someone, for example, a boyfriend or girlfriend kind of love, there's the brotherly or sisterly type of love, the motherly and fatherly type of love, and finally, there's the grandkids type of love, so you see, there's all types of feelings of love and with different degrees of intensity.

Okay, it's time to talk about what true love is. True love is an intense and tingly feeling of affection that we feel for someone. True love is based on our own personal beliefs. Judgments, and experiences, in other words, feelings of affections are based on how we portray others, for example, we might find someone extremely attractive and desirable and that is when our bodies will take over. In other words, our bodies will reinforce what our mind already knows: that this person makes us feel good on the inside. This type of love is a physical attraction that we feel for a man or a woman, it's a different type of feeling then the one we feel for our parents or our kids.

One important fact that we need to remember is that true love is unselfish. True love always brings out the best in all of us, and we always want to make others happy, in other words, true love will make us do good things for them, but without wanting something in return, true love is going to makes us want to protect the people that we love, true love is going to makes us feel a sense of belonging and it's going to makes us feel safer in our own environment, true love is going to makes us feel connected to others as well. If we genuinely love someone (and it's obvious) we want to make that person feel special and loved, furthermore, we only want to meet that person's expectations. We must remember that without the feelings of love, we will be feeling a tremendous amount of emptiness on the inside. Without the feeling of love, we are going to feel depressed, scared, and lonely.

True love is not just about loving someone. It's also about trusting each other. It's about acceptance, respect, kindness and compassion, it's about putting our egos aside and recognizing the values that we provide for each other. One of the most important thing to remember is that true love is a two-way relationship and I'm not talking about fifty-fifty responsibility here, rather I'm talking about sharing all responsibilities and being committed to each other one hundred percent. If our love for someone is pure and sincere then we are going experience what true love really is. Furthermore, when we experience true love, we only want to do nice things for the other person. We want to make that person feel good about themselves. We want that person to be happy and in return, we want to be happy as well. We must remember that if we genuinely love someone, then we must be honest with one another. We must never hide our feelings from the people that we love. We must not lie, play games, or hide the truth from them.

We must share everything, including the good and the bad equally. True love is about trusting each other to do the right thing.

Remember that if we are not in love, then we won't be able to feel connected with that person, and instead, we will create a false sense of love for them, when we are not in love we will not speak with the truth because we are thinking more about ourselves rather than thinking about other people's needs first. When we are not in love, we are only looking to fulfill our own needs and our own pleasures first. When we are not in love, we will be lacking the respect for others. We should never hold on to a person solely for the purpose of fulfilling our own personal needs.

When we are truly in love, we must be willing to give and receive equally. We must learn to accept others for who they are. Remember that when we are truly in love, we will see the good things in others and not the bad things. When we are in love with someone, we must treat them as our equal and not as someone lower than ourselves. When we are in love, we must not, physically, or verbally abuse that person. Love is unselfish. Love is giving something to others, but without expecting anything in return. It's important to remember that true love doesn't appear overnight, it's something that must be developed overtime and it's because true love needs time to grow.

Love is remarkably similarly to a fruit tree; they both need time to grow. Normally when we think of a fruit tree, we don't think about how that tree got be so tall. Well, that fruit tree had to be planted by someone, and it all started with a seed, in other words, a fruit tree would not have come to be if someone had not planted that seed.

However, planting a seed in the ground doesn't mean that it's going to grow into a big, beautiful fruit tree. It's going to need water in order to grow and produce fruit, it's not going to grow on its own, although it's possible, however, everything will have to be aligned just perfectly, it's going to need enough water and the right amount of sun. If we want a seed to grow into a beautiful fruit tree, then it must be cultivated, and as I said before; it will need water and pruning on a consistent basis. It's only then that we will see the fruit of our labor. Now! We know that true love and fruit trees have a lot in common, they both need time to grow.

We know that we must plant the seed of love in our hearts and give it time to grow because love needs to be cultivated slowly and it's the only way that love is going to grow into something beautiful.

Remember that we can't truly say that we love someone until we have spent many years together. It's only then that we can truly say that we genuinely love someone.

Chapter Fourteen

Life in the Fast Lane

Nowadays, most people are living their lives in the fast lane. They are forever rushing to get somewhere, and everything starts early in the morning. We wake up to the sound of the alarm, then we shower, and if we have kids, we need to wake them up too, we cook them breakfast, or maybe just waffles, then we have to make sure that they are properly dressed and well-groomed before they are off to school. As an adult, we also need to make sure that we put something in our stomachs, perhaps some hot cereal or a cup of coffee, then we must rush to the cars, and as soon as we are in the car we take off to drop off the kids at school. Afterwards, we drive like a bat out of hell towards the freeway entrance, but as we are driving, our minds start to wonder whether we forgot something. Our minds are going a hundred miles an hour and so is our cars, well, maybe not a hundred miles an hour but close to it. The point here is that we are not in total control because our minds are all over the place, we are driving way too fast so that we can get to work on time. Most often than not we don't even take into consideration that other people are trying to accomplish the same thing.

Sometimes we are weaving all over the freeway looking for an opening or looking for the fastest lane, and on top of that, we have the radio on full blast distracting us even more. Finally, we get to work safely, thanks to God. We got out of car and rushed into the building and lucky for us, we made it to work just in the nick of time.

But now the hard work is just about to begin, we probably have a million things that we need to take care of, for example, unfinished projects from the previous day. We probably also have hundreds of voicemails and emails that we need to take care of. Now! As for the rest of the day, we will be sprinting from one place to another, trying to finish our daily tasks or projects but as we are trying to do our work, we are thinking about our spouses and kids and hoping that they are doing well and not getting into trouble. We are also thinking towards the end of the day when we must rush back to school, pick up the kids, go back home and get them ready for sports activities. It's a constant circle of life that never seems to end.

We are living our lives in the fast lane, always going excessively fast, it's like we are racing to a never-ending finish line and it doesn't matter how fast we are going, it seems that there's never enough time to do everything that we need to do. It's understandable that in today's world, everything must be done fast. We are living a fast life because everything that we do must be done fast. Our computers are faster and faster every day, our cars are fast, our microwaves are fast, and our air travel is even faster, we want everything done as fast as possible. We are becoming a society of super speeders. It's no wonder that our lives are constantly in disarray.

We must learn to take total control of our lives, but the only way that we are going to accomplish such a task is by slowing down a little bit, otherwise, the years will pass us by and we are going to miss out on finding happiness.

Not so long ago our lives were completely different, it was a simple and uncomplicated life, everything was much easier to accomplish, going places and going to work was done at a much slower pace. In the old days, we went to work, then came back home and still had plenty of time to sit around the front porch talking to family members and friends. We talked for hours at a time, again, life was plain and simple. One would think that with all the new technological advances our lives would become easier, but apparently that is not the case, on the contrary, it made our lives that much more difficult because nowadays we must do everything fast.

We need to realize that by living a fast life, we are going to eventually develop all types of health issues for ourselves. We need to remember that excessive worrying and stress is going to weaken our minds and our body's immune system and consequently we will develop a tremendous amount of anxiety.

Most often than not, we feel as if our lives are spinning out of control and it's because no matter how hard we try, we always seem to come up short in trying to make our lives a little more relax and enjoyable. Everything is so overwhelming at times and we just don't know how to stop it. So, what can we do to improve our situation? Well, the first thing that we need to do is to slow down because this will allow us to reorganize our lives and our thoughts, in other words, it's going to help us to take control of our lives forever.

Whenever I find myself living my life in the fast lane, I immediately stop doing whatever I'm doing and I tell myself: "slow down, it's not worth getting stressed out over nothing." It really works for me and I see no reason why it shouldn't work for you too. It's embarrassing that sometimes we don't have enough time to spend with our families or friends and that is not a good thing because most of what we do is for our families, but yet, it seems like we are going in the wrong direction. It seems that there's never enough time left on the day to spend with family and to do all the things that we need to do, but no matter how fast technology gets, or how fast we go, we will never be able to catch up, so why worry? Know that if we always try to do our best, then we will be okay.

More about technology. I consider myself less than an average person as far as technology is concerned. I know that I will never be able to catch up to it no matter how hard I try and it's because of my lack of time. Sure! I try to keep up with some of the new technology, however, it's almost impossible, unless of course you have all the time in the world or you are a computer genius, otherwise, you will never be able to catch up to technology and it's because it's constantly changing or being updated, so I rather work on slowing down my fast life and try to enjoy life to its fullest, but at a much slower pace.

I want to make it crystal clear that technology is changing way too fast for me, and it's not that I can't learn it, it's just that I promise myself I wouldn't use all of my precious time on trying to learn it. I will try to learn as much as possible whenever time allows me, however, there's no way that I will be able to catch up to It. so I'm not going to worry or stress over it. It's unfortunate that I started learning way too late, so again, I won't be able to catch up to it any time soon, because it will be an impossible task. Perhaps I will be able to catch up a little bit more later on, when I'm done with my book.

Again, we live in a fast-paced world where everything must be done fast. It's a rat race, going towards the finish line, but unfortunately, there's no finish line. Remember that when we live a fast life, we are going to miss out on lots of exciting and fun things, like family time, social events, and many other pleasures that life has to offer.

Are you aware that sometimes we can't even enjoy a pleasant conversation with someone else because we don't have enough time and we are always on the run? Sometimes we don't even have the patience to listen to other people because we are thinking about our busy lives or our busy schedules, so we simply ignore them or tell them "sorry I have to go". We just overthink everything way too much.

Sometimes we want to slow down because we feel that our lives are spinning out of control, and we come to realize that by slowing down we will be able to accomplish a lot more and with less stress. Even if we were able to slow down for a day or two, the reality is that we will forget very quickly about slowing down and we will revert back to our old way of doing things and that is to: live a fast life. We must remind ourselves on a consistent basis that we need to slow down.

There's a couple of things which is contributing to our anxiety and it's a combination of new technology and economics. Well, it's more about economics than technology. Again, life is a rat race, we are forever racing from place to place, from activity to active and consequently we are depriving ourselves from enjoying many wonderful things, and at the same time we are depriving our bodies from eating healthy meals. We are depriving our bodies from physical exercise, and we are depriving our brains from reaching its true potential because of the lack of nutritional food which includes, vitamins, minerals, and nutrients.

Living a fast life is never a good thing because as we continue to go faster and faster in our accelerated world, we will sacrifice our very own happiness, and as we move faster and faster ,we will eventually run out of patience and not only with ourselves, but with others as well. It's so sad that as time goes by, we have become less and less patient.

I have a wonderful plan in place that I use for myself daily. You see, I'm always conscious that some things need to be done fast, however, I also know that not everything needs to be done fast. My plan is simple. Basically, we have three different gears. We have slow, medium, and high gears. The plan here is that we need to learn to use all three gears. I'm going to give you an example, if you find yourself driving on only one gear all of the time, then you are going to burn yourself out. We must never forget that we have two other gears which we can use anytime, anywhere, therefore, we must learn to use all three. Another good example will be a freeway…a freeway has more than one lane and in many cases six or seven lanes, therefore, we always have a choice of changing lanes, we can go slow, fast or we can even go faster, it all depends on which lane we are driving, we don't need to stay in one lane forever. The same principles applies to our daily lives. Always remember that we have more than one gear speed which we can use, so don't ever forget that we have choices and that we don't always need to go fast in order to accomplish whatever we need to accomplish.

I think it's a great plan that everyone can use to help them to slow down their busy and fast way of life. This plan it's only going to work if you put it into action every single day of your life. Does my plan make sense to you? It does to me and that is why I'm forever using this plan because I know that it works. This plan which I have in place for myself is a reminder on my part that I need to slow down, well, that is if I want to enjoy life to its fullest.

I'm aware that when we are young, we want to live our Live's in the fast lane. We never want to stop because we have way too much energy. We just want to keep on going like some type of energizer bunny. Most people don't want to slow down no matter what happens to them and even if they wanted to slow down, they wouldn't know how. Sometimes only father time will teach us that it's time to slow down.

As We Get Older

It's a well-known fact that as we get older, we slow down, and it isn't because we want to. We slow down because we have no other choice. Like I said before, we have Father Time to thank for that. One of the main reasons we slowdown as we age is because we have lived a long time. When we get older, our bodies no longer have the same strength and energy that they used to have.

Another reason as to why we slowdown as we age is because we learn that in order to enjoy life to its fullest, we need to slow down. Furthermore, we slow down because we have accumulated plenty of knowledge which plays an important role in everything that we do. We know that by slowing down, we will be able to enjoy more of the little things than the bigger things. Furthermore, as we get older, we just simply learn to use our time wisely and more effectively.

Remember that at some point in our lives, we will slow down whether we want too or not and I'm not talking about slowing down physically or mentally, rather, I'm talking about not living our lives in the fast lane. We need to realize that we don't always need to live our lives in the fast lanes in order to be happy. I'm a person fortunate enough to have learned to slow down at a much younger age and I owe it all to hundreds of books which I read throughout my life and because of that, I have accumulated a wealth of knowledge.

Even though I accumulated vast amounts of knowledge, and I will be honest about it, I wasn't always immune to living my life at a fast pace. I was forced throughout my life to ask myself tons of questions, for example, whenever I found myself driving too fast, I would ask myself the following: "where am I going in such a rush and what do I hope to accomplish?" So afterwards, I slowed down because I realized that going too fast was not in my best interest. It wasn't a good idea for me, and it wasn't a good idea for anyone else.

Perhaps the number one reasons as to why people are living their lives in the fast lane is because they want to accomplish a lot in a very short time, like in my case, I wanted to accomplish some of my dreams and goals as fast as possible; it was as if time was going to pass me by very quickly, and therefore, I wanted to accomplish most of my dreams while I was still young. I can't think of a better reason as to why sometimes I was living my life in the fast lane.

Even though sometimes I was living a fast life, I always tried to remind myself to slow down, and so I learned to slow down, however, it took me several years before I was able to really get the hang of it. Even now, I still try to do some things too fast, but again, I always do my best to remind myself, that I need to slow down, because when we slow down, we will learn to appreciate life more, and as a result, we are going to be happier than ever before.

Again, we need to learn to slow down our fast way of life, so that we can take control of our lives before it is too late. We don't want to look back and regret some of the things that we did or didn't do. Life goes by too fast; we are always going from place to place in such a rush trying to accomplish some of our goals that we fail to act as human beings. We forget our manners and behave selfishly at times. Sometimes we have no disregard for the safety of others. It's always about a *"me first"* mentality that takes over our good judgment.

We are in such a rush most of the time and it's because we don't want to die unfulfilled, and without having accomplished some of our goals and dreams. Remember that we will accomplish better and greater things when we learn to slow down. When we think things through and we have a plan in place, we will accomplish so much more. We must think about the big puzzle here. We must think and analyze all the possibilities, and we must think about what the end results will be.

Life is all about choices, therefore, we must never make any decisions or choices based on first impressions. We need to sit down. Analyzed everything and tried to figure out what our next move is going to be. We must make our choices based on true facts because the next choice we make is going to have, either positive result or negative results. Again, when we make our choices based on impulse and without knowing the facts, it might bring us some devastating results. Remember that at the end, the result is what matters. Whether the results are good or bad, it will have a positive or a negative effect on our lives and on our entire family as well.

Whenever we decide to do something, we must ask ourselves, how is this going to affect me and my family?

We must ask ourselves the following question before we decide to embark ourselves on a mission "what are the consequences for my acts going to be if I make the wrong decision vs. making the right decision?" If we make the right decision it might bring us big rewards and happiness, but on the other hand, if we make the wrong decisions, it could potentially be devastating for ourselves and our families. Furthermore, we must ask ourselves the following question when making any decisions "Do I really like this decision which I'm about to make. Am I really going to like the way things will turn out?" Remember that only you have the power and the will to change your thoughts before is too late.

Imagine for a minute how much more we will be able to enjoy our lives by simply slowing down a little. We have the power of our minds and the capacity to get creative and solve any arising problems. Our knowledge is our best weapon so we must learn to use it and we must learn to use it wisely. Always keep in mind that when we live a fast life, we will be shortening our life. We will age faster and therefore, we will die young and without having fulfilled some of our dreams, so it's vital that we pace ourselves.

Furthermore, we know now that as we age, our bodies will slow down, our thinking process will slow down, and our reaction time is not going to be what it used to be, like when we were young, but why is that? Well, there's several reasons as to why we slow down as we age. The first reason is obvious; we just simply cannot keep on doing the same physical and strenuous activities as when we were young because our physical strength diminishes as the years go by. Our bodies just won't have the same energy and it has to do with the fact that we mistreated our bodies our entire lives. We smoked, drank alcohol, we didn't sleep enough, and we didn't exercise enough either. Staying mentally and physically healthy is the key for prolonging our lives, but unfortunately most of us don't stay very active throughout our lives, maybe because in our minds we think that we will live forever.

Another reason as to why we slow down as we age is because our brain connections break down overtime between our two hemispheres. Apparently, we seem to have excessive crosstalk between our two brains and this in turn will affect our response time. It's like a circle of confusion. Another reason as to why we slowdown as we age is because the blood flowing to our brain has decreased, and finally, we age more rapidly as we get older, because we start to lose some of our brain cells and it's because we don't replenish those them with new ones by eating the right foods.

However, not everything has been lost, there is hope after all, just because we get older doesn't mean that we must accept our fate of reacting in a slow manner. There's a few simple things that we can do to keep our bodies and minds in good working condition. First, we need to stimulate our brain cells on a day by basis daily, but the only way that we will accomplish such a task is by reading and learning new things every single day. We must continue to increase our endurance by doing daily physical exercises. We must boost our immune system by providing our bodies with all the essential vitamins. Nutrients and minerals that it needs and if we do this on a consistent basis, we will enable our bodies to stay young and strong as we age. I know that it's easier said than done, but it must be done.

We must remember that as we age, we will increase our self-awareness. Our self-reflection and our reasoning, but unfortunately, as we get older, we will also lose some of our mental and physical health as well and that is why it's so important that we start taking care of our bodies at an earlier stage. Getting older is something that we must all go through. It's an unpleasant fact and there's no way we can escape it. Time is something that we can't stop, however, there are things that we can do in order to prolong our life. It's possible that we can prolong our lives and live a healthier life by stimulating our brain with mind games and doing some physical activity such as exercise or some type of sports. Any type of sports or any physical activity is going to maintain our bodies healthier and at the same time, it's going to give our bodies the ability to fight many diseases. Illnesses and infections.

Both, our bodies, and brains will benefit from mental and physical exercises. It's important that we do both physical and mental activities because our brain will take care of our body and our body will take care of our brain, it's a win…win situation.

Mental activities are especially important for our brain, because it's the food that our brain needs to keep itself young and sharp. There's a lot's of brain games out there for both, young and old that we can all play to help us keep our brains young and healthy for a longer period. Mind games can play an important role in our lives. They can help us in preserving our intelligence well into the late sixties. Seventies, eighties, nineties and even after we turn 100 years old. The sky's the limit, and the possibilities are endless. Always remember that it's never too late to start a regiment of both, brain and body exercises. Young and old can both reap the benefits of brain games and exercise.

The younger generation can benefit by helping the older generation by simply playing mind games and spending as much time as possible with them. Together we can prolong the aging process and help slow down some of the devastating diseases like Parkinson's. Alzheimer's and dementia.

Again, remember that exercise it's not only going to benefit our brains, but it's also going to help our bodies. Remember that the more we move, the more nutrients we intake, the more blood and oxygen is going to travel through our bodies and that is a good thing for our brain. Exercising has tremendous benefits, but one of the most important benefits is that our bodies will be able to get rid of some of the bad sugars and cortisol in our bodies. Sugar and cortisol are believed to be implicated for worsening Alzheimer's and Dementia. Both, our physical activities, and brain activities are of equal importance when trying to stay young and healthy.

It's very important for us to remember that: as we get older, we need to keep learning new things in order to help our brain stay young and sharp. We must never stop playing games just because we are getting older, in fact, we need to let the little kids inside us come out and play. Just because we get older doesn't mean that we must lay down and die. On the contrary, we must always think of ourselves as being young, we must always fight for every bit of life because life is precious.

We need to enjoy every single minute of our lives by stealing a moment of peace, at least once a day because as we get older life becomes more difficult to enjoy and it's because our movements are much slower. Our speech is much slower, our hearing will diminish much faster and we can't see as well and it's because our eyesight has diminished throughout the years.

Furthermore, as we get older, our quality of life seems to diminish. We no longer enjoy life as we used to, we no longer experience the same joy that we used to experience as when we were growing up, our motivation is not what it used to be, in other words, our motivation it's not the same as when we were younger. We used to get excited about many things, but now, we just don't seem to care as much.

What happened to our lives? We used to enjoy life a lot more, but now, as we are older, we seemed to no longer enjoy life as much as we used to and as we get older and older, it will become even more difficult to enjoy it. Our minds and our bodies will get tired, and we will lose the desire to live longer. We will become immune to a lot of things, and we will also become immune to what is going on with our surroundings. Perhaps the real reason as to why we feel this way is because we think in our minds that we have seen and done everything that life has to offer. We must never let the joy and the good feelings of love that we use to have disappear from our lives.

Sometimes my body feels tired and old and so is my mind, but there's one thing that I will never do, and that is to never quit. I will never surrender; I will never go quietly into the night. I will keep on fighting because life is just too precious to let it go to waste. Even if we are old, we should always try to enjoy every minute of every day.

I do believe that our minds do get tired and that we have done and seen many things within our short life. Sometimes we feel like we no longer can contribute to society as much as we used to, but we shouldn't think this way because it's the wrong kind of thinking, it's the type of thinking that will diminish who we are as a human being.

I really think that this is where the problem lies, it's our way of thinking which prevents us from enjoying life to its fullest. We really underestimate ourselves. In fact, I think that we have much more to offer and contribute now than ever before. We can offer our knowledge to our younger generation.

We need to remind ourselves, every single day, to set our spirits free and to take every opportunity to find a new love for life. New joy and new happiness. It's a matter of recharging our minds and re-training them with new and exciting ideas.

One last thing, I hope that there will be no confusion as to what I'm talking about in this chapter. You see, when we are young, we need to slow down and not live our lives in the fast lanes and doing reckless things. Remember that as we get older we don't have to live a boring life, in other words, we must remember our youth and do some of those things that we used to enjoy doing and I'm not talking about doing reckless things, rather, I'm talking about doing some enjoyable and fun things.

Chapter Fifteen

Replacing Old Ideas with New Ideas

Our old ideas most likely are not going to work in today's modern world, therefore, we need to replace them with new ideas, but the only way we are going to accomplish such a task is by changing our way of thinking and by changing the way we do things. We must retrain our minds so that we can become more creative, in other words, we need to come up with fresh ideas, and I'm not suggesting that we go ahead and get rid of every old ideas completely, after all, they are part of who we are, however, we can combine them with new ideas, so that we can create super new ideas for ourselves. Again, if we want to achieve our goals in today's modern world, we need to combine our old ideas with new ideas, however, we need to put those new ideas into action. I'm not only talking about coming up with ideas for new inventions here; I'm also talking about new ideas which are going to help us to accomplish our goals. New ideas that will help us thrive, new ideas that will help us to deal with other people as well.

When our old ideas no longer work, then it's time to replace them with fresh ideas, in other words, we must leave them behind because if those ideas didn't work in the past, chances are that they will not work in today modern world. It will be unproductive on our part and it will be a waste of our time trying to make those old ideas work for us.

We should never get stuck in a place that we don't like just because we are trying to make our old ideas work for us because it will be unproductive on our part. Never worry about old ideas that never worked, got rejected or crushed by others. If those old ideas never materialized anyway, than why worry about them? If in the past, we felt that we were let down by other people because of our old ideas, then we must not feel bad or sorry for ourselves, it's possible that it happened because of our inexperience and lack of knowledge. Regardless of what happened to us in the past, we need to keep moving forward without hesitation, but at the same time, moving forward with an open mindset to new ideas.

On an average day, we are bombarded with millions of new and exciting ideas; some of those will be our own ideas, however, sometimes the best ideas will come from other individuals or by simply observing them putting their own ideas into action. Remember that new ideas will come from many different places and they can be a combination of old ideas and new ideas.

I must remind everyone that, at the end, it doesn't really matter where those ideas come from. What matters is how we put those ideas to work for us. Knowing what to do with those new ideas is going to either, make us or break us. Do you have an idea, but you don't know what to do with it? Well, the first thing that you need to do is to store that idea into your memory bank, afterwards you need modify that idea and finally, you must put that idea into action, an idea is just an idea and it does nothing unless you put it into action.

Our very own survival depends on acquiring new ideas; therefore, we must choose carefully how we are going to put those ideas into action. When we have a good idea and we choose to do nothing with it, know that nothing is going to happen because if we don't move, then nothing else is going to move. We must become consciously aware that for those of us who refuse to adapt to new ideas, our survival will not be guaranteed. New ideas is going to contribute to our survival because we will become better adapted to any environment. We must remember that as human beings, we are very capable of adapting to any new situation. If animals are constantly adapting to new environments, then we can do the same thing. Now! That is a great idea.

Keeping an Open Mind

Are you an open mind individual? Are you able to listen patiently to what others have to say, are you willing to ask for advice when you need it? Individuals who approach life with an open mindset are more successful than those who don't. But why is that? Well, because they want to progress, in other words, they want to better themselves in every way possible. For those individuals who learn to listen to others with an open mindset, they are the ones who are going to be successful in their careers. They will be successful in life and they will be successful at anything that they want to accomplish. Keeping an open mind to new suggestions or new ideas given to us by those individuals, who know how to be successful in life is going to allow us to accomplish our goals, so don't be the one who chooses not to listen to others because you won't like the results.

Close-minded individuals don't like their ideas to be challenge because they think that their ideas are the correct ones. Close-minded individual are more interested in trying to prove that they are in the right, and because of that, they are going to miss out on improving their knowledge. The only ways that we are going to be successful in life is by listening to those who know how to be successful, in fact, we need to associate ourselves with them. furthermore, it's of great importance that we form alliances with them so that we can accomplish a higher level of success. Minimizing our efforts through cooperation is going to increase our financial power and our survival as well.

For those of us who refuse to listen to other people's suggestions or ideas and refuse to form alliances with them, we are going to be doomed. We will be left behind and I'm sure that no one wants that. People's lives will be so much easier and fulfilling, but only if they learn to listen and associate themselves with people who have the right knowledge.

A world of caution: when listening to other people's ideas and suggestions we must be careful and only choose those ideas which are correct. Remember that we don't need to incorporate every idea or suggestion into our lives given to us by others, and we don't need to put those ideas and suggestions into action without first knowing what the outcome is going to be, so always be on the alert. Always ask yourself if those ideas or suggestions given to us by others are truthful and honest.

Remember to always listen to other people's ideas and then we can make up our own mind as to whether those ideas are the right ideas or not. If those ideas and suggestions are correct, then we can go ahead and put them into action. Remember to always use good judgment and be on the alert for a possible bad situation or a possible good situation. I'm not saying or suggesting that everyone in this world are bad people, I'm simply saying that there are good and honest people in this world, but we must be careful because there's also bad or dishonest people out there.

One thing to keep in mind is that some people are not truthful because it's in their nature. Sometimes, they will pretend to like us and be our friends, but what is really going on here is that they will lie and say anything that we want to hear. They want us to put down our guard so that we can become vulnerable, and that's when they will take advantage of us. They are trying to trick us so they can manipulate and get what they want from us. Most often than not, they will lie so that they can separate us from our money. We must remember that money is the root of all evil and that people will do anything for money, so always be on the alert. They want to control our mind. They want to control our thoughts and they want to control our actions. Be careful of other people's suggestions, but do not be so careful that we will fail to recognize when a good opportunity is going to present itself.

Again, some people have good intentions to do good things, but good intentions are just that…good intentions. We must get past our procrastination and our good intentions and put those good intentions into action. Remember that sometimes, we find ourselves in difficult situations because of our lack of knowledge. It's a sad human condition that we need to overcome sooner than later.

We must not wait for something good to come our way; we must go out there and make it happen. We must create our own destiny, in other words, we must never leave it to chance. Some people say that good things will happen to those who wait, but I will tell you that this couldn't be further from the truth, rarely do good things happen to those who wait and it's just by mere coincidence that something good happens to us.

The reality is that good things will happen to those who are knowledgeable. Good things will happen to those people who do not wait for good things to happen to them; rather, they go out and make them happen. Good things will happen to those people who don't wait and it's because they don't sit around hoping that something good is going to happen out of thin air. Again, they go out and make things happen. They move and because they move, they are creating something else to move.

Furthermore, we must never wait for someone else to give us an opportunity or a break. Instead let's go all out and create our own opportunities. Never allow anyone else to dictate or determine our destiny. We must create our own destiny and our own future.

We must learn to use our imagination and wake up our stagnant mind because a stagnant mind is a wasted mind. When we approach life with an open mindset, tons of new and fresh ideas and opportunities will come rushing back to us from many different places.

Our minds will become more alert with greater speeds and alertness. We will become more efficient and enthusiastic about life as well. We must approach life with an open mindset and the burning desire to learn and to conquer our goals.

Chapter Sixteen

Self-Confidence, Self-Control, Self-Discipline

SELF-CONFIDENCE- What is self-confidence? Self-confidence means that you value yourself and the things that you do, it means that you feel good about yourself. Now! Do you know how high your degree of self-confidence is, is it high, somewhere in between, extremely low or nonexistence? Most people have some level of self-confidence, however, there are those who have little confidence in themselves. Lack of self-confidence in oneself will prevent us from taking risks, and consequently, we won't be able to achieve our goals and find happiness. Self-confidence in oneself is important for everyone because without it, we won't be able to excel in accomplishing our goals. Again, without self-esteem or a positive self-image of ourselves, many great opportunities will pass us by, our social life will suffer, and our credibility is going to suffer as well. Remember that the higher our self-confidence is the more likely we will succeed in achieving our goals.

If our degree of self-confidence is low or nonexistent, then we need to do something about it, but how are we going to find our self-confidence? There are a few things that we can do which is going to help us build our self-confidence. For example, we must never think of ourselves as losers, instead, we need to think of ourselves as loveable, energetic, and strong individuals. Furthermore, we need to pay close attention how we conduct ourselves in front of others. What else can we do to help us build our self-confidence? Well, we need to educate ourselves, in other words, we need to have the facts straight before we engage in a conversation with other people so that they know right away that we are well-inform about the subject matter. Being knowledgeable about the things that we are talking about will increase our self-confidence tremendously.

Believe or not, the following things will help us to build our self-confidence by leaps and bounds. For example, wearing nice clothes will increase our self-confidence because we are going to look good and at the same time, it will make us feel good about ourselves. Sometimes, all we need to do is to wear clean clothes to make us feel good and gain confidence. However, there's other things that we can do to help us build our self-confidence, for example, paying close attention to our hygiene by taking regular showers. Brushing our teeth, trimming our beard, brushing our hair, exercising regularly, eating the right foods, and getting enough sleep. Believe or not, all these things will help us regain the self-confidence that we have been missing for so long. But why is that? Well, because anything positive that we do for ourselves is going to make us feel good on the inside, and that in turn is going to help us build our self-confidence tremendously. Remember that when we look good and feel good our self-confidence will be at an all-time high.

Sometimes we are missing the courage, the determination, and the knowledge and that is going to prevent us from achieving our goals. When we have all these things in place, we will gain the necessary self-confidence in ourselves to go out and accomplish our goals, whatever those goals might be.

Remember that without self-confidence, we won't be able to accomplish much of anything. Sometimes we find ourselves dreaming about going on vacation to a tropical and beautiful island or wanting to start a new business venture, but then doubt starts creeping in on us, and consequently we stop thinking about it. Did you see what just happened here? Our confidence level just went down to zero, but not to worry because although sometimes we are lacking the self-confidence we can always get it back, like in this situation, if we really wanted to go on a trip or start a new business venture by ourselves or with someone else, then we would find a way to make it happen and its by having the courage; the self-confidence and a little imagination. The possibilities are endless, but it's only going to happen if we put our imagination into action.

Remember that the lack of self-confidence in ourselves it's only going to make us feel bad. It's going to make us feel that we are not worthy; it's going to make us feel as losers and I must tell you, it's not a good feeling. Furthermore, lacking self-confidence it's going to make us feel down on ourselves, in other words, it's going to make us feel inferior and it's going to make us feel as if we don't belong. More often than not, I have experienced firsthand the feelings of disappointment in the past because I felt like I didn't belong, in other words, I felt left out and I felt intimidated by others most of the time, but now, I no longer feel the same way, I'm no longer feel inferior. Now I walk with confidence, I walk with my head up, I walk with a sense of pride and I walk with a sense of belonging. We can all learn to become self-sufficient by practicing our self-confidence and we can accomplish this by having the knowledge, the courage, and the determination. Everyone can learn to walk through life with self-confidence and with their heads-up. Remember that we need to let others know that we are individual with self-confidence and that we know what we are doing.

There are several more reasons as to why sometimes we feel defected and unable to become the person that we were meant to be. However, the number one reason is because of our lack of self-confidence. Sometimes we feel inferiors because we don't have as much money as other people do. Furthermore, we feel inferior or intimidated by famous people because they have the money, the power, and the self-confidence, they also have the knowledge, and we don't. We should admire those people for what they have accomplished in their lives, however, none of those things should make us feel inferior because we have the same capabilities that they have. We just need to learn to trust ourselves and have a little self-confidence. Then and only then, we will be able to accomplish what we want. Remember that we should always walk with confidence no matter what the circumstances may be, no matter what life throws at us. We can overcome anything that life throws at us because we are all geniuses. We just need to let the genie out of the bottle, in other words, we need to let our imagination out and let it run wild.

I believed that all men and women are created equal, so we must never think of ourselves as better or worse than others. I have a tremendous amount of respect for other human beings, but at the same time, I don't feel inferior because we are all created equals in the eyes of God, whether we are rich or poor. Good looking or not so good looking, tall or short. We must never forget that beauty is in our hearts, beauty is in the way we think and not in our physical appearance.

We must never fall into the trap of feeling inferior; instead, we need to build our self-confidence which is going to help us achieve our goals. Our self-confidence is going to be the key which is going to open the doors to success. We must be careful and never lose track of our self-confidence, because If we do, it's going to disappear forever if we don't use it on a regular basis. Not having the necessary self-esteem is going to lead us into inaction, and inaction is going to lead us into loss of desire and ambition. Sometimes being poor can be an advantage because it's only then that we will be forced to learn and develop new skills that we didn't have before. Remember inaction is going to lead us to weakness and therefore, our ambitions will be few. Furthermore, our willpower is going to be diminished because of lack of confidence, so we must never let this happen to us.

Self-Control, Self-Discipline

First, I want to make it crystal clear that self-control and self-discipline is not the same thing. For example, deciding to stop smoking and start a regiment of exercises are two separate psychological functions. Deciding to stop smoking takes self-control, in other words, self-control means red light, or stop whatever we are doing. Self-discipline means green light or go. Deciding to start exercising takes self-discipline. Self-discipline also means that we must take the necessary steps to help us improve whatever we are doing. Whereas self-control means that we must remove the things that make us ineffective. The best way for us to improve our self-control and self-discipline is to put ourselves in a positive frame of mind. Self-discipline will help us to regain control over our feelings and emotions, thereby, allowing us to make the right choices. Now! How much self-control and self-discipline do we really have? Self-control and self-discipline, it's not an easy thing to accomplish, but with a little practice and patience on our part, we will be able to accomplish it. When we have self-control and self-discipline, we will be able to control most of our bad behaviors, our obsessions, and our additions much easier.

Life is always full of temptations, we face them every single day of our lives, but often, we don't know how to deal with them and its because we are unprepared. Sometimes, we have some type of self-control and self-discipline, but other times, not so much. If we want to defeat our temptations, we need to have self-control and self-discipline, otherwise, we will do the very next thing: we will give into them. Most of our temptations are usually minor and normally we are able to overcome them with ease because it doesn't required a tremendous amounts of self-control and self-discipline, however, there are some powerful temptation that we will encounter that we won't be able to overcome because our self-control and self-discipline it's not what it should be, and therefore, we will give up in trying to overcome those temptations. In other words, we will give into our desires.

We are constantly bombarded with an array of temptations, but as human beings that we are, we don't always know how to deal with them, we don't know how to overcome them and therefore, we just simply give up and stop trying because we know that our self-control and self-discipline is not strong enough.

Is there anything else we can do to help us defeat our temptations? unfortunately, the only three things that I know which is going to help defect our temptations and bad habits is our self-control, self-discipline, and self-confidence. Self-control is basically telling yourself, "No, don't do it" and self-discipline is saying, "Yes, go ahead and do it."

SELF-CONTROL: means that we can stop ourselves in the middle of doing something, for example, it will stop us from overeating. Self-control is going to challenge our bad habits because self-control is more about our emotions. Our actions and our reactions. Self-control it's not about being in total control of our thoughts. Our emotions and our physical sensations. Self-control means that we are not going to be affected as much by the events happening around us, such as: being emotionally hurt by someone, in other words, we will be able to maintain our composure and our balance by not getting upset or angry, furthermore, self-control it's going to allow us to think clearly when face with danger.

It sounds confusing. However, self-control doesn't mean that we must have control over everything. It simply means that we should have our thoughts, feelings, emotions, and reactions under control. Does this make sense?

SELF-DISCIPLINE: is something that we use to help us start something, for example, starting a new career or saving money for a vacation. Self-discipline is going to keep us from overeating the next time around. Self-discipline is about being consistent with our plans, being on time and accept responsibility. Self-discipline is basically having control over conscious decisions and behaviors. For example, whether to buy ourselves a new car or a new dress. It's all about what we are thinking at any given moment.

When self-control and self-discipline are used wisely, we are going to achieve a tremendous amount of success. Self-control and self-discipline will help us in overcoming most of our self-destructive, obsessive, and compulsive behaviors. Both, self-control, and self-discipline are qualities that we should have at our disposal twenty-four hours a day. Both, self-control, and self-discipline will help us find peace of mind and happiness

It's of great importance that we learn self-control and self-discipline because it's going to allow us to accomplish more of the things that we desire and less of the things that we don't. We need to consistently reminder ourselves that we need to have our feelings and emotions under control.

I know that it's easier said than done, but nevertheless, we must follow this path if we want to be successful in achieving our goals. We must understand that nothing comes easy; nothing is given to us, unless we earn it, and it's only with hard work and dedication that we will be able to accomplish it.

It's imperative that we master our self-control and self-discipline, because if we don't, we are going to be at the mercy of our bad habits, furthermore, we are going to be at the mercy of other as well. We must make a conscious decision to improve our lives and find true happiness. We must keep in mind that our worst enemy is no other than ourselves, therefore, we are going to need all the help that we can get which we are going to get from self-control, self-confidence, and self-discipline.

We all need to have more self-control and more self-discipline because they are two immensely powerful weapons which we can use to help us to overcome uncontrollable anger and bad behaviors. The beauty of having these two powerful weapons in our arsenal is that it doesn't cost millions of dollars, it's free, and since it doesn't cost anything, other than some effort on our part, we should put them into action whenever possible. We must take advantage of these two weapons every time we find ourselves in any stressful situation. Mastering our self-control and our self-discipline is the key that is going to open the doors to living a happy life. It's the key which is going to help us to defeat our worst enemy: our bad behaviors.

Furthermore, mastering our self-control and our self-discipline is going to open the doors to a whole new world that we have never seen before. When we learn to master our self-control and our self-discipline, we will have the opportunity to defeat all other forms of self-destructive behaviors and emotions. There are plenty of self-destructive behaviors and emotions that we have, for example, anger, selfishness, greed, revenge, fear, rage, hatred, envy, and jealousy. All of these are self-destructive behaviors that will impact our lives in a negative way when they are not under control. If we want to be successful, and if we want to accomplish our goals, we must master our self-control and our self-discipline first.

Remember that our lack of self-control and self-discipline it's going to prevent us from finding happiness, but how is that going to help us? Well, for example, whenever we find ourselves in a bad situation or we are having an argument with another person and we can't seem to find a way out of that situation, then the only thing that we need to remember is that we are the bigger person. We have the advantage because we have the self-control, but most importantly, we have the self-discipline that we need which it's going to allow us to simply walk away from any bad situation. Remember that we have the power to control the outcome. We can decide if we want to continue arguing with that person or put an end to it by using self-control and self-discipline.

We must remember that if something is not working according to our plans then we need to move on to greener pastures because it would be unproductive on our part to try and make things right. No matter what type of situation we find ourselves in, we always have the option to walk away from them by using self-control and self-discipline. Always keep in mind that the road has many twists and turns and that even if we practice self-control and self-discipline every day for the rest of our lives, there will be times when we are going to fail because as human beings that we are, we do not always going to win.

Remember that we are going to win some of our battles, but we also going to lose some of them. Remember that no human being is perfect, and from time to time we are going to struggle. We are going to fail because we cannot have total self- control and total self-discipline all the time, but that is okay, it's part of the process of learning.

Can you imagine for a minute if we were able to completely have total control over everything that we do? It would be an amazing and exciting thing to accomplish, but again, let's be reasonable. Let's be content with some of the things that we will accomplish by simply having self-control and self-discipline. If we keep on trying and never give up, we will never fail, but even if fail, we will win. We must remember that failing is a big part of the learning process and that there's no learning without failing. We can control our own destiny, but only if we learn to master our self-control and self-discipline. Knowing that we have things under control is going to give us the strength that we need to keep us moving forward. We must remind ourselves, constantly, that we can accomplish anything that we want if we only use our minds. Our imagination, our self-control, and our self-discipline.

Remember that if we want to achieve success in life, we need to fail first. It's only by failing that we will be able to become successful. We must never be afraid of trying new things because we are afraid of failing; in fact, I encourage everyone to fail from time to time because it's going to help us to build our characters.

I have learned many valuable lessons throughout my life, I learned that when things don't work out the way I wanted it, then I needed to change the way I was doing those things. We should never try to make something work if we know in our minds that it's never going to work. In other words, we should try taking a different approach when things are not working according to our plans. Sometimes we try to be too perfect in everything that we do and consequently, we lose our focus, plus the fact that it's going to drive ourselves crazy.

Many years ago, I found myself having panic attacks which turned into anxiety and it's because sometimes we get stuck in stagnation. We get stuck in quicksand and we don't know how to get out of it. We forget to think in a rational manner and instead we panic.

I tried many things throughout my life. I work in many different places, probably more than I can remember. All those decisions I made in the past seem like the right thing to do at the time, but you know what? Those things that didn't work out for me as I planned, those are the ones that taught me some of the most valuable lessons because I learned from them. Sure, I regret making some of those decisions, however, in today's word, I would have done some of those things differently because now I know that I have self-confidence, self-control, and self-discipline.

Whether it was a good lesson or a bad lesson, I did learn from them and perhaps it took me a long time to realize it. Life will teach us many valuable lessons, some of us will learn from those lessons, but others not so much because they will keep on making the same mistakes, and therefore, they will keep on getting the same results.

From now on, I'm going to take my own advice. I'm not going to try to be perfect every single time, don't get me wrong, we should always thrive for perfection, but we must keep in mind that things don't always work out the way we want. We must never forget that we are in-perfect human beings and that sometimes it doesn't matter how hard we try; we won't always going to be successful. Am I being contradictory here? Yes, I am, but you see, sometimes we must trust other people to help us achieve success, we hope that they will do their part, however, when they fail, then we are going to fail as well because these are outside forces that we can't control. The following four things will help us to achieve our self-confidence self-control and self-discipline and it's by control our emotions: our feelings our thoughts and our actions. Let's not get stuck in a cluster of bad mixes of anger. Emotions and feelings which can come back and hurt us in many ways. When our unhealthy thoughts. Feelings and emotions are present in our minds; they will drain our energy from our bodies and our ability to think rationally.

Chapter Seventeen

Who Do We Trust?

Who do we really trust and why? All human relationships are based on trust, honesty, and collaboration. Trust is the foundation of every human relationship, whether that relationship is between a husband and wife, parents and their kids, brothers and sisters, romantic or friendships relationships, it doesn't matter, trust must be present in any relationship in order for that relationship to work.

When we put our trust in someone, we expect them to be honest about everything, but when that trust is broken for whatever reason, then there can no longer be that mutual trust between those people. I know that we must trust other people. We must trust that they will be honest with us and that they will do the right thing and at the right time. Remember that a broken trust can make or break a person.

We must make hundreds of decisions every single day of our lives and one of those decisions is to put our trust in other people; we must trust that those people will be trustworthy and that they will do the right thing. We must trust that they are not going to put other people's life in danger, we must trust that they will drive in a safely manner, we must trust that they will take their responsibilities very seriously, we must trust that they will obey the rules because the same rules applied to everyone and not just for a few people. Trust must be an unbreakable bond between two or more people because without trust nothing can be accomplished, our entire civilization, including our government, our community, our church, our culture, and friendships...are all based on trust and honesty.

It's unfortunately that too many people will break that bond of trust and honesty at one time or another and it's because no human being is perfect. No human being is immune from breaking that trust which exists between two or more people or the trust that exists between two countries. What is the main reason as to why we can't always trust each other to do the right thing? Well, there's lots of reasons as to why that is, but the number one reason is… Greed, greed will kill the bond or trust which exists between two or more people. Secondly, sometimes we cannot trust one another because we have weaknesses, and yes, we all have weaknesses whether we realized or not.

Remember that Greed will trump everything. Greed is a powerful weakness which we all have, and it's something that most of us won't be able to overcome most of the time. In fact, Greed can sometimes be more powerful than love. Again, Greed will kill the trust between two people, and it will kill most relationships in general.

When we place our trust in other people and those people betray us, then our trust becomes less and less as the years go by, we will become less trusting and it's because we don't want to suffer, we don't want the pain associated with betrayal. Our human capacity to trust is not what it should be and although it's true that we can trust some people from time to time, but the real question here is: who do we trust?

If we can't trust family members or friends, how are we supposed to trust strangers? Again, who do we trust? Well, I would definitively put my trust in family members first, because they would be more trustworthy to me. They will be more reliable, and they will be more trusted to do the right thing. Unfortunately, not all family members can be trusted to do the right thing. I'm someone who has felt the pain of betrayal in the past and I must admit that it does hurt. Every time we are betrayed by someone who we love, our trust becomes less and less because it's not an easy thing to overcome, but does this mean that we are never going to trust another human being again? Of course not, we must give people the benefit of the doubt because everyone deserves a second chance and besides, I like to think that there's still hope for humanity, I like to think that I am open to the possibility that someday people are going to change their ways. I like to think that they can be trusted once again.

Sometimes trusting other people becomes a big struggle for me, especially, when I have no other choice but to trust them. My expectations are always high, so therefore, I'm counting on other people to do the right thing, but don't get me wrong, I want to trust others. I want to find the good things in them and not the bad things because I think that there's something good in everyone. Again, I'm an individual who will give others the benefit of the doubt. I don't want to lose my faith in humanity because I like to think that we can always turn our lives around. I'm always looking for something good in everyone. Something that is going to make me feel good on the inside about trusting them. Remember that sometimes we must trust some people, but others not so much, because we never know if their intentions are good or bad. Some people go through life lying and cheating, thinking that they can do anything they want. They think that they can get away with anything, but it's only because they don't know any better.

I really have a hard time dealing with dishonest people, especially when they spent their entire lives' lying and cheating, therefore, those people are not to be trusted. You would think that those people should know better by now, but unfortunately, they don't and even if they knew that lying, cheating and stealing was wrong. They will continue to do the same things because they cannot help themselves. It's in their nature. Furthermore, I'm not surprised by their actions at all because we live in a world dominated by greed, deception and manipulation. Most bad things happening in our world are being done by unscrupulous individuals who have no respect for themselves and for others; they have no respect for life itself, they have no honor, they have no honesty.

Always remember that the mischief of someone is an open door for others to benefit for personal profit. We must be honest with ourselves and with others, especially, if we are faced with the opportunity to benefit from the misfortunes of others. It's cruel and unethical and there is no glory in it for either party. Remember that it's a well-documented fact that whatever action we take against other people, whether is a good action or a bad action, it's going to come back to us tenfold. It's karma in action; it's the law of the universe, period. We must learn to overcome our desire to take advantage of another person's misfortune.

I personally believe most human beings on our planet have the capacity to do accomplish great things, but at the same time, they also have the capacity to do many bad things. For me is all about trust and honesty. It's a matter of principals. It's about having a conscious mind. It's about caring and respecting others. For those people who can contain themselves from dishonestly. They will have my respect and my admiration forever.

Nobody can blame me for not wanting to trust most people on the face of our planet because when I put my trust and faith in someone else, I end up getting hurt or disappointed, whether it's an economical or emotional trust, it doesn't matter. Some people cannot be trusted to do the right thing, especially, when there is money involved. People will say anything to get what they want because everything they do or think about is for themselves and nobody else and that is what I called being selfish and unconsidered. I'm not saying this just for the saying, but it's a true reality and without exaggeration on my part.

Life must go on and as we go through life, we will encounter all kinds of people. Good, honest, and trusting people, however, we are going to encounter bad, dishonest, and untrusting people, but nevertheless, we must learn to trust others because trusting others to do the right thing is vital to our survival. It's only by integration that we are going to be able to thrive. Sometimes we have the need to trust other people; however, we must be careful and choose only those people who we can trust the most.

We must make a stand against all injustices. We must make a stand for our freedom, our health, our suffering, and our pain. We have the power of imagination and we have the power of knowledge which is going to help us to separate the facts from lies. We have the power to put an end to the deceit because we are no longer a bunch of unsuspecting sheep running into the hands of Mr. Wolf. Our world must not be clouded by lies and deceit. We must work together towards making our world a better place for everyone. A world where our trust and our honesty is not going to be doubted or challenged.

The Power of Imagination

We can say that a person who "knows" is a person who is conscious of his or her own world, in other words, they are conscious of their thoughts, their actions, their surroundings and their knowledge. But can a person who has enough knowledge be successful merely because of their knowledge? Remember that in order to be successful we must put that knowledge that we possess into action because without action nothing is going to move.

A successful man or woman are the ones who know how to use their knowledge and it's because they put that knowledge into action. They believe in themselves and they believed they can accomplish success by simply putting that knowledge into use, and with enthusiasm. People who have the knowledge know that knowledge alone is not enough. It doesn't guarantee success; they know that they must put that knowledge into action. They also know that we must use the power of imagination in order for that knowledge to work. Imagination is the source of power and once it's understood is going to be used as a weapon to accomplish anything that we desire.

Some people say that necessity is the mother of all inventions and it's true, however, I happened to believe that necessity by itself does not constitute an invention but combines the power of knowledge. Necessity and imagination and we have the power to change our lives forever. When we finally understand the power of imagination and how it works, we going to benefit tremendously in many ways. We will be able to conquer and solve most of our problems and difficulties by simply using our imagination. Our imagination is something that we have been using (perhaps unconsciously) for thousands of years, and it's something that we can use anytime we desire. It's one privilege that we possess that cannot be taken away from us by anyone.

I honestly believe that most human beings are not consciously aware of the tremendous powers which we possess. Knowledge is power, self-control is power, self-discipline is power, self-confidence is power, and imagination is power. When we finally learn to use these powers and put them into action, our limitations will be next to none. By using our imagination, we will be able to put an end to many problems which are affecting humanity. By using our imagination, we can end poverty and misery for millions of people around the world. By using our imagination. We will be able to find cures for many diseases. Imagine if we eliminated all types of cancer and other illnesses around the world. That would be an amazing accomplishment! So, let's start using our imagination and get to work.

Once we discover the power of imagination that we didn't know we had, our world is never going to be the same for us. We no longer going to be the same person because we are going to be aware of everything, we are going to be in total control of our thoughts and actions. I'm not going to exaggerate, but quite possibly, we can all become geniuses, in fact, we are geniuses already, it's just that some of us know it, but others do not. So, unleash the power of imagination. Release the genius inside you, let it come out and play.

We must make the transformation from a dormant to an active imagination and we must make it a daily priority. We must remind ourselves every single day, right after we wake up that we need to have the desire to make the transformation in our lives from a dormant imagination to an active imagination.

For all of those who haven't yet discovered the power of imagination, I want you to know that it's there waiting for you. It's in a dormant state of mind and it's going to stay that way, unless we go ahead and wake that imagination and start using it. Remember that we can use our imagination anytime anywhere we so desire. Any time is a good time to start using our imagination, so why not take advantage of this powerful tool. It's free and it doesn't cost money.

Remember that imagination is the engine that will creates new ideas; it's the creative power of the mind. Our capacity of achievement is our imagination. Therefore, we must arm ourselves with this powerful weapon of imagination, and if we do that, our capacity of achievement will have no barriers and no limitations.

Overcoming Our Weaknesses

It's without a doubt that we all have some hidden strengths, but we also have hidden weaknesses within ourselves that we have yet to discover. Most people don't like to talk or be reminded about their weaknesses because it's something uncomfortable and unpleasant for them. It's something that we rather not talk about because it's going to embarrass us, we rather hide them deep inside us. So, what is the solution, how are we going to be able to defeat our weaknesses if we don't want to talk about them or we don't want to bring them out into the open? We must remember that avoiding our weaknesses, it's only going to hold us back.

If we want to get rid of our weaknesses, the first thing that we should do is to figure out what they are. It's important to remember that there's no shame in admitting that we have weaknesses, we all have them, so we mustn't be afraid to bring them out into the open, in other words, we need to talk about them, either, among ourselves or with a friend. We don't need to talk to others about our weaknesses if we don't feel comfortable, however, we need to acknowledge them so that we can learn to defeat them. Again, there is absolutely no shame in talking to someone about our weaknesses. Remember that the only way to build our confidence and grow stronger is by getting rid of our weaknesses.

We must never underestimate ourselves because we have many abilities and strengths that we can use to help us overcome our weaknesses, for example, we can use our self-control, self-confidence, and self-discipline. These are powerful tools that we can use to help us overcome our weaknesses and other afflictions that we might be struggling with.

Some of our weaknesses are never easy to overcome because we had them, perhaps since we were kids, however, we have less severe weakness that we can overcome with much less effort on our part. As for the more powerful weaknesses; it will be more challenging for us because they will need more time and effort on our part, in fact, some of our weaknesses can become so powerful that it's almost impossible to get rid of them, but nevertheless, we should never give up, we must keep on trying even if we are not successful at first. Remember to never give up and never give into your weaknesses.

I must point out that some weaknesses are good, and some are bad, and I'm going to explain why. For example, I have a weakness for loving my family too much and although it's a good weakness to have, this weakness can become a liability if someone from my family decides to take advantage of the love and generosity that I have for them. Believe me, it will happen sooner or later. Some people will exploit our weaknesses for their own benefit because they will see us as weak or softies.

I like to think that I'm neither weak nor soft, maybe a little soft, but it's only because it's in my nature to love and to help others unconditionally. I much rather have a few good weaknesses than a ton of bad ones. I'm well aware of what my weaknesses are and I'm not afraid to admit it. Indeed, I do have good weaknesses, but at the same time I have some bad weaknesses or should I call them… bad habits. One of my weaknesses is the fact that I smoke cigarettes. This weakness is enormously powerful, in fact, is one of the hardest weaknesses to overcome for any human being. I know for a fact that we are intelligent human beings with the capacity to accomplish many great things, so getting rid of our weaknesses is no exception. Okay, so I have yet to overcome my additions, but maybe it's because I don't really want to do it. One thing that I know for sure is that I'm able to keep my additions under control and that is by not smoking or drinking in excess.

Another one of my weaknesses is the fact that I like to drink beer, and I don't know if I can call it a weakness because I really enjoy drinking beer. It helps me to relax, especially after I had a rough day, but I also know that I must keep this one under control. Some days I don't drink at all, in fact, as I was writing this chapter, I decided to test my will power by not drinking for three days, and you know what? I did it and I'm proud of myself. Furthermore, sometimes I don't drink for as many as ten days, but normally I drink a few beers every other day.

I must say that it's not an easy thing overcoming our weaknesses, but nevertheless, we must keep on trying until we can become successful in conquering our weaknesses. I have gotten rid of most of my weaknesses, but I still got some that I'm working on. Some of our weaknesses are sometimes stronger than ourselves and at times we feel defeated, but we must keep going and perhaps next time we will be victorious. Again, we must never give up. We must never surrender to our weaknesses.

If we want to defeat our weaknesses, then it's important that we use the greatest weapon that we possess: our minds. The way we think is going to determine how successful we will be in defeating our weaknesses in the future.

What about you? Have you thought about what your weaknesses are, and if so, do you know how you will overcome them? Perhaps you are thinking that you have no weaknesses and that you are perfect, however, nothing can be further from the truth. The sad reality is that we all have weaknesses, but we don't like to think about them. Perhaps the reason as to why we don't want to think about them is because they are hidden deep inside us, so out of sight, out of mind, right? Sometimes we are consciously aware of our weaknesses, however, on occasions we choose to not think about them because we know that we won't have the will power to get rid of them as easily as we wish we could, so we just do what comes naturally, we ignore them.

Furthermore, sometimes we are consciously aware of our weaknesses, but we feel powerless and unable to do anything about it. It seems that all our efforts are in vain because we just can't seem to get rid of them no matter what we do, so it brings me to my next question "what can we possibly do, which is going to help us to get rid of our weaknesses?" Well, the first thing that we need to do is to never try to do too much too fast, we need to start by conquering one weakness at a time because if we try to conquer all of them at the same time, we will fail miserably.

Instead of trying to get rid of our weaknesses first. We should try to know ourselves better instead and we can accomplish this task by simply knowing what our strengths are. We must get to know ourselves a little bit more, but most importantly, we must admit to ourselves that we have some weaknesses that we need to overcome and that alone is a victory. It's only then that we will be able to move forward and work towards getting rid of most of our weaknesses.

Remember that it takes a big man to admit that he is wrong and that he indeed has weaknesses. It's a big step admitting that we are not perfect and it's a big step that we must take if we want to conquer our weaknesses. Again, knowing what our weaknesses are is going to help us in determining our future, our success, and our happiness. Most people don't think about their weaknesses; therefore, they are going to limit themselves from achieving a higher rate of success.

Now! we must remember that everything we do in life requires a tremendous amount of effort on our part, but there's one thing that we must never do, and that is to never come up with excuses not to do something because most often than not, we are the masters of excuses. If we keep making excuses for ourselves, then we might as well give up now. Keep in mind that we are human beings and that we are weak at times and that we are going to make mistakes, and that it's okay because to error is human, but at the same time, we need to minimize our weaknesses and our mistakes. Always be brave and be proud of yourself.

Let's all start a new beginning. Let's start by not going through life stumbling and falling, instead, let's come up with new ideas that will help us overcome our weaknesses. Knowing and admitting our mistakes and our weaknesses is going to help us in changing our destiny. When we have the desire, the power, and the knowledge, we will accomplish anything that we desire.

Again, getting rid of our weaknesses is not an easy task. It's something that we must work on a consistent basis, because it's going to take time to make radical changes to our old way of thinking. Remember that if we apply our knowledge, and we commit ourselves, we will conquer our weaknesses, eventually. Remember that we are in control of everything that happens in our lives, we have an unlimited potential to create a new and better world for ourselves and for other as well.

By using our minds, we can change the things which are not working for us and we can also change the things that we don't like about ourselves.

We must change the way we think, and we must change the way we do things. We must use all our abilities to help us make wise decisions so that we can create for ourselves a new future and a new reality. We can do anything that we want because we are more capable than we think.

Remember that when our will is weak, and we suffer from low self-esteem, overcoming our weaknesses is going to be difficult, therefore, it's important that we maintain a high degree of self-control, self-confidence, and self-discipline at all time. We must be conscious that we can overcome any difficult situations by using the power of our minds. We also need to demonstrate that our will is greater than our weakness, and that we need to approach life with an open mind to anything and everything because it's the only way that we are going to achieve success. When we approach life with an open mind, we are not only going to gain valuable knowledge, but we will be able to come up with new solutions to problems that we previously didn't know how to solve.

We must remember that our greatest enemy is no one other than ourselves. We set our own limitations upon ourselves. We are the masters of creating our own success or creating our own failures.

Sometimes it's not what we do, but what we don't do that will limit our true potential. Remember that there will be peaks and valleys and that we are not always going to be successful in achieving our goals, but we must never get discouraged by the outcome; all we are doing right now is gathering information and acquiring knowledge for the future.

Healthy Boundaries, Are They Important?

Healthy boundaries are extremely important because they are the ultimate guide to successful relationships. Without healthy boundaries our lives will be chaotic- there will be no personal or mutual respect between one another. I like to believe that most people understand what boundaries are, however, there are those who know what they are, but they chose to ignore them, and because of that, they will create feelings of resentment, anger, and disappointment among themselves and other people as well. Healthy boundaries will set the limits for acceptable human behavior. It's important to remember that there are different types of personal boundaries, for example, physical boundaries, which refers to our personal space, physical touch, privacy, and body. Emotional boundaries- refers to our feelings and thoughts. Sexual boundaries- refers to the physical aspects of sexuality, in other words, it will protect us from any unwanted physical touching activities from others. Intellectual boundaries- refers to our thoughts, values, ideas, opinions, and beliefs.

Material boundaries- will protect our personal materialistic possessions, such as our homes, our cars, our furniture, and our money.

I'm not only talking about our personal behaviors towards other people or talking about personal property, like a house, although having boundaries for personal property is essential for peace of mind, and for the neighborhood. What I'm really talking about here is the type of boundaries that we impose upon ourselves that will prevent us from achieving our goals

To better understand what boundaries are, it's important to know that there are two types of boundaries that we impose upon ourselves- the first one is a healthy type of boundary, and the second one is an unhealthy type of boundary.

Defining boundaries are important because it will help us to understand who we are as a person. When we set healthy boundaries for ourselves is going to let others know that we have self-respect, and that we are self-worth, otherwise people will never respect us if they think that we have no respect for ourselves. It's important that we trust ourselves; it's important that we believe in ourselves, because If we don't believe in ourselves than no one else will either. We must spend the time to get to know ourselves. We must know what our desires are, we must know what we want or don't want out of life, and we must know what our true values are.

Knowing what our boundaries are is going to help us achieve our goals, but on the other hand, unhealthy boundaries will prevent us from reaching those goals. We must set healthy boundaries for ourselves and others because they will keep us safe. They will keep us in good physical and mental condition. Unhealthy boundaries that we knowingly or unknowingly impose upon ourselves are boundaries that will prevent us from accomplishing most of our goals. Unhealthy boundaries will prevent our potential to meet or exceed our expectations.

You see, it's all about our mind set, if we think that we can't accomplish our goals, then we won't be able to accomplish them because in our own mind we already accepted defeat by setting limitations to what we can accomplish. We should always set healthy boundaries for ourselves and others, however, we must never set boundaries that will prevent us from reaching our goals. We must allow ourselves to succeed, we must not sabotage ourselves before we even begin. Healthy boundaries are those boundaries that will make us stronger in the long run. Healthy boundaries are those boundaries that will allow us to use our abilities but without outside forces interfering with it.

Unhealthy boundaries are those boundaries that will show the weak side of us, for example, not knowing what we want out of life; showing others how weak we are by pretending to be needy or pretending to be the victim. We must set personal boundaries for ourselves, but they must be the type of boundaries that will help us thrive.

Healthy boundaries will protect us from being manipulated by others because as you may already know, when people sense that we have weaknesses, they will take advantage of us. They will use our weakness against us, and they will violate who we are as a person. We must never allow others to manipulate us in any way, shape or form because we deserve some respect, but at the same time, we need to give others the respect they deserve, it's a win-win situation for everyone. We must never demand respect from others unless we earn it. These are important healthy boundaries that we must put into place if we want to command the respect that we deserved from others. We have the power to decide how others will treat us in the future and it's only by setting healthy boundaries for ourselves and others. Remember that it's our responsibility to accept or reject how others will treat us. We need to understand that setting healthy boundaries for ourselves it's going to protect us from any type of physical or emotional danger. Healthy boundaries will protect us not only from dangerous animals, but from dangerous people as well.

We must make it crystal clear to others that we have boundaries and that we deserve respect and that we will respect them in return. Don't be like those people who have weak boundaries or have no boundaries because those people will violate, not only their own boundaries, but they will violate our boundaries as well.

Most of the time we are responsible for whatever happens to us, but it's only because we sabotage ourselves, in other words, we sabotage our efforts to succeed. Sometimes we sabotage ourselves because we drink too much, we get involved in abusive relationships, we use drugs, we drive too fast, we don't listen to reason, we hang around with the wrong crowd, and finally, we sabotage ourselves by self-negative talk or negative thinking.

All these negative things that we do will have an adverse impact on our lives. They will prevent us from reaching our goals, they will prevent us from doing the things that will make us happy, they will minimize our ability to perform at a higher level, and they will prevent us from taking care of ourselves as we should. Another way of sabotaging ourselves is by being procrastinators, and yes, procrastination will prevent us from doing the things that we need to do to accomplish success. It's like a disease or a plague that we can't get rid of.

Are you one of those people who put off doing things for later? We all know how that works, you put off doing most of the important things that you need to do today... until tomorrow, but tomorrow never comes, so they never get done, it's a good way to sabotage our very own happiness.

We must remind ourselves that healthy boundaries are put into place by us to protect ourselves from being hurt, and not only from ourselves, but protecting ourselves from others as well. We need to be careful not to set too many unhealthy boundaries for ourselves because we might not be able to coexist with others. We must be careful and only set up boundaries that will protect us from getting hurt psychically and emotionally, so it's important that we draw the line somewhere.

If we want to find happiness, then we must set boundaries for ourselves. However, those boundaries must be within reason. They must be boundaries which we can live with. We must not set boundaries that will prevent us from achieving our goals or prevent us from finding happiness. It's important to set healthy boundaries at home, at work or in our social lives. We need them because they will help us to achieve healthy relationships with others. Healthy boundaries is something that we must set for ourselves and other people to help us keep our behavior in check. In other words, it's going to help us set limits as to how people will treat us. It will help everyone to maintain a healthy relationship with coworkers, family kids, and friends.

A word of advice...if you want to reach your goals and find happiness, you must set healthy boundaries for yourself. You must stop procrastinating and do the things that you need to do today... not tomorrow. Finally, you must not live your life according to someone else's expectations, instead, you need to live your life according to your own expectations.

Chapter Eighteen

Our Human Abilities

It's a well-known fact that we possess many human abilities. We have the power to control our minds, our emotions, and our thoughts. Some people have the power to control other people's minds. Others can predict the future, read other people's minds, and are able to heal their bodies quickly. We also have the capacity to reason which sets us apart from the animal kingdom. Some of us have a tremendous ability to solve complex mathematical equations and others have "intrapersonal intelligence" which means that we have the capability to understand ourselves, in other words, we have the ability to analyze our desires, thoughts, and emotions. We understand our thoughts, our emotions and we are self-motivated individuals. Furthermore, people who understands intrapersonal intelligent are always in tune with themselves, they want to know everything that there is to know about themselves- they want to know why they think, feel, and act the way they do. They are highly self-motivated individuals who have a tremendous amount of self-discipline to go get what they want. By the way, I thought it would be a good idea mentioning that most people lack the understanding of what intrapersonal intelligence was, but, I hope that you will know by now because I just finish explain it very briefly in this chapter.

Everyone has the mental ability to learn from our past experiences. We have the mental ability to adapt to new situations, and we have the mental ability which is going to help us solve most of our problems. We have a tremendous ability to enhance, to control and to change our thoughts. Our human abilities will allow us to change the things that we don't like about ourselves, and we also have the ability to help others do the same.

We all have many human abilities, but unfortunately, most people only use a small percentage of them, but why is that? Is there a good reason as to why people don't use their abilities more often even when they know they have them? There must be an explanation as to why people don't put their abilities into action, perhaps it's because they don't know that they have them, it's that simple. Even if they knew they had those abilities, sometimes they just simply don't know how to put those abilities into action, or even worse, they are afraid to use them. Most of our abilities are hidden inside ourselves and that is why most people don't know that they have them. In order for us to be successful in life, we need to bring out those abilities and put them to work for us, and if we do, we are going to open up a whole new world full of wonderful surprises. We are going to learn new things, acquire new knowledge, and we are going to be much happier which is going to allow us to smile more often.

We need to realize that when we put our abilities to work for us- that there will be many big rewards coming our way, so why not start using those abilities right now which is going to make our lives more enjoyable. There's absolutely no reason as to why we shouldn't be using our abilities. The one thing that can really stop us from using our abilities is if we are afraid to use them. Another good reason why we are not using our abilities is because we get lazy or because we don't want to invest our precious little time that we have left in them.

If we want to improve our lives, then we must put our abilities to work for us, because the rewards will be many and soon enough, we will be able to collect those rewards. When we use our abilities and put those abilities into good use, we will be able to change our entire life forever.

We possess the ability to think and react properly. We possess the ability to transform our lives forever, we possess the ability to remove barriers which are imposed upon ourselves or by others. We have an unlimited pool of creativity and imagination locked inside waiting to be discovered. Let's not waste any more time and start putting our abilities, creativity and imagination into action. We will be surprised by all the wonderful things that we will accomplish, but only if we put our abilities into action.

It's a sad reality that most people's dreams are never going to materialize because they don't want to take the time and put those abilities, imagination and creativity into action. If only they knew that their lives were going to improve tenfold, then, I'm sure that they wouldn't even think about it for a second, they would do it instantly. We can come up with all types of excuses as to why we don't use our abilities more often, for example, our lives are way too busy and there's never enough time in the day to do anything else. Sometimes we put our abilities into action, but we just can't seem to get the result that we are looking for, and therefore, we stop trying. Well, we need to keep in mind that sometimes that is going to happen because there are outside forces that will prevent us from accomplishing our goals. We are going to encounter too many roadblocks, but that doesn't mean that we should stop trying.

We must remind ourselves every single day of our lives that life is never easy and that we must work hard, physically, and mentally for everything that we want to accomplish.

Life is all about learning new things every single day, life is about experimenting with different things, life is about developing our senses, life is about putting our abilities to work for us. Life is about not giving up at the first sign of trouble, life is about growing strong each day, and finally, life is about never giving up no matter who or what is trying to stop us. If we give up every time, we find ourselves with roadblocks, then we are never going to accomplish any of our goals. We must keep on pushing ourselves forward and never look back, we must never have any regrets and we must never surrender to laziness. We need to reorganize our lives and make the necessary changes if we want to improve our lives.

Remember that we are creators. We are innovators and we are inventors, so let's put our abilities to work for us. Nothing can stop us from achieving our goals if we use our imagination and our abilities. We have the choice to change, not only our own lives, but the lives of those who we love as well. We must remove the barrier which prevent us from achieving our goals, but the only way that we are going to accomplish it is by putting our abilities into action.

Changing Our Behaviors

Most often than not our behaviors are good which are good qualities to possess, but we also have many bad behaviors that can come out at any time. Furthermore, sometimes we don't even realize that we have such bad behaviors until someone, or something points them out to us. Bad behaviors can and will be a liability, they will work against us in many ways. Our bad behaviors will hold us back from loving relationships and from being promoted in our jobs, but that is just the beginning. We must become aware of our bad behaviors so that we can achieve a higher rate of success in everything that we do.

I want to mention that we are not born with bad behaviors. We learn them as we grow up, we learn them from our parents, our friends or from watching others behaving badly, so keep this in mind because it might help you change your bad behaviors into good ones.

The following are examples of bad behaviors: Talking behind other people's backs- we criticized them without giving them the benefit of the doubt. We use manipulation to get what we want from others. We have bad manners. We interrupt others when they are talking. Sometimes we lie. We are constantly yelling at our parents, our kids, and our friends. In general, we yelled at most people for no good reason. We are forever breaking our promises to ourselves and to others. Sometimes we are unfriendly with other people. We skip work for no good reason. We lose our temper quite easily. We complain or become too critical about everything. We like to annoy other people on purpose. We argue too much and for no good reason, maybe it's because we want all the attention for ourselves. We also drink too much. We smoke too much. We are forever eating unhealthy foods. We don't exercise enough. We overspend on unnecessary junk and we shop on impulse. We procrastinate, and finally, we negative self-talk ourselves out of the good things.

These are only a few examples of our bad behaviors or bad habits that we possess, but believe me, there's a lot more within ourselves. The good news is that we have other bad behaviors which are of less consequence, they are small behaviors and habits that will not have as big impact on our lives, but don't get me wrong, they are still bad behaviors, but with lesser consequences.

The following bad behaviors are examples that will impact our lives on a much smaller scale: Picking our nose in front of others, biting our nails when we are nervous, spending too much time watching television or on our phones. Not taking care of ourselves. We don't shower and brush our teeth enough and we don't take care of our physical bodies either. Nobody is immune from developing bad behaviors or bad habits, including myself.

We need to realize that our bad behaviors will push other people away from us and it's because they don't want to hand around people who don't have much self-respect for themselves. Again, most people don't want to hang around with people who behave badly, because bad behaviors are contagious. The only ones who want to hang around people with bad behaviors are those with bad behaviors themselves, in other words, the people who act the same way as they do because as you may know by now, like attracts like, after all.

Why do people keep behaving badly? I really think that some people enjoy doing it because it's like a high for them, either that, or they honestly don't realize that they are acting in such a manner. Is there something that we can do to help us combat our bad behaviors? Well, it's not enough knowing that we have bad behaviors, we need to know exactly what they are, in other words, we need to identify them first. Afterwards, what we really need to do is to never give ourselves the permission to act in such a manner, then we need to visualize ourselves changing those bad behaviors for good behaviors. It's obvious that it's going to take some time to get rid of our bad behaviors and it's because we have been doing it for too long. Again, it's going to take some time for us to change our bad behaviors and turn them into good behaviors. Who wants to hang around people who have bad behavior, anyone? Our bad behaviors will push people away from us. Furthermore, it will create problems at work, with our marriage and with our social life. We must remember that our bad behaviors will reflect our true personality, in other words, it's going to shows our true character and our maturity to the rest of the world, so we must be careful how we conduct ourselves in from of other people.

There are different things that we can do to help us keep our bad behaviors under control, but the most important of them all is by taking control of our thoughts, our emotions, and our feelings. Throughout this book I explain how important it is for us to take control over our thoughts, feelings, and emotions because that is the key which is going to help us defeat our bad behaviors or our bad habits. We need to have a good understanding of the things that we are doing at any given time, so that we can prevent ourselves from acting badly in front of others. When we become self-aware of the bad things that we are doing, we are going to create more opportunities for ourselves. For example, we are going to improve our relationships with our spouses, our parents, our kids our family and friends. We also going to improve our relationship with our bosses which is going to create new opportunities for ourselves.

It's a sad reality that we are forever trying to change other people's behaviors instead of concentrating on changing our own behaviors first. We are forever telling others that they need to changes their current way of life, we are telling them how they should live their life, we are telling them to change their diet to a healthy diet, we are telling them to exercise, we are telling them how to dressed, how to speak, how to think, how to cut their hair, how to conduct themselves in public, we are telling them what movies or shows they should watch, we tell them what types of friends they should be hanging around with, we are telling them not to drive too fast or too slow, we are forever telling people not to drive and text at the same time. Perhaps our intention are good when we tell other people how they should live their lives, but I'm guessing that people will eventually get tired of hearing the same words coming out of our mouth time after time, so they stop listening to us.

It's always easier to try and change other people's bad behavior than our own, but why is that? Well, maybe we are doing it unconsciously or because we are so preoccupied telling others what to do that, we forget about ourselves.

Remember that when we work on changing our bad behaviors, then others will follow. We don't always need to tell others what to do because they will follow, but only if we set a good example. How can we expect others to make a change when we are not willing to make those changes ourselves? It's unreasonable and un-logical on our part.

We need to prepare ourselves for a better life now, but the only way that we are going to accomplish it, is by our willingness to change. I know that we are not programmed to make changes to our lives and it's because we don't like changes, we are too accustomed to our old ways, but nevertheless, we are quite capable of changing our way of thinking and we can also take our way of thinking to another level by getting rid of our bad behaviors or bad habits. I know it's not an easy thing to accomplish, but it can be done, so let's get started. You don't need to change your life or change all your bad behaviors overnight, but you can start by making little changes to your way of thinking, because whatever you are right now is the direct result from your old way of thinking.

Why Do We Have Fears?

What is fear? Fear is an emotional feeling that occurs when we are face with eminent danger, in other words, it's a response signal which our brain sends to the human body so that we can be prepare ourselves to face a threatening situation. Moreover, it's important to understand how this takes place- first, our brain sends a signal to the suprarenal glands which releases adrenaline which is a type of hormone that increases our heart rate and respiration which occurs as part of our body's fight-or-flight response to any potential danger which might put our lives in danger.

It is only natural that we feel fear, and perhaps it doesn't happen often, but it does happen to everyone on occasions. Fear can happen in less than a blink of eye. Fear is a constant companion for everyone, in other words, it's never going to go away, but not to worry because I have good news for everyone, there is help on the way. I promise that everyone will see the light at the end of the tunnel, and I'm going to explain why, so bear with me. Fear is an emotion which is pre-program into every human being. It's a pre-program instinct which is going to prevent us from getting hurt. It's an instinctual response to potential danger. In other words, it's a physical response to fear. Furthermore, fear is a protective mechanism that will kick-in every time we are faced with any type of danger which is a good thing because it will increase our chances of survival.

There are different types of fears that we will experience from time to time, for instant, the fear of dying; fear of flying, fear of crossing a bridge, fear of going through a tunnel, fear of being in public places, and the fear of public speaking, but that is just the beginning. There are those who will fear just about everything, they are afraid of failing, afraid of rejection, afraid of commitment, afraid of driving, afraid of making any type of changes to their current way of life, they are afraid of the dark, afraid of height, and afraid of dentist.

These are only a few of the different fears that we will experience at any given time or place. Fear is something that most people do not completely understand, and it's because they don't have enough knowledge about it, and therefore, they don't know how to react to it when they are put into a situation where they don't feel comfortable. Understanding what fear is and how we came to acquire them, is going to allow us to keep them under control.

Most people are afraid of the unknown, I know I am, well, sometimes. We fear the things that we don't understand, we are afraid of future events that perhaps never going to materialized which is an unfounded type fears, in other words, they are imaginary fears; they are fears that we unknowingly create in our minds, they are the type of fears that will end up crippling us from time to time. There are two types of fears. The first type of fear are imaginary fears or adaptive fears. This is the type of fear that is never going to materialize. The second type of fear is called "primal fear" or inborn fear. It's part of our survival instincts at work. This type of fear is one that we need to keep because it will save our lives when in time of danger.

Fears can be tremendously powerful-they will steal our happiness if we do not keep them under control. Our fears have the potential to disrupt our daily lives in many ways. We must learn not to panic when we are faced with unrealistic or irrational fears. Remember that our fears will turn into panic and panic will turn into anxiety to the point where we won't be able to breathe.

Children have fears too- they have a fear of being left alone by their parents, they have a fear of the dark, and they have the fear of the unknown, therefore, we must be careful how we deal with our fears in front of our kids, in other words, we must be strong for our children. We need to keep our fears under control when our children are present otherwise our children will acquire the same fears that we have.

Again, why do we have fears? Well, do not fear no more because some of the answers to our fears will be revealed in this book. As I mention at the beginning of this chapter-fear is an unpleasant emotion caused by our erroneous beliefs that something or someone is dangerous and it's likely to cause us pain and anguish. Fear is a survival response mechanism that will kick in when we are faced with danger. We must understand that this type of fear is valuable to us because it's going to help stay safe.

I hate to keep repeating myself, but I must, because it's only by repetition that we are going to learn. Remember that most of our fears are unfounded fears that most likely are never going to materialize because there is no actual threat to us. It's all in our heads. It's all imaginary. Now, there will be actual fears that we are going to experience, for example, let's say that we are highking in the woods and suddenly we are faced to face with a big black bear, what would you do, would you panic and start running or would you put your thoughts in motion and try to find a different solution? I can assure you that running it's never not the best idea. Now! That is imminent danger or a situation where we expect to be seriously harmed or even cause our deaths.

It's important to remember that most of our fears are already built inside us, they are inborn fears or fears that we were born with. There are other types of fears, but these types of fears we learn as we got older, in other words, they are adaptive fears. Obviously, some of our adaptive fears will protect us from danger, but unfortunately, the majority of our adaptive fears are imaginary fears, those are the ones that we must try to stay away from because they are dangerous to our health and wellbeing.

We need to understand that if we didn't have fears, we would survive for too long. We probably would be eaten by a tiger, a lion or we could fall off a cliff. Our inborn fears have been built into us to keep us from getting killed. Inborn fears will trigger our fight-or flight response, which is going to possibly save our lives when we are confronted with a dangerously situation. Most of our fears are learned later in life, for instant, we learn to be afraid of heights. I was never afraid of heights when I was young, it wasn't until I was about twenty-five years of age that I developed a fear of heights, but before that, I was never afraid of jumping from a second story building, but now! I'm afraid of jumping from the second or third steps from our house stairway, but why am I afraid to jump when I know that it's not a dangerous situation? Well, maybe because I'm much older and do not want to break any of my bones. It's a natural response. It's a survival mode that kicks in. I guess we can say that I have a fear of heights. Remember that most of our fears are not going to manifest themselves until years later, when our brain has matured enough.

Again, most of our fears we learn later in life and they are very quickly adapted by us and it's because our brain is fully developed. It's not going to be an easy task getting rid of our fears, and it doesn't matter if they are in-born or adaptive fears, in fact, they will stay with us for the rest of our lives. However, we can learn to keep them under control.

We learn early in life that we must avoid certain things or animals that can potentially hurt us, in other words, we learn very quickly to avoid any potential danger, but not everyone feels the same way, some people have very few fears or none at all. People who don't have fears are called "fearless", In fact, some of those people thrive on fear because it's exciting for them.

As I said before, there are many types of fears, and I can go on forever, however, I'm not going to, but I will name a few more: Some people have the fear of open or closed spaces, for example, they have the fear of elevators because, either, they are afraid of heights or because they don't want to get stuck in one if the light where to go out. Others will fear tigers, snakes, rats, spiders, clowns, or bugs.

Is there such a time when being afraid is a good thing? Of course, there is. Sometimes having certain fears is a good thing because it's going to prevent us from getting hurt or dying. Fear is a vital response to any physical or emotional danger. If we didn't have fears, we wouldn't be able to protect ourselves from danger. Sometimes our fears will take over, even though there's no actual danger for our lives.

The reason we have fears is because there are many things that we don't understand, and therefore, it's only natural that we feel fear when we are faced with the unknown. Now! we know that having certain fears is a good thing to have because they will protect us from dangerous situations, it's like a survival kid that we have inside, however, we must learn not to be so fearful about everything and everyone because if we let our fears take over our minds- then are going to missed out on doing lots of fun activities with our families.

Furthermore, our fears will prevent us from discovering new places where we can go, have fun, and enjoy ourselves. Sometimes our fears will prevent us from having a normal relationship with our families and it's because they are so powerful that they will paralyze us completely. In other words, our fears will steal our freedom, our lives, and most importantly, they will prevent us from finding happiness. When our lives are overcome by fear, we are going to be limited as to how much we are going to accomplish in our lives, we will be limiting ourselves from reaching most of our goals. Furthermore, unknowingly, we are sacrificing our freedom because our fears are preventing us from doing the things that we normally love to do. Fear is a terrible thing to live with.

As human beings, we will avoid doing the things that we fear the most because we live in a world controlled by fear and that is why we are always fearful and cautious about everything that we do. Our lives are turned upside down because of our fears, but nevertheless, we must learn to keep them under control, or even better, we must learn to let go of our unfounded fears. We must take control of our lives; we must take control of our fears before they turn into anxiety and before they can cause irreversible damage. We must stop living our lives in fear because fear is a negative emotion that is going to drain our mental and physical energy. We must turn around these negative energy and turn it into positive energy instead.

The only way that we are going to be successful in conquering our fears is by stop our negative way of thinking. By using the power of positive thinking, we are going to be able to get rid of most of our unfounded fears.

Every human being on the planet, at some point or another, has been afraid of something or someone and I am sure that some of us will denial it. We will deny it because we don't want to appear as weak in front of other people. Denying or hiding our fears is not going to help us to get rid of our fears, talking about them to someone might.

Okay, so fear is always in our minds, but that doesn't mean that we must hide in a dark place and never come out, we must make the effort, we must come out of that dark place and slowly challenge our fears face to face. We must try to overcome those ugly feelings of fears which are making our lives miserable. We must never allow our minds to be in a fear state of mind, instead, our minds should be in a calm state of mind.

Again, if we want to conquer our fears, our state of mind must be calm, it must be completely relaxed. Furthermore, we need to be in total harmony within ourselves and the universe. But how are we going to accomplish such a task? Well, that is a good question. We can accomplish this task by meditating on a regular basis because meditation is going to help us to understand that our fears are just a survival human response to real threats. We must understand that real treats are few and far in between. It's important to remember that most of our fears are unfounded fears and most likely they will be of no consequence to us because they are imaginary threats.

The best way to get rid of our unfounded fears is by being self-aware that we are not actually in any real danger. Furthermore, we must ask ourselves the following question: "what I'm I afraid off?" We must remind ourselves that fears are just fears and if we face them head on, they will become weaker and weaker, and eventually, our fears will be under control.

Anyway, we must understand that fears are part of our daily lives, and even if we were to get rid of most of our fears, we are always going to acquire new ones because it is what makes us human. If we were robots, then we would not have any fears at all. Sure, we all have fears, but fears should not stop us from accomplishing our goals, having fun, enjoying our lives to its fullest and finding happiness.

I personally believe that everyone has the power to conquer their fears, and it's by defending ourselves, in other words, by attacking them instead of them attacking us, we must face them directly and with tons of determination. We must go out into the world and face them one at a time until we learn to keep them under control. I want to make it crystal clear that we are not going to always be successful in conquering every one of our fears, but we will conquer most of them. As for the rest of our fears, you know, the ones that we are not going to be able to overcome, but at the very least, we will be able to keep them under control. Remember that we must not fear the unknown. We must not be afraid to embark into new journeys just because we are afraid of the unknown. We don't like to make changes to our lives because we are in a comfort zone and anything outside our comfort zone will make us be fearful.

Change doesn't always come easy, but nevertheless, we must make a change in our lives because our minds and bodies are screaming for those changes and it's because they were not designed for stagnation. Let's listen to what our minds and bodies are telling us, let's listen to what our conscious mind is telling us. Let's not shut them down because our own happiness depends on it.

We must try our best not to be afraid of the unknown, and it's only natural for us to be afraid of forces that we don't understand, but we must do our very best to overcome our fears. President Franklin D. Roosevelt once said, "We have nothing to fear but fear itself." Furthermore, I believe that Jesus once said, "Always walk without fear because I'm walking by your side" These are powerful words that we should always remember. We must learn to control our fears and we can accomplish this task by controlling our thoughts because when we learn to control our thoughts, we will learn to control our fears, and only then we will be able to regain total control of our lives.

We were born with incredible abilities, including the instincts which is fundamental to our survival. We must remember that we were born without fears (except for our inborn fears) and that we learn to develop those fears from our parents, our surroundings and by observing others, in other words, our parent's behaviors and beliefs become our own. We can change our fundamental behaviors, our bad habits, our beliefs, and our attitudes which we learn from others as we were groin up by simply changing our way of thinking.

Our fears have the potential to destroy our lives; they will help us into making bad decisions because we are making those decisions based on fear alone and not on logic. We must remember that as human beings we tend to overreact when faced with imminent danger, we forget to think in a rational or in a logical manner.

Is there anything else we can do to help us move forward? Well, overcoming our fear is not an easy thing to accomplish, however, we can train ourselves not to panic when faced with imminent danger, and again, it's not an easy thing to do, but if we learn to control our fears, then we are going to be happier than ever before.

My recommendation for everyone reading this chapter is that: if you have any type of fears or phobias and if you want to conquer or defeat them, then you must find a nice quiet place where there's no distraction of any type because you will be doing some meditation, and in order to do that, you need a nice quiet place where you can relax so that you can meditate without any interruptions, It could be any place that you feel comfortable with, it could be in your car, inside your home, outside your home or at the park. When you find a place where you feel comfortable, you will sit down, and you will close your eyes because you are going to completely clear your mind of every negative thoughts, feelings and emotions that you might have. I always preferred meditating outside when it's not too hot or too cold, in other words, the temperature must be just right, with the right amount of breeze and the right amount of sun, and believe me, it works wonders, it's the best feeling in the world.

Okay, let's move on. After you close your eyes, you will breathe in slowly through your nose and exhale out through your mouth. You need to do this several times before you start to feel the calmness and serenity that you are looking for. Afterwards, you will feel in peace within yourself, you will feel the gentle breeze caressing your entire body, and finally, you will feel the nice gentle rays of the sun warming up your entire body. You must keep doing this for at least fifteen minutes. You must remind yourself that you don't need any negative thoughts, feelings or emotions in your life.

There's another way which is going to help you to keep your unfounded fears under control, and that is by reading as many books as possible on the topic. Reading fifteen to thirty minutes per day is going to help you tremendously and it's going to keep your mind sharp. You can always read a book for thirty minutes a day, but make sure you do it before you begin your meditation. Don't forget that you need to keep doing the same breathing exercises at least two or three times a week. These exercises are going to help you to get rid of some of your unfounded fears.

I do other things besides meditation, for example: I remind myself every single day that I need to live my life like if it was my last day here on earth, I remind myself that life is precious and short and that I shouldn't waste it on meaningless tasks. We must remind ourselves every single day that we deserve to be happy and that we are worth it. We must remind ourselves that we are a better than what we think we are, and that from this day on, we will try to be the best person that we can possibly be.

Chapter Nineteen

The Miracle of a Smile

We all have something to offer to others, and it doesn't always have to be about money, fortunately, there's an abundance of other things of value that we can offer, for example, we can offer some of our precious time, we can offer kindness, compassion, sympathy and we can also offer some of our skills. There is one other thing that we can offer to others, and perhaps this is one of the most important of them all, I'm talking about a "smile" If we don't have anything else to offer to others, at the very least, we can offer them the miracle of a smile. Yes, sometimes the miracle of a smile can go further than any materialistic thing. We all have a magical smile within ourselves waiting to come out. A smile can brighten someone's entire day, especially a sick child. Smiles have the power to mend broken hearts, but most importantly, it will bring new hope where there was none before. We need to smile more often because those who smile on a consistent basis (and it's a fact) are much happier than those who don't, furthermore, smiles are magical, they have a type of energy and light which is contagious, it flows from place to place brightening other people's lives.

It's undeniable that we all had bad days in the past, I know I have, in fact, I had many of those days when everything seems to be going wrong, but you know what! When my days are not going the way that I want them to go, I immediately start smiling on the inside. Furthermore, whenever I go to the store and I'm about to open the door to get inside and I see that someone is approaching I wait for them, I hold the door open and also wish them a wonderful day, but I also do it with a smile on my face. Remember that when we smile others will smile back.

Often, when we smile at someone, they will smile back, and when that happens, it makes our days that much more special. Sometimes, when I'm having a bad day and someone smiles at me, right away my entire day changes from a bad day to a good day. It completely brightens my entire day. For example, there's a lady that works at a McDonalds located near my house, in Lincoln Ca, and even though she probably doesn't make a whole lot of money, she always has a big smile on her face. She welcomes everyone with such a big smile that I have no other choice but to smile back because her smile is contagious, it seems that nothing ever bothers her. She also has such a good attitude that makes me want to be just like her, because her smile and attitude is contagious.

Unfortunately, I can't say the same thing about other people who works at other fast-food restaurants. For example: There's a girl working in a nearby fast-food restaurant, and it's only a few blocks from the other restaurant, and OMG, her attitude really sucks. One time I order a meal and she was going to charge me close to ten dollars, so I mention that it was too much, I told her that I wanted the six dollars meal and not the expensive one, to which she replied with anger: "well, next time you have to let me know which one you want" her bad attitude ruined my appetite, and so that is why I like to hang around with happy people. People who always have a smile on their faces. I honestly don't like hanging around grouchy people because most likely, they are going to ruin my day. By the way, I thought it was worth mentioning that I continuously meet people with a horrible attituded-they have no sense of humor whatsoever.

Anyway, a smile has the power to heal whatever ailment we might be experiencing, so therefore, it's important to remind ourselves, every single morning that we need to smile throughout the day regardless of how our day is going. I'm constantly reminding myself that I need to smile as much as possible, furthermore, I remind myself that every day is going to be a beautiful day and that I must enjoy every single minute of every day. We must remember that life is too short to be wasted on unproductive and meaningless tasks, so, let's start smiling more often.

Again, smiles are contagious, and I don't mind getting contagious with a ton of smiles. When we smile more, we will look more attractive, and we will be much happier. A smile from someone has the potential to lift our spirits up and our moods as well.

Smiling is good for our health because it's therapeutic, plus the fact that it doesn't cost anything. Every time we smile, we are sending signals to our brains, in other words, we are activating neural messaging which help our bodies heal whenever we are experiencing any type of sickness. Furthermore, when we smile, we are activating or releasing neuropeptides which will help us fight off stress.

Neuropeptides are molecules that allow neurons to communicate with each other. Perhaps the biggest benefit that we get when we smile more often is the fact that we will have less time to be sad, angry, depressed or stressed. When we smile more often, our bodies will be in total relaxation, which in turn, is going to help us lower our heart rate and high blood pressure. As we can see by now, smiles have tremendous beneficial.

Smiles are one of the best medicines in the universe, but the best thing about a smiles is that it doesn't have any bad side effects. Smiles serve as antidepressants, in other words, it's a mood lifter. Smiling more often is going to increase our chances of living longer and happier.

Again, it's obvious that when we smile more often, we will be much happier, and we will feel better about ourselves. Remember that when we smile more often people are going to treat us differently because we are going to be viewed as more attractive people, more reliable and honest. When we smile at someone, we should be getting a smile back from them, however, when they don't smile back it's because they are perhaps scrooges. Remember that our entire world is going to be a much better place for everyone if we just smile more often.

There's a good reason as to why I like to associate myself with people who smiles a lot, and it's because it makes me feel good on the inside. It makes me feel alive, it makes me feel happy, and most importantly, it makes me forget about my problems. Again, the people who smile a lot will feel more attractive than the ones who don't. Smiles are like magnets; it just draws you in.

Why are we drawn to people who are always smiling? Is it because a smile has physical attraction? Well, there's no denying that there's a physical attraction link to the act of a smile, but for me it's a little bit different. I like to hang around people who smile a lot because it makes me forget about most of my worries. A smile from a child. A smile from our loved ones and even a smile from a stranger is going to make our day much less stressful.

We must remind ourselves that we need to smile every single day because when we smile more often, we are going to get rid of our stress, and yes, smiling relieves stress, so when we are feeling lots of stress on the inside let's try to smile more often, and if at the end of the day we are still stressed out, then we need to smile some more.

Smiling and laughing is contagious and if you don't believe me, try smiling at someone, I guarantee that they will smile back. Remember that Smiling more often is going to boost our immune system, in other words, our immune system is going to function more effectively. Remember that when we smile on a consistence basis, we will be more relaxed and it's going to make us look and feel younger. Smiling more often is going to help us stay positive and become more successful because we will have more confidence in ourselves.

We need to learn to smile more often and we need to leave our laziness behind. Remember that our laziness and lack of exercise will shorten our life span. Exercising regularly will keep our minds sharp and our bodies healthy and fit. Staying active, exercising, and smiling more often is the foundation for living a longer and healthier life. The more active we are, the longer we will live. We must learn to smile more often because people who smile more frequently are the happiest people on the planet. Everyone in this world has been blessed with a good smile, so let's not be afraid to let it all out. Let's all smile more often.

Paradise

Where is paradise? Is it a place in heaven or a place here on earth? Most people believe that paradise does exist. People say that paradise is a place where we go after we died, and perhaps it's true, however, I also believe that paradise is here on earth, and I'm not talking about Paradise California which is north of Sacramento, although my heart goes out to all those people who last relatives and friends in the horrific fire of 2018.

I'm also not talking about paradise in the state of Nevada; south of Las Vegas, no! Rather, I'm talking about paradise here on earth. According to the bible, at the beginning of time there was an actual paradise here on earth, it was mankind's first home, it was the garden of Eden. The garden of Eden was a place where Adam and Eve lived free from any diseases and death, however, Adam and Eve decided to disobey God by eating the forbidden fruit, and consequently, they lost their home because of their disobedience. Furthermore, the bible says that paradise will be restored once again, here on earth, so there is hope after all.

You see, depending on our state of mind, we can either choose to think of earth as paradise or we can choose to think of earth as hell on earth, and as far as I'm aware of, there's no other planet like ours in the entire universe. Again, the bible mentions that paradise is here on earth and that when Jesus comes back, we are all going to continue living here on earth, we will forever live in peace and harmony, here in paradise.

Earth is the most beautiful and colorful planet in our solar system. We have breathtaking islands throughout the planet, we have some amazing jungles and colorful forests in most of the seven continents. Some continents have more forest or jungles than others, but nevertheless, every continent has an abundance of islands and forests which we can all learn to enjoy instead of destroying them. We also have an abundance of exotic plants thought-out the forests of the world, mostly in the spring and summer time. We have rolling hills and meadows full of colorful flowers blanketing the land and we also have an abundance of wildlife for us to enjoy. I can go on and on describing all the wonderful and beautiful things that our planet has to offer, however, it will take me a long time, so I'm leaving it up to you to discover more of our beautiful paradise here on earth.

It's unfortunate that some people don't realize that we are living in paradise. Again, our planet is the most beautiful planet in our solar system, it's a paradise that we need to explore more often.

Focusing on Living Rather Than Dying

For the first forty-five years of my life, the thought of dying was in the back of my mind most of the time. Day in and day out, wondering if there was an after-life, but now, I no longer think about dying, no longer the thought of dying crosses my mind, at least not often. I no longer think about dying, instead, I focus my energy into living for an exceptionally long time. It's only when a family member dies that those thoughts of dying start to creep up again, but I know that I must be strong, and I must try to concentrate my thoughts on something else.

We must not think about dying, at least not that often. When we think about dying it's only going to zap our mental and physical energy out of our bodies, instead, we must use our energy to focus on living longer and taking care of ourselves, physically and mentally. We must think of ourselves as young and strong, instead of old and weak. Thinking of ourselves as youthful and vigorous is going to allow us to live longer. There's absolutely nothing wrong on our part in thinking of ourselves as staying young for a very long time, believe me, it's not a sin. When we think of ourselves as old, we will feel old and defeated, but on the other hand, if we think of ourselves as young and strong, we will feel and stay young for an exceptionally long time. This is yet another way for us to challenge ourselves and our minds.

We must reprogram our minds to think of ourselves as young rather than old, but is this possible? Absolutely, I know that everything is possible when we challenge ourselves and challenge our minds. We must remember that our minds and our bodies are separate from each other, however, they work together as a team like a perfectly well-oiled machine.

We must focus our precious energy into stopping the aging process, but we can only accomplish it by not thinking about death, instead, we must focus our energy on life itself. We must focus on living for a long time.

With a positive attitude. A positive way of thinking and the power of our minds, it will be possible. At the very least, we can retain youth much longer. We must clear our minds from any negative thoughts that we might have because our negative thoughts have the potential to kill us at a much younger age, in other words, our negative thoughts will cut our life short.

From a young age, we were programmed to believe that everyone, eventually, is going to grow old and die. Such seed was planted deeply into our minds by everyone and even though it is true. We must not give into dying, at least not until we have fulfilled most of our goals and dreams. If we believe that we will die young, then most likely, we are going to die young, but on the other hand, If we believe that we will live for a very long time, chances are that we will live for a very long time.

The Sun

As human beings we take a lot of things for granted, but perhaps one of the biggest things that we take for granted the most, is the Sun. The sun gives our bodies the energy that it needs to survive. The sun gives the plants the energy that they need so that they can grow. The very same plants or trees that we grow which give us the food that we eat on a day by day basis. The sun is a big contributor to our existence, because without the sun, we will not be able to survive for too long. The sun gives our bodies the energy that it needs, and it gives us the food that we eat, it gives us the warmth that we need when we are cold, in other words, the sun is life itself. Without the sun, we will not be able to exist. The sun is an enormous ball of fire or a gigantic lamp that illuminates our daily activities. The sun gives the light that we need during the day, it's the light that enables us to see what's in front of us.

The sun is a big contributor to everything that exists on our planet earth, and of course, there are other important factors that contributed to life on earth; for example, without pollination from the bees, the flowers and plants that give us the food that we eat would not be able to survive. The sun has many hidden benefits, for example, it gives our bodies the energy that it needs in order to survive. Furthermore, the sun gives the plants and the trees the energy that they need in order to grow and produce fruit.

Most people are aware that the sun has many healing benefits, however, some people are not aware of that fact. Normally the winter months can be depressing for some people and it's because we are lacking vitamin D, which is produced by the sun and consequently, people will feel lonely and depressed. Some people are more acceptable to committing suicide during the winter months due to the lack of the comforting warm from the sun. I have experience, firsthand the nostalgia and the sadness throughout the winter months, so nobody is immune from it.

The sun is a good stimulant for good health for people who are depressed because they will find some relief, comfort, excitement, and a good sensation of well-being. The warm ultraviolet B rays of the sun will help us in the production of new and exciting feelings. The sun will stimulate our thinking, our thoughts, and our bodies with new energy. Whenever I experience the warm rays of the sun on my body, it makes me feel good about myself. The sun helps in restoring the human body with new energy and new hope.

Most often than not we take the sun for granted or even worse, we forget that there's a sun out there. A sun that we can all feel and enjoy. I'm guilty as charged, I do forget about the sun from time to time; I forget that the sun has the power to warm me up when I'm feeling cold, furthermore, I forget that the sun has the power to make me feel better whenever I'm feeling lonely or depressed.

Today I have re-discover the power of the sun. I forgot that there was a sun out, but why did I forget about the sun? Well, I was too preoccupied working on my book, when suddenly I started feeling tired and cold and that's when it hit me, I had the urge to step outside into the balcony where the sun was shining. After fifteen minutes of sunshine I was feeling reenergized. My entire body was full of new energy once again, so I went back inside and continued working on my book.

I actually didn't forgot about the sun outside the balcony, I knew it was there, but I couldn't bring myself to stop writing, I was too preoccupied with my own thoughts about writing my book that I just wanted to keep on writing, I didn't want to stop, I just wanted to keep on going like an energizer bunny.

I finally realized that I had to get my body outside and enjoy the warm rays of the sun. I forced myself to go out there, and let me tell you, it was an amazing feeling. The warm rays from the sun made me feel at peace once again. It also made me feel warm, but not only on the outside but on the inside as well.

As I mentioned earlier, one tremendous benefit that we get from the sun is vitamin D, and by the way, vitamin D is the "sunshine vitamin." The human body does very well in storing vitamin D in the summer months, and any excess of vitamin D which our bodies get from the sun during the summer months is stored in our bodies for the winter months. Vitamin D is also essential for our teeth and our bones' health. A daily dose of sunshine for about fifteen minutes during the day will allow us to get about ten thousand international Units of vitamin D and that is more than enough to keep us going for the entire day, but of course, some people get more than enough vitamin D in thirty minutes, however, any extra vitamin D is stored in our bodies for future use.

It's of great importance that we get at least fifteen minutes of sunshine daily. However, if we are not able to do it daily, then we should try doing it for at least three to four times a week. The vitamin D that we get from the sun is not the only source of vitamin D, but it's the most important one because our skin produces vitamin D from the ultraviolet rays of the sun. Warning: we must be careful not to expose our bodies to the sun for too long because it could potentially cause cancer in the long run.

God is a good architect, he knew that without the light of the sun there would be no life on earth, our planet would be nothing but a big ball of ice. There's always a purpose for everything. There's a purpose for the sun, there's a purpose for the moon, and there is a purpose for everything else that exists in the universe, so let's not take anything for granted, let's all go out and enjoy the sun as much as possible or whenever possible.

Chapter Twenty

We Can Accomplish More by Working as a Team

If we want to be successful in accomplishing our goals and bringing peace to our world, we need to join forces with other people. Working as a team, we will be able to accomplish our goals in less time than working by ourselves. By working as a team, we can change our world, and we can start by getting rid of the deceit, greed, corruption, and suppression that we have been subjected to for millennials.

As a team, we will be able to move mountains. As a team, we will be able to move forward and get closer towards achieving our goals. We all dream of a better world, but unfortunately, there are those who don't care about what happens to our planet. They also don't care what happens to other people. It's a well-known fact that: as long as people get what they want, they won't care much about anything else because their greed is stronger than their will to do something good for others. Greed will take over people's minds preventing them from becoming the person that they were meant to be, a person with honor and integrity: A person who knows how to control their thoughts, their emotions, and their actions. Often people forget about one of the most important aspects of our lives, which is to find happiness. We must remember that without happiness nothing else is going to matter. It's important for us to remember not to let our greed prevent us from finding happiness, in other words, we must never let our greed cloud our rational way of thinking.

We don't always need to get everything that we want in order to find happiness. You see, when we become greedy other people will suffer along the way and it's because every decision that we make in our lives is going to affect others, it will impact our entire families in many ways. Our bad decisions will impact our friends, and the rest of the world's population. We must keep in mind that with every action there will be a reaction. We can always better ourselves economically, however, we must never, and under any circumstances, make others suffer, after all, we are in this together.

We need to get rid of our me first mentality if we are going to survive as human beings in our world. If we do not work as a team, and change our way of thinking, we are never going to achieve total happiness. By working as a team, we will accomplish much more, but faster.

By working as team, instead of working against each other; we are going to discover new technologies, which in turn, is going to help us to discover new worlds in record time, but before we can work as a team, we need to get rid of our unhealthy way of thinking, including, our unhealthy emotions, unhealthy thoughts, and self-defeating behaviors.

Can you imagine for just a few minutes if everyone on the face of the planet could work closely together, and in complete harmony? Wow! One can only hope. We must keep in mind that if we work as a team, we will be able to conquer most adversities, furthermore, we will live more productive lives. Working as a team, we will be able to overcome most of our problems, and at the same time, we will take on new and greater challenges. It's a win-win situation for everyone.

Preying on Others

It's a well-known fact that through-out history we inherit the tendency to prey upon our fellow man, and not only economically, but physically as well. What is the number one reason as to why we behave in such a manner? Why do we sometimes behave like wild animals? Well, I know for a fact that our animalistic survival instincts kick in, in other words, it's the survival of the fittest mentality, but it doesn't need to be that way because we are intelligent human beings capable of solving most of our problems in a rational manner, but only if we work together. I'm aware that back in the Stone Age, we needed these survivor skills in order to survive, however, in today's modern world that type of behavior is unnecessary. We supposed to be civilized and rational human beings, but sometimes we forget to act as such. We can't continue to have the same mentally that we had back in the Stone Age, tens of thousands of years ago, but it doesn't need to be this way because we are intellectual human beings with the tremendous capacity to think and act in a civilized manner. We are capable human beings with the power of reasoning on our side, yet, for some unexplained reason, we are still carrying a big club on our shoulders.

I know for a fact that our ancestors were cavemen and supposedly, we are their descendants. But nowadays there's a big difference between a caveman and a modern man. Caveman did not have the tools that we have today. They also didn't have the knowledge; they didn't have the technology and they didn't have the ability to put their thoughts into proper working order.

Now days we have the capability to be stable, calm and deliberate, but most of the time we are not, we should be using logic, but we are not, we supposed to be collected in the face of adversity, but we are not, we are supposed to be sensible and thoughtful to others in need, but we are not, we are supposed to use common sense and be level headed, but we are not.

My final conclusion is that: as human beings we can't always be trusted to do the right thing, we don't always speak with the truth, the sincerity and honesty that we all deserve, I just don't see it happening any time soon. It seems that our mere existence is based on lies and greed. I have asked myself the same question a thousand times, why are we so unbalanced and sometimes reckless? Again, I think that our bad behaviors have to do with the fact that we were program to be hunters, we were program to bring home as much kill as possible and it didn't matter how much food we bring home, it was never enough, we wanted more, in other words, we were never satisfied with what we had and in today's world, not much has changed.

In today's world, man acts just like our ancestors, and it's because we were programmed to accumulate as much as possible. There's one difference between the Stone Age and the modern man, the caveman used to go hunting, because they were program to bring home "or cave" as much food as possible, but in today's modern world, man is program to accumulate as much money and materialistic things as possible and that is the only difference between the modern man and our ancestors...the caveman. Again, it's never enough, we always want more. We are programmed to accumulate as much riches as possibly, and without any regard for others. Our mentality has not changed much throughout the millenniums.

I'm not saying that every man and woman acts and behave in such a manner, however, most people will behave badly when they are tested to their limits. I'm guessing the fear of poverty will make us behave in an irrational manner. Not having enough money or food is going to tempt us into committing all types of atrocities; for instant, lying to others in order to get what we want. Furthermore, when we are tested to our limits, we are capable of cheating, robbery, rape and even murdering someone. We are all capable of committing all types of human violations, but at the same time, we are also capable of doing many good things for humanity.

Throughout the millennials, men inherited a great deal of distrust against each other. It has been building among men for too long, but we can put an end to it right now! It's time for mankind to put an end to our distrust, it's time for mankind to make a change and to put an end to the nature of the beast. We must become real men of honor, integrity, and respect for the sake of humanity.

Every Day is a New Day Full of Wonders

Every day is a blessing because it gives us the opportunity for a new beginning. Every new day is full of excitement, every new day gives us the opportunity to move forward with more confidence towards achieving our goals. With every new day we should be moving forward, but without the memories of our past failures holding us back. The only thing which is going to hold us back from moving forward is: ourselves.

We must leave our bad habits and old patterns behind, otherwise they will continue to hold us back from becoming the person that we were meant to be. We should never let our past prevent us from reaching our goals and from finding happiness. We must free ourselves from the illusions that we created for ourselves, furthermore, we need to free ourselves from the illusions that others created for us as well. We must not let the illusions of deceit hold us back and we must never look back and revert to our old beliefs.

We must learn from our mistakes. We must not keep on making the same old mistakes time after time. We must learn our lessons and move forward leaving the past behind us. If we use our previous experiences and use them to justify the wrong conclusion about ourselves, then we are going to let our past dictate our future, therefore, we must never let the past dictate who we really are. Remember that we are the only ones who will determine our future.

Every day is a new day full of wonders, therefore, we need to get inspired every single day of our lives, but we can only accomplish such a task by creating new goals for ourselves. We must focus our energy on our new goals, and new attitudes, rather than focusing on our limitations. We must remind ourselves daily to let go of old ideas and instead try to create new ideas for ourselves.

With each new day, our love for life must continue to grow because each new day is a blessing, each new day is a miracle. Each new day is going to give us a boost of new energy. With each new day, our energy is going to renew itself and it will flow through our bodies like never-before. Our bodies, our souls, and our minds need new energy on a consistent basis because this new energy is going to allow us to focus on the positive side of life and not the negative side of it.

With each new day, our desire to get healthier and live longer should be increasing by leaps and bounds. Each new day is going to bring us an abundance of new things to enjoy and experience; it's going to bring us new ideas, new desires, new discoveries, and new horizons to explore.

Life can be full of wonderful surprises, but only if we learn to overlook the ugly side of it. We must learn to live our lives in harmony and enjoy the good things that life has to offer. Furthermore, we need to let go of our previous bad experiences. We must never give up on life and we must not give up hope because with each new day there will be hope for a better tomorrow. We should always look for new and exciting things to do so that we can keep our hopes alive.

We must step out of our comfort zone and venture out into the unknown because it's the only way that we are going to meet other people which is going to open the doors for something new and exciting for us to do, plus we might find out that we are going to enjoy it as well.

Life is beautiful, just look around you and you will see that there's so much going on around us, but unfortunately, sometimes we fail to recognize it because we are so preoccupied with our own, and sometimes, meaningless thoughts. We really need to wake up from our dormant state of mind and become more aware of our surroundings so that we can learn to appreciate and enjoy life to its fullest.

We must not let time slip by us because time is precious, and we must not waste it on meaningless and unproductive activities. We only have a limited time to enjoy and experience all that there is to experience in our lifetime. Let's not waste that precious time that we have here on Earth and start enjoying it by doing positive activities with our families and friends. Remember that as we get older, life will become a burden, but it doesn't have to be that way, instead, let's find new and enjoyable things to do.

The secret to finding happiness is to wake up every morning with a positive attitude, with passion and enthusiasm to learn new things. Remember that we only have one life to live and that one life is not enough to experience all that there is to experience, so we must take advantage of every opportunity and live every day like if it was the last day of our lives here on Earth.

Our time and energy should be invested on the search and development of something more fulfilling, such as…spending more time with our family on fun loving activities. It's unfortunate that most of us don't have the luxury of enjoying more time with our families because our jobs won't allow us to do so. Often our jobs require us to work too many hours, so there will be little time left on the day for other activities or spending time with our families, our kids, and friends. Remember that any spare time that we have should be spend with our family doing exciting things.

Our Beautiful and Enigmatic World

We live in a beautiful world full of wonders and beauty. A world where life thrives and flourish, a world full of miracles happening all around us every single day. Our world has many beautiful things to see and enjoy, so many oceans and lakes to navigate, so many rivers to travel, so many waterfalls to see, so many mountains to climb, so many forests to explore, so many sunsets and sunrises to enjoy, so many different and exotic animals to see and photograph. I believe that everyone should try to enjoy all the beautiful things that our planet has to offer us instead of trying to destroy it.

We also need to learn enjoy and love our families and friends more with each passing day because we don't know how much time we have left to enjoy them. We must try to get along with one another, and yes, even with strangers because somehow, we are all connected to each other. Oh! and please don't tell me that we are not connected because we are more connected to each other than we might ever know, we all depend on each other to survive, furthermore, tell me if we are not connected to each other somehow, for example: The farmers grow most of the food that we eat. They grow the fruits and vegetables that we eat daily, they feed the cows that give us the milk that we drink- the milk that we turn into chocolate milk- the milk that we use to make our mash potatoes- the milk that we use for our cereal in the mornings before we go to school or before we go off to work and the milk that we use for our coffee.

Furthermore, farmers feed the cows, the chickens and the pigs that gives the meat that we eat. These are a few examples of how well we are connected but wait a minute! There's more, we are connected to the truckers who deliver most of the food that we eat. We are connected to those people who build the cars that we drive and that we love so much, we are connected to those who build our roads, we are connected to those who build our homes, we are connected to those who mow our lawns, and we are connected to those who supply us with electricity and so on.

You see, we are all connected, so don't tell me that we don't depend on each other for survival. If anyone out there thinks that he or she is not depending on others to survive, then they are one hundred percent wrong. Our mere survival depends on each other, we are indeed well connected.

We are indeed connected in so many ways, but unfortunately, there are those who don't even have a remote idea of how well we are connected to each other. We must remember that our actions will impact, not only ourselves, but it's going to impact the rest of the population, so remember to be kind to yourself and others, furthermore, remember to always stay humble.

Back to our beautiful world... It's unfortunate that we are too busy and too preoccupied with our own thoughts and our own greed that we fail to recognize how wonderful and magical our world is indeed.

We live in a fast-paced world where everything needs to be done fast. It's a very demanding and exhausting world and it's because of that, we have no time left to do the things that we really love to do...the things that will bring us joy and happiness or the things that we really care about the most.

Are we doomed forever, are things going to get worse as time goes on, is there any hope for humanity for the future, are we going to allow ourselves to fall into stagnation forever? Of course not, we must refuse to fall into stagnation at any cost because we are intelligent human beings capable of accomplishing many great things, but only if we learn to slow down and stop being greedy.

We can accomplish anything that we so desire, but only if we stop ourselves from blocking our rational way of thinking. We must stop being so greedy, we must stop doing the things that will prevent us from reaching our goals and find happiness. We must remember that: when there is so much greed in this world, there cannot be complete happiness and enjoyment in our hearts. I cannot emphasize enough that greed, money, and power is the root of all evil and I also think that most people know this, but having said this, most of us can't help ourselves. We cannot control ourselves because greed can be something powerful for us to overcome, greed will make us go blind, greed will make us become immune to other people's needs.

Somehow, we must find the time needed for recreational enjoyment, but in order to accomplish such a task is by slowing down a bit and think about the decision that we are about to make. We must stop the madness and stop driving too fast, we are always going from place to place in such a rush that forget to smile, we forget to enjoy life to it's fullest, and we forget to enjoy our beautiful world.

I know that most people don't have the time for personal enjoyment because of their demanding work or perhaps they don't have the desire because they have no strength or energy left at the end of the day, but we must remember that there are no excuses big enough for not trying. Remember that if we have the burning desire to be happy and enjoy life to its fullest, we will be successful. With a little effort on our part, we can become the person that we were meant to be...a happy person.

We must remind ourselves that we live in a perfect world and that when we get ourselves into trouble, it's not the world's fault that we get in trouble. It's not the world fault that we are so unhappy at times, rather, it's our inability to learn from our mistakes because we keep on making the same mistakes over and over, so remember that it's not the world we should be blaming, instead, we should be blaming ourselves for our misfortunes. Perhaps it's the human species that can't get along with each other and that is what makes our world seem like a troubled world. We have no one to blame but ourselves. We are the ones that should be working together to try and make our world a better place.

As of right now, our world is a world in trouble because there's plenty of anger, hate and crime among each other. There's wars which kills millions of innocent people around the world. There's terrorism, there's corruption, there's misery, there is jealously, and there's selfishness among us, and it's all because of our greedy nature.

Furthermore, our lives are full of stressful events, most people live in poverty, in fact, seventy percent of the world's population lives in poverty, that is an astonishing revelation to me, there's a high rate of unemployment in many parts of the world and that makes people uneasy and desperate. We are also encountered with health issues and problems between families, but perhaps the biggest problem that we all face constantly is the fact that we don't have enough money to feed, dress and put a roof under our families heads. There's never enough money to go around and as a result, we become angry and irritable and this in turn is going to follow with more anger and desperation. Our minds will, eventually, be invaded by anxiety and when anxiety invades our bodies, everything will stop, we will lose our focus, we will lose the desire to accomplish our goals and we will lose the ability to love and care for others.

I'm not going to judge or blame others for all the problems and ugliness which afflicts our world because we are all guilty, we are all responsible for what happened in the past, and we are all responsible for what is going to happen to us in the future. There's not one easy answer as to how we can solve all our problems, however, there are little things that we can start doing right now which will make our planet a better place for everybody. We can start by doing the little things that don't cost anything, in other words, they are free; for example, we can start by being nice to each other, we can be polite, we can say thank you, we can smile more often, we can stop being so greedy and we can donate some of our time to help others in whatever they need.

What else can we do to make a difference? Well, for example, if someone has offended us in any way, shape or form, the first thing that we should do is to never wait for the other person to make the first move into apologizing, we must take the initiative and talk to them, and maybe things will work out for the best, but we are never going to find out if we don't make the first move. You and I can make a big difference in people's lives. We must take charge of our own destiny right now before it's too late. We must not wait until tomorrow because tomorrow might never come. Most often than not we will tell ourselves, "I will start tomorrow" but unfortunately, tomorrow never comes. We must be responsible and be accountable for our own actions, but we need to start now. We must try to solve our differences or our difficult situations between one another today. Not tomorrow.

We must take the initiative and start doing the little things that will make a difference in our lives and the lives of our families, friends, and strangers.

Perhaps, we can start by smiling more often to others, a smile can go a long way because it's going to brighten someone's day. I know my days are much brighter when someone smiles at me or tells me something nice, so don't wait for others to smile first, take the initiative and start smiling more often. Remember that our future is in our hands, but it's in someone else's hands as well.

Another thing that we can do now to alleviate some of the ugliness in our world is to be honest with one another, this would help tremendously because honesty can go a long way. Honesty is going to help us in building the trust and confidence that we need between one another but remember that before you and I can be honest with each other, we need to be honest with ourselves first. There's a perfectly good reason as to why we need to be honest with ourselves first because if we are not honest with ourselves, then we are not going to be honest with other people either, does this make sense to you? I know it makes sense to me.

How to Become Successful in Life

If we want to become successful in life and in business, we need to observe, study, and follow the ones who know how to get things done, but why do we need to imitate or follow them? Well, because they have the knowledge and the experience which is require in order to be successful. Yes, those are the people who we should be following because they have been there and done that.

If we want to be successful in everything that we do, then we need to do what other successful people are doing, in other words, we don't follow people that we don't respect and admire. We don't follow people who are toxic, we don't follow people who are lazy, and we don't follow people who don't have respect for themselves and others, because if we do, they are going to bring us down to their level.

There are many true stories about successful people who became Millionaires. For example, Mr. Warren Buffet. As of 2019 he is worth billions of dollars. However, I am not going to get into the details of why he is so successful because it would take a while for me to explain it. The only thing that we need to know about Mr. Warren Buffet is that he has the knowledge and experience which is one of the main reasons as to why he has been so successful in business. Mr. Warren Buffet does things the right way, in other words, he knows exactly where to invest his money.

Mr. Warren Buffet is perhaps the best person that we should be following when we want to invest some of our money, and it's because he has been successful most of his life. He is the one who millions of people are keeping their eyes on, they watch every move that he makes, and when he makes a move, everybody follows him.

Restaurants and grocery stores is another good example of successful stories and I will explain why, you see, when a restaurant comes up with an exotic and delicious dish that people loves to eat, almost immediately other restaurants will follow with their own similar dish, in other words, they copycat that delicious dish, however, they give it a differently name, but they also make some small changes to the recipe and for obvious reasons. They don't want to be sued by the restaurant who came up with the original recipe.

Moreover, the grocery stores copy each other, but they do it in a different way. They copy each other's advertising by selling the same items for a lower price and that in return is going to attract more customers to their store. Sometimes a grocery store comes up with an ingenious way to advertise, promote or sell a certain product and since it works for them, then other stores will follow with something similar, so why do they do it? Well, because it works. We must follow or imitate those successful people or corporations, well, that is if we want to be successful in life and be successful in business as well.

Again, we don't follow unsuccessful people because they don't know how to create wealth. We don't follow people who behave badly or do bad things because those people are only going to get us in trouble, furthermore, we don't follow people who do drugs because those people, most likely will want us to intake drugs too, unless of course, we want to intake drugs, the choice is ours to make.

I'm a firm believer that if I want to be happy, then I need to follow happy people, furthermore, if I want to be successful in accomplishing my goals, then I need to follow successful people. We also don't follow those who are going to make us feel bad about ourselves. We don't follow unsuccessful people who don't know how to create wealth for themselves, and we don't follow those who don't know how to create happiness for themselves. There are plenty of people who only knows how to create chaos, misery, desolation, and unhappiness for themselves and for everyone else, in fact, they only want to bring us down to their level of lifestyle, so we must be careful who we choose as our friends.

I'm an individual who doesn't like to judge others because of who they are or what they do, I'm simply saying that every man and woman have the same opportunity to learn and to better themselves, economically, mentally, and physically. Again, some of us choose to become successful in accomplishing our goals, but others not so much. I do understand that some people are lacking the knowledge or to be more precisely, they are lacking the right knowledge which is need it in order to make the right decisions in their lives.

There are those who are lacking the desire to get ahead in life. They are lacking the desire to become great achievers, but nevertheless, these individuals, the uneducated ones, have the same opportunity as everyone else to try and accomplish the same things that successful, powerful, and rich individuals have accomplished, if indeed, is what they genuinely want. Everyone has the right to thrive for the same things that other successful individuals have accomplished, but in order to accomplish such a task is by educating ourselves. Educating ourselves by acquiring new knowledge is going to make all the difference in the world. Remember that knowledge is power.

There are two types of people in the world, the doers and the non-doers, the doers are the ones that go out and do what they say they are going to do. The non-doers are the ones that will stay home. The non-doers are the dreamers. The doers are the non-procrastinators, the non-doers are the procrastinators. The doers are those who don't leave anything to chance, they don't leave the things that they need to do today until tomorrow, they do wherever they need to right now! The procrastinators leave most of the things they need to do now, until tomorrow, and as everyone knows by now, tomorrow never comes.

So, what type of person would you rather be, the doers, the non-procrastinators or the non-doers and procrastinators? The doers are the ones that get all the glory because they don't let anything stop them from achieving their goals, and the non-doers are those who let everything stop them from achieving their goals. Anyone can achieve their goals and dreams by simply imitating those who know how to be successful. Unsuccessful people must learn from successful people, they must learn to do things the right way and without hurting other people in the process. We must never take advantage of other people's misfortunes by stepping over their toes. Furthermore, we must never, under any circumstances, degrade other people in any type or form or treat them like if they have a plague or had some type of contagious and incurable diseases. We must conduct ourselves with integrity and respect in front of others.

We have power within ourselves, we have total control over our actions, and we also have the knowledge, so, why not use it to make a better life for ourselves and at the same time help others so that they too can accomplish their goals. The individuals who have the knowledge and the desire to better themselves, they are never going to quit when confronted with obstacles. They will simply keep moving forward, in other words, they don't let obstacles get in the way from accomplishing their goals. They simply remove those obstacles, or they find a solution to their problem, but one thing they would never do is to give up on their dreams.

People who are successful don't see a high mountain which they must climb, instead, they see a small hill. People who are successful have a clear understanding of how things work, they see the light at the end of the tunnel, instead of the darkness, they know that there is light at the end of the tunnel and it's because they have a clear vision of what they want to accomplish, in other words, they look at the future instead of the past.

We were all created to be achievers, we were all created to be successful human beings, we were born with a powerful mind along with a lot of imagination, and we were born with an incredible capacity to think rationally. We have all the tools that we are ever going to need to help us in our search for a better life. Those tools were given to us by our creator so that we can achieve our goals. We were not created by our creator just so that we go through life falling on our faces. We were not created so that we can suffer and be in pain. Remember that if sometimes we suffer is because of our own doing. We were created so that we can become the person that we were meant to be, a happy person. We were created to become the creators of good values for ourselves and for others because we are the future assets of society.

If we want to dramatically improve our way of life, then we need to learn new knowledge so that we can do things differently. because the things we are accustomed to doing are no longer working. We must educate ourselves by reading new books and by imitating others. It's only by educating ourselves and imitating others that we will be successful in achieving our goals.

We are only going to be achievers of great things when we start asking ourselves the following questions, "What makes me happy, what makes me unhappy, why do I behave the way I behave, why do I become angry at times, and for no good reason whatsoever, why do I feel so much disappointment when things don't go the way I want them to go?" Well, if you must know, I'm going to tell you why, and it's because most of the time, we are lacking the knowledge, we are lacking self-discipline and we are lacking self-control.

We are always searching for something that will make us happy. Something that will make us feel good on the inside, something that is going to give us the deep-warm feeling of joy and happiness, but unfortunately, we are never going to find out what that something is, unless, we figure out what we want. The reality is simple, it's not that complicated, we need to find out what things are going to make us happy and then go out and do those things.

There is a perfectly good explanation as to why we are not successful in life, and it's because instead of thinking about success, we are thinking about failure most of the time. If we want to be successful, we must imagine ourselves being successful, if we want to be happy, we must imagine ourselves being happy, we are not going to achieve happiness by imagining ourselves being miserable. We become successful by imagining ourselves being unsuccessful. We become what we think, so we must be careful what we are thinking right now because whatever we are currently thinking, that's exactly what we will get in return. We will attract whatever we are wishing or thinking about the most, so having said this, why not imagine ourselves being successful and happy all the time, why not do some of the things that will make us happy and go after them?

Chapter Twenty-One

Photography

Today I decided to write about photography because photography is one of my passions in life. It's such a joy for me taking pictures of landscapes, nature, wildlife, and seascapes, but occasionally I like to photograph people as well, but not as often as I do with nature. I take my photography seriously because that is what I enjoy doing the most. Photography is something that I always wanted to do since High School. I had photography classes in High School for two years and during those two years I was able to learn to develop my own black and white images.

Back in those days I didn't have the luxury of having an extra room in my house where I could set up a dark room, so I did the next best thing, I converted a small closet into a dark room. Again, it wasn't much of a space, but it was big enough to allow me to do my work. It just goes to show you that when we use our imagination, anything is possible. Anyway, I was happy because I was able to develop my own black and white images in that little dark closet.

During my years in High School I learned to mix my own chemicals. It was an exciting time for me because I was able to buy chemicals and white photographic paper from the "Kodak Store" which allow me to develop black and white images. I remember spending countless hours developing pictures, and sometimes I stayed up well into the morning hours, in fact, sometimes I only had a couple hours of sleep. The reason as to why it was such an exciting time for me was because it seem as if time didn't exist, in other words, time was standing still for me. My life was all about photography and soccer, but that is another story, anyway, whether I was outside taking pictures or developing in my little dark room, I was always having fun doing it.

Thirty-two years have passed since high school and during those years, I never did much with photography, however, from time to time I would pull out my instant Polaroid Camera and snap a few pictures and that was as far as I got with photography during those years of inactivity. It wasn't until 2011 when me and my wife Norma went on a trip to Oregon. We went to visit my sister in-law Connie and her husband Eugene Powell in Curtin Oregon. Curtain is a small community near Cottage Grove, which is located about fifty miles from Eugene Oregon. Anyway, it was then that I rediscovered my true passion for photography.

Eugene Powell loan me his camera because I had a film camera and his was a digital one. Digital cameras are more efficient in many ways. They are faster, and we don't have to waste any time going to the store to buy film, chemicals and paper and spend countless hours developing those images. I must say that I had a blast taking pictures of some beautiful places in Oregon, especially the waterfalls. They are amazing. Oregon and the state of Washington have a lot to offer, the sceneries are breathtaking, it's a paradise for photographers.

After I got back from our trip, I enrolled myself in college because I wanted to learn more about digital photography. I went to Mission College in Santa Clara, Ca for one semester and that's when I finally brought myself a new digital camera: the D700 Nikon, and by the way, I'm still using that same camera. It was one of the best Nikon Cameras at the time, it's been a great camera overall because it did everything that I needed to do.

The following year I decided to try a different college, so I enrolled myself at De Anza College in Cupertino, Ca for another semester.

Okay, moving on, but before I do that I want to mention that I acquire a taste for other types of art, and one of them was oil paintings, in fact, the reason as to why I develop a taste for other types of art is because I bought an oil painting of Mr. Heinie Hartwig "a listed artist" at a local art store. A few months later I bought another piece by the same artist, and so I became an aficionado of his work, however, I decided that I wasn't going to keep paying retail prices for his work, so I contacted Mr. Heinie Hartwig himself. He invited me over his house, and I started buying more of his art pieces. So, throughout the years, I end up buying about a dozen of his oil paintings on board. By the way Mr. Heinie Hartwig and I became good friends. He is an amazing artist.

Now is 2020 and I still have the same camera but eventually I want to update my old camera for one with at least twenty-four megapixels because I need those extra pixels which are required for panoramas.

For the last two or three years I have been thinking about going back to Oregon and Washington State, but this time around I want to be well prepared. The last time I was up in Washington State it was almost a complete failure because most of the images which I took from Mount St. Helen, were ruined. You see, there was a major volcanic eruption which happen in 1980 and consequently, there was a lot of volcanic dust in the vicinity. It was a very windy day and because of that the dust got inside my camera and ruined most of the images, but nevertheless, it was quite an experience. My wife and I went back to Oregon a year after and I took some breathtaking images along the beautiful coast of Oregon, and I must admitted, I loved it, so now I want to go back yet again, however, this time around I want to make sure that I'm well prepared, I have a lot more experience now than I had eight years ago.

When I'm photographing nature, landscapes or wildlife, I feel like I'm in a tunnel, all my focus and concentration is on taking pictures. I can spend all day taking pictures and not worry about the time. Perhaps it has to do with the fact that whenever I'm photographing breathtaking sceneries I totally forget about the outside world.

Whenever a photographer is out and about taking pictures, we must think about many different scenarios which might happen as we are shooting, for example, we must think about the time of day, we must think about where the light is coming from and adjust our camera accordingly, in other words, we need to constantly make changes to our camera settings, and if we are photographing animals, we must be ready for action. We must anticipate their moves and be ready to take the shot because if we are not ready for them, then we will miss an opportunity to capture a great shot.

The reason I love photography so much is because it makes me feel free, alive, and happy. It makes me forget about the world, at least for a while. Photography makes me feel free, especially when I'm out somewhere in the wild taking pictures of amazing waterfalls, mountains, rivers, animals or exotic flowers. The possibilities for photography are endless because we can pretty much photograph anything, anywhere and at any time. Photography is fun, but at the same time it can be challenging; for example, one day I decided to go to a nearby lake which is located only about a mile from my house in Lincoln, Ca. Anyway, this small lake or pond is full of wildlife, at least most of the time. I went there several times within a year, but I wasn't able to see much other than the usual ducks, a turtle and some birds, so

I stop going for a while. The following year I decided to go back yet again and to my surprise, I found an abundance of wild life; I found the usual ducks and birds but I also found a snowy egret, a blue heron, a green heron, and a bunch of turtles sunbathing on top of the rocks, so you see, you can never say that you don't want to visit the same place twice because you never know what you are going to encounter. Oh! I forgot to tell you; my Granddaughter was with me that time, so I let her snap a few pictures as well. The following page contains a few of the images that I took that day.

Good Luck, Bad Luck

I strongly believe that most people accept failure because that is all they ever know. Failure is accepted as a curse which is the wrong kind of thinking which is going to prevent most people from trying new things. I do not believe in curses; however, I do believe in good luck and bad luck. Good luck and bad luck comes and goes, in other words, it doesn't have a timetable, both, good luck and bad luck will manifest itself without any notice. I know about good luck and bad luck because for the first 45 years of my life I felt as if I had the worst luck in the universe, I just couldn't win at anything, especially at slot machines. I could never win no matter what I was playing.

I didn't know it back then, but when I turned twenty-one years of age the worst part of my bad luck was about to begin. It was the day that I was finally able to legally gamble. I remember that day well because I was so excited. I was so happy that I could hardly wait to get to Reno Nevada, but little did I know that for the next twenty-five years bad luck was going to follow me whenever I gamble. Anyway, for the next twenty-five years I never won a jackpot more than a couple hundred dollars, imagine that, and I want to make it crystal clear, I don't have a gambling problem because I know how to control myself. I know when to quit, I just like to enjoy myself by having a couple of beers while I'm playing. The main objective for me is to have fun whenever I'm gambling. It's not about winning for me, however, when I do win something, it makes me feel good. There's no denying that too many people have gambling problems. Mostly, they go to a casino thinking about winning rather than having fun, but the reality is that very few people ever win something big. My advice for everyone out there is that: whenever you go to a casino, don't just think about winning, instead, go and try to have fun, in other words, enjoy yourselves because if you are thinking about winning most of the time, than chances are that you are going to be disappointed.

Anyway, all those years without winning much of anything made me think that someone put a curse on me. I was always unhappy and disappointed every time I didn't win. I was always complaining about my bad luck.

I realized now that I was wrong, I was approaching life with the wrong kind of attitude. I was being negative most of the time, so I decided that I was going to change my negative way of thinking because all those years of gambling; all I can think about was winning and not about enjoying myself. You see, when we only think about winning and not having fun, we will miss out on having a good time. all those years I prevented myself from having fun and instead I was miserable. We must remember that our negative way of thinking will prevent us from having fun. When we have a negative attitude like I did back then, we are not going to win, and we will not have a good time either. Well, I'm not going to denied it; I did have fun occasionally.

You see, twenty-four years later my bad luck change into good luck, and may I mention that twenty-four years is a long time of bad luck, but what I didn't realized back then was that bad luck can change in an instant, so after I turn forty-five, I started noticing little changes in my life, I began to win bigger jackpots, well, not that big, but nevertheless, they were much bigger than before. However, my real good luck came about three years later when I turned forty-eight years old, and I must say that it didn't happen in Las Vegas or in Reno; it happened when I brought six two-dollar scratchers. Anyway, I scratched all six tickets, but I only won twelve dollars, so I decided to go back home with my twelve dollars, but as I was walking out the door, I thought to myself, oh! What the heck, I'm just going to buy a few more two-dollar tickets, and so I did. I scratched the first ticket, but I didn't get anything so then I scratched the second ticket and I realized that I had won twenty thousand dollars I could not believe my eyes, so I had to show the lady behind the counter the ticket to see if I really had won. She verified that indeed I had won twenty thousand dollars. It was an exciting day for me because I knew that my bad luck was no more.

About eight years later my good luck struck again, I brought some more two-dollar tickets and hit another twenty thousand dollars. Near that time, I also won several jackpots in a single day for a total of nine thousand dollars.

I think one of the reasons why my luck changed so drastically was because I changed my way of thinking, I started thinking in a positive way rather than a negative way. It might not work for everyone. However, it's worth a try. Changing our attitude towards life can make a big difference.

Anyway, I decided to make a change in my life, so I became a positive thinker and I started by changing my old way of thinking, I decided that whenever I was going to gamble in the future that I was going to have fun and enjoy myself first and if I won something then that was a bonus. One of the things that helped me change my way of thinking was by reading as many books as possible. Mostly I read books about self-improvement. Furthermore, I educated myself about many different topics and therefore, I started increasing my knowledge with each passing day.

What about you, do you still think that you are cursed or that someone put a curse on you? Do you believe in curses or is it just the lack-of education and knowledge? Luck does really exist, but it comes and goes at will, so we must be ready for when it shows up at our doorstep. There are many laws in the universe, however, only two of those laws have to do with good luck and bad luck. It's important that we think about good luck rather than bad luck. By thinking of ourselves as lucky we might be able to attract good luck for ourselves. Remember that we need to always think positive whether we win or lose.

Honesty

What is honesty? I'm assuming that we all know what honesty is, but do we really practice it on a day-by-day basis? Most people would like to believe that they are honest, but the true reality is that everyone lies from time to time, even if it's an innocent little lie, we just can't help ourselves because it's in our nature. We must remember that lying to others it's only going to hurt us in the long run and in many ways. We could potentially lose people's respect, trust and admiration for us, furthermore, we could potentially lose our reputation as being an honest person, furthermore, we will be viewed as liars. Remember that lying is never a good thing, because even if it is a small lie, it has the potential to damage our reputation forever.

Although there are many compelling reasons to lie, we must refrain ourselves from lying or cheat just to gain an advantage on the competition. Even large and small companies will lie to their customers, but I'm not going to talk about the big companies right now, instead, I'm going to talk about small businesses. There's millions of small businesses around the country who provide services to homeowners, but unfortunately, half of those small business owners lie to their customers, they make promises that they don't intent to keep and some of them overcharge by as much as 200%- 500% more for their services, in other words, they want to get rich quick at the expenses of unsuspected customers.

I'm not just saying this because I want to hurt those small businesses, on the contrary, I want to help them because I know that small business are the backbone of our country, however, they should charge customers a fair price for their services, they should never take advantage of the poor and unsuspected people who worked so hard for their money. There's a perfectly good explanation as to why I'm saying these things and it's because in the past, I have been ripped off by many of those small businesses who provide customers with home services, like home repairs.

Recently I hired a company to replace our water heater, they made several promises and they kept most of them, however, they didn't keep two of the promises and on top of that they charged me and my wife three times as much than what we would have paid someone else. I'm not saying that every small business are the same because I know for a fact that there are small companies or business out there who conduct themselves with honesty and integrity. Is there ever a good time for us to lie to others? Yes, but only when someone wants to hurt us, or our lives are in danger.

I have only one standard by which I conduct myself and that is by "HONESTY." I won't ever compromise my honesty no matter what. There are those who claim to be honest, but it's only because it's convenient or profitable for them to do so. Again, it's human nature for both man and woman to follow the path of dishonesty, but why is that? Well, most often than not, they follow that path because it's the path of least resistance, furthermore, they follow this path because it's more profitable and advantageous for them.

When we apply honesty to our lives from the very beginning of our existence, we will adapt honesty to our lives later in life, furthermore, when we applied honesty to our daily lives, most likely, we will become more successful than our counterparts. Honesty is an important quality to have because it's going to contribute to a positive mindset, in other words, it's going to help us find peace, harmony, and happiness.

People are going to instantly notice when someone is not being honest, in fact, they can smell it from miles away, I know I do. When we conduct ourselves with honesty towards other people, they will adapt the same honesty and positive behaviors toward us, it's a win-win situation for everyone.

Honesty is the essential foundation on which to build any type of relationships, whether it's a business relationship or a friendship relationship. When we are honest with ourselves, we will refrain from lying to others, in other words, we don't betray the trust they have in us. We must remember that trust is built based on honesty and when we lie to someone, that trust goes out the window.

Honesty should always be the main ingredient in every relationship, and as said before, we must be honest with ourselves first before we can be honest with other people. Our honesty and integrity is going to influence other people to do the same. Our actions will dictate who we really are as a person, so we must never tell other people what they want to hear just to make them feel good because that is not being honest with ourselves or with them. We must always tell the truth, even if it hurts.

Overcoming Our Obstacles

We all have many goals and dreams that we want to accomplish within our lifetime, however, as we start our journey into fulfilling those goals, we instantly run into obstacles or roadblocks, so we give up. However, Others view their obstacles and roadblocks as opportunities to learn and grow, but the people who gave up, see those obstacles as dangerous, they become paralyzed by fear, and as a result, they simply give up on making their goals and dreams become a reality. Some people say that if there was an easy road to follow and without any obstacles to overcome, then, it's probably going to lead nowhere, in other words, there will be no personal growth without obstacles.

It should not matter how many obstacles we encounter throughout our life, what really matters here is that we need to prepare ourselves, mentally, physically, and spiritually for whatever obstacles we might encounter. We also need to prepare ourselves with the right knowledge because without it, we are not going to be able to conquer our obstacles. We must arm ourselves with these powerful weapons which is going to help us to defeat every obstacles that we encounter.

Obstacles are part of our daily lives; they can also be overwhelming at times for most people. Our obstacles will stop us on our tracks in a heartbeat, but only if we let them. We can let our obstacles stop us from reaching our goals and finding happiness or we can convert our obstacles into minor speed bumps on the road by simply using our imagination. Again, we can overcome any obstacles that we might encounter, but only if we use our imagination, for example, when we use our imagination, we are going to be able to overcome every obstacle that we encounter along our journey. It's all up to us. We must decide for ourselves if we are going to let our obstacles stand in our way to success.

If we approach our obstacles with an open mind, we are going to defeat each one as they come. We must never try to defeat all obstacles at one time because if we do, we will become overwhelmed by them and that is going to lead us into giving up.

We all have a lot of obstacles that we must overcome every single day but knowing how to overcome them can make a big difference in defeating them. Our biggest obstacles are personal, but we also have social, and environmental obstacles that we must overcome. It's never an easy thing to accomplish but is achievable. Furthermore, there's other obstacles that we might encounter along our journey, for example, not having enough time, the lack of money, the fear of failure, not knowing what to do in every situation, being stuck in a job that we hate and not having the right knowledge or education. All these things are obstacles that we might encounter on a day by day basis which will prevent us from reaching our goals, however, we can change all this by simply changing the way we think. It's a matter of how bad we want something.

We must ask ourselves the following questions, but we must be honest about it, "are we going to let our obstacles stop us from accomplishing our goals?" Are we going to continue to allow them to control our lives and destiny? How we deal with our daily obstacles is what matters the most, so therefore, we need to learn how to eliminate our obstacles one by one. It's important for us to learn how to identify our obstacles because that action is going to help us to defeat them.

Remember that everyone is going to have obstacles that they need to overcome, but we must remember that people who address their obstacles properly are not going to let them get in the way from achieving their goals. We can defeat every obstacle or problem that we encounter, no matter how big, but only if we choose to do so. If we choose to challenge our obstacles, then we must do whatever it takes to overcome them. Again, we have many tools that we have at our disposal that we can use which is going to help us in defeating our obstacles but remember that our imagination is the most important of them all. Using our imagination is the best solution to help us defeat any obstacles, and we can use it any time, any place. Remember that we must focus our energy on finding a solution rather than dwelling on it for too long, because the more we think about it, the less energy we will have left to help us find a solution

We should see our obstacles as a new way to learn new things. Our obstacles should be viewed as nothing more than a big puzzle which we need to put together, well, that is if we want to see the final image. Solving a puzzle is a big challenge, but if we want to solve it, then we must challenge ourselves to finish it in as little time as possible so that we can see the final image sooner than later. We must not see it as an impossible puzzle, rather we must see it as a challenge for our minds. We know we can solve any puzzle, but at the same time we don't think about roadblocks or obstacles that we cannot solve, because it's only a matter of time before we are able to put all the pieces together. Overcoming our obstacles should not be any different than solving a puzzle, furthermore, we must not see our obstacles as threats or barriers that we can't overcome, instead, we should view them as a challenge and nothing more. It takes a lot of patience and dedication to put a puzzle together and we know in our minds that we can put it together, so why can't we approach our difficult situations or roadblocks with the same mentality as building a puzzle?

It should be a matter of imagination and not a matter of fear of failing. We must never let our minds be invaded by doubt and painful thoughts when we are faced with difficult situations or roadblocks. We should never retreat when faced with obstacles which have the potential to deprive us of our happiness. We must never fear the unknown, we must never hide from any difficult situation, we must never fear any obstacles because a road without obstacles is going to probably lead us to an unexciting place.

If we can't overcome some of the many obstacles that we might encounter when trying to achieve our goals, than we must go around them, but we must never give up because if we give up at the first sign of trouble, we are never going to accomplish much of anything, and if we are too tired to continue going forward, then we must stop, take a break, and come back tomorrow with new energy. The same principles are applied when we are trying to solve a puzzle, for example, when we are too tired to continue, what do we do? We take a break or just simply stop, then, we will come back to it when we are ready. When we have new energy, and when we can think clearly, but one thing that we should never do is to quit. We just don't quit and give up because we are not quitters.

We know that there will be many obstacles in everything that we do, so therefore, we must learn to accept them because when we learn to accept them as a part of our daily lives, we will be able to defeat them in less time than never before because we are now conscious that those obstacles will exist. We must accept and know that without obstacles, we would not learn much of anything, so, let's not fall back into complacence which is going to prevent us from finding a solution in solving our problems.

Chapter Twenty-Two

Our Irrational Beliefs

Why do we have so many irrational beliefs and where do they come from? First, we are not born with irrational beliefs or bad habits. We start to develop them right from the beginning of our childhood. We develop our irrational beliefs by observing other people, we learn from our parents, our brothers, our sisters, our friends, strangers, and we also learn from a long-life of experiences.

Our irrational beliefs are tendencies or patterns of thinking that are not true. They are cognitive distortions, in other words, they are distorted thoughts and beliefs which is a misinterpretation of the real facts. Again, I want to make it crystal clear that we are not born with our irrational beliefs. Our irrational beliefs are unknowingly reinforced by our brain overtime, furthermore, they will continually reinforce themselves throughout our lives, unless of course, we stop them. Okay, but how are we going to stop our irrational beliefs from becoming permanent? Well, we can start by making small changes, for example, we can start by changing our old way of thinking, but we can only accomplish it by gradually leaving our irrational beliefs behind, in other words, we must replace them with rational beliefs.

Our irrational beliefs come from within our brain, and even though, our brain is right most of the time, there are occasions when our brain is going to send us the wrong information, and it's because, overtime, our brain develops some type of faulty connection. But how are we going to know what our irrational or faulty beliefs are? Well, we need to figure it out, and we need to do it quickly, it's not that difficult. The first thing that we need to do is to challenge our beliefs. We need to find out which ones are rational beliefs and which ones are not because if we don't, they are going to affect our lives in many negative ways.

We all suffer from irrational beliefs from time to time and it's because of the way we think. The number one reason as to why sometimes we behave in such irrational manner is because, unknowingly, we put ourselves in that situation, furthermore, we put ourselves under a tremendous pressure to succeed in everything that we do, but no matter how much we have accomplish in the pass, it's never going to be enough, so therefore, we must be careful not to overstress ourselves with insignificant little things which have the potential to derail our lives forever. Our irrational way of thinking is going to affect our lives in many ways, for example, it's going to affect our relationships with everyone that we love and care for, furthermore, it's going to affect our lives at work and at home.

We don't always need to be loved by everyone in the world, we don't always need to have everyone's approval, and it's okay if sometimes we get rejected by other people, we don't always need to be perfect, we don't always need to succeed in everything that we do, we don't always need to get all of the things that we so desire. We must remind ourselves that we don't need to put all this extra pressure on ourselves. All that really matters here is that we do our best to succeed and if sometimes we are not successful, then we have the option to keep trying, but the one thing that we must never do is to put ourselves in a situation where we are going to lose our minds.

It's of great importance that we pay close attention as to how we use our thoughts and our beliefs. We need to think clearly and free ourselves from unnecessary junk. We must learn to recognize or identified our erroneous beliefs, we need to put them through the thinking process so that we can make modifications accordingly, otherwise, they can and will be very damaging to our health, physically and emotionally.

We must never jump into conclusions before knowing all the facts, for example, we must first figure out if the information our brain is sending us is correct or incorrect, and then, we must decide for ourselves if that information is right or wrong. It's in our best interest to take the necessary time to think and to process all the information which our brain is sending us so that we don't misinterpret the truth about the real facts.

When someone says something to us, whether it's a good thing or a bad thing, our first reaction will be of the negative type, most of the time, but why is that? Well, the main reason as to why we react in a negative way is because we have not taken the time to process that information, we don't know if that information is right or wrong, we just simply react in a negative way because we are not thinking properly and correctly.

We mustn't be so sensitive, and we must never jump into the wrong conclusions, in other words, we must first let our brain process that incoming information because once we do that, we will be able to think in a rational manner which is going to allow us to make the right decisions based on rational thinking rather than irrational thinking.

A good example of when wrong information can be devastating to our health is when someone tells us that we are ugly, now! are we going to believe them knowing that, in fact, we are not ugly? We know deep inside our minds that we are not ugly, so why do we let it bother us so much? Well, it's a very simple answer, and it's because we all want other people to like us, and when they say something that we don't like, it's going to make us feel bad about ourselves even though it's not true, but the fact that someone told us that we were ugly can make us have doubts about ourselves, and consequently, if we are not careful, we will end up believing it.

You see, when someone tells us something, even dough is not true, our minds will send that information into our subconscious mind and if we are not careful we will start believing it, and in most cases, we tend to trust what our brain is telling us.

We must never think of ourselves as ugly. We must never think of ourselves as dumb or stupid just because someone tell us. Remember that other people don't know us as well as we do. They don't know what we are capable of accomplishing. Furthermore, we must never think of ourselves as failures because we know deep inside that we are not, in fact, we are very capable of accomplishing many great things. We must not dwell on a single negative failure or a comment made by someone else, including, our Dads, our Moms, our spouses, and our friends. We should, and under any circumstance, feel hopelessly lost just because someone said something negative about us. It's at times like this that we need to remind ourselves that we need to ignore all negative comments made by others because we are stronger than what most people think we are. We are more beautiful than what most people think we are.

Now you are aware that our brains make hundreds or even thousands of connections from the things that people tell us, from the things that we see, from the things that we hear, from the things that smell, from the things that we taste and from the things that we feel. All this information enters our brain. They are connections between our thoughts, our ideas, and our actions.

Just remember that It's never in our best interest to feel anxious or depressed about unpleasant current and past events, we must stay focused, we must stay in total control, we must retain our healthy thoughts and beliefs at all times. We must let go of our irrational beliefs and demand of ourselves much more, but in a well-controlled and peaceful environment. We need to challenge ourselves strongly and persistently by disputing our irrational thoughts and beliefs. If we apply this method consistently throughout the years, we will be able to change our irrational beliefs, and eventually, we will be able to get rid of our bad behaviors, and that is by controlling our irrational beliefs. Never again we will be defected. Never again we will be slaves of our irrational thoughts, beliefs, or fears.

Our irrational beliefs can make us very unhappy. They can also be deadly if they are not under total control by us. We need to reverse our irrational beliefs and turn them into rational beliefs because it's unproductive to hold on to them. If we choose to hold on to our irrational beliefs, we are going to be miserable for the rest of our lives.

We must remember that there are thousands of different distortions or irrational beliefs that enter our brain daily, but the most important thing to remember is that no matter how distorted our irrational beliefs may be, it's about how we interpret them.

When we get anxious, depressed or angry, we develop many distortions and it's because of the way we think and therefore our irrational beliefs start to change from positive to negative, but remember that there is always hope because we can reverse those distorted or irrational beliefs into positive ones. When we finally learn to identify our irrational beliefs, we will be able to change our lives forever.

Why Do We Think and Act the Way We Do?

I have been thinking about this question for quite a long time and I have concluded that there are a couple good reasons as to why we act and thing the way we do. First and foremost, every human being on the face of the planet is unique, in other worlds, we are all different from one another in more ways than we can even image, for example, we have different likes and dislikes, we have different needs, we have different personalities, we have different tolerances for pain and that is what makes us different from each other. Can you imagine for just a minute how boring our lives would be if we all think and feel the same way?

One reason as to why we think and act the way that we do is because of our genetics. Genetics play an important role in the way we thinks and act. We are all born with slightly different genetic codes, in other worlds, every human brain is unique, we think and act according to our past experiences and our generics. Furthermore, our instincts, our emotions, and our intellectual level, plays an important part on the way we think and act as well

Another reason as to why we think and act the way we do is because we were programmed to think and act a certain way and it all started from the very beginning of our existence, in other words, we were programmed from the time that we were born (mostly) by our parents, our teachers, but we also learned by imitating others. I completely understand where we are coming from, but nevertheless, if we want to improve our lives, than we must make a conscious effort to improve our way of thinking and doing things, unless of course, we are happy with being who we are right now.

As for the rest of us, it's not going to be an easy task breaking away from our old habits, our old way of thinking and breaking away from our old way of acting, after all, it's all we ever known for most of our entire lives. We must keep in mind that it's in our human nature to stay put in one place because we like who we are, and we are too comfortable staying in one place. Let's face it, most of us don't like changes and when changes do occur, whether it's our choice or not, we will feel very uncomfortable.

Regardless of how we feel about making changes, we must change our old way of thinking, change our old habits, change our old beliefs, change our old way of acting, well, that is if we want to advance into the next level of super thinkers. Never forget that we need to learn new things every single day so that we can keep our mind sharp and fresh. We also need to adapt ourselves to new environments and new circumstances if we want to survive in the new world. Furthermore, we must adapt to a new way of thinking because the way we think right now is the cause of most of our afflictions. We must remember that our remarkable brain has the capacity to adapt and to overcome difficult circumstances. Our miracle brain has the capacity or the ability to adjust to new habits and new beliefs, so therefore, nothing should hold us back.

If we persist in holding on to our old way of thinking and acting we will be left behind, just like old technologies, we will be the forgotten people and only because we didn't want to make the necessary changes needed to keep up with the rest of the world. We must remember that changes are good because it's going to help us break away from our boring routines in which we are stuck right now. For those of us who don't want to be stuck in the same old place, let's make some much-needed changes to our way of life, let's not be afraid to evolve into superior human beings. New changes will bring us new energy, plus the fact that we are going to feel better as human beings knowing that we know new things. Remember that with new changes there will be new and exciting feelings which otherwise we would have never experienced.

When we no longer have the desire to learn, we will be punishing our brains from learning and that is never a good thing. We should never let our brain starved from much needed knowledge and excitement. Remember that our brain was designed to be challenged and to learn new things every single day of our lives because our brain needs to consistently acquire new information on a day-by-day basis in order to stay young. Any new information that we feed our brain is going to be the food which is going to keep our brain young and healthy for a long time to come. Without this food our brain is going to be hungry and consequently is going to fall back into a sleep mode and it's going to stay that way until we feed our brain new information once again.

We must keep in mind that our current way of thinking and acting could potentially impact our overall health. It doesn't take a genius to realize when our thoughts are not well-rounded, they can and will make our bodies sick with diseases, so we must be careful about what we are thinking at any given moment. We can take total control of our lives by simply changing the way we think and act, furthermore, if we change our old way of thinking we will be able to make rational and well-rounded decisions. Remember that any decisions we make today is not only going to impact our lives, but it's going to impact the lives of the people that we love, and probably for the rest of our lives.

Encouraging Our Children to Learn New Things Every Day

I believe most parents encourage their children to learn new things every day, however, there are some parents who don't encourage their children to learn new things on a daily basis, but I understand why that is, and it's because of their busy schedule. I cannot emphasize enough about how important it is to take a little time every day to teach our kids new thing, especially when they are toddles because that is when they are eager to learn. I can see it in my 1 and 3-year-old Grandsons, they are eager to learn, in fact, sometimes I think that they understand everything that we are saying.

It's important to remember that learning new things will promote self-improvement and personal growth in our kids now and in the future, furthermore, it's going to increase their self-confidence. Children will adapt to new situations very quickly, so we must never stop their progress by limiting their education. If we teach our kids new things every day, then, they will be well prepared to solve any problems or conflicts at a much younger age.

We need to teach our kids important social communication skills at a younger age. It's important that we don't wait until they are adults to teach them positive behaviors. We must not wait till our kids are adults because by that time it will be much harder for them to adjust to a new way of life. Remember that our children are our future and if we don't teach them all that they need to learn while they are still young, they will suffer the consequences.

Sometimes as parents, we don't have the knowledge or the time to teach our kids new things every single day, nevertheless, we must make the effort to teach them as much as possible so that they can have a productive and happy life. Sometimes we prevent our children from learning new things, and it's not because we don't want our children to learn new things, on the contrary, as parents we want our children to learn as much as possible, but most often than not, we succumb to laziness.

I believe that we should give our children a little more freedom to experiment new things by themselves, but at the same time with the proper adult supervision. Exercise is especially important for our children and it can be a lot of fun for them, but unfortunately, many parents don't have the time or the energy to do it.

As parents that we are, we are forever telling our children, don't do this, don't do that, please stop or you will be punished, or you will be grounded. I believe that the only time parents should prevent their children from experimenting with new things is when they are unsupervised by an adult and it's because they might get injured, but other than that, parent should set their children free; we should let them explore the world, we should let them learn new things every single day, so that they can evolve into super little human beings.

Again, the only time parents should tell their children not to do certain things is when they might be in danger of getting hurt, otherwise, let the children explore, let the children gain some valuable knowledge while they are still young because this is the time when their brain is at it's best, as far as being able to learn quickly. We must never forget that a child's brain is like a sponge which absorbs everything.

As parents, we must encourage our children to learn and to think for themselves, we must let them fly, (not literally) we must not stop their progress and set them free. I don't mean to imply that kids should do whatever they want, whenever they want to, especially when there's the possibility that they might get hurt doing dangerous activities, but again, with proper adult supervision they should be okay. Furthermore, parents should always be there for their kids, every step of the way to guide them. Kids will accomplish some amazing things, but only if we let them thrive.

Raising a child is all about giving them every possible opportunity to succeed, and by giving them the necessary tools which they need so that they can become successful. We must never punish our children with too many imposing rules because they will feel suffocated by them and that in turn is going to diminish their ability to learn.

We must find out what types of activities our children like to do, in other words, find out what they are passionate about and then put a well-thought-out plan and put it in place for them. Remember that every sacrifice we make for our children is going to be rewarded later in life, after all, is it not why we get married? To have children, to raise them properly and become a happy family? It's only fair to mention that when we get married, we will lose our freedom to do the things that we were accustomed to doing. Now! We must remember that most of the things that we do are for our kids. We get up in the morning and go to work for our kids and our spouses, and both of us work for our kids, in fact, mostly everything we do is for our kids.

We want to teach our children new things every day, however, we must resist the temptation to impose our will on our kids, instead, we must let them speak for themselves, in other words, we must give them the freedom to speak their mind, at school and at home as well.

We must teach them to adapt to new circumstances and to look at everything from a different perspective. We must let them use their own imagination, we must teach them to use reasoning when they trying to find a solution to solve a problem by themselves, we must let them explore new ideas. We must set high standards or expectations for ourselves and for our children, but at the same time, we must be careful not to overwhelm them. We must give them the time and space which they need, and eventually, they will figure things out by themselves. Remember that we need to always be there for our kids, every step of the way, including, emotionally available and responsive for their needs.

We must never forget that in life, as adults and as children, we will fail many times. We are going to take two steps forward and one step backwards, but that is the only way in which we are going to learn and grow strong together. We must learn to let our children experience the feeling of failures because it's the only way they are going to learn valuable knowledge and build their own character.

It's not always an easy thing to fulfill every child's needs, in fact, it's one of the most difficult things which a parent must do on a daily basis that at the end of the day we are exhausted and we are left with little energy to do other tasks. As you might already know, kids have such a tremendous amount of energy and they need to somehow find a way to get rid of all that energy, and that is when we come in. We must find a way for our kids so that they can get rid of all that energy. My kids are older now, but I do have grandkids and even though my energy is not what it used to be, I still need to play with them, normally I'm exhausted within the first fifteen minutes. I learned throughout the years how to deal with their needs in different ways, for example, when my granddaughter wants me and my wife to take her to the zoo, I immediately put into play my reverse psychology, I tell her that instead of going to the zoo that we should go to the park near our house, and she will say yes every single time, it's not that I'm tricking her into doing whatever I want her to do, instead, is more of a compromised solution, either way, she is just as happy. I do this because she has so much energy and I don't, although I wish I had more energy so that I can do more things with her. I do enjoy playing with her, she is funny, and she makes me laugh. I also have two Grandsons; one is 3 and the other one just turn 1 year old. Let me tell you; they are full of energy and it's hard for me to keep up with them.

Anyway, there is a perfectly good explanation as to why she wants to go to park instead of going to the zoo, you see, when I talk to her about going to the park instead of the zoo, I get really excited about it, I tell her that we will have a lot of fun and I also tell her that, eventually, we will go the zoo, when is not so hot. Both her and I know that I keep my promises, well, most of the time. Kids nowadays are super smart. They never forget a promise, so we must be careful what we promise them because they will remember when we fail to keep our promises.

Sometimes we must let our kids make their own choices, in fact, they love it when they are able to make their own decisions, they thrive on it, so give them some freedom to explore. Remember that being a good parent is not only about the child's behavior, rather, is about the parent's behavior, we must not obsess ourselves with trying to be perfect, therefore, we should never expect perfection from our children either or we will become even more exhausted than we already are.

Let the children play. Playtime is important for our children because it's an opportunity for them to learn new things. Playtime is also an opportunity for our children to learn and to negotiate with other kids for some of the things that they want, furthermore, they will learn that sometimes they must adapt to new situations. Playtime is a good time for our children because it's going to help them to develop their skills, acquire new skills. Playtime is going to teach our kids how to solve conflicts between other children. They will learn to compromise, and they will learn to negotiate about which games they want to play.

Furthermore, we must never physically or emotionally abuse our kids, instead, we need to teach them good manners, we need to teach them how to share some of the things they have, including toys. We need to teach them about life itself, we need to teach them that sometimes they must work hard in order to earn what they want, we need to teach them that if they work hard, they will be compensated for their efforts. I know, some of you might be thinking, oh! that is plain wrong. Why do we have to compensate our kids for doing what they are supposed to be doing in the first place, but in the real world, we all want to be compensated for our hard work. That is what life is all about, isn't it? It's not any different for our children. We all want to be compensated for our hard work, especially at work. We work hard at our jobs hoping that someday we will be compensated for our hard work and dedication. Furthermore, if that wasn't the whole purpose of life, then why do anything at all, why should we bother? In life, we do things because we want to accomplish something and if we are not going to accomplish anything by doing it, then what is the purpose of doing it?

Our Mental State of Mind

Have you ever wondered about your mental state of mind? And if so, Is it in a good place or in a bad place? Our very own happiness depends on whether our mental state of mind is in the right place or not. When our state of mind is in a positive mode it will allow us to have a positive attitude towards life, in addition, we will become more energized, which in turn is going to allow us to focus more of our energy on new opportunities in life. When our state of mind is in a good place, we are going to be able to get along with other people with ease and comfort and at the same time, we will be able to manage stressful situations more efficiency.

Whenever we find ourselves in a negative state of mind, we are going to feel miserable; we will feel discourage, frustrated and unable to function properly, in addition, we will feel as if our lives have no meaning, however there is no better time for us to reflect or become self-aware of our current state of mind. This is the perfect opportunity for us to change our negative state of mind and turn it into a positive one.

Depending on our mental state of mind, we can either perceive the world as the most beautiful place in the universe or we can perceive it as the most disturbing place. Sometimes our state of mind it's at a high level of self-awareness, when we feel in harmony within ourselves and the universe, it's a time when we feel a warm sensation of calmness and wellbeing, it's a time when we see other people with kindest, it's a time when we feel good about ourselves and it's because we know that our state of mind is in a good place where everything flows smoothly.

Now! what happens when our state of mind is not in a good place? Well, most likely we are going to feel moody; depressed, disappointment, regret, anger, or we are going to have feelings of unworthiness, how are we going to see the world then? It's obvious that we will see the world differently because our state of mind is not in the right place which is why we should try to put our state of mind back where it belongs: in a calm state of mind.

It's important to remember that we have good feelings that make us feel good on the inside, however, we also have bad feelings that make us feel miserable, but the good news is that we can change those bad feelings into good feelings any time if that is our desire. We have a choice of how we want to feel and how we perceive the world at any given moment, any time of day or night. It's all about the state of mind in which we want to be, we can either choose to see things in a positive and exciting way or we can choose to see them in a negative and unexciting way, it's all up to us. We must decide for ourselves in which state of mind we want to be, and if we feel that we are in a negative state of mind right now, then we must change into a positive one, but we must do it quicky and we must retain that state of mind throughout the day.

Some people might be wondering or asking themselves, but how can we change our state of mind in an instant, and is it possible? Well, my response to that is that everything is possible, but only if that is what we really want. We have the power within ourselves to change the things that we don't like about ourselves. We have the power to change our negative state of mind into a positive state of mind, we have the power to change how we are feeling at any given moment, believe me, I do it every single day, in fact, it's one of many daily routines which I practice daily and it does wonders for me.

We must remember that if we want to feel good and look good, then, we must change something about ourselves. For example, if we are feeling tired after a long day at work, we simply don't come back home and sit on the cough for the rest of the evening, sure we want to relax for a while, but if we really want to completely feel good, then we must get up and re-energize ourselves by taking a shower and believe me, we will feel good afterwards. Now, let's say we took a shower and we are feeling good about ourselves and suddenly we decide that we want to go for a ride, but what happens when we get in our car and we realize that it's filthy on the outside and the inside is full of trash? Well, it's not going to make us feel good, I know I wouldn't feel good. I wouldn't feel clean, it would make me feel uncomfortable.

I don't know how other people feel about getting into a filthy car, but I normally like to keep my car clean because it will make me feel good, especially after I shower and want to go for a ride. When we get home from work, we probably will feel physically and emotionally exhausted and without much energy left to do anything else, however, if we take a nice warm shower, we are going to feel in a state of relaxation afterwards. Unknowingly, we have accomplished two things here, first, we will feel good about ourselves. Secondly, we will completely change our state of mind from feeling tired to a peaceful state of mind. There's plenty more that we can do to help us feel good and to help us take our state of mind into a whole new level of peacefulness. For example, meditation or exercising.

Changing our state of mind from a bad place to a good place or from a negative state of mind to a positive state of mind doesn't really require much energy on our part, but it does require us to have the desire to do it. Whenever negative feelings invades my mind; I immediately begin to reverse my way of thinking, in other words, I put my mind into a positive way of thinking. I will begin by thinking about the good things and not the bad things-the fun loving things which I love to do, I start thinking about all the beautiful things and places on our planet, and immediately, I start to feel better about myself because I'm letting go of all the negative thoughts roaming inside my mind, I'm replacing them with more pleasurable thoughts which is going to make me feel happy. We must make a conscious effort to redirect our thoughts towards the things that will make us feel good. The things which are going to make us happy the most.

Our state of mind is controlled by how we are feeling on the inside at any given moment, our feelings and emotions play a big part as to how we will act and react in the real world. The way we are acting right is because of something that we are thinking about at this precise moment. Our good or bad mental state of mind does not appear in our mind out of nothing, there's always something that triggers how we feel at any given moment. Everything in our brain comes from somewhere, including the way we think, our thoughts, our feelings, our emotions, our disappointments, our happiness, and our anger, they are all triggered by something or someone, therefore, we must be careful about how we are feeling at any given moment.

Again, everything that we are thinking now is caused of something, that we hear, by the things that we see, by the things that we smell, by the things that we touch, by the things that we physically feel, and by the foods that we eat. Furthermore, our state of mind is also affected by other people. By the things that they say to us, and I'm going to give you an example of how sometimes the things people say to us will impact our state of mind, for example, as I was writing this chapter, my wife was talking on the phone with a coworker, she stay home due to a cold, and may a say that she hardly ever stays home whenever she is sick, anyway, I just couldn't concentrate, I tried and tried, but with no avail, it completely put my state of mind out of whack, so, I stop writing and instead I went to the gym to exercise for about an hour.

Afterwards, I cooked myself some eggs for breakfast, took a shower and after the shower, I felt like a totally different man, my state of mind was in a better place, I was able to continue writing.

There are many environmental events that will affect our state of mind, and it can happen at any given moment. These environmental events or disasters will affect everyone on the planet, for example, different weather patterns, including global warming or extreme heat, cooling periods, floods, polluted air water and soil, overpopulation, deforestation, ozone layer depletion, acid rain, and water pollution. All these environmental events will affect everyone. It's going to affect our state of mind in many ways, now and in the future.

But how can environmental events have such an effect on our state of mind? Well, when we hear about these environmental events through the news or through someone else, these news will travel through our nervous system as electrical signals to our brain and once this information is register into our brain, then it's going to be after us to process it for interpretation, and depending on how we interpreted that information, it will have an impact on our state of mind, it's either going to put us in a positive state of mind or is going to put us in a negative state of mind.

There is a tremendous amount of information which is constantly entering our brain, but not to worry because our brain can process that new information at incredible fast speeds. The important thing here is that this information is going to affect the way we think and feel. It's going to affect our state of mind in a good way or in a bad way, and I must say that it's going to affect some people more than others, but it's going to impact everyone.

We must decide when, how, and where we will put into practice the information which our brain is receiving from different areas, however, there is one thing that we should never do and that is to never act merely on impulse because as we already know, acting on impulse can and will be very costly to all of us in many ways, for example, it can be damaging to our pocket book, and to our overall health, furthermore, it's going to have a negative effect on the way we think, and it has the potential to bring diseases to our bodies as well. Some people say that knowledge is expensive, but ignorance can be much more expensive, believe me, I know from experience because it has happened to me many times in the past.

Making decisions without going through the thinking process is not a good idea. We must always think about our decision making before we put that decision into action. Once we know for sure what our next decision is going to be, we must put it into action and hope that this action taken is going to be of great benefit for ourselves, for our health, for our state of mind, and for our bodies.

Our brain is where we have the power to think, our brain is where we can visualize our next move, so therefore, we must make our next decision, not based on impulse responses, but in a well thought and rational manner. Remember that if we act on pure impulse and we make the wrong decision, we could potentially bring sickness to our Physical bodies, and to our mental state of mind. It can potentially bring diseases, stress, tension, irritability, worries frustration and depression, but most importantly, all these things can and will turn into anxiety if we are not careful.

Furthermore, we could potentially increase certain chronic conditions, such as asthma, allergies, and even rheumatoid arthritis and all because we overloaded our mind and body with stressful situations. Our minds and bodies will eventually break down, if they are not able to catch up with the overload from our daily stressful situations, furthermore, our immune system will become weaker, causing even more problems, for example, depression and lack of energy and if we lack the energy, we will lose our ability to concentrate, in other words, it's going to impact our state of mind, furthermore, when we lose our ability to concentrate, we will lose our ability to be more productive.

It sounds scary, doesn't it? I don't mean to scare anyone in any way. We must not get too concerned about all these outside environmental events or get too concerned about the things that people are saying about us. I'm not insinuating that we shouldn't care about the things that people say about us or our environmental issues, we should care, after all, it's our planet. It's our home. We must not let all these concerns stay in our minds for too long because if we let them hang around, they will grow into worry and worry is going to eventually grow into stress and stress is going to turn into anxiety, it's a never-ending vicious cycle.

We can put an end to all these concerns, but the only way that we will be able to accomplish such a task is by changing our mental state of mind. In other words, we must take our mental state of mind from a bad place to a good place.

Chapter Twenty-Three

Simplifying Our Lives

Now more than ever, we need to simplify our lives. I know it's not an easy thing to accomplish, but nevertheless, we must find a way to eliminated not only our cluttered homes from materialistic things, but we need to declutter our minds from emotional junk as well. We must remember that possessing less stuff, the more time we are going to have available for other activities. A well organized and clean house is going to safe us time and space, furthermore, we are going to save precious physical and mental energy which we can use to spend doing the things that will make us happy. Now days, we tend to work longer hours and if that wasn't though enough, we must deal with an abundance of other things that need to be done on a daily basis, for example, taking care of our children daily activities, and making sure that all their needs are taken care off.

So, you see, there isn't enough time during the day to do all the things that we need to accomplish and that is why is so important for us to learn how to simplify our lives. I don't know about other people, but for me, a cluttered home will give me a feeling of uneasiness. I try my best to keep our house organize because I like to know were everything is when I'm looking for something. It saves time, energy, and keeps me from becoming frustrated.

Okay, so what to do and how are we going to accomplish it. First, we need to unclutter our houses inside and out from the things that we no longer need. Secondly, we need to organize the rest of our things, including our closets, pantries, kitchen cabinets, bathrooms, storage places and finally the garage. Lastly, we need to write ourselves a list of things to do for the entire month and we must tackle one thing at a time so that we do not overwhelm ourselves with too much too fast. We need to remind ourselves that we do not need to declutter our entire house in one day.

Nobody ever told us from the beginning of our existence that we should try to live our lives as simply as possible. But why is that so important? Well, normally by the time we are forty or fifty years of age we are mentally and physically exhausted and it's because we didn't know how to simplify our lives from the very beginning, and as time went by, our lives got more complicated and as a consequence, we become overwhelmed and unable to function properly, mentally and emotionally at full capacity. Furthermore, our happiness was compromised along the line because we were too preoccupied trying to do too much in as little time as possible. We were also trying to make everyone happy and consequently, we prevented ourselves from living a normal, or uncomplicated life.

It's important for us to understand that simplifying our lives will allow us to live a more productive life because we will have more time to take care of ourselves, in other words, we are going to be able to do the things that are going to make us happy the most. Furthermore, by simplifying our lives we will have more freedom to experiment with other things that we never got to experience before.

Again, simplifying our lives is not an easy thing to accomplish, nothing is ever easy, but we can start by decluttering our lives from materialistic things or as I like to call it "materialistic junk." I don't want to insult anyone, but half of the possessions which we own are most likely junk. They are things that perhaps we are never going to use again, so why are we holding on to them? I understand that we have many things that we use on a daily or weekly basis which are essential, for example, Lawn equipment, chest toolbox, folding tables, chairs, and ladders. Furthermore, we have plastic bins full of precious memories which are obviously important for us to hold on for our kids.

The best way for us to get rid of the things that we no longer need is by giving them to someone who is going to use them. Believe it or not, those materialistic things that we possess sometimes will prevent us from moving forward with our lives-they are preventing us from finding our very own happiness. We must keep in mind that owning too many materialistic things it's only going to complicate our lives even further than what they already are, so let's start by getting rid of unnecessary junk today. Believe me, you won't regret it, I promised.

Most often than not, we love to buy things that we do not need, and we buy them because we have the money, but the real question here is, do we really need such things? Sure, it feels good being able to buy whatever we want at any given time, however, once we have them in our possession, it's no longer that exciting and we will soon forget that we have them.

Now, let's talk about kids toys. Every kid want a brand-new toy every time we go to the store, so what do we do? We end up buying it for them, they will play with it for a few days, but soon after, they will forget about them and it's because they have hundreds of other toys laying around. Every time we go to the store kids want yet another toy. It's a vicious cycle that never ends, so in the meant time, we keep on accumulating more toys. Don't get me wrong, I believe in buying kids bran new toys every now and then, however, we must draw the line somewhere.

We must remember that having fewer things to worry about will free up more time and space for us which in turn is going to allow us to do other important things, for example, spending more time with our kids, and grand kids playing some of those games or toys that we brought for them and teaching them how to play with them. Most often than not, we buy our kids toys, but we don't teach them how to play with those toys and it's because we are overwhelmed with an abundance of daily chores that we need to get done. Never forget that the less junk we have, the more time and space we will have to play with our kids, now! That is an important quality time.

Moreover, sometimes we buy new things to impress other people, for instant, a brand-new car, but maybe it has to do with the fact that we want other people to know that we are successful. We don't always need to accumulate materialistic things in order to impress other people. I rather impress other people by being a good neighbor; by being honest, by being their friend or by helping them whenever possible.

I talked a bit about how important it is for us to unclutter our lives from materialistic junk, but now, I'm going to talk about the most important thing, "our emotional and mental junk." Yes, our minds are clutter with all types of unnecessary junk, therefore, we need to clear our minds from these devastating mental illnesses which is holding us back, causing stress and preventing us from finding happiness. Most people don't realize that our minds are filled with so much junk which is occupying precious space in our brains.

Wouldn't it be nice if we were able to learn new ways that will allow us to live a more fulfilling life, a less stressful life, a life where we are not going to feel overwhelmed, anxious, and depressed? Our entire lives can change dramatically by simply making small changes like decluttering our minds from unnecessary mental junk and by decluttering our houses from any unnecessary materialistic junk. If we only do these two things, then we will simplify our lives tremendously. By simplifying our lives we are going to be able to have more control over our lives, we will have more time to do the things that we really love to do, instead of wasting time and energy on doing the things that we don't enjoy doing.

Okay, so we know how to declutter our homes from materialistic junk, but how are we going to declutter our minds from emotional and mental junk? Well, there is one thing that we can all do which is going to help us to get rid of our mental junk or mental blockish, that thing is called "meditation." I know, it sounds simple, and it is, but if we start making excuses for ourselves, then we are creating even more junk for our minds because we are telling our minds that we don't have the time or we don't want to do it.

We really need to start doing the things that we like to do instead of the things that we hate doing. Think about it for a minute, why should we do those things if we don't like doing them? Anyway, there is one thing that we absolutely must do, well, that is if we want to declutter our precious mind from junk, and that is through meditation. We must learn to meditate even if we don't like doing it because it's the only way for us to clear our minds from mental junk.

As human beings, we normally don't think about simplifying our lives by decluttering them from unnecessary junk because we are not aware of what is happening to us, in fact, we don't even think about all the junk which enters our minds on a daily basis and that is why is so important for us to become aware of our situation. Our minds are not automatically programmed to get rid of the clutter. They are only programmed to gather information and store it and that is it. It is after us to become aware and find a way to get rid of all the junk or bad information that enters our minds.

Unknowingly, we simply like to feed our minds with junk or unhealthy information and because of that, our minds get clumped with bad information, and consequently, our lives will become full of worries and anxiety. We need to declutter our homes from materialistic possessions, but most importantly, we need to declutter our minds from mental junk and I'm not implying that we should get rid of every materialistic possession that we own, I'm basically saying that occasionally, we need to do some materialistic spring cleaning, but most importantly, we need to do some spring cleaning for our minds, but on a more consistent basis.

Normally, it is not until we are much older and wiser that we start to think about slowing down and simplify our lives, but it doesn't have to be this way because if we learn to simplify our lives at a young age, then, our lives will be that much more enjoyable.

You see, when we are young, we don't even know what simplifying our lives means, all we care is about having fun, working hard and playing hard, in other words, we just want to go fast, we do not want to slow down, we want to conquer everything and everyone.

I must admit to myself that when I was young, I did not think about slowing down either, I used to accumulate or collect just about everything, and I still do, however, now I'm very particular as to what I buy or collect, but nevertheless, I'm just as guilty as everyone else. Now, as far as my mental state of mind or my "emotional mental junk" I know how to declutter or free my mind from unhealthy feelings and emotions, at least most of the time. The way I get rid of my emotional mental junk is through meditation, and I'm able to do that because I'm a conscious individual, in other words, I'm aware of my situation, and therefore, it's much easier for me to accomplish it. Remember that "meditation" is the best option that we have which is going to help us to get rid of most of our afflictions.

There are other things that we can do that will help us to simplify our lives forever. For example, we can get rid of some of our debt and we can accomplish this task by simply stop using our credit cards, and by paying them off one at a time. Yes, being in debt can complicate our lives. It will clutter our minds with mental stress and fatigue. Decluttering our minds from too much debt is not an easy task to accomplish, however, we must try to do our best. We must make a conscious effort and try to pay off our debt, and not just any dept, but all our debts if possible. Furthermore, we can start by paying off those high interest rate credit cards first which are eating a good chunk of our paychecks.

Currently I have a credit card with a high interest rate, in fact, I had it for over twenty years and it was making me mentally ill knowing that I had two pay roughly two hundred dollars a month on interest alone, which is roughly about forty eight thousand dollars on interest over that time span. Wow! that is mind boggling. Anyway, my wife and I are still paying twenty five percent interest on that credit card, however, I cut my card in little pieces, so I no longer use it, we will only use it for a real emergency. Anyway, it was taking a toll on our checkbook. There is absolutely no good reason why we should be paying an extra couple hundred dollars more a month for a credit card that we can normally get through a credit union with a much lower interest rate rather than a credit card from a major bank.

Paying up to fifteen percent more on interest every month it's not in everyone's best interest. We have a couple other credit cards with an average of 10% interest. This is the type of emotional clutter that we need to get rid of because it will allow us to have more money in our wallets and less emotional clutter in our minds.

Paying off our debts can alleviate some of our worries, but most importantly, it will alleviate some of our mental clutter from our minds. Believe it or not, paying off some or most of our debts is going to allow us to be less stressed, I call that "decluttering our brain from unnecessary junk." Remember that debt can be a big contributor in cluttering our minds with emotional junk.

Furthermore, getting rid of our negative thoughts, negative feelings, and negative emotions is going to help us to declutter our minds from mental and emotional clutter. Now! Let's talk about our materialistic things a little bit more. Cleaning our desks and our garages of unnecessary junk is going to give us peace of mind, and I'm not talking about just rearranging them, no, I'm talking about getting rid of all unnecessary junk because that is going to help us to simplify our lives.

Sometimes we like to hold on to things for our kids, hoping that when we died, they will keep them and treasure them forever, but the sad reality is that our kids too have been collecting things for many years, and therefore, they are not going to keep but a few things which are important to them, for example, family pictures, documents, and perhaps, a few other things. Now, as for the rest of our materialistic junk, they are going to dispose of them, therefore, it makes no sense to try and save it for our kids.

Again, I'm not suggesting that we get rid of everything that we own, after all, we will need some of those things. I'm simply suggesting that we get rid of the things that we haven't used for years. Remember that in this case, less is better. The less things we have, the less we need to worry about.

Simplifying our lives does not need to be complicated because all we really need to do is reorganize our thoughts and we can accomplish this task by meditating. It's the only way for us to let go of our emotional junk from our minds.

How to Reach Our True Potential

There will be plenty of obstacles which are going to prevent us from reaching our true potential, however, there is one obstacle that will prevent us from reaching most of our goals and that obstacle is our own "ignorance." But, having said that, I don't mean to imply that we are lacking normal human intelligence or that we are incapable of reasoning, on the contrary, we are indeed very capable of accomplishing many great things, but only if we put our minds into motion.

We can easily turn around our lives and the lives of those who we love by simply educating ourselves, but the only way to accomplish such a task is by reading as many books as possible and by living our laziness behind, because as you may already know. You must know that laziness is a killer of all good things. We must keep in mind that it's through self-improvement that we will get the most out of life.

We must keep in mind that we are unique individuals, in other words, every human being on the face of the planet see's the world differently. We don't think the same things and we don't like the same things, however, one thing I know for sure is that we all want to improve our lives, mentally, physically and economically.

Can you imagine for a minute if we all think the same way or if we think about the same things? Wow! that would be boring. We don't always need to think the same things and we don't need to see the world in the same way in order to make a difference, we simply need to be in a good place. A place where our minds will be able to reach its true potential.

The only way for us to reach our true potential is by learning new things every single day because it's going to allow us to acquire new knowledge which in turn is going to help us in reaching our true potential. Furthermore, we will be able to apply this new knowledge to our advantage in many ways. We can apply our new knowledge to solve most of our problems, so let's not waste that opportunity. Remember that knowledge is going to help us overcome most obstacles that we might encounter in the future.

There are an abundance of reasons which that will prevent us from reaching our true potential, for example, the lack of motivation, the commitment, the desire, the passion, and the energy which is required to help us overcome those obstacles. These are some of the essential tools that we have at our disposal to help us overcome most difficult situations, furthermore, without these tools, we are never going to reach our true potential, and therefore, we will fall short of expectations almost every single time. We must never let any obstacle stand in our way from reaching our true potential and finding happiness.

It's obvious to me that most people are content with what they have achieved so far, but not me, I always want to learn more. When we become satisfied with what we know, we will get complaisant, we will stop learning, our lives, unknowingly will become boring and there will be no more desire to better ourselves. The true meaning of our lives is to learn and to be the best that we can be, therefore, we should never stop learning new things. We must never stop feeding our brain with new information because if we do, our brain is going to go into a dormant state of mind. The same principle applies to our bodies, if we stop feeding our bodies the food that it needs, it's going to become weak, and eventually it's going to die.

For those individuals who want to learn new things and better themselves, they need to remind themselves that they need to have the right tools, for instant, self-motivation, commitment, desire, passion, and energy.

The same principle applies for cooking, if we don't have the right recipe or the right ingredients, then we won't be able to cook much of anything and that is why we must arm ourselves with the right tools. Having the right tools is essential for any type of job, whether we are trying to better ourselves or trying to build a house. Our goals, dreams and expectations must never fall short of expectations because we don't have the right tools to work with.

Every profession must have the right tools which are needed in order to do a good job. A construction worker does not go to work without the right tools, and if he does, he is going to be disappointed, in other words, he is not going to be able to finish his projects without those essential tools.

In order to help us along with our journey, we must arm ourselves with the right knowledge. Knowledge is power and if we use it wisely it will help us reach our true potential. Possessing the right knowledge and applying it in the right way is going to help us find a solution to most of our afflictions. Furthermore, knowledge is going to help us to understanding how our minds works. We have the knowledge hidden within ourselves, we just need to extract it, and then apply it to our daily lives.

It's important for us to understand how our minds works, and we must understand how all things work in order for us to achieve success, moreover, it's not enough knowing how things work, it's not enough understanding how our minds work, and it's not enough knowing ourselves, so in order for us to be fully successful, we must put our knowledge into action. If we applied our knowledge and use the right way, our projects will be accomplished in little or no time at all, and it's going to improve our quality of life, it's going to increase our abilities and it's going to help us enjoy our lives to its fullest.

For centuries, our minds had restriction which prevented us from reaching our true potential, but now is time for us to let go of those restriction. Now more than ever, we need to evolve into super-human beings so that we no longer depend on others for leadership. The veil has come off, we are no longer tied down by those restrictions which is limiting our way of thinking, no longer our freedom will be in jeopardy, no longer there will be restriction preventing us from expressing ourselves freely, no longer we will be limited by our inexperience. Remember that we were born to be value creators, not value destroyers.

Taking Advantage of Every Opportunity

It is a well-known fact that most people will fail to recognize new opportunities when they present themselves, therefore, it is of great importance that we get better at spotting those opportunities, otherwise, we ware going to miss out on experiencing new and exciting thrills, in other words, we are going to miss out on a chance of a lifetime. Sometimes opportunities come our way, but unfortunately, we are not ready to take on new challenges, or worst yet, we are afraid to embark on new journeys. We must prepare ourselves and never be afraid because some of those opportunities might never come back, and sure, there's always new opportunities coming our way, but perhaps we already miss out on the greatest opportunity or the change of our lifetime. My personal advice is to always be ready and willing to take on new challenges, but without being afraid of the unknown.

When we challenge ourselves, venture out into the unknown and take advantage of every opportunity, then we are going to discover new and exciting places that we never seen before; we will experience new trills, we will meet new people which in turn is going to allow us to learn many new things. We must take every opportunity to expand our horizons, however, one thing that we must never do is to come up with a myriad of excuses not to do it. Let's not wait until we get older and realized that we missed out on creating a better live for ourselves and our families because we were too complacence with what we have.

We all have passed on many new and exciting opportunities in the past, but sometimes it's only because we fail to recognize them, however, we should not feel bad because even some of the greatest minds in the past have committed the same mistakes.

When I'm talking about taking advantage of an opportunity, I'm not only talking about taking advantage of monetary opportunities that come our way, I'm also talking about other types of opportunities, for example, finding the love of our life or the person that we will marry and live with for the rest of our lives. Furthermore, if we fail to recognize an opportunity when it presents itself, then is possible that we might miss out on a new and exciting career, but most importantly, we are going to miss out on finding happiness.

We must be ready for any type of opportunity, whether that opportunity is to find love or an opportunity to better ourselves, economically, physically, or emotionally.

Again, most of us go through life not knowing or not recognizing an opportunity when it presents itself, and therefore, we are denying ourselves from finding some much-needed happiness. But how are we going to recognize those opportunities? First, an opportunity is often a matter of perception, so it matters how we perceive the world because it will reflect who we are as a person. Sometime opportunities will present themselves by pure luck, but most often than not we must create our own opportunities and it's by preparation that we are going to accomplish it, in other words, we need to educate ourselves first and once we do that, then we are going to be able to recognize them. Moreover, opportunities are everywhere, but in order to recognize them we must have the ability to scan our enviroment, afterwards, we must create a plan, and then follow with action. Again, we will be able to recognize an opportunity by simply being aware of our surroundings in other words, we must be aware of everything that is happening around us. Remember that we must answer the call when an opportunity knocks at our doors.

Sometimes we don't take advantage of an opportunity because we didn't know how to recognize it in time and afterwards, we become angry at ourselves for not recognizing it in time. When we fail to recognize or take advantage of an opportunity, for whatever reason, we will start bargaining for much less. We don't want to fall into a depression state of mind because we failed in recognizing and taking advantage of such opportunities, however, there's hope because starting today we will not limit ourselves by accepting our past failures, and we are not going to accept that we have been defeated by our own ignorance.

From now on, we are not going to deny ourselves the opportunity from learning, growing, and achieving complete happiness. We are not going to deny ourselves the opportunity to learn new and exciting things. There is no doubt in my mind that everyone holds the key to their own happiness. His own success, and his own health.

Why Do We Do the Things That We Do?

The nature of human behavior, how it works and why we do the things that we do. In the first place, the number one reason as to why our behaviors never changes is because we are not aware that we need to update our old way of thinking on a consistence basis. It is a human condition for mankind to keep on doing the same old boring things over and over and it has to do with the fact that we think that all information within our subconcious mind is correct, but we could not be more wrong. We need to change our old way thinking, in other words, we must replace our thoughts for new thoughts. In a sense, it's like having one of the first computers that were invented back in the early eighties. You see, nowadays, those old computers are no longer of much use to anyone because all the information which is stored in them is old information, plus the fact that they are too slow, in other words, they are dinosaurs. In today's modern word we have super-fast computers capable of accomplishing many tasks in little or no time.

To be successful, in today's modern world, we need to consistently keep up with new technology, but in order to accomplish that we need update our computers, in other words, we need to replace our old computers with new computer which are much faster now than never before. New computers are not only faster but they have been updated with new information. The same principle applies to our old way of thinking, we need to replace old information from our subconscious mind with new information. We must adapt to new ways of doing things and we must change our old way of thinking.

We need to constantly update our old way of thinking because our old way of thinking and doing things no longer works efficiently. We must be willing to let go of some of our past information which is stored in our subconscious mind, however, if we insist on holding on to our old ways of thinking, then it's going to hold us back from moving forward into a brand-new future full of excitement and happiness. We need to adjust to new trends or make changes to our old ways of thinking and we must do it on a consistence basis. We are constantly updating our computers, our phones, and televisions, so why not do the same thing to our way of thinking? Why not give our brain some new and updated information?

It's a well-known fact that most people don't like making changes to their old style of life because they are too comfortable being who they are. However, sometimes people will make those changes but only because they are forced to do it by someone else, however, they feel extremely uncomfortable making those changes. Yes! we are all going to feel uncomfortable when we make changes to our way of thinking and to our daily routines, but it has to do with the fact that we are in a comfort zone and we don't want anything new in our lives to interfere or break our daily routines. Nevertheless, we must come to the realization that we need to make some changes to our old way of life so that we can keep up with the modern world. Remember that: in the long run, we will be better off, we will feel better about ourselves because we will have new and exciting things to do.

Occasionally, we try to make changes to some of the things that we don't like about ourselves, but we end up failing miserably, but why is that? Why do we fail so miserably? Well, the problem lies way down deep in our subconscious mind, you see, everything that we ever learned in the past is stored there, but we don't know how to change that information, or better yet, we think that all that past information stored in our subconscious minds is good information, but we couldn't be more wrong because not all information is good.

Every bit of information or knowledge stored in our subconscious mind began way back when we were first born, and it kept accumulating as the years went by. Again, every bit of information and knowledge that we learn from a lifelong of personal experiences was a slow process. It was a lifelong of learning new things every single day, furthermore, as we kept on getting older, even more information was being recorded into our subconscious mind, it sits there waiting to be put into action.

Some of the information entering our subconscious mind as we were groin up, and as mentioned before, was the wrong information and that is why we need to update that information. We must understand that all information in our subconscious mind is never going to go away because that information or knowledge that we have accumulated throughout the years is encrusted into our subconscious mind. However, we have the option to replace some of the wrong information for new and improve or updated information every time we want.

Again, old information stored in our subconscious mind is the number one reason as to why it's difficult for us to make any change to our old way of life, and it's because that's all we ever known, however, it doesn't mean that we can't make changes any time we want to, it simply means that it will take an enormous amount of effort on our part. Again, it's going to be a difficult task to accomplish and it's because we are so accustomed to doing things based on old information.

It might sound contradictory to what I'm saying here, but it's of great importance that we retain some old information or knowledge, whether it's right or wrong because we will be able to draw that information and compare it to new information, and by doing so, we will be able to come it with the right information. Remember that acquiring new knowledge or new information is going to help us to make better decisions in the future.

Again, the information store in our subconscious mind has been there for many years which means that we are set in our ways as adults, however, it doesn't mean that we can't make adjustments because we are capable of that, and much more.

We cannot insist on doing the same old things in the same old-fashioned ways and expect to get different results, we must change the way of doing things to a new and improved way. We must remember that our computers are in constant need of attention; they need repairs, they need updates and so is our subconscious mind.

We must remind ourselves every single day that we need to do better for ourselves, but the only way for us to be able to accomplish it: is by changing our old way of thinking. We must ask ourselves the following questions "How can we improve our lives? How can we get rid of our daily habitual and boring routines?" We need to remind ourselves that everything is possible, but only if we make the necessary adjustments in the way we think. We can change the way we act as a human being, and we can change the way we conduct ourselves at any time as well.

These are some important factors that we must practice on a day by day basis and should not be taken lightly because these factors, in the long run, are going to help us to better understand who we are as a person. We must help ourselves to better understand why we do the things that we do. These factors will help us to understand how our thoughts work and how they are processed in our mind.

There's only one way for us to learn and that is by always questioning everything that we do. We need to question our decision-making process every single day. Furthermore, we need to "always" ask ourselves tons of questions before we decide to put into actions our ideas. We must ask ourselves "what quality of life do I want to live? Do I want to live a happy life or an unhappy life? Do I want to live a boring life or an exciting life? Do I want to live a healthy or a life full of diseases? Do I want a good paying job which is going to help me buy a home? A job that will help me buy a car, a job that will help me pay my bills, a good paying job which is going to allow me to save enough money for my retirement?" These are questions that we must ask ourselves because it's going to help us improve our current way of life?

Nobody wants to experience the pain and the misery that comes from having made the wrong decisions. Nobody wants to experience or feel the pain from a life full of unhappiness or a life full of unhealthy conditions. Nobody wants a life full of anxiety, nobody wants a life full of sadness, nobody wants a life full of anger, and nobody wants to live their entire lives under any emotional pain because of our erroneous way of thinking which lets us make bad decisions.

We must make a total transformation within ourselves, but the only way to accomplish such a task is by changing our negative thoughts to positive ones. We must change our negative attitude towards life and replace it with a positive attitude. If we want to leap into a new future full of wonderful and exciting things, then we must change our entire behavior pattern, we must break away from our old way of thinking, in other words, we must free ourselves from any type of mental slavery. We must free ourselves from our old ideas, old behaviors, old thoughts, and old patterns. There is a way for us to be much happier in the future and that is by getting rid of our old way of thinking, it must be replaced by a more updated one. Again, we must break away from our old way of doing things to a new and more efficient and improved way.

There are many things that we can do to improve our lives and the lives of those who we love, but the most important one is to pay close attention to our thoughts because our thoughts will make us or break us if we don't adjust our thoughts according to our needs. We must remember that when our thinking is toxic and irrational, we will not be able to live a happy and fulfilling life, so, it's vital for us to trade our toxic and irrational thoughts for non-toxic and rational ones.

Big success comes from repetition, in other words, we must constantly keep our thoughts in check so that we don't fall back into stagnation. We also need to keep our actions in check because if they are not under control, we might do things that perhaps will regret later, so, it's important that we have complete control of everything that we do and think.

Changing our old way of thinking will create an array of new thoughts which is going to allow us to experience some of the most wonderful feelings that we never experience before; it's going to bring joy and happiness to our hearts like never before.

I'm not suggesting that we change our entire way of thinking or our entire way of doing things overnight, I'm merely suggesting that we need to start by making little changes, and in return, we are going to prepare ourselves for much bigger changes in the future. It's always a good idea to start slow at the beginning, in other words, we should start by taking baby steps, or should I say, "we must learn to crawl before we can learn to walk." We must make the necessary changes on a step by step basis because by doing it this way, we will be able to absorb more information, also, we will be able to retain that information much longer.

By leaving some of our old habits, old thoughts, and old way of thinking behind, we will be able to improve our perception, our awareness of our surroundings and our environment, and the same time, is going to allow us to regain total control over our actions, and if we can accomplish that, then we will no longer going to have feelings of regret, despair and anxiety, furthermore, no longer we will have so many negative thoughts which are going to hold us back. This is the right time for us to move forward, but without looking back at our past failures.

Everyone on the face of the planet, at one time or another, have experience feelings of anxiety, failure, anger regret, unworthiness, and feelings of desperation, but we must never think of our feelings as negative or failures, instead, we must think of those feelings of failure as a way for us to learn new things which it's going to give us the opportunity grow in wisdom.

There are many types of feelings that we have from time to time. Feelings that cannot be easily explained, feelings of sadness, frustration, and feelings of disappointment. Again, these are feelings that we cannot always explain because we do not completely understand them, but we must keep on moving forward and eventually, if we search for answers hard enough, we will find the right answers.

We must remember that there are no impossibilities for mankind, and that there is nothing that we cannot accomplish when we put our minds into action. However, it will require dedication, effort, self-control, self-discipline, consistency, and finally, it will require a strong desire and the wiliness on our part to make those changes in our life.

What are some of the requirements that will allow us to make a change in our lives? What will it take for us to learn new things and to develop new social skills? Well, in the first place, we need to get inspired, and not just inspired, but highly inspired. Secondly, we must use our imagination, and thirdly, we need to do some soul search. Now that I think about it, soul searching should be the first step that we need to take because it's going to help us learn who we really are.

Life is full of wonderful surprises, but we are never going to be able to experience them, unless we make a change to our way of living. We must expand our horizon and knowledge because right now, we know what we know and that is it, or at least that is what we think, and it's because we were programmed to think in a limited kind of way.

Deciding to make a change in our lives is the easiest thing, but doing it, it's a whole different story. We must ask ourselves the following question: "How strong is our desire and our wiliness to change?" We must keep in mind that most people are too comfortable being who they are, so therefore, they will not welcome any new changes, however, if they want more out of life, then, they must make the necessary adjustments.

Changing our old way of thinking and our old way of doing things it's not going to be an easy task, but with a strong desire, determination, and some passion on our part we will succeed, eventually. Again, it's not an easy task, but it's possible to reinvent our old selves into a new person. We must remind ourselves that we can become whoever we want to become because it's our choice and nobody else's, but ourselves. It is a matter of looking into the mirror and examining ourselves and then we can decide if we like what we see, if we like what we see, then we don't need to do much about it, but if we don't like what we see, then it's obvious that we need to make some change so that we can become who we were meant to be: *A better person.*

Remember that we need to interrupt the flow of negative thinking, furthermore, we need to let go of our old bad habits and our old erroneous thoughts. If we want to accomplish happiness, then, we must explore new possibilities and gain new knowledge on a consistent basis. We must also keep in mind that things just don't happen because we want them to happen, nothing falls out of the sky right into our laps. Instead of wishing for something good to happen to us, we must go out and make it happen, in other words, nothing is ever going to move until something, or someone moves first.

We need to understand that if we are going to be successful in everything that we do, then we must make some adjustments to the way we think and act. Changing our old way of thinking and leaving our bad habits behind is going to allow us to find happiness much faster.

We must be aware of every thought that runs through our minds, every minute, every hour, and every day until we are able to master a new way of thinking. We cannot change our way of thinking, our bad habits and our behaviors for a day or two and then forget about it. Surely, we need to take a break from time to time to meditate and let our mind relax for a while, but it doesn't mean that we will take a break forever. We must continue to improve our lives on a day by basis regardless of the circumstances.

Wishful thinking is a good thing. However, we cannot always hope or wish that things are going to change for us without any effort on our part. We need to keep in mind that it's only by repetition that we will be able to become master at whatever we do. After we have mastered our skills, our way of thinking, and the way we do things, then, everything will become automatic.

How to Be Happy and Successful at Work

First, we need to remember that happiness is a choice and whether we choose to be happy at work or at home, it's going to totally depend upon ourselves to make it happen. It all sounds simple, doesn't it? The reality is that it will be a difficult task to accomplish but not impossible. There is one thing that we need to do every single morning, and that is to remind ourselves that we are choosing to be happy for the entire day instead of miserable. Remember that starting our day on a good note is going to determine what the rest of our day is going to feel like for us, in other words, it's either going to be a happy day or it's going to be a miserable day. We must be on the alert and never let anyone or anything get in the way of our decision to be happy.

Furthermore, if we want to be happy at work, then we must do the following, but we must do it every single day, and that is to remind ourselves to let go of any negative thoughts that we might have about ourselves and other people as well. Whether it's at work or at home, we need to let go of any jealousy, anger, and envy. But, on the other side of the coin, we need to get excited about our jobs, we need to be passionate about the type of work that we do, and we must never get discouraged when things go wrong. We must try to always be happy people who are open minded because happy people are more fun to be around with.

Secondly, we need to keep in mind that if we a are not happy at home, then it's obvious that we are not going to be happy and successful at work either, and that is why it's so important that we try our best to find happiness at home first before we can find happiness at work. But how can we possibly find happiness at work? Well, first of all, we have no business working at a place where we are going to be miserable or unhappy most of the time, so therefore, it's important for us to find the type of work that we love to do because if we like what we do, then most likely, we will be happy and successful and not only at work, but at home as well.

We need to constantly focus our thoughts and energy on the things which are going to make us happy the most, in other words, we need to have a clear vision of what we want to accomplish in our lives. We all have goals and dreams that we want to accomplish, but the only way to accomplish them is by believing and trusting in ourselves to do the right thing. Furthermore, how can we be happy and successful at work? Well, we can start by being on time, then we can follow by putting our minds into what I call "in a working mode state of mind" this means that we must pump ourselves with new energy every single morning, and leaving our laziness behind. We also need to have a plan of action or a list of things that we need to accomplish throughout the day, then we must follow through with a ton of determination so that we can get things done. It's important to remind ourselves to utilize our time wisely and not waste it on unproductive tasks,

Furthermore, if we want to be happy and successful at work, then we need to master the details of our jobs and absorb every responsibilities. We must never blame others because our state of mind is not in the right place, instead we must become leaders rather than followers, we must learn to create new opportunities for ourselves and for others.

We must unleash our imagination so that we can discover our true potential. We need to create opportunities for ourselves and not wait for others to create those opportunities for us. We need to become what we were meant to be: self-leaders because when we learn to become self-leaders, we will be able to control our own destiny. We must not focus all our energy and attention on only one project, we need to focus some of that energy and attention on creating new and exciting projects for ourselves as well. We must not let ourselves fall into stagnation because our minds were not built for stagnation, rather, our minds were created to be stimulated every single day.

When we use our imagination, we will be able to overcome most of our obstacles with ease. We must always keep moving forward, and we need to consistently come up with new ideas and new projects. Remember that the human mind has no limitations, we can achieve so much more than what we have accomplished so far, but only if we use every available resource. We must look at things differently now. We must look beneath the surface perception at work, at home, in the news and in our social life. From now on, we need to look for common denominators so that we can come up with new concepts.

Chapter Twenty-Four

We Have the Power to Control the Outcome of Our Actions

Our future will be determine by our actions today, so, we need to put our minds into action and start making good decisions which is going to allow us to control the outcome of our actions, however, we must use all our abilities, including our precious mental and physical energy on making good sound decisions today so that we can create a better tomorrow for ourselves. We must remember that the past does not matter as much as the future because the things that we have done in the past are not going to impact our future as much. As human beings that we are, we normally focus our thoughts on yesterday rather than tomorrow, and yes, we can learn from the mistakes that we have made in the past and that will help us to not make the same old mistakes time after time.

Again, future results will depend totally on our ability to make good sound decisions today. We have the power to control our own destiny, well, that is if we make the right decisions followed by the right actions. But how are we going to know if we are making the right decisions and in the right order? Well, for starters, there's a few things that we absolutely must have, and that is knowledge, awareness, wisdom and common sense, but unfortunately, these things only come with age, and I'm not suggesting that young people cannot make good sound decisions, on the contrary, throughout my life, I have seen many young people make good decisions which creates desirable outcomes for their future, for example, it's going to create an abundance of happiness, joy and self-fulfillment for them.

Normally, young people are not able to make all the right choices but it's because they are missing the knowledge and the experience which is required in order to be successful. Now, as for the rest of the word population, know that being older doesn't guarantee any success either, unless we learn to expand our awareness, in other words, we must be aware that some of the things that we wish for will be obtainable and some will not, so we must keep that in mind.

Furthermore, we must be aware that our lives will always be full with difficult challenges, and for the most part, we will be able to overcome most of them, however, some of those challenges will be a lot more difficult to overcome because they are challenges which are beyond our control, in other words, they are outside challenges or forces that we cannot control. For example, we cannot control what other people think or say about us, we cannot control what they are thinking in general, period, and we cannot control their actions either.

There are an abundance of things that we can't control, for example, we can't control many natural disasters related to the natural process of the earth, like earthquakes, floods, volcanic eruptions, floods, tornadoes, tsunamis, avalanches, forest fires due to lighting, extreme heat and mudslides due to excessive rain.

Furthermore, our space is full of natural wonders, but it does have some threats that could potentially wipe out all life here on earth, for example, asteroids, solar flames, gamma-ray radiation bursts, supernova powerful explosions, and according to scientist, we also have black holes that could potentially devour the entire earth. All of these are examples of natural disasters which can happen at any time, but we shouldn't worry too much about them because we have no control over them, so why worry about it, it's only going to increase unnecessary stress and anxiety.

Whenever I find myself thinking about natural disasters, I immediately turn my switch from an on positions to an off position and instead, I turn a different switch, the one which is going to help me to put my mind in a relaxed state of mind, that switch is called "calmness switch" We must never live our lives in fear, instead, we should always try to be as happy as possible because life is too short and we must not waste our precious time thinking about the things that we can't control. We don't have the power to control natural disasters or control other people's actions, but we do have the power to control the outcome of our own actions. These are examples of outside forces in which we have no control, so therefore, we shouldn't spend too much time worrying about them because worrying about the people or the things that we can't control can potentially affect our health in many ways. We basically only have the power to control our own destiny, and it's by controlling our own actions. Furthermore, we have the power to choose if we want to be happy or not, we have the power to control our thoughts, we have the power to control our attitudes, and we have the power to believe whatever we want to believe, whether is good or bad.

Our daily challenges have the potential to make or break us, therefore, we must be careful how we react whenever we are faced with any type of difficult situation. How we decide to handle our daily challenges will make all the difference in the world, either is going to make us stronger or it's going to make us weaker. We need to focus more on the things that we can control and not the ones that we cannot control. About the only thing that we can do when we find ourselves in a bad situation in which we have absolutely nothing to do with is to try our best to control ourselves.

Again, we will face many events which will take place within our lifetime, but unfortunately, we won't have any control over them and it's because they are events or forces which are outside of our control, so therefore, we won't be able to control the outcome. Most of these challenges and future events will put us in a difficult situation, by giving us unnecessary stress, frustration and anxiety, in other words, it's going to negatively affect our lives in many ways, furthermore, it could potentially impact our physical health and our mental state of mind, but only if we let them.

We don't need to worry about future events in which we absolutely don't have any control, and I'm not suggesting that we shouldn't worry, for example, we should worry about climate changes or global warming, we should worry about those things, after all, it's our planet. It's our home, however, we shouldn't worry in excess that we will jeopardize our ability to function properly.

The one thing that we should worry about the most is to try to control the outcome of our own actions. If we do this, we will be able to put our mind in a positive state frame of mind instead of a negative one. We might not be able to control other people's actions and reactions or control what happens with outside events that we can't control, but we can always control how we choose to respond to those stressful events by preparing ourselves, and that is by controlling our own thoughts, and our own actions.

We are human beings capable of thinking in a rational manner, and if we can control our thoughts, then we will be able to control the outcome of our actions. The power of rational thinking is enormously powerful. It's one of the most precious gifts that we possess and it's something that we can put into practice every single day. We must remember that if we learn to control our thoughts and not let any outside influences dictate our actions, then, we will have total control of the outcome, and whatever that outcome may be, we know that we are responsible and no one else.

Our thoughts are a product of either, self-suggestions or suggestions said directly to us by other people. Any suggestions whether are coming from within ourselves or from other people will pass through our brain for interpretation and if we are not careful, those suggestions could possibly turn into actions thereby leaving us with the responsibility of the outcome. We have the power to accept or decline any suggestions whether they are our own or not. If we decide to accept any outside suggestions and put them into action, it's only because we have fully examined them.

It doesn't make sense to worry about the thousands of things that we can't control, in fact, most people worry more about the things they can't control than the things they are able to control. But why do we worry so much about the things that we cannot control? Well, because there is a lot to think about, for example, our lives are full of many wonderful surprises, however, life has many unforeseen and complicated surprises as well, not everything is fun and games.

I really believe that we can control mostly everything that we do in our lives, for example, we can control our thoughts, our emotions, our feelings, and our actions, now! that is called "self-control". When we have self-control, we will be able to make good decisions, thereby, giving us total control of everything that we do, and if we can accomplish that, then we won't have to worry so much about future events that we can't control, and instead, we will worry about how well we prepare ourselves for those events, whether we have control over them or not.

We must remember that our past reality was created by way of our thoughts, our beliefs, and our feelings. Our future reality it's not any different, it is to be created the same way and that is by way of our thoughts, our beliefs, and our feelings, it's something that is never going to change no matter how much everything else changes. There is only one thing that we can change in the future and that is to change the way we think, act, and react. If we can manage to remember these three things, then we will change our future reality.

Remember that we are who we are because of our past experiences which are recorded into our subconscious minds, therefore, we must never allow our subconscious mind to fall into the belief that we were created with limitations, on the contrary, we were created to be value creators. We were created with tremendous abilities; therefore, we must never accept that our minds were created with limitations.

Love Will Heal Our Minds and Bodies from Diseases

We don't always need to take medicine to heal some of our physical and mental illnesses, in fact, most often than not, taking medicine it's only going to create more negative side effects than our bodies can handle. Our bodies were not created for eating, drinking, or inhaling many foreign substances, especially, clinically made drugs. When we eat, drink, or inhale these chemicals, the results will be devastating for our bodies, therefore, it's of great importance that we be careful what we put in in them. We don't always need to take drugs in order to heal our bodies because our bodies have some tremendous healing powers.

The human body is a remarkable machine, it has the power to heal itself, but only if take care of it and eat the right foods. What I'm trying to say here is that: our bodies must have all the right vitamins, minerals, and nutrients but when we fail to provide our bodies with healthy food and the right ingredients, then our bodies will become weak. They will not be able to fight off diseases because they will be lacking the necessary strength that they need in order to do the job they were intended to do.

There are plenty of things that we can do on a day by day basis which is going to help us to keep our bodies healthy and in good physical condition. The next three things are essential for a healthy body:

1. Eating the right foods.
   I know that eating healthy isn't always possible, especially when we are on the road, but nevertheless, we must be consciously aware of the things that we eat. We all love to eat hamburgers, fries, ribs, or steaks, however, we must try to eat other things, for example, fruits, vegetables, and nuts. As far as food goes, there must be some type of balance within our bodies. We cannot keep on feeding our bodies junk food our entire lives or our bodies will suffer the consequences.
2. We must exercise daily.
   even if it's for a short period of time, some exercise is better than no exercise at all, and believe me, our bodies will thank us later in life.
3. We must intake vitamins.

It's a well-known fact that the foods and vitamins that we intake are depleted of vitamins, minerals, and nutrients because of the rigorous process that they put them through. It's extremely important that we eat the foods that will give us the most vitamins, minerals and nutrients. It's recommended by most experts that we fuel our bodies with some healthy foods before we turn to supplements because eating healthy foods is going to give our bodies and our brains what they need for them to work properly and efficiently.

We must educate ourselves as to what type of vitamins we should be taking, and if we don't want to take vitamins, then we must decide on what type of foods we should be eating, well, that is if we want our bodies to get the right vitamins, minerals, and nutrients. Eating a good healthy diet, including fruits and vegetables along with exercising and taking vitamins is going to help us to keep our bodies fit and healthy, but it is not enough, we must also have a very important ingredient and that is "true love".

It might sound a little strange to some people, but true love has some tremendous healing powers. Yes, true love is the missing link to reaching maximum health, but why is love so important for our health? Well, for example, when we are in love with someone it's going to make us feel good on the inside, furthermore, when we are in love, we are going to be much happier than people who are not in love. We will feel more energetic throughout the day, more enthusiastic about life itself; we will feel more enthusiastic about experimenting with new and exciting things and it's all because we are in love. Love can be a powerful weapon in healing our bodies and our mind from many ailments and diseases.

Love can be manifested in many ways, for example, the love we feel for our spouses is different than the love we feel for our parents, brothers, sisters, grand-kids and friends. Love is a powerful human emotion. It's an emotion with different degrees of intensity. Love is something that we have been craving from the very moment of our existence. The love we feel for our spouses is the sensual or romantic type of love and it's best described by the Greek word "Air" which originated from the mythological god of love. The love we feel for our family is called "storage." It's a Greek word that describes the love between parents, children, brothers and sisters. The love we feel for a friend or any other human being is called "Philia." Philia is practice among most Christians; it's the kind of love people feel towards each other. Love is an emotional bond between friendships, furthermore,

Philia is a Greek word that describes some of our most powerful human emotions towards our human brothers and sisters, for example, compassion, goodwill, respect and there is the love we feel for God.

We must remember that happy people are more fun to be around with. Now! Which person do you rather want to be around, a happy person with a healthy mind and body or an unhappy person with an unhealthy mind and body? But, wait a minute, you are probably telling yourself that you already knew all of this, and that it's nothing new for you, however, you must remember that not everything has been writing, not everything has been said, and not everything has been discovered. Remember that there is always something new and exciting to learn and discover, something that you have never seen or read before.

I'm aware of the things that we must do in order to accomplish happiness and keeping our mind and bodies healthy. I know that we must consistently maintain a high degree of self-awareness because that is going to allow us to do the things that we need to do which is going to help us to maintain a healthy mind and body.

I know for a fact that most people (including myself) are doing the things that we should be doing to keep our minds and bodies sharp and healthy, however, there are some people who are doing the right thing almost every single day, in fact, I see it all the time with my own two eyes, they are more conscious about their health and their bodies now days than ever before. Are you taking the necessary steps towards accomplishing your happiness, are you taking the necessary steps towards accomplishing a healthy state of mind, and a healthy body?

Okay, moving on, not only love has the power to heal many diseases, but love can also heal loneliness, depression, anger, anxiety, and many more ailments which are afflicting our minds and our bodies. We know for a fact that when we are in love, we see the world differently, for example, we are more capable of showing our love and compassion for other people more often, we appreciate the things that we do have more. Furthermore, when we are in love, when we are happy, and in good health, we will show more appreciation for life.

People who are in love are much less acceptable to catching colds and illnesses and it's because their white blood cells are happy and when their white cells are happy, they will perform at full capacity. People in love are much happier than those who are not because being in love gives people the necessary energy which they need to fight off diseases.

Now we know that we don't always need to take drugs to cure some of our physical or mental illnesses. Sometimes all we need is a little love from someone to help us feel better about ourselves. Again, love is the best medicine we can take and not only for our bodies, but for our minds as well. Sometimes we find ourselves with no one to love, but if we really feel true love in our hearts, then true love is going to find us, well, eventually. True love is everywhere, but most importantly, true love is in our hearts, so we must challenge ourselves and go find that missing link: love. We should always try to show our true love which we have deep inside ourselves…love that we can give to others, instead of anger and hate.

As I mentioned before, as human beings, we are always looking for love and affection from others, in fact, it's what every human being on the face of the planet thrives for. True love from others is what keeps us going strong, therefore, we need the love and affection from others to be able to survive in our environment.

There's a couple of things that we need to remember when it pertains to love. In the first place, in order to love someone else, we must learn to love ourselves first because if we don't love ourselves, then, how are we going to be able to love and show our affections for other people? The chances of loving someone else is going to diminish tremendously when we don't know how to love ourselves first.

Secondly, true love needs time to develop, and it can only be developed overtime. True love is a powerful weapon, but unfortunate most of us do not know how to tap into that power.

Whether we are aware of it or not, true love has the power to heal most illnesses and it does it by restoring our health, harmony and by bringing our bodies back into balance and when that happens, we will be able to feel loved, feel secure and be accepted by other people. Love is also going to help us to get rid of our isolation, unhappiness, and loneliness. Anyway, love has the power to heal all wounds, and love has the power to make us stronger and more confident.

As human beings we have the tendency to hold back our love and affection for other people and it has to do with the fact that we are afraid of getting rejected, or even worse, getting hurt, and as a consequence, we end up building walls around us to protect us from harm. If we learn to let go of our insecurities, then we are going to be able to bring down those walls which are holding us back and preventing us from finding happiness. We must use some of our mental energy and redirect that energy towards finding true love, and if we can accomplish that task, then we will find true happiness.

Moreover, we are social animals by nature, therefore, we need to constantly associate ourselves with other human beings because we are incapable of living in isolation for a long period of time. People who live by themselves are more prone to develop some type of mental illness, in other words, no human being can live on an island by themselves for too long.

Furthermore, when people do not have any human contact with other human beings, it's going to affect, not only their mental state of mind, but their physical bodies as well. Being alone from all the bustle and hassles can be a good thing, but only for a little while, however being alone for too long will have a negative effect on our mental state of mind and I'm not saying that people will go crazy, but it's possible because we will lose touch with reality. We must have some type of human contact most of the time.

Should We Let Other People Influence Our Thoughts and Ideas?

About the only thing that we can control without outside influences is our thoughts and ideas. It's, therefore, that we need to make sure that our thoughts and ideas are not being influenced by others for evil purposes. We must not let others influence our thoughts and ideas unless they are of great benefit to us.

Most often than not, people will try to influence our thoughts and our ideas, only because they want to take advantage of us. Sometimes people will try to deposit their own thoughts and ideas into our brain because it's going to benefit them, in other words, it's a simple form of brain wash if you ask me, and I'm not just saying this for the saying because it happen to me many time in the past, so we must remember that people will say anything that we want to hear so that they can take advantage of us. We must always be on high alert when listening to other people's ideas and I don't mean to imply that we shouldn't listen to their ideas or suggestions. What I'm saying here is that we must be selective and only choose those ideas which are good ideas.

My philosophy is that: we need to listen to what other people have to say because it's a good way for us to learn new things, however, it doesn't mean that we should do everything they are suggesting, again, we must be selective. We have the need to listen to other people's ideas, but we must be careful who we listen to. We must be careful which ideas we are willing to put into action, furthermore, we must never let any undesired ideas enter our mind suggested by others. However, when a good idea is given to us by someone else, we should not give it a second thought, we must put that idea into action right away, or at the very least, take that idea and store it into our memory bank for future use.

We must never feed our brain with junk ideas, just like we will not feed our body with junk food. When we give our bodies junk food, they will become sick, and eventually, they will die prematurely. If we give our bodies healthy foods, they will act accordingly and the same principle applies when it comes to our brain, give our brain some good ideas and our brain is going to respond accordingly.

We have the power to control what goes inside our brain. Our thoughts and ideas will bring us success and happiness, or failure and misery. But how are we going to take total control over our minds? Well, the answer is simple. We are the controllers of our own thoughts and ideas. Therefore, we will be able to control our own destiny. Isn't this amazing? If our thoughts and ideas are the right ones, then we will be successful in life.

Our thoughts and ideas are the most important tools that we own, so therefore, we must use them wisely. Our thoughts and ideas are delivered from our imagination, from observing others, and from listening to others. Our thoughts and ideas are the source from which we will acquire tremendous power. Success or failure lies within our thoughts and ideas, and the results we get from putting them into action is going to determine who we will become in the future.

I believe that if we train our minds to think and to coordinate our thoughts and ideas, we are going to accomplish most of our goals. We must use our abilities not only to create values for ourselves, but for others as well. We must never let anger, greed, dishonesty, laziness or let any external negative authority affect our state of mind in any negative way. Our actions must always be directed by love and compassion towards others.

Seeing Through the Illusions

What is an illusion? Well, there are different types of illusions, but the main three type of illusions are as follow "Optical illusions" which deceives the eyes through visual images, "Auditory illusions" which misleads the ears through sound waves, and finally, there is "Tactile illusions" which is an illusion that affects our sense of touch.

However, the illusion which I want to talk about is an illusion that people invent in order to deceive someone, in other words, it's a misrepresentation of the truth and therefore is false information. I'm also talking about the illusions that we ourselves create sometimes in order to misrepresent or keep the truth from someone else.

Again, an illusion is something that is not true. It's a fabricated illusion; it's a fantasy or an impression created by us or by someone else. Sometimes an illusion it's an invention from our own imagination and is something that we invent when we don't want to face the truth about something or someone.

Moreover, why do we invent so many illusions? Well, there are several reasons as to why we invent them, and it's not that we unknowingly invent illusions for ourselves, but we do invent them from time to time, however, most of those illusions are invented by others to keep us in check, to distract us from the truth. We also invent illusions or lies to protect ourselves from any type of danger, either, for something that we don't fully understand or to protect ourselves from other people.

Another reason why people create illusions is because they want to deceive someone, in other words, they want to take advantage of their weaknesses or their lack of knowledge, and the only way that they will get what they want is by distorting the truth. It's the way of life for some people and they will never change because that is all they ever know. Sometimes people create illusions and use them against us, and other times we create illusions or lies and use them against other people in order to get what we want. It's a never-ending vicious cycle.

Furthermore, we create illusions because sometimes we do not fully understand the real facts or the truth about certain things and therefore, we replace the truth with our own opinions as to what the truth is, so we invent what we think is the truth and trick ourselves and our minds into believing otherwise.

When we are unable to explain the truth or the real facts and we fabricate a lie, we are creating an illusion in our minds, we are creating a distorted truth with a lie in our subconscious mind and eventually, we end up believing that what we are creating is nothing but the truth. We must be careful as to what type of information we are feeding our brains because when we are creating or fabricating lies, we are preventing our minds from progressing.

When we create illusions for ourselves, we are denying ourselves from being our true selves, we are imitating someone else, we are creating a false image of our true selves and eventually, we will lose our true image of ourselves because our fabricated illusions will create long-term mental confusion. Remember that illusions are created by us when we try to misrepresent or distort the truth with lies, and eventually, if we are not careful, our true self is going to disappear forever. We must stay true to ourselves. We want to exist as our true selves, we do not want to disappear, and we don't want to be pretenders either. Furthermore, we want to be who we were meant to be in the first place and that is to be our true selves.

Most often than not, Illusions are created when we don't know the true facts about something or when we are under pressure from others to perform at a higher level. We must not let others influence our true way of thinking. We must not let others force us into being someone other than our true selves. We must never allow ourselves to be used for someone else's self-interest, we must always be on the alert.

It is only from the fully and honest state of mind and most importantly, seeing through the many illusions created by ourselves and by others that we will be able to see things for what they really are, it is then that we will be able to make the jump into the next level of super humans. With super minds, creating super values for ourselves and for others.

We must make the jump into the next level of higher thinking and become super achievers. We are not going to become the next wave of geniuses that will save the world from destruction and save ourselves from ourselves from extinction by lying, cheating, and creating illusions for ourselves and for others.

Chapter Twenty-Five

A Positive and Healthy Attitude

We all have the option to wake up every single morning and decide for ourselves whether we will start our day on a positive note. In other words, we have the choice to choose between a positive and healthy attitude or a negative and unhealthy attitude. Why would anyone want to choose an unhealthy negative attitude is beyond my comprehension. Take me for example, the first thing that I do when I wake up is to remind myself that I need stay positive no matter what happens throughout the day, and if along the way something negative happens to me, for example, someone might say something about me which I don't like, most likely is going to make other people unhappy for the entire day, but not me, because I know myself; I know that if I stay mad it's going to ruin my day, so whenever I start having thoughts of negativity, I immediately change my negative attitude into a positive attitude. The benefits of having a positive and healthy attitude throughout the day are many, for example, we will be much happier, we will be more resilient, we will improve our relationship with our family, friends and others, furthermore, it's going to improve our relationships at work with co-workers.

It's important that we maintain a positive and healthy mental attitude throughout the day. It's in our best interest not to spread our negative and unhealthy thoughts to our love ones and to our co-workers. Remember that nobody likes to interact with negative people, but on the other hand, everybody likes to hand around positive and energetic and happy individuals, in other words, positive people attracts, well, positive people.

A positive and healthy attitude have tremendous benefits vs having a negative and unhealthy attitude, for instant, it will raise our energy levels to an all-time high, we will be more inspired than ever before, we will achieve more of our goals much faster and it's because we are in a positive state of mind. Furthermore, a positive and healthy attitude will boost our confidence to new levels; it will help us to overcome our obstacles much faster.

Remember that having a positive and healthy attitude and smiling on a consistent basis is going to increase our chances to succeed in accomplishing our goals. We must keep in mind that happy people with a healthy attitude will attract other happy people. Again, nobody likes those people with a bad attitude, and that is a fact. Having a healthy and positive attitude is going to make us feel good and it's going to make us look more attractive to other people, and if that wasn't enough, we will be able to prolong our lives because as we all know, happy people live longer than unhappy people.

It's of great importance that we have a daily routine, for example, a routine reminding ourselves that we need to start our day with a healthy and positive attitude towards life. A positive and healthy attitude, along with positive thinking will help us to make good sound decisions throughout the day. It's going to help us in believing that everything is going to be alright, in addition, our healthy attitude is going to increase our motivation and it's going to help us forget about our past failures, furthermore, our roadblocks will be much easier to overcome when we have a positive and healthy attitude.

I know for a fact that sometimes we forget about our healthy and positive attitude towards life, and it's understandable, after all, there are too many things that can go wrong thought out the day. We have so many things that we need to take care of that sometimes we lose track of our healthy attitude, but we must continue to improve on building a healthy and positive attitude for ourselves no matter how difficult our lives might get. But how do we keep our motivation and our healthy and positive attitude strong throughout the day? Well, we can start by surrounding ourselves with positive people who will help us to lift our spirits up, especially, when we are feeling down. Remember that we need to associate ourselves with people who like to have fun, people who are funny, people who likes to smile a lot, people who share our points of view, people who have new and exciting ideas, and people who love their jobs. There is an abundance of things that we can do to help us maintain a positive and healthy attitude, for example, listening to music, going for walks, and at same time enjoying what nature has to offer, we can also try to be more friendly with other people. We must remember that even if we fumble the ball on occasions, we know deep inside that we have the power to bounce back at any time because we have the power of positive thinking on our side.

Again, having a healthy and positive attitude is going to improve our overall relationships with other people. Having a positive and healthy attitude will increase our chances of becoming successful in the workplace, at home and in our social lives and it's because people will notice, and in return, they will start imitating us. A positive and healthy attitude is the key which is going to open the doors to a whole new word for us. It's one of the keys which is going to help us to accomplishing our goals and dreams, but we must remember that a healthy and positive attitude is going to start with self-talk, therefore, we need to learn to talk to ourselves on a consistent basis. When we have a positive and healthy attitude, we will look at the world and the people in a positive and not in negative way. When we have a positive and healthy attitude, good things will happen to us instead of bad things. It's important that we look at the world and the people in it as beautiful and kind rather than ugly and unkind.

When we have a positive and healthy attitude towards life and everything that we do, people will respect us, and in return, they will change their attitude about how they see the world as well. Furthermore, it's important that we learn to have a little more patience with those individuals who have bad attitudes because we don't want to take a step back, rather, we want to slowly move forward so that we can improve our relationships with everyone.

Again, there are an abundance of things that we can do to help create a positive and healthy environment for everyone. For instance, we can start by being kind to others, we can smile more often because people will smile back and that is going to help everyone to keep a positive and healthy attitude. Remember that whatever we do now, it's going to have an impact on future generations. We must remember that our kids and grandkids will continue to live on this planet after we are gone, therefore, we need to leave them in a good and healthy environment.

We can help create a good healthy environment for everyone, any time, any place on the planet, no matter where we are, no matter where we go, we can always make a difference. We can make a difference when driving, by being civil to each other. We can make a difference at the park, at the store or at the mall. We can make a difference by being nice to people and finally, we can make a difference by respecting each other's ideas and point of views, even when they are wrong.

One final thought, we need to surround ourselves with family and friends who are loving, uplifting, honest and helpful. We do not need to surround ourselves with a negative and depressing social environment. Negative people, friends and family will sap the pleasures and happiness out of our lives, sure, we will try and help them whenever possible, but as I said before, some people are never going to change their ways, and I'm not suggesting that we should abandoned them, but we cannot devote our entire life trying to help them when it's obvious that they don't want to be helped, instead, we must use our energy on those individuals who want to be helped.

Inspiring Others to Do Better

If we want to inspire other people to do better for themselves, then we must work on inspiring ourselves first. But how are we going to find that inspiration? Well, by following the people who we admire the most, and it could be anyone, for example, our spouses, family members, friends, our bosses and even people who we don't know. We need to follow those individuals who have accomplished many great things in the past, in other words, we follow the people who are successful, people who are enthusiastic about life, people who love their jobs and their families. Furthermore, we need to follow those people who are physically healthy because they take care of their bodies by exercising daily, we also need to follow those people who enjoy their hobbies. These are the people that we must follow because we are going to draw the inspiration and the energy which we need in order to make a better life for ourselves. Remember that we must follow the people who we admire the most because they are the ones who will teach us how to thrive and take our motivation to a whole new level.

Once we have accomplished such a task, then, we will be able to encourage others to do the same. Other people will draw the inspiration they need from us and that is why it's important that we conduct ourselves with honesty and integrity. In order for people to follow us, we need to set a good example first because when people see that we are people of honor, then they will follow, they will listen to what we have to say.

People will not follow us, if they think we don't believe in ourselves or we don't stand for something good. Furthermore, we need to be honest, we need to be strong in the face of adversity, and we need to always speak with the truth. It's only then that we will be able to encourage others to try new things.

There are different ways in which we can inspire others to better themselves, for example, we can encourage them to change their destructive behaviors, change their way of thinking, and change the way they do things. Most people have the desire to change and improve their lives, but unfortunately, they don't have the know how or the knowledge that they need in order to be successful, and that is when we can step in and use our knowledge to help them, assuming that they want our help.

Most often than not, people do not have a role model they can follow and trust. Someone who will inspire them to be the best they can be. A successful and happy person. When people don't have the support and the encouragement they need from others, it's going to be hard for them to get inspired, and because of that, they will probably fail in their attempt to make a change in their lives.

For over forty years I tried to help other people, but I realized that I was not going to be one hundred percent successful. I was not able to persuade a whole lot of people to transform or change their lives. I do have to admit that there were those who managed to make a few small changes to their way of life, however, their changes were minimum, they were not enough to completely turn their lives around, but nevertheless, even making a small change is better no change at all.

I always try to help, teach, praise, and encourage others to do better, I will continue to praise others for the things they have accomplished so far. We must praise others instead of criticizing or condemning them for their failures, but whatever we do, we need to make sure that we are being honest and that we really mean it from the bottom of our hearts. I found out that it is better to praise others for their accomplishments than condemning them for their failures. We need to praise others for all the things that they have accomplished, but not only for the big things, we also need to praise them for the slightest improvements, especially young children because they thrive on the support from the adults.

People are most likely to do better when we praise them instead of criticizing them. By encouraging others to do better, they will feel better about themselves and we will feel better as well, but most importantly, when people feel better about themselves, they will try to do better in everything that they will do in the future. Remember that everyone likes to be praised whenever they accomplish something good. We all crave recognition, and appreciation from others.

The appreciation, the recognition, and the praise from others is the food that feeds our soul and when we don't get it, our self-esteem will suffer. We need the recognition from our parents, our husbands, our wife's, other family members, and we need the recognition from our friends in order to keep us going. Remember that we need the recognition and the appreciation from others because we feed off the nice compliments that we get from them, it's a true reality.

No human being likes to be ignored or feel unappreciated, especially, our spouses, and our kids, therefore, we must learn to appreciate and recognize the efforts and the work they do on a day by day basis, whether at work, at home or in our community.

All it takes to make someone feel good about themselves is a word of praise, a word of appreciation, and a word of recognition. Again, the best way to help others is by inspiring and praising them for the things that they have accomplished. When people are inspired, there will be no limitations to what they will be able to accomplish, so, let's not stop ourselves from inspiring our kids and other to do better. As parents, we must never allow ourselves to stop our kids from learning and thriving. We should always encourage our kids and others to do better and to learn new things every single day. We are the only ones who can stop our children from becoming who they were meant to be, furthermore, we must remember that our planet is going to be a better place for everyone, but only if we encourage ourselves and others to learn new things.

In Need of Appreciation

We don't always appreciate others for what they have done for us, in fact, most people probably don't even care at all. This is one area in which I feel proud of myself and it has to do with the fact that I never forget when someone does me a favor. I am really an appreciative person. Moving on, we are imperfect human beings because we don't always do the right thing, however, not everything is a total loss because we have the capacity to change our ways and learn new things.

Showing our appreciation towards someone else is something that doesn't require much effort on our part, however, most of the time we fail to appreciate or recognize other for what they have done for us. We need to constantly remind ourselves that we can say nice things to others. We need to remind ourselves that we are capable and that we indeed appreciate others when they do things for us. I understand that it's hard to change overnight, but we need to start by taking little steps towards being nice and appreciative to one another. It's important that we learn to appreciate others for the things they do for us, after all, they took the time from their busy schedules to help us.

There are several reasons as to why we might not always appreciate or complement other for their good deeds, for example, we are too preoccupied with our own thoughts, we are having a bad day, we might be feeling tired and uninspired or maybe we just don't care enough to say something nice to others, but whatever the reason is, it's not good reason to ignore other people's feelings.

Let me remind everyone that the best time to pay someone a compliment is when we are having a bad day, and it doesn't matter if that person is a stranger, it's not that difficult to say a kind word. There isn't a good enough reason not to complement others, unless we are selfish or plain and simple, we just don't care. I can assure you that being nice and appreciative to each other, it's going to make everyone feel a whole lot better about ourselves. Believe me, it's going to help us grow and mature as human beings. It's going to help us to get rid of our arrogance.

Whenever we are dealing with a business transaction, we must make it a win-win situation for everyone who is involved with the transaction. When everyone benefits and is rewarded, then everyone goes home happy and that in turn it's going to open the doors for us with new business opportunities. As human beings, we are constantly trying to outdo each other that we forget the most important thing in the word, we forget to act in a civilized manner. Again, we need to learn to appreciate others for what they have done for us, either as a favor or in a business transaction.

We can all win when we unite our forces and fight for a common cause. We must keep in mind that it's not totally our fault that we are the way we are, we were not born this way, we were not born selfish and unappreciative, we were thought by watching other people throughout the years. I'm not going to blame the parents or the teachers because I do believe that parents and teachers will not teach kids how to be selfish. On the contrary, they teach kids how to be nice, share their toys, show their love and appreciation towards others by saying something nice, for example, thank you.

The good thing about all this is that we can change our ways. We can change the way we are feeling, we can change the way we think, we can change our thoughts and we can change our selfish acts any time by simply giving other people some of the things that don't cost money, in other words, they are free, for example, our time, our appreciation, our respect and our recognition. We must remember that anything we do unto others, whether it's good or bad it's going to come back to us, it is also known as Karma.

Everyone at one time or another likes to be recognized for their efforts and their good deeds. We are in a never-ending search for praise, affection, and recognition from others, in fact, every time we do something good or extraordinary, we want others to know about it. But why do we feel the need to be recognized for our amazing accomplishments? Well, because as human beings we crave the recognition and attention from others, in fact, we thrive on that recognition and when we don't get it, we will feel unworthy.

Sometimes, we like to do something amazing in order to get the attention from others, however, if nobody knows about it, then why do it? I know, we should be doing it because we will feel proud of ourselves, and it's going to make us feel good knowing that we were able to accomplish such a task. However, most of the time we like to do some amazing things, but it's only because we want to get some recognition and appreciation from others and it's something that most human beings crave for. We like others to tell us good things about ourselves because it makes us feel good. It makes us feel warm and cozy inside, and it makes us feel proud of ourselves.

We must remember that nobody likes to hear unpleasant things about themselves. Nobody likes to hear ugly comments from others, comments that will hurt our feelings. Nobody likes their feelings hurt, period. Criticizing others, especially, because of their human condition or their human appearance is not welcome by most people. Sure, we all know that some people are somewhat shorter than others... some are taller than others. Some are skinnier than others. Some people are smarter than others, but only because they have the knowledge, and they know how to use it. Some people are physically better looking than others, but others not so much, but may I remind everyone that beauty has nothing to do with the physical part of the person... beauty is on the inside.

A person can be overweight and not so attractive on the outside, however, that person might be beautiful and kind on the inside and that is all that matters to me. I have met many people in my life, but let me tell you, I have met beautiful people on the outside, however, they hold a lot of anger and selfishness on the inside and therefore, it makes them appear ugly. I have seen people not so attractive on the outside, however, when I got to know them, they were beautiful and kind on the inside. Again, we must never forget that everyone likes to hear nice things about themselves, occasionally.

The Power of Suggestion

What is "the power of suggestion?" The power of suggestion is a psychological process in which we are manipulated by comments, statements or ideas given to us by other people. In other words, it's simply a tendency to believe something that is repeated many times, but it doesn't necessarily mean that it's true. Suggestions, whether they are autosuggestions, meaning that they were created by ourselves, or they came from someone else have the power to influence our behaviors in many ways.

Everyone is susceptible to manipulation and it's because we are bombarded with an array of ideas, comments, or suggestions on a day-by-day basis by other people. However, most ideas are created by us, in other words, they are autosuggestion or ideas that we created for ourselves. Autosuggestions ideas is not something that pops out of our minds out of thin air, they are ideas created by us through our physical senses, for example, something that we saw, something that we herded, something that we smelled, something that we touched, or something that we ate.

Whether we realized or not, the power of suggestion is a powerful weapon that we can use anytime, anywhere, but we must use it the right way. We must never use it to tell others what to do, instead, we must use it to self-talk ourselves into making the right decisions. Unknowingly we have been using the power of suggestion our entire lives to make decisions which will impact our lives, either in a good way or in a bad way. We must never use the power of autosuggestion in a negative kind of way, in other words, we must never use it in a way which is going to hold us back from accomplishing our goals.

The power of suggestion is most often used to convince or entice other people to buy something, for example, a new car, a new house or in the case of a child, a new toy. However, the power of suggestion is mostly used by us to convince ourselves that we can accomplish anything that we desire. The power of suggestion can be used to improve our overall health, build our confidence, improve our concentration, or help us to relax when we are experiencing stress or anxiety. The possibilities will be endless when we finally learn to harness the power of autosuggestion. We also possess another powerful weapon which is our "imagination" and if we combine them both, we will be able to accomplish many wonderful things for ourselves. We can use autosuggestion for ourselves to improve our lives and we can use suggestions to help others so that they can improve their lives as well.

Furthermore, we can use suggestions with people at work. We know that nobody likes other people to tell us what to do, it's a human condition that we all have, so don't feel bad if you have that condition. We have had that condition since the very beginning of our existence. Ever since we were kids, our parents were telling us what to do and when to do it. I remember my parents telling me "don't do this," "don't do that." It's no wonder we don't like other people telling us what to do. No one likes to take orders from others. No one likes to be bossed around like a puppet, and it doesn't matter if that other person giving the orders is our own boss. I believe that there must be some type of balance or some type of compromise between us and those who hold the power to tell us what to do.

I strongly believe in "THE POWER OF SUGGESTION" because it's an amazing tool that we can use when trying to convey a message to others. We must never tell other people what to do, rather, we should make some suggestions and that is it. The proper way to ask someone to do something is by using the power of suggestion, we don't tell people what to do. We don't demand others to change or do things which they might not be willing to do. It's always better that we make suggestions to others, instead of demanding, and at the end, both parties will feel much better about themselves, and who knows, they might even appreciate the suggestion.

Normally, we have many tasks that we need to accomplish at work, however, if we don't do our jobs as we should, then there will be consequences, for example, our bosses have the obligation to tell us what to do and how to do it. They are no longer suggesting to us, they are demanding that we get our work done. I know that most people don't like that, but if we do our jobs the right way and on time, then our bosses will be happy. Occasionally, we are going to deviate from performing at our best, perhaps we are doing something the wrong way and we are not getting the results that we are looking for and that is when our boss can step in and suggest, not demand, but suggest to us that there's a different way to accomplish a better result, in other words, it's a nice way from them to try and get someone to do their job in a more efficient way, it's a win, win situation for everyone.

I strongly believe that this is the best solution for everyone when there is an issue which needs to be resolved, especially when there is a dispute or disagreement between two or more people. In fact, I think this is the best solution for almost every situation. Again, we can only suggest to others, we can't order, demand or boss people around, after all, we are all individuals with pride. There is absolutely no need for any type of demanding behavior. We want to treat people with respect, and in return, we will be respected. We want to treat others the way we want to be treated, it's not that difficult. When everyone puts their egos aside and starts behaving in a mature way, we all win.

We need to try and give people ideas in the form of a suggestion on how to do their jobs in a more efficient way, but never, ever, order them to do it our way or try to impose our will upon them. Again, we can make some suggestions at work for our employees, for example, "if this is not working, then maybe you should try something different" or "what do you think about this idea?"

There are many techniques that we can use to help people do what they need to do without making them feel bad about themselves. We want people to be on our side, not against us, furthermore, we want them to be our friends instead of our enemies, it is a technique that works most of the time and it's a technique that works for everyone.

Moreover, when people make a mistake, we don't tell them that they made a mistake or scream our heads off, instead, we can suggest that if that didn't work for them, then, maybe they should try something else. We can suggest to them to write down two or three things that might work for them instead. By suggesting to others instead of demanding, we are saving them from embarrassing situations, and we will save ourselves from being the bad guys. Furthermore, by doing it this way, we are letting them learn from their own mistakes. By using different techniques that don't put people to shame, we are giving others the feeling of being important to us, and at the same time, we will save their pride.

We all have the desire to be recognized by others, for example: when we do a good job at work, we need to hear from our bosses that we are doing a good job. When we are doing a good job at home, we need to hear from our families that we are doing a good job as well. As human beings we need the encouragement from others because we thrive on the encouragement that we get from them, and it should not matter if we are getting paid for doing our job or not. It's not a matter of getting paid for it, it's a matter of hearing that we are being appreciated for our hard work.

If only our bosses were a little more aware that if they treat everyone with respect, in return, people will be a lot more productive because they will be happy and content. I think there are a small percentage of bosses that really care about their employees and it's because they know how to use the power of suggestion, also, they have the knowledge and they know how to use it, furthermore, they know that by treating their employees as human beings and not as numbers, then they will get so much more out of them. When our bosses treat us as friends instead as an employee, we must never take advantage of that situation, we should do the job we are supposed to do regardless. When everyone does their share, it's a win-win situation for everyone.

Whether we like or not, there will be a lack of appreciation and gratitude on behalf of our bosses, however, for those bosses who know how to treat their employees, the rewards will be that much greater for them. When we demand of others to do the things that we want them to do, it's only going to make people go into a state of rebellion, along with a sense of resentment against the person giving the orders.

Always remember to use the power of suggestion when dealing with people. We can use the same technique at work and at home, in fact, we can use the power of suggestion any time anywhere. We can use it with our spouses, our kids, and our friends. We can use the power of suggestion on the road or wherever we might be and whomever we might be with. The appreciation and recognition towards our employees will motivate them to always do better. We must keep in mind that the power of suggestion and appreciation is a thousand times more powerful than the power of criticism. Appreciation and recognition is the medicine that we need for our souls.

We must try not to get too down on ourselves if our bosses are those individuals who don't know how to appreciate our hard work. If we don't get the appreciation or we don't get the recognition that we so much desire, then, there are other things that we can do to make us feel good about ourselves, for example, switching careers. One of the things that we can do to make us feel good about ourselves when we are feeling unappreciated is to read a book. Reading a good book is one of the best medicines for our lack of self-confidence, for the lack of feeling unimportant and for the lack of appreciation by our peers. Reading a book is going to help us to lift our spirits up. I really appreciate reading a good book, especially when I'm having feelings of unworthiness. When I'm having feelings of not being appreciated by other people, when I have done something good for them and they don't show any appreciation, and when I'm having those feelings in which I feel that I'm not in control of my own feelings. Reading a good book helps me tremendously when I'm feeling down, it helps me in rebuilding my confidence and self-esteem.

One last thing...as an employee, we must never take advantage of our bosses when they are kind and caring bosses. We have a job that we must do, so we must do it, furthermore, we have a responsibility and that is to do the best possible job that we can do. We must be one hundred percent responsible for our jobs, and we must do it well and without taking advantage of the situation. Just like there are bad or uncaring bosses, there are also bad employees that will take advantage of certain situations. My suggestion for everyone in the workforce is to take responsibility for your actions because doing a good job will be vital in climbing the ladder for a better position. Remember that when we take responsibility for our actions, our minds will continue to take over greater and greater chunks of business.

When My Motivation is Not Present

Today I decided to talk a little bit about my motivation. The reason as to why I wanted to talk about my motivation is because for some unexplained reason I woke up feeling uninspired. No matter how hard I tried, I wasn't able to start writing on my book; I wasn't able to focus because my mind was completely blank. Now that I think about it, I'm sure that it had to do with the fact that for the last two weeks I was not able to do my regular exercises. The main reasons as to why I was unable to worked out was because of my book. I wanted to finish it as soon as possible and that prevented me from working out.

I'm not trying to make excuses for myself because I normally don't like to make excuses for not doing what It needs to be done. I normally worked out at least three to four times a week and I know that sometimes is not enough, however, I always try to do my best. One of my favorite exercises is walking on the treadmill and I try to do it for a at least thirty minutes, but I preferred working out for an hour. Sometimes when I don't feel like working out on the treadmill I go for a walk at the park. Other times I like to change the scenery so I'm always looking for new places to walk, and I must admit, it does wonders for my state of mind. One of the most helpful exercises which I enjoy doing every morning is "yoga" You see, yoga is good for our bodies, but most importantly, it's good for our minds because it will allow us to relax throughout the day.

Anyway, as I was saying earlier, I couldn't get myself motivated earlier this morning. I was feeling tired and sluggish. I had no desire to do much of anything, however, after a few minutes of pondering about how I was going to get back on track, when suddenly, an idea popped into my head, I decided to come up with a daily morning routine which consisted of the following: a little bit of yoga and stretching, get dress, eat something light, then work out on the treadmill for about an hour, fallow by a cool off period, then take a shower, which by the way, it does wonders for an aching body, put on some clean clothes and finally comb my hair and voila! I would feel like a million dollars again.

This routine works for me; however, it might not work for everyone. My personal routine helps me to elevate my energy level, I feel relaxed, and my motivation level is at an all-time high as well. This is exactly what I need to do when my motivation is not present because afterwards, I feel good about myself, and that will enable me to start writing once again. Anyway, I was excited to add something new to my book and I was able to do that because my motivation was back. You see, the exercise, the breakfast, and the shower were all contributors in getting my motivation back on track. I was able to think clearly and I was no longer feeling tired.

The lack of motivation is perhaps one of the biggest reasons as to why people are unable to get going in the mornings. We must remind ourselves on a day by day basis that somehow, we need to get motivated so that we can get inspired to do whatever we need to do for the remaining of the day.

We should ask ourselves the following questions every single morning "what is my desire today; what do I need to accomplish, furthermore, how high is my motivation?" You see, the best time for us to get inspired and get motivated is first thing in the morning because it's when we are at our best. Furthermore, we should try to get motivated when we are feeling tired, when we are feeling like we can't move. This is the best time for us to recharge ourselves with new energy and we can do it by going a walk, or taking a shower, and believe me, afterwards, we are going to feel better about ourselves; we will finally have the motivation and the energy that we need in order to help us get to through the day.

We need to find out what type of exercises we like to do and then make it a daily routine. We also need to find out what type of things will get us motivated or inspired; what gets us going every morning and then we must follow with action, but we must do it on a consistent basis. We must try different things and see what works best for us. I always remind myself that in order to feel good, I must look good first.

Chapter Twenty-Six

A Death in the Family

2018 was a rough time for me and for the rest of my family. You see, several family members die this year. First, one of my uncles died earlier in the year and even though we were not that close, it was hard for me to digest. Whenever there is a death in our family or any other family for that matter, we cannot help ourselves but to think about our own mortality. It makes us realize how strong we can be at times, but at the same time, it remind us about how fragile we can be as well. When a family member dies, all our emotions and feelings come out. It's like an emotional roller coaster for the entire family.

Another family member died in 2018, it was my cousin's wife, she lived in Mexico. The last time I saw her was about 40 years ago, however, I have a vague image of her face in my mind, but the real reason as to why I didn't saw her was because I never went back to Mexico to visit them, again, we were not very close either, perhaps, it was because of the great distance between us.

Another family member died a few months later, it was my brother's grandson, and I can only imagine how hard must have been for him, his wife and the rest of the family. Furthermore, I can even begin to imagine the pain and the suffering that my niece had to go through because losing a son or a daughter it's something that no human being ever forgets. It stays with us for the rest of our lives, but nevertheless, we must keep moving forward with our lives hoping that they are in a good place forever. I am sure that my other two nieces were affected as much by his passing, it seems that he was a very loved young man by everyone. Again, I was not close to him either, I only saw him a few times while he was alive, but that doesn't mean that he won't be missed by me either.

A few months later I received some more bad news. I got a call from one of my nieces in Las Vegas, Nevada. She told me that her dad, my brother-in-law, died. He had heart complications. This was kind of unexpected news because he was released from the hospital a couple weeks earlier.

A few months later, another family member died, it was my sister in-law. She was battering cancer for some time and even though we all try to help her in many ways, it just wasn't enough, all we were able to do was pray very hard for her, but at the end, she couldn't overcome the terrible and debilitating effects of the chemical radiation treatments, she was gone fairly quickly, she will forever be in our hearts. She was a funny and kind person, in fact, I don't ever remember her being in a bad mood, she was always cracking jokes, she made everyone around her laugh with her jokes and her good sense of humor. Everyone misses you.

2018 was not a good year for our family, but nevertheless, we must hope for the best for everyone, we must keep on going with our lives and at the same time, we must try harder to get along and be nicer to each other, in good and in bad times. Before 2018 I have not been to a family funeral in many years because, as everyone knows, I used to suffer from panic attacks and anxiety, so therefore, I was not able to attend previous family funerals. Nowadays, I am eighty percent cured from my anxiety or as doctors call it "disease." Now I'm able to do a lot of the things which I couldn't do for many years, so I'm grateful for that.

A few years ago another nephew pass away and I wasn't able to go to his funeral either because of my anxiety, however, when my brother in-law passed away in Las Vegas I decided that it was time for me to face one of my biggest fears, so, I thought about it for a while and I decided that I wasn't going to let my anxiety defeat me any longer, I decided that I was going to overcome my fear of funerals, so I made up my mind to go, and so I did, it wasn't easy, but nevertheless I went. I must admit, I had some help from my wife Norma, she encourages me to go. One of the things my wife said to me was that I must go and support my sister; she suggested to me that I should be there for her, and so I did. It was hard for me at first, but after the first day of being there, I reminded myself that I had to stay strong not only for myself, but for my sister as well.

My sister was devastated by my brother-in-law's death. They have been together for forty-two years. I was a little bit closer to him because we saw each other about three to four times a year. Now I realized that we should have been a lot closer than we were, but unfortunately that didn't happen and the only thing that we can all do now is to try harder to become better human beings by loving each other even more.

When a family member dies, it always feels as if someone dump a bucket of cold water on our bodies, and by the way, it only re-enforces what I have been writing about all this time and that is that: life is too short to be wasted on meaningless tasks. Life should be enjoyed to its fullest, life should not be wasted foolishly. Life should be enjoyed with family members to its fullest by caring for each other, by loving each other and by spending time with each other.

Every minute counts and we should all do our best to do good deeds and to enjoy our families while we are still alive because everything else doesn't matter as much, especially money. Money is only important because it will help us to buy food or materialistic things. Money does not buy love, and it does not buy true happiness. We must remember that money doesn't buy beautiful smiles from the people who we love either.

Dealing with Our Feelings and Emotions after a Loved One Dies

Dealing with our feelings and emotions after a family member dies it's never an easy thing to overcome. We all cope with our feelings and emotions in different ways when someone we know suddenly dies. Some of us will cry or get angry. Others will find different ways to stay busy to lessen their pain, others will drink, others will go shopping, or overeat. We are all different and that is why we show our feelings and emotions in different ways. Furthermore, there are others who don't show any emotions or feelings whatsoever, but it doesn't mean they don't care, it's just their way of showing their feelings and emotions.

Everyone feels something different on inside when someone that we love dies, but just because we don't show our true feelings or emotions doesn't mean that we don't care, it's our way of showing or coping with our situation. Grieving is a long process; in other words, it will take a long time for us to be able to heal from our emotional pain. It is something that is not going to heal overnight, so we must give ourselves plenty of time to heal. It's important that we don't try to cope with our feelings and emotions by ourselves. We need to reach out to family members or to a friend for comfort and support, we do not need to keep all that pain inside by ourselves. Again, we must reach out for someone and slowly let that emotional wound heal.

There is absolutely nothing that anyone can do to prepare us for the passing of a family member, it's always tough no matter what, but regardless, we must stay strong. It's important that we work on re-discovering the bond and the love that we used to have for our family members because we never know how long we have left here on earth to enjoy them. We need to re-establish our love and mutual respect once again. We must also put aside any differences that we might have with a family member before it's too late.

A word of advice: Whenever there is resentment or anger inside us that we are holding onto for a family member or someone else, it's important that we learn to let go of them before it's too late. We must not wait to make things right. We must not wait to mend our broken hearts, we must not wait to tell someone that we love them because if we wait, and that person passes away, then it's going to be too late to do anything about it, well, it's actually never too late, per say, but why wait? Why not do it when we are alive?

Remember that any resentment or anger that we have against someone who dies will go away because it doesn't matter anymore. Why is it so difficult for us to let go of resentment and anger when the person we love is still alive? Is it because we take everything for granted? We must learn to make peace with each other while we are alive, it is not that difficult, besides it's FREE, in other words, it does not cost anything, but perhaps a little pride.

Why Are We So Resistant to Change?

As I mentioned before, there are plenty of reasons as to why most of us are resistant to make changes to our way of life, for example, the lack of understanding about the need to make those changes. Whether we realize it or not, change is already happening all around us, in fact, life is all about making changes. Life is all about being able to adapt to new trends, new jobs, new situations, and new technologies.

New changes are happening all around us every single day, but sometimes we simply don't notice them, or even worst, we choose to ignore them, but they are happening whether we want to acknowledge them or not. Most changes are being made by our peers and sooner or later we must adjust to those new changes because it will be in our best interest. Sometimes we do make changes to our way life, but it's either because we make them out of necessity or someone else make them for us whether we like it or not.

Sometimes we don't welcome new changes which are imposed by others because we don't like them, however, there are other changes that we welcome with open arms because they are of great benefit to us. It's always better to be prepared for new changes whether they are created by ourselves or by others. In fact, it's always a good idea that we embrace them, rather than to ignore them. We must remember that changes will happen whether we want them or not, so why not prepare ourselves for them.

Resistance to change is a normal human response and it's because we are so accustomed to doing what we already know, and therefore, we don't want to jeopardize or lose what we already have, in other words, we want to do the things that we already know; the things that will make us feel secure and comfortable and anything outside our comfort zone it's going to make us feel very uncomfortable.

Changing our habitual or daily boring routines is never an easy thing to accomplish and it's because it will require a tremendous amount of energy and effort on our part, and I completely understand that, however, we need to understand that making a change it's only going to benefit us in the long run. Furthermore, it's going to help us grow as human beings, plus the fact that we are going to acquire new knowledge, which in turn, is going to help us make better decisions in the future.

There are plenty of reasons not to make changes to our current way of life, for example:

FEAR OF THE UNKNOWN- Fear of the unknown is perhaps the number one reason as to why most people don't welcome any new changes to their way of life, but we must remember that with changes comes more personal growth, more knowledge and with new knowledge, there, will be more flexibility to do, or experience new things that we never experience before. Furthermore, we must remember that fear is just a negative thought in our subconscious mind which is trying to prevent us from reaching our true potential, in other words, fear is the killer of all good things.

Normally when we are afraid of the unknown it's because it makes us feel extremely nervous, thereby, preventing us from trying new things. Only those of us with a clear vision of the future are willing to risk making changes because we know that if we make those changes it is going to bring us many big rewards.

FEAR OF FAILING- Most often than not, we are afraid to make changes to our comfortable way of life because we are afraid of failing, and again, it's understandable, but we must remember that if we never fail, then we will never be able to learn new things. We must never allow our fear of failure (also known as: ATYCHIPHOBIA) stop us from achieving our goals, we need to let go of our fears and take a chance from time to time.

LACK OF KNOWLEDGE- The lack of knowledge is another reason as to why we don't like to make changes. Most often than not we are afraid to experiment with new things because we do not possess the knowledge, which is required in order to be successful, so we rather not try. Perhaps, in our mind we think that if we obtain new knowledge that our lives will get more complicated and challenging, however, I think that most people will welcome new knowledge with open arms because they are consciously aware that knowledge is power and they know that with new knowledge, their chances of becoming successful will increase tremendously.

There is absolutely nothing preventing us from acquiring new knowledge, the only person that can stop us: is ourselves. We must remember that new knowledge is going to allow us to become successful in everything that we do in life. Knowledge will help us to understand ourselves better. It will help us to discover our strengths and our weaknesses, so we must always keep that in mind.

LACK OF SELF-CONFIDENCE- The lack of self-confidence will stop most people from making a change, but not to worry because there are things that we can do to help us build our self-confidence once again, for example, our perception of ourselves need to improve, we need to visualized ourselves as successful individuals and not as failures. Often, we form an image of ourselves as losers instead of winners, but we can change that by visualizing ourselves being successful instead of failures. One thing to keep in mind is that we are not born with self-confidence, we learn it as we grow up.

FEELINGS OF INFERIORITY- in the first place, let me remind everyone that nobody is perfect, we all get those feelings of inferiority from time to time, and it doesn't matter if we are successful, smart or good looking, we are still vulnerable to those feelings. There are those who believe that they are unsuccessful, dumb, or not so good looking, in other words, no one seems to find their happy place. All those feelings of inferiority which we get from time to time is a byproduct of our own imagination. So, how are we going to overcome those feelings of unworthiness? Well, there are a few things that we can do to help us deal with our feelings of inferiority, for example, we can start by not worrying so much about what others might think about us, especially if those people are not our good friends, so why worry about it, instead, we need to surround ourselves with positive people who will uplift our spirits. People who will appreciate us for who we are because that is going to help us to build our elf-confidence. We also need to be more assertive of ourselves. We need to walk with confidence, in other words, we need to show the world that we are confident individuals. We must never allow ourselves to be afraid, instead, we should show others that we are confident individuals.

FEAR OF CRITICISM- Whether we like it or not, sometimes we are going to be criticized by others, perhaps, for something that we have done wrong, but we must remember that we are imperfect human beings and that we are going to make mistakes. We shouldn't be afraid of criticism, especially when it's constructive criticism. We must never run away and hide inside a cave and hide forever, on the contrary, we should use that criticism as a motivational tool for us to learn new things, and at the same time, eliminate our weaknesses.

My advice to anyone who is reading this book, is that no matter how difficult life might get at times, we must never give up on trying to improve our lives. Remember that there will be big rewards, but only if we don't quit. Furthermore, we must lift our heads up and walk with confidence and without fear of the unknown.

Most often than not, decision making is going to be the number one source of our stress. It's not an easy thing to always be conscious and responsible every minute, every hour and every day, but it's mostly because our minds don't like stress, so sometimes in order to avoid stress, our minds will seek the path of less resistance.

We must remember that our resistance to change will keep us from reaching our goals, well, that is if we have any goals that we want to accomplish. Again, most people will take the path of least resistance to avoid decision making. We must let our own knowledge guide us, but without any external guidance or authorities. We must be self-sufficient and self-aware of everything which is going on with our lives. We are all very capable individuals of processing our own thoughts and without any outside forces.

Another reason as to why some of us don't like changes is because we are set in our old ways of thinking, so we don't want to be bothered by new changes. Again, we normally don't want to make change or learn new ways of doing things and it's because we are hard wired to the past, in other words, we are emotionally connected to the people and things from our past, and if we suddenly make a changes, then we will lose what we had.

Resistance is a normal response to new changes and it's because most people can't get over the fear of change, new changes will cause people to doubt themselves because of their inability to adapt, it can be scary for some people. The fear of change can sometimes paralyzed people, so they stop themselves from trying new things. Fear of change in most cases will stop us from acting. The simple though of new changes will give us anxiety and self-doubt and these are the types of feelings that we all need to overcome because they are holding us back from finding our true selves.

A Healthy Body Equals a Sharp Mind

If someone were to ask me if I wanted to have a perfect body, and at the same time have a sharp mind, my response would be, and without any hesitation, "yes." It's obvious that everyone wants to have a healthy body and a sharp mind. But how are we going to accomplish such a task, how are we going to improve our overall health, and keep our bodies in good physical condition at the same time?

Most people already have a good idea of what it takes to reach such a goal. It's not a secret, but just in case some people don't know that yet, I'm going to explain it in more detail. In the first place, we need to have the burning desire and the mental energy in order to achieve such a goal. Secondly, we need to have a plan, and then we must follow that plan with action because it's not enough to have the burning desire. Desire alone is not going to give us what we want, we must have a plan an then execute that plan, in other words, we must put that plan into action, or our desire to have a healthy body and mind is not going to materialize. It is a simple formula that we must follow.

Whatever we wish for can become a reality, however, it will take hard work and dedication on our part. Sometimes we wish for something good to happen to us and we end up getting our wish, but it was by pure coincidence or luck that we got it.

It' important for us to remember that in the real word, nothing is given to us, unless we earned it, so we must get our wheels in motion and go after what we are looking for, for example, if we want a healthy body, then we need to stimulate our bodies with exercises, but at the same time, we will be stimulating our brains. When we exercise on a consistent basis, our bodies will stay healthy and our minds will stay sharp as well. It's a win-win situation. If we take care of our bodies… our bodies will take care of our minds, and if we take care of our minds… our minds will take care of our bodies. Remember that we must stimulate our bodies with exercises and our minds with new information on a consistent basis in order for them to stay healthy for a long time to come. We must remember that our brain was created to be challenged on a day by day basis, and that we don't need to worry about overloading it with tons of information because our brain was created to store billions bits of information per second.

Now! There is one thing that we must never forget and that is to be aware of the things that we eat, so if we feed our bodies healthy foods, then our bodies will stay healthy and they will respond accordingly. When we neglect our bodies and don't give them the exercise and healthy food which they need in order to stay healthy, then our bodies are not going to maintain their good health and appearance for too long and the results will be catastrophic; they will get sick and eventually die. The same principle applies when it comes to our brain, if we feed our brain nothing but negative thoughts, then we are going to attract negative thoughts in return, in other words, we are what we think. Remember that if we neglect our bodies, then we are neglecting our brain and it's because they feed from each other.

Again, when we feed our bodies healthy food and plenty of exercise, then we will be taking care of our brain as well, in other words, we will provide our brain with new energy which it's essential for good mental health. I really believe that at the end, we will like the results. Furthermore, by taking good care of our bodies and our brains, we will be keeping them free from diseases. Once again, our bodies and our brains are inseparable. They work together, in other words, they are a team, one cannot survive without the other.

A word of advice: We must never start a regiment of exercises; feed our bodies nutritional foods and suddenly decide to stop because we are not feeling it, or we are feeling tired. We must never get complacent, in other words, we must not let ourselves be overcome by laziness. We must do what we were intended to do and that is to exercise so that we can keep our bodies relatively healthy and our minds sharp. Remember that laziness is like a disease, and therefore, it should be banned from our lives, but that is only my opinion. I know very well about laziness because I felted it many times in the past. It's obviously that whenever laziness invades my body and mind, I don't feel like exercising, however, I always try to motivate myself by thinking about all the great benefits which I'm going to get from staying active. Furthermore, I know that whenever I am feeling lazy, it's the perfect time for me to get myself motivated again. By the time I'm done exercising and taking a shower, I know for a fact that I'm going to feel good all over again. I'm going to feel physically stronger, and my mind will be in a state of relaxation.

Our Physical Bodies Must Stay Active

Our physical bodies were not designed for inactivity, they were designed to accomplish many physical challenges, but sometimes, we get lazy and therefore, our bodies will suffer because of our inactivity. Not only our bodies will suffer because of our inactivity, but our minds will suffer and be in danger of contracting many psychological setbacks. When our bodies are weak, due to the lack of physical exercise, it's going to bring us a lot of chronic stress, in other words, they are not going to function in the way they were intended for.

Furthermore, when our bodies are not in a good physical condition, we won't be able to get a good night sleep because of the tremendous tension in the muscles and it is because we are not in a complete state of relaxation. When our immune system gets compromised, our bodies will suffer, and therefore, they will not function properly, they will become weak and we will be struck by diseases.

If we really think about it, we gain absolutely nothing by stressing our minds and our bodies. In our minds, we worry about everything; we worry about little things, we worry about big things and we worry about nothing because we let our imagination run wild, and therefore, we are stressing our bodies unnecessarily. We are a nation of people who worry way too much and for no good reason. It is of great importance that we stop worrying in excess, especially about things which might never happen.

Our physical bodies were designed to overcome many chronic stresses; however, they do need our help. It's important that we take care of our bodies with physical exercises and a healthy diet so that it can stay healthy.

The human body can accomplish many physical tasks, but they also have the capability of healing themselves and it's because they were designed to stay strong and healthy. Our bodies have their own healing mechanisms in place, they have an internal flowing energy that runs along energy meridians and by stimulating that flow of energy, our bodies own healing system is activated. It's unfortunate that we spend our entire lives abusing our bodies by not exercising, sleeping enough and by not eating healthy foods, and may mention that I'm guilty as charged, but I do try my best to keep my body healthy.

In order to be successful in achieving a healthy mind and body, we must stay active, we must find some type of activities that we enjoy doing, for example, working out at the gym with some weight lifting, walking on the treadmill, running in place, and if that is not your thing, then running, walking or hiking will do just find, oh! I almost forgot, for those of you who have a pool, swimming it's an amazing exercise because it will trigger relaxation afterwards.

The important thing to remember here is that we must try to stay active most of the time. However, one thing we must never do is to come up with excuses for not exercising, even when we are surrounded by little people jumping and screaming their heads off, regardless, we must try to do our best to keep our bodies in good physical condition. Furthermore, we can always take our kids to the park for a long walk, it will do wonders for them and for ourselves.

The tremendous benefits that we get from physical activities, will bring us joy and satisfaction. Physical exercise will help our bodies in releasing many happy endorphins and chemicals that will act as painkillers. They are the happy hormones which our bodies need daily. Exercise is not only good to help us improve our sleep, but it's going to help us with minimize our anxiety and it's because our bodies are releasing anti-anxiety hormones or happy hormones when we exercise.

There are many things that we can do to help us achieve a healthy mind and body, for example, we can find time for self-relaxation, we can try to enjoy the things that we do daily a bit more, but most importantly, we must make time for relaxation. We also need to find fun things to do, something that is going to make us feel good on the inside.

We also need time for yoga and meditation which is going to help us to slow down our fast way of life. In fact, I believe that we should start our days with five to fifteen minutes of meditation. Meditating is perhaps the best medicine that anyone can take to cure just about anything that is bothering us. Meditation is going to help us to overcome many psychological issues that we might currently have. Meditation will help us in reducing stress. Meditation will help our bodies to heal and our minds to relax

When our bodies are in a completed state of relaxation, our heart rate will drop, furthermore, our muscles will relax allowing us to think clearly and to be more in control of everything, in other words, it will allow us to be conscious of everything that we are doing, it's going to allow us to use our logic more efficiently, it's going to allow us to solve problems easier and faster. Remember that meditation is going to bring our minds some clarity, in other words, meditation is going to bring us the wisdom that we are lacking right now.

Exercising in moderation can be of great benefit, it will keep our bodies and our brains healthy, but we need to be careful because too much exercise can cause inflammation that will send toxins into our brains and we don't want that. Our bodies are designed to withstand enormous amounts of physical exercises and other activities, however, they do have their limitations too, so therefore, we must be careful not to push them over their limitations. When we push our bodies to perform beyond their capacities, they will start to produce cortisol which is going to stress our brain.

The truth is that we all think better when we take the time to exercise, in fact, physical exercise is one of the forms of therapy for stimulating our brain into active mode. We must always try to ease and focus our minds with pleasurable sounds and exercise. Remember that staying active with a good exercise routine and a good healthy diet is going to bring joyful results not only for our brain, but for our bodies as well.

Chapter Twenty-Seven

Replacing Our Old Habits with New Habits

Breaking our old habits is not an easy thing to do, in fact, it is one of the most difficult and challenging tasks that any human being can overcome. Why is it that we cannot break away from our old habits? Well, you know what people say. Old habits die hard, and it's never been so true because we are used to doing things the old fashion way and sometimes, we don't realize that there are better and faster ways to accomplish the same results. Breaking away from our old habits is something that we must learn to overcome.

We must learn to let go of our old habits by replacing them with new ones. We must go on to bigger and better things because we were born to be achievers, we were not born just to be born, grow older, die and that would be the end of our existence, no, I refuse to believe that. We were born to be value creators, to be inventors, we were born to learn and develop our senses, we were born so that we can learn and develop our true characters, we were born so that we can discover who we are as a person and lastly, we were born so that we can gain new knowledge.

It is without a question that we need to meet our old bad habits face to face and try our best to defect them. To put it in another perspective, we must challenge our old habits. We must conquer them, and we must leave them behind. I can even imagine for a second of the wonderful rewards that will come our way, when we finally learn to defeat our old habits and acquire new ones. I get so excited just thinking about all the possibilities.

We have been living with our old bad habits for our entire lives and that is why they are so powerful and it's because that is all we ever know. These forces of nature cannot easily be conquered, but nevertheless, we must find a way to defect them once and for all. One thing which is going to help us defeat these forces of the universe, and I'm not suggesting that they will be easily defeated, but it's double, you see, everything starts with a strong desire to change and if we have the desire to change, then everything is possible. All that is required on our part is our undivided attention or total concentration, it is only then that we will be on our way to becoming a new person.

The secret here is that we must not over-worry too much about our old habits for now because if we worry about them, then we won't have the time, the energy or the desire to make those changes, so instead, we must focus on creating new habits for ourselves. However, we must never try to make too many changes too fast. We need to start by making small changes at first, one small change a day is a good start because we don't want to overwhelm ourselves with too many changes too fast. If we take our time, we will be successful. We must remember that any changes that we make to our current way of life is going to be better than no changes at all.

We must not waste our precious energy on our old habits because if we continue to focus every bit of our energy on feeding our old habits, then, not much will change for us. Again, we must re-direct our thoughts and our energy towards a new beginning. I'm sure that our old bad habits are going to start disappearing as soon as we begin building new ones.

Our brain is linked to our old thoughts, old ideas, and old habits and that is why our old habits die hard because we are creatures of habit. We must remember that our brain is like a computer which is linked to old information which was previously entered by a computer programmer, however, what happens when there is no new information entered into that computer? Well, nothing will happen because we can only retrieve the same old information. If we want new information, then we must enter new information into it.

The same principle applies when it comes to our brain, currently there's only old information store in it, in other words, is information that was previously recorded by us through our life experiences. Again, our entire past information and knowledge which is stored in our brain was the result of many years of experiences. Throughout our lives we will experience many events which are going to be recorded in our subconscious mind for future use. All these events are new experiences that will be picked up by our senses, and in turn, this information will travel to our brain through our nervous system to be stored in our database.

We must remember that our habits are created by our past experiences, by our environment, by our surroundings, by the places we visit and by the people that we associate ourselves with. Our environment is the source that supplies our brain with new information through our five senses, seeing, hearing, smelling, tasting and feelings. Therefore, we must get creative and do something different every time, something that we have never done before, we must use our imagination and venture out into the unknown. Finally, we need to build new habits so that we don't fall back into stagnation.

It's sad when we become slaves of our old thoughts, our old ideas and our old habits. I see it in many people every single day, and even though I try to help them, sometimes they do not want to hear it, instead, they ignore me as if I was a plague. Oh well! there is absolutely nothing I can do for those people who are not willing to change, willing to find new things to do and willing to find new knowledge.

I really don't see any reason as to why we should become slaves of our old bad habits. I will continue to try and help those people who are willing to learn new things by teaching them that life can be that much more exciting when we discover our own true selves. We need to learn to defect our old bad habits, but the only way that we will be able to accomplish such a task is by creating new habits and by learning to master them. We must not walk the same old path that takes us to the same old place. We must find and create new paths that will take us to new and exciting places that we never been or seen before. We must not walk the path of least resistance; we must find new paths that will take us to new horizons.

It's important to remember that not all of our old habits are bad, in fact, we have some good habits along with a lot of bad habits, but the habits we need to concentrate on the most…are our good habits and not the bad ones. The good habits are the ones which require our total attention. Good habits are worth keeping because they will be the platform, the starting point for creating new habits and creating a new beginning. Again, there is no need to replace our good habits, however, we do need to get rid of our bad habits, the undesirable ones and replace them with new ones.

It's not going to be an easy task for most people, but for those who want to make a change, they will be able to do it, but only by having a ton of determination and courage. If we focus most of our energy on our good habits, we will achieve victory, eventually, and when we do, then the rewards will be more satisfying than we can imagine. Remember that if we apply ourselves, we will be victorious.

A world of caution! In the future we will encounter ourselves face to face with the temptation of reverting back to our old bad habits, however, we must resist such a temptation. We must keep in mind that temptations will be around every corner, however, we must fight it with all our strength and will power.

Again, If someday, we find ourselves wanting to revert back to our habits we must remember that we have come a long way and that we have defected our old bad habits, so we must do it one more time. We must not panic because now we know that we will be able to defect them time after time. We must remember that it is only by repetition that we will be successful.

Okay, now we know that we have found new paths which will be engraved in our mind forever, however, we are not quite done yet because as we travel through new pathways, we will discover even more new pathways, and this in turn will make us even stronger. We must remember that once we master our new habits, they will become permanent habits, they will be encrusted in our mind just like our old habits, however, this time around, we want to keep those new habits forever. Our new habits will be the blueprint by which we will live for the rest of our lives. We must select our new habits carefully, and we will be able to accomplish this task by selecting the type of environment in which we want to live in.

We must create our own world by creating ourselves a clear picture in our minds of the type of life that we desire.

Replacing Our Old Beliefs with New Beliefs

Whether we are consciously aware of it or not, our beliefs make us who we are, they influence our lives in many ways, for example, they influence the way we think, and the way we do things. Our beliefs are something that we perceive, in our own mind to be true, however, it doesn't mean that it's necessarily true. Sometimes we believe what others are telling us because we trust them, but we hope that they are telling us the truth, and sometimes they are, but other times they are not, so we must rely on our intuition to find out what the real truth is, and that is how our beliefs are formed. Our beliefs are formed by what we know. Our old beliefs have the potential to hold us back from evolving into higher beings, and that is a good enough reason for us to question whether our beliefs are the right beliefs. But how do we know if our old beliefs are correct or incorrect? It's actually very simple, we must challenge ourselves to find out if indeed our old beliefs are right or wrong.

It's important that we challenge our beliefs and discard the ones which are not beneficial to us, in other words, we need to get rid of our untrue beliefs and replace them with new beliefs. Most people go through life without ever questioning whether their beliefs are true or not, maybe it's because they think that their beliefs are all correct. Furthermore, they never challenge their own beliefs before, so why would they start now? We know that some of our beliefs will be the right beliefs, which is a good thing for us, however, the rest of them are not going to be the right beliefs. We must keep in mind that our beliefs will determine our happiness, furthermore, they will determine our actions, and the actions we take will determine our future and our lifestyle.

We must challenge our old beliefs from time to time to determine if we are on the right path to happiness. Sometimes our inability to challenge our own beliefs is because of our lack of knowledge. In our current word everything is forever changing, so therefore, our lives are constantly in need of change. We must remember that most of the things that we have done in the past are no longer in line with the new way of thinking,

Changing our old beliefs for new beliefs will allow us to prepare ourselves for the future. Our world is constantly changing so we must keep up with the world, especially, with our technological word. Technology is forever changing, and if we are not willing to change with it, then we will be left behind, and we will suffer because of our unwillingness to change.

We Shouldn't Be Afraid of Failing

We all fail at one time or another, in fact, most of us fail more than we would like to, however, we must come to the realization that failure is a big part of our lives and that there is no way that we can completely avoid failure, sure, sometimes we are going to be successful in accomplish our goals, however, we need to keep in mind that we are going to fail on occasions because we cannot be successful one hundred percent of the time.

Take me for example, I can't remember how many times I have failed in the past and I'm not afraid or ashamed to admitted, in fact, I probably failed thousands of times within my lifetime, furthermore, failure is going to keep happening to all of us because it's something that no matter how hard we try to avoid it, it's going to continue happening because failure is part of our daily lives whether we like it or not.

It sounds as if I'm being somehow negative, but let me assure that it's not the case, on the contrary, I'm always thinking in a positive way, and I'm always hopeful that everything I do is going to be a success, but I'm also aware that things don't always work out as we planned, and therefore, we will fail at times.

We must keep in mind that the only time we will not fail is when we don't take any risks. We mustn't be afraid of failing, and even if we fail time after time, it doesn't mean that we are losers, on the contrary, if we keep on trying and never give up, then we will always going to be winners, regardless of what other people might think. We must remember that the only way to learn is by failing.

I know for a fact that nobody likes to fail. Nobody likes to feel disappointed. Nobody likes to be embarrassed in front of others, however, we must not see failure as something negative, instead, we should see it as an opportunity to learn and start over.

Again, we must keep in mind that there will be the possibility of failure in some of the things that we do, but we must look at those failures as bumps on the road. We should never be afraid of failing, we must never give up on our dreams, we must keep on pushing ourselves until we accomplish what we set out to do.

It's kind of amazing because as I was writing about not giving up, I decided to take a little break from it. I wanted to take a break so that I could rest my eyes, and at the same time clear my mind from clutter. Anyway, as I was resting outside my balcony which is overlooking the pool, I saw a spider web between the rails, and I must admit that it wasn't the first time I saw the same spider web, in fact, I saw it several times before, I know this because for an entire week, I kept on knocking it down with a broom, but the next morning the same spider web reappeared, and I'm assuming that it was the same spider which was rebuilding it.

So, what does this have to do with never giving up? Well, you see, the little spider never gave up, she kept coming back during the night to rebuild her web because that is what spiders do, again, they never give up, furthermore, what would happen if she gave up? She would die of starvation because the web is a way for her to catch her food. So, that just goes to show us that we should never give up either.

Even though the little spider cannot think, she never gives up, she uses her instincts instead and that will prevent her from dying of starvation. The little spider was never afraid of failing, so why should we be afraid of failing. If we really think about it for a minute, failing is only going to make us stronger in the long run. The little spider story was a valuable lesson for me, and it should be for everyone else.

Rich and famous people got what they wanted, not because they were always successful, but because they failed many times before. Every rich and powerful man or woman has gone through failures, in fact, I believe that if they fail and they didn't keep on trying, then, they would not be rich, famous, or powerful. This is the number one reason as to why they became rich and powerful, in other words, they never gave up on making their dreams come true. The man and woman which I am talking about never gave up just because they failed before. Perhaps, they didn't succeed at first, but they never gave up, they kept on pushing until they accomplished what they set out to do. They never took their eyes off from the big prize.

Sometimes the only way to succeed at something is by failing time after time. The man and woman who I am talking about failed many times before they became successful and because of that they turned their failures into success. Sometimes failure is not an option, and when we need to win, then we must win, however, we are not going to win all the time, believe me I have failed at most things which I tried to accomplish in the past, but one thing is for sure, I never gave up.

Nowadays, I continue to push hard for what I believe in, no matter how many roadblocks or bumps I might encounter on the road.

There will be times when we are going to fail, but it's only because we want to fail. You see, if in our minds we have already made the decision to fail, then we will fail for sure, in other words, we will fail before we even try. We all know that success does not come easy, and we also know that sometimes we will fail many times before we can become successful in achieving our goals and dreams.

Furthermore, there will be times when some of our failures will not be totally our fault because sometimes there will be outside forces that we cannot control, in other words, they are forces which will prevent us from achieving our goals. These outside forces, in which we have absolutely nothing to do with, are forces that are imposed upon us by others to prevent us from becoming successful. These outside forces are by design. They are not by pure coincidence. Sometimes we have no other choice, but to put our trust in others, and therefore, we put ourselves in a vulnerable position because we are giving them the power to act on our behalf and most of the time, those individuals will take advantage of our situation.

So, now we understand that there will be circumstances and events which are out of our control, but it doesn't mean that we should stop trying, we just need to be more careful who we trust. When we fail at something or we make a mistake, we must be ready and willing to learn from it, and we must be willing to be thought by others, but only by those people who know how to be successful because they have been there before.

We must remember that there will be no failure for those who try and fail, but there will be great failures for those who never tried. For those who will remain strong in the face of adversity, their faith is never going to be destroyed by others. Remember that if you think that your life is going to be a failure, then most likely, it will be a failure, but on the other hand, if you think your life is going to be successful, then most likely, it's going to be. We must never drive ourselves to poverty and misery only because of our past failures, rather, we need to drive ourselves to new heights, and we can accomplish this task by learning from our mistakes.

Failure Can Be a Good Thing for Kids

Often, our behavior as adults it's nothing more than a reflection of what we have learned in the past from different people, and it all started way back, since the very beginning of our childhood. We were influenced by our parents, our teachers, and by our environment. Most often than not, we blame one of the parents whenever our kids are misbehaving, but the true reality is that both parents are responsible for the education of their own children, they are both equally one hundred percent responsible.

Most parents try to teach their children good values which are also reinforced through our school education system. As parents, we hope that whatever we teach our children will be enough, but unfortunately sometimes that is not good enough because our children will be influenced by other kids in a good way, but also in a bad way. We must understand that each of our children will be different. They will develop their own personalities, or their own characters whether we like it or not, but most often than not our children will turn out okay.

There is an abundance of good things that we can teach our children as they grow up, for example, we can teach them good values, how to express themselves, how to take constructive criticism, how to solve problems, how to develop their hidden abilities, how to be social, how to be resilient, and how to have integrity, but most importantly, we can teach them that failing is a good thing and that they can learn from their mistakes. We need to teach our children from early on that if they fail at something that it's going to be okay. When parents allow their children to fail, they will learn to overcome adversity by themselves, they will learn how to deal with stressful situations, anxiety, and they will learn to conquer their fears, Well, eventually.

We need to remind our children that if we did not fail, that there would be no opportunity to learn from our mistakes, and therefore, there would be no recovery or progress. We must teach our children that sometimes failure is a good thing and that they need to accept constructive criticism because when gracefully accepted, they will be able to learn how to handle feedback later in life. As parents, we need to teach our kids to be proud of themselves when they try something new and fail. We need to teach them to be honest with themselves and others as well. We need to teach them about respect and teach them about sharing their toys with other children.

One thing that we must never do as adults, is to treat our children as if they were already adults, furthermore, we must never rule our children with an iron fist because it's only going to make them resentful towards us later in life. We must never give them everything they want, instead, we can teach them that if they want something, they need to earn it by doing some chores. Now! Those are good values.

There must be some type of balance when raising our children. We need to make sure that we treat them with respect and listen to everything they have to say because it's very important for them to know that parents are listening.

Furthermore, as parents, we must never lose our cool every time our kids want something, instead, we must learn to deal with our kids' needs in a different way than we are accustomed to. For example, as a grandparent, whenever my granddaughter wants something that perhaps she shouldn't have at that time, I play a little reverse psychology with her, for instant, whenever she want to go to a fun place and I know it's kind of far, like the zoo, I tell her that instead we should go to the park which is closer, and by the way, she joys going to the park also. Furthermore, when I mention that it will more fun at the park instead of the zoo, she gets super excited because she likes the park, but she is not the only one getting excited about it, I must get excited about it too because If I am not excited about it, then she is not going to be excited either. Remember that if we make it sound exciting for kids and tell them that we will have lots of fun, they will respond accordingly. Furthermore, as soon as she agrees to go to the park, she has already forgotten about going to the zoo. It's not about tricking her, instead, it's about getting out of a sticky situation because it's not possible at that time.

Being a parent is completely different than being a grandparent, you see, as a grandparent we have a whole life of experiences under our belts per say. We have already dealt with our own kids. We already had the experience about which things worked or not work with kids. Furthermore, as grandparents we learned that we need tons of patience when dealing with kids, but as young parents we are inexperienced, and we have yet to master the art of patience. Patience is the key to everything.

Constructive Criticism

It is a well-known fact that most people do not accept constructive criticism very well, and it's totally understandable, however, constructive criticism has a place in our society, in the workplace, in our homes, and in our social life. Normally, when we get criticized, our pride gets hurt, but other than that, there isn't a good enough reason not to accept constructive criticism from others. How are we going to learn new things if we cannot handle or accept constructive criticisms? I am aware that constructive criticism is a good thing, not only for myself, but for everyone else because it is going to allow us to learn at a faster pace, and at the same time, we will gain valuable knowledge. We must remember that if we learn to accept constructive criticism, we will become mentally stronger as time goes by. Furthermore, we must get rid of our pride if we want to become successful in business and in life.

I am a firm believer in accepting constructive criticism, and rarely do I get upset when someone points out my mistakes or points out that I am acting foolishly. I know that sometimes it is not a good feeling being criticized by someone, however, I try my best not to get upset when someone criticizes me, especially when I know that they are in the right. Now! When people are trying to fabricate lies or they are trying to rattle my cage, then it's a different story, but even then, I always try to hold my composure because I know that getting upset is not in my best interest.

Again, constructive criticism has a place at home and at work and we should never get mad or get offended by it. We must learn to accept criticism from others because it is going to improve our performance at work and at home. If we want to become good future leaders, then we must be able to accept constructive criticism with grace.

Constructive criticism is something that we need to learn and embrace, after all, it's something beneficial that we can use to give us a competitive edge at work and in our social life. We must remember that constructive criticism is only another way for people to give us feedback about the things that we are doing wrong. As human beings, we would like to think that we are doing everything right, but unfortunately that is not always the case, and if we don't take the time to listen to others, then how do we really know if whatever we are doing is indeed correct? Again, nobody likes to be criticized by other people, after all, we have our pride, however, if we don't learn to accept constructive criticism then we are never going to be promoted at work, in other words, we will never be able to make the leap into a higher form of life.

Sometimes we will feel as if we are being attacked with negative criticism because we think that it's something personal, and it might be true, however, we must keep in mind that most constructive criticism we get from others will not be personal, especially criticism from our bosses. We must keep in mind that as a professional, we must be able to take criticism, well, that is if we want to get promoted into a higher position.

Our first natural response when we are being criticized by others is to put our guard up, we get defensive, we get angry and sometimes we want to physically attack those who are giving us feedback. We must learn to refrain ourselves from becoming agitated or becoming violent, we must learn to calmly accept constructive criticism from others no matter what. Constructive criticism is just that... Constructive criticism and if not done with malice, we should accept it as just that...constructive criticism and nothing more. We must come to the realization that constructive criticism it's only going to allow us to become stronger in every way.

We must remember that constructive criticism is going to add tremendous value to our lives, it's going to benefit us in many ways, it's going to improve our social skills and our productivity is going to increase by leaps and bounds, both at work and at home. When we learn to accept constructive criticism, we will benefit ourselves tremendously, and we will improve our relationship with others as well. Remember that criticism is a good thing because it's only going to enrich our future and our lives with new opportunities.

Chapter Twenty-Eight

Delicious Superfoods for the Brain

We all know that if we want to keep our bodies strong, we need to eat healthy foods. But what about our brain, does it deserve the same attention? You bet it does, in fact, it probably needs more attention than our bodies do because our brain is where everything starts, after all, without our brains our bodies will be nothing more than just an empty body. We need to eat some nutritious foods which are going to keep our bodies strong and our minds sharp for many years to come.

The following are just a few delicious foods that we should be eating to accomplish a healthy body and mind.

Blueberries

Blueberries are delicious, sweet and they are very nutritious, they will help us to protect our bodies and our brains from oxidative stress. Blue berries may also help to reduce some age-related effects such as Alzheimer's or dementia diseases. Furthermore, blue berries will protect our cholesterol in our blood from becoming oxidized.

Blueberries are labeled by many people as super foods. They are low in calories, and they are rich in some antioxidants, but the most potent antioxidant compound in blueberries is in the family of polyphenols antioxidants called flavonoids. Antioxidants will protect the human body from free radicals. Free radicals are a type of molecule which are very unstable, they can cause chaos in the human body by damaging our cells. These free radicals also contribute to aging and many other diseases. Blueberries also contain fiber, vitamin C, vitamin K, manganese, and other nutrients.

Wild Salmon

Wild salmon, or Alaskan salmon is rich in omega 3. Omega 3 is crucial for our health because It has fatty acids, which are essential for brain function. Omega-3 contains anti-inflammatory substances. Alaskan salmon also contains vitamin B12, Vitamin B6, Pantothenic Acid (vitamin B5), Niacin (vitamin B3), Riboflavin (vitamin B2) Thiamin (vitamin B1), Selenium, Phosphorus, potassium, and magnesium.

Nuts and Seeds

Nuts and Seeds are packed with vitamins, minerals, and fats. Nuts will help in lowering our LDL cholesterol levels, they are also rich in fiber. Nuts and seeds is a good source of vitamin E, but we must also remember that nuts are loaded with calories, so we must be careful not to consume too much.

The following is a list of nuts and seeds that we should be eating.
1. Almonds
2. Cashews
3. Brazilian Nuts
4. Flax Seeds
5. Pumpkin Seeds
6. Sunflower seeds.
7. Pistachios
8. Peanuts

Peanuts

Peanuts are rich in energy, they contain nutrients, minerals, antioxidants, and vitamins. Peanuts contain monounsaturated fatty acids that will help with lowering LDL which is bad cholesterol and instead helps with our HDL which is a good type of cholesterol, which will prevent coronary disease and strokes. Peanuts also contain a source of dietary protein, amino acids which are essential for growth and development. Peanuts contain a high concentration of polyphenolic antioxidants which might help to reduce the risk of stomach cancer. Peanuts also contain "resveratrol" another type of polyphenolic antioxidant which will help protect against cancers, heart diseases, generative nerve disease, for example, Alzheimer's disease, and viral-fungal infections. Peanuts are also an excellent source of vitamin E which helps to protect the body from free radicals. Peanuts also contain several B vitamins. Like, riboflavin, niacin, thiamin, pantothenic acid, vitamin B6, and folates. RDI of niacin helps with the blood flow to the brain. And finally, peanuts are rich in several sources of minerals, for example, copper, manganese, potassium, calcium, iron, magnesium, zinc, and selenium.

Pumpkin Seeds

Pumpkin seeds are loaded with magnesium. Which is vital for converting food into energy.

Avocados

Avocados are a fatty fruit that contains monounsaturated fats which is good for healthy blood flow and lowering blood pressure. But be careful with the calories. Recommended 1/4 to 1/2 daily.

Eggs

The yolk is rich in choline, a B vitamin nutrient.

Red Wine

Red wine has some good benefits, it has antioxidants that might prevent coronary artery disease which is a condition that leads to heart attacks. Antioxidants might increase your HDL cholesterol which is the good cholesterol. Red wine must be consumed in moderation.

Kale

Kale is a member of the cabbage family and it is the king of all the healthy greens. Kale is perhaps one of the most nutritious foods on the planet, it's loaded with many beneficial compounds. Kale contains vitamin A, vitamin K, vitamin C, vitamin B6, manganese, calcium, copper, potassium, magnesium, vitamin B1, vitamin B2, vitamin B3, iron and phosphorus. Kale contains truly little fat.

Coffee

There are some good benefits that we get from drinking coffee, for example, it can improve cognition by improving short-term memory and speeding up the reaction time. Coffee will aid in weight loss, it will boost our energy level, it will reduce the chances of diabetes, it will increase liver protection and it might prevent certain types of cancers. Consuming coffee with moderation will decrease the chances of developing Alzheimer's and Dementia in elderly people, drinking coffee will lower the chances of getting affected by Parkinson's disease.

Whole Grains

Brown Rice-Whole Wheat Bread-Quinoa-Bran Flakes-Oats, and barley. Boost cardiovascular health.

Beets

Reduces inflammation and they are high in cancer protecting antioxidants which helps to get rid of toxins in our blood

Bone Broth

Boosts our immune system, improves joint health, and food allergies.

Broccoli

Broccoli has high levels of vitamin K and choline, it is also rich in vitamin C.

Coconut Oil

A natural anti-inflammatory. Suppresses the cells responsible for inflammation. It helps with memory loss as we get older.

Dark Chocolate

Dark chocolate is full of flavanols, powerful antioxidants and anti-inflammatory properties. Make sure it is 70 percent cocoa.

Extra Virgin Olive Oil

Contains antioxidants known as polyphenols. It helps to Improves learning, it improves memory and reverses the age and disease related changes. Helps against ADDLs, these are proteins that are toxic to the brain that induces Alzheimer's.

Toxic Relationships

As human beings, we are becoming more health-conscious about our toxic external environment than ever before. We know that is becoming more and more toxic as the years go by, in addition, we are becoming more health-conscious about the type of foods that we are consuming which are toxic, but yet, many people do not realize that they are in a toxic relationship, but why is that? Why can we not learn to recognize when, indeed, we are in such a relationship? Well, to the best of my knowledge nobody likes to be in a toxic relationship, yet, I see it all the time and it's because as we were growing up, we learn many things from our parents and teachers, however, no one educated us on how not to be a jerk in a relationship, so it's up to us to figure out on our own whether or not we are in a toxic relationship.

Nobody deserves to be in a toxic relationship. A toxic relationship will create many damaging health effects, for example, emotional stress, depression, and anxiety which can weaken our entire immune system, therefore, creating many physical medical problems, like heart diseases, including heart attacks, strokes and even dying. Those are good enough reasons not to be in an unhealthy relationship, but wait, there is more, an unhealthy relationship has the power to suck the life out of most people, it has the power to drain our physical energy. It has the power to completely drain us emotionally and leave us feeling empty on the inside, in addition, our peace of mind and the trill that we once had for life is going to diminish tremendously.

A toxic relationship has other negative side effects, for example, it will prevent us from becoming the person that we were meant to be, in other words, it will prevent us from growing and evolving as human beings. We must learn to let go of any unhealthy relationships because life is too short to be wasted on toxic relationships which can make us miserable and unhappy for the rest of our lives. It is always better to get out of any toxic relationship than to continue living with bad company. We must remember that the true purpose of life is to find true happiness, and therefore, we must never waste the one and only opportunity that we might have to find happiness.

When we think of a toxic relationship, the first thing that comes to mind is a relationship between a man and a woman, a husband and a wife, or a boyfriend and girlfriend, However, there are other types of toxic relationships out there, for example, parent/kids relationships, toxic friendships, and occupational or toxic coworker's relationships. Sometimes human tendency is to unconsciously seek toxic relationships, perhaps because as children, we were in a toxic relationship with our own parents, and as we grew older, that relationship was carried over to our adulthood. Those past experiences will stay in our minds forever, and as adults, sometimes we unknowingly stepped right into a toxic relationship because that is all we ever knew.

I'm going to agree that most toxic relationships in our society could have been avoided, however, there are many reasons as to why we enter into a toxic relationship, for example, we are too young to know any better, we don't have the experience, we are blinded by love and we all know it. Love is blind. Okay, so that was then, but what about now that we are older, how can we avoid falling into a toxic relationship? Well, one of the things which is going to help us to avoid falling into such a relationship is our "self-awareness" or being able to recognize any psychological disorders in the other person which we are so crazy about. Even though we are not trained to diagnose the imperfections that other people might have, there is still something that we can do, and that is to always pay attention to how that person makes us feel. For example, does that person make us feel that we are worth it, does that person make us laugh, does that person make us feel comfortable within our own skin, furthermore, do we feel relaxed, happy and content? These are good qualities that we should be looking for in someone that we are romantically involved with.

Now! if on the other hand the person who we are romantically involved with makes us feel uncomfortable or uneasy, or critiques everything that we do, then most likely that person is going to be a control freak.

Sometimes people who have a problem with relationships are not aware that they have such a problem, in other words, they are not self-aware of the situation, they don't recognize that: indeed, there is a problem with their relationship. Another reason as to why people are toxic in their relationships is because that is all they ever known and it's also possible that others were constantly putting them down, they were always being judged by others, and as a result their confidence diminished to an all-time low

There are other reasons as to why a person is toxic in their relationship with their partners, family, friends, or coworkers. For example, SELFISHNESS-selfish people do not care enough about their partners; it is all about them and almost never about the other person. Selfish people do not care about anyone else but themselves because they are blinded by their egos. CONTROL FREAKS-control freaks normally do not acknowledge other people's feelings. AGGRESSIVE-when aggressive people are confronted about their problems, they instantly get very defensive.

Normally, when someone is in a toxic relationship it is easily spotted by others, however, most often than not, people who are in toxic relationships are not self-aware of the situation. So, are you in a toxic relationship? Perhaps it's hard for you to distinguish between a normal relationship and a toxic relationship because you have been in such a relationship for a very long time and you don't realize it or perhaps you are aware of it, but you don't know how to get out of such situation, or perhaps you became so accustomed to it that you no longer care.

Again, how do you know when you are in a toxic relationship? Well, there are many signs which will indicate whether you are in such a relationship, for example, there are signs of aggression from your partner, there's physical violence, mental abuse or emotional abuse, there's jealousy, there's lying, there's criticism, and there's cheating. When you are constantly frightened or intimidated by your partner, you will lose yourself, you will lose yourself steam and eventually, you will lose sight of who you are as a person. You must never let this happen to you.

Moreover, there are other signs which are going to let you know whether we are in a toxic relationship, for example, excessive rage or anger, blaming, avoidance, negativity, resentment, and uncaring.

All these are signs that will indicate that we are in a toxic relationship which is going to prevent us from finding happiness. Furthermore, a toxic relationship is going to make us feel as if we do not belong, as if we are not enough, it is going to make us feel unworthy and unhappy. We are all capable of showing signs of aggression and many other unpleasant bad behaviors at one time or another, and it doesn't matter if we are male or female, we must refrain from inducing the people we love with any type of physical or emotional pain, well, that is if we really and honestly love that them. I'm not saying that we should give up on our relationships with our significant others, in fact, we should always try to work out our differences between one another, after all, was that not the intent when two people decided to join their lives?

Furthermore, we must do our best to try and workout any toxic relationship which we might have with our cow-workers, our bosses, our family members and our friends, but if that doesn't work, then, we must move on. We must remember that if we have been in a toxic relationship for a long time and nothing has changed over the years, then most likely nothing will change in the future. Sometimes no matter what we do or say, things are never going to change, so therefore, there is no point in staying together any longer.

In everyone's lives there is always something worth fighting for, however, in this situation, staying and fighting will be a losing battle and it is not in our best interest. There is absolutely nothing wrong admitting that we are in a toxic relationship and that we have nothing worth holding on to.

We all have the power to decide on our own, whether we want to continue living in a toxic relationship for the rest of our lives. We have the power to decide if we are going to continue living a miserable life or we will try to get out of that unhealthy relationship and try to find happiness somewhere else. We must remember that the real purpose of life is to find happiness. We deserved so much more out of life than what we have right now.

Signs of a Non-Toxic Relationship

Everyone knows that no relationship is ever perfect, but we also know that any normal and healthy relationship is going to make us feel good inside, at least most of the time. When we have a normal relationship, whether is a romantic relationship, a friendly relationship or family relationship, we always want the best for that person, we want to raise their spirits and cheer them up when they are feeling down. We always want to have their backs no matter how complicated our lives might be. In a healthy relationship there must be loyalty and trust between two people. We must trust that our partners or friends will do the right thing for us and vice versa. Healthy relationships are the ones which is going to bring out the best in everyone.

We must remember that if we want a relationship to work, then we need to develop our communication skills between us. Good communication skills is perhaps one of the most important attributes which both parties need to have because without them, there will be nothing but chaos and disappointments.

In a healthy relationship, there must be trust in each other because without that trust, there will be nothing to hold people together. I really believe that when two people lose the trust and respect for one another, they will lose everything else, they will lose the love, they will lose the good feelings sensations of being in love and when this happens, there will not be much to hold on to. Once that trust is broken there will be not much left for us to do to improve our situation, nothing is ever going to work because the trust and the respect that we once had for each other does not exist anymore.

Remember that there's got to be mutual respect and honesty between two people who love each other in order for that relationship to work. Furthermore, without honesty there will be no trust and we all know that honesty is always and without a doubt, the best policy." There must be openness with each other, there must be freedom to express each other's feelings and without any criticism or intimidation from the other person, furthermore, there's got to be equality for both parties. Both parties must share the responsibilities one hundred percent because that is why people call it a partnership.

When there is true love between two people, there will be no anger. There will be no tension, there will be no criticism, there will be no cheating, there will be no jealousy, there will be no disrespect, there will be no misunderstanding, and there will be no dissatisfaction, instead, there will be mutual respect, honesty, trust, equality, support, fairness, good communication skills and encouragement. We always know when we are in a healthy relationship because we always try to make each other as happy as possible, and we not only say it with words, but we also show it with action. Furthermore, when we show it with action, we can rekindle our love for each other and at the same time bring back those warm feelings of love which we use to have for each other when we first meet. We must try to please each other, but with mutual respect. Furthermore, we must respect each other's personal interest, hobbies, opinions, and friends. We must not get jealous of each other's friends nor be so critical either.

In a healthy relationship there will be no retreating into isolation and loneliness when things get rough, rather, we need to feed off each other's strength, instead putting up walls between us. We must leave our selfishness behind because not everything is about me, instead, it's about both of us, it's about you and me.

It's said that people's happiness or unhappiness is reflected by their facial expressions, but it's people's eyes which will tell us a lot about the person's state of mind, for example, we will be able to see people's expressions of love, happiness, and contentment by looking in their eyes, unfortunately, we will be able to see unhappiness and sadness in their eyes as well.

I prefer to surround myself with positive people who will lift my spirit up when I'm feeling down, people who I admire and respect, people who are naturally happy and outgoing, people who will make me laugh, people who are fun to be around.

Any toxic relationship, whether that relationship is with our spouses, friends, or coworker most likely is going to bring us down because any toxic relationships will be physically and mentally exhausting, it will drain us of our precious energy.

Loving Feelings

Love is the pivotal stimulation for our brain; without those loving feelings of good sensation, our mental strength is going to diminish as time goes by, we will be less capable of coping with every day difficult situations without those loving feelings of good sensations, and that is why it's so important for us to not let our love for life fade away. It's important that we bring back those "loving feelings and devotion" that we used to have for each other. We must always stay vigilant about our feelings and emotions because it's easy for us to lose our focus in the middle of our chaotic life.

Love is the stimulation which our brain needs in order to survive, and when that stimulation is missing, our brain will not be able to trigger other emotions. We need to consistently remind ourselves that we must stimulate our brain with new excitement on a day by day basis, for example, we can think about warm feelings of love about our families, our friends and humanity. We must not let those feelings of joy and happiness get away from us because, if we do, we will live a life full of regrets and unhappiness.

We must have a purpose in life, and we do, however, it's not all about accumulations of materialistic things, money and power, instead, it should be about finding ourselves, it should be about finding out who we really are as a person, in addition, we must have the desire to thrive, the desire to love and the desire to be loved by someone.

We need more of the good things which life has to offer us, for example, feelings of love, and warm feelings of good sensations. We must never forget why we are here on this planet. We are here to find ourselves, we are here to grow as human beings, we are here to find happiness, and we are here to explore and experience many wonderful feelings of love.

Life is all about experiencing many new things, for example, finding love for the first time or experiencing the feeling of joy when we achieve some of our goals. We must explore our choices and our desires. We must seek new ways to make our lives more enjoyable for ourselves and our love-ones. We must stimulate our brain with new ideas, but at the same time, we must learn to enjoy the things that we have right now.

We should never be ashamed to wish for a better life for ourselves, and may I remind everyone that it is not a sin, however, we must do it with honesty and hard work. God never said that we must be born, grow up and die without having to experience many wonderful things. God did not create us so that we can suffer, rather, he created us so that we can grow as human beings, and at the same time, learn and experience many wonderful things. Again, I believe that God put us here on this earth for a purpose, and that is to learn, grow, build our characters, and learn from our many mistakes.

I know that at any given moment, we are all capable of triggering our capacity to love again and at the same time bring back those feelings of love, feelings of compassion and feelings of enjoyment that we use to have for someone. All these wonderful feelings are beautiful and precious moments that we must bring back into our lives, in fact, we need more of those wonderful warm feelings of love in our lives. We do not need feelings of negativity which is going to make us feel bad about ourselves.

Chapter Twenty-Nine

Our Wondering and Inquisitive Mind

I believe that every human being on the face of the planet has an inquisitive mind, but what is an inquisitive mind? An inquisitive mind is a curious mind, one which is constantly asking questions, one that is always searching for answers, and it is obvious that; the more we ask, the more we will know. It is only logical that we let our minds wander into the unknown because we are forever curious about everything. Our inquisitive minds want to know how everything works. Our minds have an insatiable curiosity to learn new things every day, in fact, it is one of the biggest reasons which keep us going, and therefore, we will never stop asking questions.

When did all this curiosity begin? Well, it all started way back, when we were first born. As babies everything was new to us, so we started to develop a desire to explore, to learn, to hear, and to see new things, we were always looking around, exploring our surroundings. Our brains were constantly searching and wondering about all the new things that we were seeing, hearing, touching, and feeling.

Scientists say that in the first three years of our lives we learned the most because our minds are in the developing stages. Scientists also believed that we stop learning at the age of eighteen years old, however, scientists recently concluded that our human brain never stops learning after all, even as we get older our brain is capable of learning new things. Perhaps we learn at a slower pace, but nevertheless, we keep on learning new things, even at the age of one hundred years old and beyond, and I must admit, I'm completely in agreement with them because I'm sixty years old and I'm still learning new things every single day because my desire to learn is never going to die. I am always looking for something new to experiment with and it's because I have intrapersonal intelligence, meaning that I want to know everything that there is to know.

I am not surprised that we have a wondering mind, we were born to be explorers, we were born to challenge our minds on a day by day basis. Now we know that ever since we were babies, our minds started to wonder, constantly asking questions, noticing many new things within our surroundings. We were forever asking the proverbial questions, "what is this, what is that" and how does it work? Some people say that having a wondering mind is not a good thing; they say that having a wondering mind is the enemy of concentration, they say that it can get us in trouble, and they are partially correct, however, it's not a bad thing, as long as we don't let our minds wonder into undesirable or unpleasant places.

If we have dreams of accomplishing our personal goals, then we need to have an inquisitive mind because it's the only way that we will accomplish most of our goals and desires, furthermore, without a wondering mind, we will never be able to accomplish much of anything.

When we stop wondering or stop dreaming, we will be diminishing our brain capacity and diminishing our abilities to learn new things, so again, we need to let our mind wonder into the unknown. We need to feed our minds new information by asking lots of questions, because at the end, the rewards will be many. We must always keep our minds sharp, but the only way for us to accomplish such a task is by feeding our mind new information every single day, however, we need to make sure that such information is the right information.

We need to remind ourselves that we need to occasionally stop, take a break and give our minds a break, furthermore, if we allow our wondering mind to rest, then it's going to allow us to put our thoughts back in order. Again, we need to give our minds a break every now and then. Furthermore, we must never put our minds in a state of chaos, confusion, and distress.

It is of great importance that we keep on challenging our minds throughout the decades because it is going to allow our minds to stay young and healthy, but the only way that we are going to accomplish such a task is by learning new things every single day, for example, we can put puzzle pieces together; this is a tremendous mind game which is going to help our minds to stay sharp for a long time and it's because we are stimulation our brain to think in many different directions. Remember that when we challenge our minds to think and experience new things, and in return, we will be allowing our brains to build new brain cells, and that is quite an exciting thing for me.

Some people's minds are always sharp because they have jobs which requires them to do plenty of thinking throughout the day, they are constantly working, and therefore, they are allowing their brains to create new brain cells, furthermore, they are helping their brains and bodies to stay young and healthy for a longer period of time then those who have jobs, but are not require to do a lot of thinking. For those people who have jobs which does not require a lot of thinking, do not panic, because you too can have a sharp mind, but only if you put your mind into action. Remember that you can let your mind wonder into the unknown anytime, anywhere, in other words, it does not need to be at work.

We must stimulate our minds with mental exercises, but we must make it a priority to challenge our minds on a day to day basis. We must remember that our wondering minds are nothing more than our brain in action.

To better understand how the human mind works, we first need to know that there are two types of thoughts running through our minds. The first type of thoughts which we find ourselves experiencing from time to time are called "stimulus-dependent thoughts" or (SDTs).

Dependent thoughts are the ones which are triggered by individual tasks, in other words, all our attention is focused on solving a specific task, furthermore, our minds are completely engaged in solving that particular problem, and therefore, our minds have no time to wonder off somewhere else. Again, our stimulus-dependent thoughts or focus thoughts are thoughts which are completely engaged in a single task, such as cutting the lawn or changing the oil in our cars.

Now, the second type of thoughts going through our minds are "stimulus-independent thoughts" or (SITs). Our stimulus independent thoughts do not have a complete focus point, in other words, it doesn't not concentrating on any specific task for too long and that is why our minds wonders off from place to place or from topic to topic and this is when we must be aware and not let our minds wonder or day dream indefinitely. It is a well-known fact that we spend about fifty percent of our time daydreaming or letting our minds wonder off.

I actually enjoy letting my mind wonder off into the unknown from time to time, in fact, I do it all the time, and maybe the reason I do it so much is because I know how to control it, I know that I have total control of what my mind is doing, well, most of the time. For example, during the day, I try to use stimulus dependent thoughts, I am so focused on what I am doing that I hardly have time to let my mind wonder off. Now! at nighttime is a completely different story, I struggle a little bit trying to fall asleep and it is because I let my mind wonder off into different directions. Sometimes I forget that I have the power to control my thoughts, it might take me an hour or two, but eventually I am able to shut down my mind from wondering off. I completely shut my mind off by putting my mind into blank mode, in other words, I think about nothing. Furthermore, when I can't control my thoughts fast enough, then I turn my attention to something else, for example, I concentrate on watching television because it will help me take my mind off from wondering, and I must say that it works tremendously well for me, at least most of the time.

Our wondering minds can be a blessing, but only if we are thinking about pleasant thoughts and not unpleasant thoughts. Our thoughts must be pleasant and happy thoughts because it is obvious that happy thoughts are better than unhappy thoughts. If we must let our minds wonder off, then we must let them wonder off into a land of pleasant thoughts and not the land of unhappy thoughts because people who let their minds wonder about pleasant thoughts will be happier than those who don't, so keep that in mind, and besides, who wants to think of unpleasant thoughts? I know I am don't.

What Are We Passionate About?

It seems to me that most people are passionate about something, however, more than fifty percent of the people on our planet are unhappy with their current way of life. Some people are unhappy with their jobs and that will translate into being unhappy at home as well. We must remember that if we are unhappy with our jobs or our current way of life that we have options, and even though sometimes we don't like changes, it's important for us to turn our lives around. Well, that is if we want to find happiness. So, what are you most passionate about? Most of us have hobbies that we like to do after work or on the weekends, but what about you; do you have any hobbies that you enjoy doing? Most people are passionate about something, for instant, becoming a great athlete, a singer, or an artist.

Take me for example, I am passionate about many things, I am passionate about photography. I also have a passion for writing and even though I am not a career writer per say, I still love to write, I have a passion for reading books on different topics. Furthermore, being a professional landscape photographer allows me to further develop a taste for many types of art as well. These are just a few examples of the things that I love to do or that I'm passionate about. As you can see, I am passionate about many things, but most importantly, I am passionate about life itself.

When people have personal goals which they want to accomplish, it means that they are passionate about something, furthermore, people who are passionate about something will live longer, plus the fact that they will be much happier doing the things that like. Being passionate about something is important in life because it gives us the motivation to thrive and to do better for ourselves. People who are passionate about something will wake up earlier than most people, not because they have too, but because they will be excited about doing the things which they love to do, for example, going to work to do a job which they like. Passionate people are always willing to do more than what they are asked to do. Passionate people always work harder at whatever they do, they also have the courage and the determination to go after the things they want.

It is worth mentioning that in life, there are the doers and the non-doers, but sadly enough, there are people who spend their entire lives daydreaming not knowing what their true passions are. Perhaps they don't realize that they are living a boring life. A life without much enjoyment, a life without much excitement or a life without much passion for anything. We must ask ourselves the following questions "Is this the type of life that I want to live for the rest of my life, a life full of unhappiness?" Perhaps we are not totally unhappy with our current way of life right now, but at the same time, we are not as happy as we should be. If we were a little more passionate about the things that we do, our lives would be more exciting, not only for ourselves, but for the entire family as well.

Again, If we are currently unhappy about the way we are living our lives, then we must do some soul searching, and if we decide that we want to make a change in our lives and follow our true passion, then we must arm ourselves with the burning desire and passion in order to succeed.

It took me many years to finally discover what my true passions were, but once I did, I never looked back. I was not living my life as it was meant to be. I was not always unhappy, but at the same time, I was not always happy either, so I decided to make a change in the way I was living my life, and so I did.

The first thing that we need to do is to find out what is going to make us happy in the future and then go do it. We need to approach life with a new attitude and from a different perspective. I believe that everyone is passionate about something, take me for example, I'm passionate about everything that I do, no matter how big or insignificant it might seem, I'm passionate about my family, my friends, I'm passionate about becoming healthier by exercising more often, I'm passionate about reading as many books as possible because reading is good for the soul, and it makes me feel good about myself plus the fact that I'm constantly learning new things. Furthermore, I'm passionate about nature, and recently I rediscovered my passion for writing, even though I always wanted to write a book, I actually never had the opportunity to follow my passion for writing until now, so now I'm doing it.

You too can follow your own dreams; however, you need to find out what your true passions are. Now, how are you going to find out what those passions are, and how are you going to accomplish such a task? Well, the first thing that you need to do is to never tell yourself that you don't want to try new things because trying new things is going to help you discover what your true passions are, furthermore, you must never tell yourself that you don't want to explore or visit new places, because you will never know where is going to lead you. By trying new things or exploring new places you might be able to discover one of your passions, but you must remember that if you don't try new things, then you will never be able to find out.

I used to be the type of person that did not want to try new things, visit new places or meet other people and It was not because I was lazy, rather, it had to do more with the fact that my anxiety didn't allow me to do much of anything. You see, I used to think that if I went to a new place which I never been before, I thought to myself that I was going to be bored, little did I know back then that I was missing on lot's of fun adventures, so I decided that I was going to conquer my fears and my anxiety, so after a few years of trying different things, I was able to conquer most of my fears and anxiety, and as a result, I was able to visit new places, I was able to experience new emotions, new experiences and new trills. From then on, I started enjoying life to its fullest. Doing something new and meeting other people made me rediscover my true self. I will never say no to visiting new places and trying new things because we never know what we will encounter.

I will give you another example of how your life can change forever. Let's talk about my passion for photography, you see, in landscape and wildlife photography, you can't say that you don't want to go back and visit a place where you have been before because as I previously said, every day is a new day full of wondering surprises, in other words, no day is going to be the same, especially when it has to do with photography, you will always find something new to photograph. I currently live in California and even though I used to think that there wasn't a whole lot to photograph, other than some beautiful beaches, but guess what? I must admit that I was wrong for thinking in such a negative way. I found out that there is plenty of landscapes and wildlife to photograph, we have the golden gate bridge, the redwoods, Yosemite, we have waterfalls, we have beautiful sunsets, but that is just the beginning. I must have been delirious for thinking that there was not much to photograph. You see, I learned that there was plenty to photograph in my backyard than I realized. I was able to use my imagination and as a result my eyes were completely open forever.

I will give you another example of how each day is always full of wonderful surprises. You see, there is a small pond in the middle of a golf course followed by a small lake in the town where I currently live which is near Sacramento Ca. Every time I go there, I find new wildlife to photograph, some days the only wild life I see is the usual ducks, and it's because they are there all the time, but sometimes I find Snowy Egrets, Blue Herons, Green Herons, Black Phoebes, Turtles, and even Mongooses. But guess what? One day I went there and I wasn't expecting to find much of anything, however, to my surprise, I encounter all of them at the same time, the Ducks were there as usual, the Snowy Egrets, the Blue Herons, the Green Herons, the Black Phoebes, the Mongooses, and the Turtles, and not only a couple turtles, there were roughly eight or nine of them.

I saw the turtles resting on the rock absorbing some of the sun heat as usual, everywhere I looked there were turtles resting on different rocks. Some rocks were occupied by two turtles and some rocks were occupied by three turtles, they must have been family, perhaps a male, female and their baby, anyway, all the turtles were sunbathing on different rocks, it was such a joy for me. I got to photograph more wild- life in one day than the previous two or three years. It was an exciting day for me because I got to photograph plenty of wildlife. My granddaughter was with me that day, and she enjoyed it as much as I did, she even snapped a few pictures herself.

So, you see, just when you think that things cannot get any better, they do, you just never know what you will encounter. This experience taught me a good lesson, it taught me that we should never miss an opportunity to explore something new and exciting every single day. It's all about how we approach life, if we think we will be bored when we go to a new place, then we will be bored, but on the other hand, if we think we will have fun, then most likely, we will have fun. We must always stay positive because every day is a new day, every day is a different day, every day is beautiful and full of wonderful surprises. We must approach life with enthusiasm, with passion, and with hope. Furthermore, we must never disregard all the little and enjoyable things that life has to offer us, we must enjoy every single day whether it is a sunny day or a rainy day. It is all about how passionate we are about something.

If we want to live a more fulfilling life. A life full of happiness, then we need to become aware of our current situation, we must rediscover what our true passion for life is. It is time for us to leave our boring life behind and start living the life that we were meant to live, a happy life, not a stagnant, boring, and unhappy life. We must approach life with the burning desire to learn new things every day. Furthermore, we must try to find joy in everything that we do. We must try to enjoy the big things as much as the little things that life has to offer.

We must expand our awareness, we must be open to new suggestions from others, we must open our mind to new ideas, new places and other people. We must remember that if we approach life with a new and positive attitude, we will open new doors which will take us where we have never been before. We must get engaged in all the things that we are interested in, and there could be hundreds or even thousands of things that we thought were boring before, but now, we might find out that we will like doing those previous boring things. Anyway, we need to simplify our lives and declutter our minds from unnecessary junk, and then, we will be able to peacefully and calmly be passionate about the things that we like to do the most, and if we can accomplish such a task, we will be able to live a happier life.

Being passionate about something will give us the energy that we need in order to follow our dreams. We must begin our day by getting excited about the things that we need to do, and not by the things that we hate doing. We must surround ourselves with positive and happy people and not negative people.

Never Give Up, Never Surrender

The thought of failing in achieving our professional or personal goals is a scary thing, and it's because when we fail at something there will be emotional consequences, however, it doesn't need to be that way, as long as we set ourselves some reachable goals, then we shouldn't have to abandon them in the middle of the process. Now! when we set ourselves unreachable goals and then we quit in the middle of the process, then we will be viewed as quitters, in other words, it's going to reflect on what type of person we are. We should never try to reach goals which are beyond our capabilities, unless off course, we have some help from other people. Furthermore, if we ever find ourselves in a situation where we set ourselves a goal that was beyond our capabilities and we know deep inside that we are not going to be able to achieve such a goal, then it's better to abandon it, because that action will free up time that we can use in other goals which are more manageable.

Regardless of how big or small our goals are, we will encounter many obstacles along the way and as a result sometimes we will give up too early, perhaps, because in our own minds, we know that we are going to fail, and therefore, we set ourselves for failure before we even begin. When we fail at something is because we stop using our imagination, furthermore, we have surrendered ourselves to the enemy and it has to do with the fact that we failed many times before.

As we all know, if we want to be successful in accomplishing our personal and professional goals and dreams, we must continue to be mentally strong, even though we failed many times in the past, in other words, we must never give up in the face of adversity. We must constantly set new goals for ourselves because it is the only way in which we will be successful. Setting new goals for ourselves is something special because it is going to give us a boost of self-confidence, especially after we are successful in accomplishing some of our goals.

It is unfortunate that some of us will not be able to accomplish most of our goals, because most often than not, we set for ourselves too many unrealistic goals, and I am not saying that those goals cannot be achieved, on the contrary, most of our goals could be achievable, but only if we are one committed one hundred percent to those goals. One of the main reasons as to why we fail most of the time in accomplishing our goals is because we are not fully committed.

Moreover, we also fail because we are not well-prepared, and we are lacking the necessary knowledge which is required to become successful. If we want to be successful in accomplishing our goals, then we must arm ourselves with the necessary knowledge which is required in order to accomplish those goals. We must remember that knowledge is power, and if we have the knowledge and the desire to succeed, then, no matter how many obstacles we must face. No matter how many walls we must climb, no matter how many hoops we must jump through, eventually, we will accomplish some of our goals. We need to remind ourselves that it is only with hard work and dedication that we will become successful.

There are other reasons as to why we are not successful in achieving our goals, for example, we are forever coming up with excuses, and more excuses for not moving forward with our projects. Coming up with excuses is much easier than to come up with new ways for us to reach our goals. Other excuses that we might come up with for not pursuing our goals are as follow: not having enough time, fear of the unknown, fear of failing, laziness, and not having a plan of action.

Sometimes, we come up with more excuses for not doing something, than to come up with excuses for doing it. Other times we will feel anxious about trying something new, our bodies will become invaded by anxiety which can paralyze us or stop us in our tracks, and therefore, we rather do nothing. Believe, I was there.

All our excuses, along with the fear factor of the unknown, plus the anxiety that comes with it, will be the real killers of most of our dreams because it will prevent us from accomplishing most of our goals. These things are the ones that will prevent us from challenging ourselves, and they are the ones that will prevent us from setting new goals for ourselves in the future. We must remember that there is nothing to fear but fear itself.

We must keep in mind that every time we tried something new in the past and failed, that we didn't actually fail because we tried our best, but on the other hand, if we never try something new because of the fear of failing, then we have failed anyway because we didn't try. We need to always stay strong and never give up, we must do our absolute best not to stop in the middle of our journey. We must never hope that: eventually, things will work out for us, in other words, we must never wait for good things to happen to us, instead, we need to make them happen, and we can accomplish it by putting our imagination into action.

We must never set goals for ourselves for the wrong reason or because someone else wants us to have such goals, instead, we need to do it because we want to do it, furthermore, we do it because we are our own man, or woman, and we do it because we know what we want out of life. When we set new goals for ourselves for the wrong reasons, we are only setting ourselves for failure because we will not have the desire and the determination to follow through, we will not pursue them because we have no interest in pursuing those goals.

It is important that we set new goals for ourselves, but most importantly, we need to have a good plan in place, and then we must put that plan into action, furthermore, we must follow through with tons of determination and desire. We must never give up, we must never surrender, especially when we are encountered with roadblocks. Most of our desires and goals can become a reality, but only if we are willing to put the time and effort into it, also, we must remember that nothing is worth having if it is too easy to accomplish. Again, remember that it is much easier to give up when we fail or when things don't work out the way we had planned than to continue to pursue our dreams and goals.

We must never stop trying to better ourselves because even though it is human nature to quit when we see trouble on the horizon, we must never surrender to our weaknesses. Furthermore, our first reaction is to quit and follow the path of less resistance, but we must never give up because giving up it's only going to show what type of person we are. In other words, it will show our true character. If we want to become successful in the future, then we need to re-energize ourselves with new energy, new desire, new determination and new knowledge because that is going to allow us to move forward with our plans, and it's only then that we will not be able to do what comes naturally for most people, and that is to quit or give up. We must remember that life is almost never fair or easy.

We must face our fears, we must face adversity head on, we must keep moving forward and it doesn't matter if we don't succeed at first because we will be gaining valuable information and knowledge that we will be able to use in the future, and just maybe next time we will be successful in whatever we are trying to accomplish. One other thing that we need to be aware of is to never try to set too many goals for ourselves at one time because we will feel overwhelmed and as a result, we will end up quitting before we reach our destination.

It is always a good idea to start with one or two goals at a time and believe me when I say that it does not pay off when we set too many goals for ourselves. When we set too many goals for ourselves, we are only going to set ourselves up for failure because there's simply not enough time to concentrate on too many goals at the same time. We must face our challenges one at a time or one step at a time.

Many years of experience has showed me that we can't solve all our problems at the same time, it is an impossible task to accomplish, We cannot climb to the top of the mountain on a single bounce, therefore, we must tackle them one at a time and if we can accomplish this, then we will feel more relax, we will feel less stress, and we will be less frustrated.

There is no denial on my part that sometimes life will deal us with a terrible hand, but it is not a good reason for us to quit and stop trying to be the best that we can be, also, there's no denial on my part that sometimes we lose our way and as a consequence we get stuck in a place that we don't belong. We are so used to doing things the same old fashion way that sometimes we forget that there are easier ways for us to accomplish the same thing. We must have an open mind and ask other people for advice, but unfortunately, most of us don't want to listen to other people's suggestions, instead, we rather give up, we rather quit on our dreams than to listen to their suggestion and therefore, we will stop learning.

We all have different methods of solving our problems, however, sometimes those methods no longer work because they are out of date, and it is then that we need to come up with a new and improved method. We must remember that there is more than one solution to solving our problems or our difficult situations. We do not need to be afraid to try something new, furthermore, we need to use our imagination and look at our problems from many different angles. In most situations, it is not the actions of others that make us quit, but our own lack of imagination, education, and knowledge which is going to make us quit. When we fail is because we are not in total control of our thoughts and our actions, furthermore, when we fail is because we are completely unprepared for life's difficult situations.

We must improve our education and our knowledge because we were born with an amazing ability to learn and to adapt to difficult situations, we were born to be creative, we were born to invent and discover new things.

When we were born, we had limitations as to what we can accomplish, however, as we get older and we learn more and more, our limitations will be fewer, and as we gain more and more knowledge, our only limitations will be those limitations that we impose upon on ourselves. Our imagination and our abilities must be put into action. We must never stop using our imagination and our abilities because if we do, then we will be putting limitations upon ourselves, and therefore, we will become powerless.

Moreover, at what point in time do we give up on our precious dreams and goals? Well, the answer is "never" we never give up on our dreams and goals, we never surrender to all the different excuses that we might come up with which will prevent us from reaching our goals.

I'm a firm believer that we never give up on our dreams, and we never give up on accomplishing our goals, and I am going to tell you why, for example, I never gave up on my dreams of writing a book and becoming a professional photographer. Sure, it has taken me about forty years to write it, but now that I'm about to finish it, I must say that it was a lot of hard work and dedication on my part, I had to give up a lot of my precious time to this book, but I am glad that I did because I am excited to finally get my book published. It has been a long journey, but I am feeling good about myself because I accomplished what I set out to do many years ago.

I am also happy about the fact that my photography skills have improved tremendously over the years, I have learned so much that I can only feel proud about myself because I have accomplished yet another one of my goals. My photography is not quite where I wanted it to be, yet, because I want to become a master photographer and not just a photographer. Once I am completely done with my book, I will dedicate more of my time and energy to photography.

I was never scared of failure because I knew that someday I was going to be able to accomplish some of my goals, and again, it has taken me a while, but that just goes to show everyone that it's never too late to start setting new goals for ourselves. We must never give up. We must never surrender to laziness. One other thing…there will be a time when it's okay to give up on our dreams, for example, if our dreams were to become a professional athlete, like a professional soccer player or a professional football player, then it's okay to quit, but is only because I am sixty years old and to think that I can still become a professional soccer player it's out of the question and for several obvious reasons, I am too old for that.

They say that when we fail in our quest in reaching our goals, it becomes a reflection of who we are as a person, it becomes a reflection of our abilities and self-worth and therefore, it translates into failing as a person, and it's true, however, now days we recognize failure as an integral tool for future success, in other words, we must first fail sometimes in order to be successful in the future.

Learning to Express Ourselves

What am I feeling on the inside right now, what causes those feelings and emotions to manifest themselves inside my brain, are they a manifestation of something that I saw, something that heard, something that I ate, something that I smelled or something that someone told me? These are important questions that we need to ask ourselves because they will help us to better understand how we are feeling. Furthermore, once we identify how we are feeling, we will be able to express those feelings and emotions correctly to other people. We should never express our emotions and feelings to others, unless those feelings are completely understood by us, furthermore, they must be under our control.

I understand that our feelings and emotions is something that happens automatically, in other words, they are meant to be felt. They were meant to be express. They were not meant to be repressed. I also understand that repressing our feelings and emotions could have a negative impact psychologically, furthermore, they have the potential to impact our physical bodies as well, for example, we can develop heart problems, breathing problems, insomnia, stress, and tension. Those are good enough reasons to motivate us to learn a little bit more about how our feelings and emotions are manifested inside our bodies. It is important that we learn to express our feelings and emotions correctly so that people can understand exactly how we are feeling.

We need to understand that our feelings and emotions are part of who we are, in other words, they are never going to go away no matter how hard we try, so it is important for us to learn to express ourselves in a way in which is not going to cause any emotional anxiety. Furthermore, we need to learn to express our feelings and emotions, not in an uncontrollable manner or on impulsive responses, but in a passive and controllable way.

Most of our happiness comes from being able to express our emotions, our thoughts, our desires, our hopes, and our ambitions. Furthermore, our success and happiness will depend totally on our ability to communicate or express ourselves, so it is important for us to learn how to express ourselves by coordinating our feelings, our emotions and our thoughts, it is only then that we will be able to integrate those thoughts and put them into action. Our feelings, our emotions, our thoughts, and our actions must be coordinated, they all must work together as a team. When we finally learn to coordinate this information, we will be able to achieve a higher rate of success and happiness.

Our feelings, emotions, and thoughts is the most important part of who we are, therefore, we must make the effort to try and identify them, afterwards, we must learn to express those feelings, emotions and thoughts in a healthy and conductive way. Knowing how to express our feelings and emotions to others is going to help us with our personal life, and it's because those feelings will be aligned with our cultural values and as a result we will be able to build healthy relationships with other people.

Our ability to correctly communicate or deliver our thoughts and feelings to others effectively is the most important part of accomplishing our happiness.

Showing our true feelings and emotions does not come easy for some people, and it is totally understandable. Communication means everything in any relationship and when we don't know how to communicate our feelings, thoughts, and emotions to others, then we are preventing ourselves from living a happy life. People who don't have good communicating skill must learn to develop those skills because that barrier of miscommunication must be torn down. We must learn to coordinate our thoughts, feelings, and emotions and then we must put them into words so that other people know exactly how we are really feeling.

Again, we have the need to learn how to communicate our feelings clearly, so that there will be no misunderstanding about how we are feeling. We must be open and sincere. We must not be afraid of showing our true emotions because holding them back is only going to make us miserable in the long run. We should never be afraid to open-up and show our true feelings to others, especially close friends, and family members, and besides, they might respect and admire us even more for sharing.

We must not allow our fears to enter our mind about expressing our feelings, moreover, we might find out that we really like opening-up or communicating our feelings with other people. One final note, if we want to improve our relationship with other people, then we need to learn to communicate better and we can learn by studying others. The ones who know how to communicate, the ones who are confident in themselves.

Finding Harmony within Ourselves

What does harmony really mean? Well, it simply means that we are at peace with oneself. It means that our thoughts, our feelings, and emotions are all in alignment. Being in complete harmony within ourselves and the universe will help us to bring back the balance that we are missing into our lives, in addition, harmony will allow us to balance our minds, bodies and souls, in other words, it is going to help us to become more conscious of everything which is happening in our inner and outer world.

When we are not in tune with oneself, in other words, when we are not in complete harmony within ourselves and the universe, we will struggle with every day difficult situations, in addition, we are going to feel disconnected from the outside world, we will feel insecure, vulnerable, ashamed or guilty, but on the other hand, if we are completely in tune with oneself, we will calmly take control of every situation that we might encounter. We are no longer going to feel anger towards ourselves or others, we are no longer going to be in a depressive state of mind because we know now that we are governed by love and compassion, instead of hate. Now we know that we are self-worth because we have expanded our hearts, we have made the transformation from our old world into a brand-new world full of happiness. A world where only love rules our lives.

But how are we going to find harmony in a world where our lives are ruled by greed, dishonesty, and materialistic things? Well, there is only one way in which we will accomplish peace of mind and that is by meditating. Meditation is going to slowly help us to let go of our old world of bad behaviors, greed, and dishonesty. We will find harmony within ourselves by letting go of our past life. By decluttering our minds from unnecessary junk and by forgiving ourselves and others for old grudges that we might have against each other. Furthermore, we need to let go of any negative thoughts, emotions and feelings which we might still have, and instead, we must focus our energy on the future so that we can build a better tomorrow for ourselves and our families.

We must remind ourselves on a consistent basis to look for the things that will make us happy, instead of the ones that will make us miserable, in addition, we need to remind ourselves that there will be more things that will make us unhappy than things that will make us happy and it's because we are thinking about the bad things more often than the good things. We must remember that it is the law of attraction in action, meaning that whatever we are thinking about the most is what we are going to receive in return.

One of the things that we need to do every morning, when we first wake up, is to remind ourselves that if we want to find peace of mind, harmony, balance, calmness and happiness in our lives, then, we must do all the things that I mentioned above.

Rather than worrying about everyday difficulties and wasting most of our mental energy on useless tasks, we should be channeling that energy towards finding harmony within ourselves and the universe. We must remember that once we find that inner peace that we so desire, we will be able to discover new and exciting things which will stimulate our senses and allow us to find happiness much faster. I cannot emphasize enough about how important it is for everyone to start making a change in their lives, but I am not talking about starting tomorrow because as we all know it, tomorrow might not come, so therefore, if we want to change our lives, then we need to start today.

I have been making small changes to my life for the last twenty years because I want to live the rest of my days in harmony and peace, in addition, I want to challenge myself to be become a better person because I don't want to look back and ask myself if was good enough, in other words, did I do enough for myself and for others, did I accomplish most of my goals?

We must remember that we have a tremendous ability to adapt to new changes. We have the ability to make changes to our lives at any given moment, in addition, we need to believe in our ability to cope with adversity, but most importantly, we need to remind ourselves not to overreact to any type of negative adversity. Moreover, when we finally learn to be in harmony with oneself and the universe, we will be able to put our thoughts in order which in turn will allow us to be less anxious when something goes wrong and it is because we will be in complete control of our thoughts, feelings and emotions. when we have our thought in the right place, we will be able to create positive images of ourselves, for example, images of peaceful places where we can go and feel a complete inner peace within ourselves.

We must avoid creating negative images of ourselves, for example, doing things that we do not want to do or creating images of ourselves being in places where we don't want to be. Creating positive images of ourselves will give us the power to lift our spirits to new heights, in addition, creating positive images of ourselves is going to help us to build our confidence, but on the other hand, negative images in our minds will destroy our confidence and our abilities to cope with adversity.

We must never waste our energy on unhealthy emotions, such as: Rage, Anger, Depression or Anxiety, instead, we need to learn to distract ourselves with suitable distractions from anxious moments by replacing our damaging thoughts with images of total relaxation.

Another thing which is going to help us feel less anxious is not to make too many unrealistic demands for ourselves at one time, instead, we can start with one or two, because once we accomplish those demands, we will be able to move onto other demands with more confidence. Another way of coping with our everyday demands is to change those demands into preferences or change them to more manageable and realistic demands.

It is important that we learn to find harmony within ourselves so that we can find the balance that we need in our lives. We must not only find balance for our minds, our thoughts, our emotions, and our feelings, but we also need to find balance at work, at play time, and everything in between. Everything in life must have some type of balance or the universe would not work properly, so having said that, our minds and physical bodies must be in total harmony if we want to find that inner peace that we have been looking for so long

Most people struggle their entire lives trying to find that elusive balance and harmony which is missing from their lives. They struggle with self-doubt, with low self-stem, and it is because their mental state of mind is in chaos, they are totally out of tune within themselves, the universe, and their surroundings.

Starting a new life is not always easy, but nevertheless, we must make that move, well that is if we want to accomplish happiness. In our new life, we will accept ourselves as a person of peace and as a person who accepts the people who we love as they are because as we know it, we cannot make them change their ways, unless we change ourselves first. In our new life, we must never allow ourselves or anyone else to make us feel as if we do not belong, furthermore, we must never allow ourselves or others to make us feel ashamed or insignificant. In our new life we will be our true selves. In our new life, we will make our own decisions and without any pressure from outside sources, in addition, we will expand our mind, expand our education and our knowledge at our own time, in other words, we will start a brand new life by allowing ourselves to be who we really want to be, we will allow ourselves to be happy, we will allow our minds to heal from our past mistakes and we will allow our bodies to heal physically as well.

Chapter Thirty

What is Our Degree of Tolerance?

Tolerance is an important quality which we need to have because it will provided us with many new opportunities which otherwise we wouldn't get if we didn't have such a quality, and I don't mean to implied that we should be tolerance with other people only because it is beneficial for us, rather, we should be tolerant because we are well aware that we are all different; we all have different beliefs and ideas, therefore, we should have respect for each other, however, it doesn't mean that our beliefs and ideas are the correct ones.

We all have a certain degree of tolerance. Some of us have a high degree of tolerance, but others not so much. Take me for example, I know that I have a high degree of tolerance, in fact, I have been accused many times before of being too passive, or too nice, and perhaps they are correct. I am an individual who tries to practice self-control every single day, someone who learned to keep his emotions under control, and let me remind everyone that I am not perfect by any means because the true reality is that no human being on the face of the planet is anywhere near perfect.

What about you, have you ever thought about whether your degree of tolerance is at an all-time high, or do you get highly irritated when someone says something that you didn't like, or even worst, they say something that you know in your heart is not true, furthermore, do you get upset when someone you know says something to you that you didn't expect to hear from a person that you know?

Tolerance is a power tool that everyone must have, and I will explain why, as human beings we normally don't pay much attention to the real meaning of our words, sometimes we simply let them come out of our mouths without thinking if those words will cause others emotional and irreparable damage. All it takes is a couple of words from us to inflict damage on to others. We must choose our words carefully when we are trying to communicate with someone else. Our words are immensely powerful, their meaning can break us or make us, therefore, we must be careful with our choice of words when we engage in a conversation with others.

It is obvious that intolerance is the opposite of tolerance. Intolerance is the barrier which impedes all forms of success; however, tolerance is the destroyer of those barriers. Tolerance must be practiced by everyone on a consistent basis until we learn to master it. Again, I like to think that I have a high degree of tolerance, however; occasionally I lose my cool and concentration. I can get upset just like everyone else. Sometimes people will make me upset, however, I will not stay upset for too long because I always remind myself that I must regain total control of my emotions. Everyone has the capacity to elevate their degree of tolerance to another level by not getting irritated so easily when someone makes them upset. We can all accomplish this task by taking control of our feelings and emotions.

In order to change who we are as human beings, we need to take our degree of tolerance to a whole new level, and I know that it's easier said than done, but we must do it, well, that is if we want to advance to another level of thinking.

If we can all take our degree of tolerance to another level, we will be helping in changing humanity forever. If only people would have a little bit more tolerance towards their human being's counterparts, the world would be a much nicer place to live in. That is how powerful tolerance can be. Half of the people which I dealt with in the past had very little or no tolerance towards their fellow man because they lose their cool faster than a bullet train, in addition, they lose their ability to concentrate, and therefore, they forget to act in a civilized manner towards others.

Yes, I know that there's a lot of people with a high degree of tolerance out there, however, it's only a small percentage of the entire world population, so I ask myself why? Well, the only conclusion that I came up with was because of the lack of knowledge and the lack of self-control. We must not forget that lack of knowledge can and will be very costly.

How Do We Measure Success?

How do we really measure success? Personal success can be measured in different ways, for example, money, power, fame, happiness, and health. However, we must decide for ourselves which of the above is more important to us, perhaps, they are all important for some people, but for others, there might be only one, maybe two or even three. I'm guessing that most of us measure success by how much money we have, however, having a lot of money does not necessary means that we will completely be happy, furthermore, money is only a piece of paper which allow us to buy most of the things that we desire, for example, food, a new house, a new car or any other materialistic items, and for the most part, we are happy when we first buy something new, however, our happiness doesn't last for too long, in other words, that happiness that we feel is only temporary because as soon as the newness wears off, we want something newer, in other words, we are never satisfied with what we have, we always want more.

Again, we all measure success differently, but for me, the most important measure of success is "health" because nothing else in the world will make me happier. You see, if I am completely healthy, then I will be able to obtain other things and it is because of my good health, furthermore, when I am healthy, I will be able to work and that in itself will allow me to earned money, which in turn, is going to allow me to buy some of the things that I want, in addition, when I am healthy I will be able to exercise which is going to help me keep my mind sharp and my body healthy. Now, as far as fame, I don't really care too much about fame, I simply want to earn the respect which I deserved. That is all I ever wanted, and as for power, I also do not care too much about acquiring power. The only power that I wish to have is the power which is going to enable me to choose my own destiny. In addition, I want to have the power which is going to help me to control my own thoughts, feelings and emotions.

Money is not going to make us happy when we are feeling lonely, depressed or we are having feelings of unworthiness. For example, if for some unexplained reason I am feeling lonely, depressed, unhappy, or miserable, then money will not make me happy at that moment. I also measure success by where my state of mind is at, you see, when my state of mind is in a good place, then I am going to feel a sense of happiness and that is more important to me than all the money in the world. I really don't believe that we should be measuring success by how much money we accumulate. While it is true that money can bring us happiness in many ways, it can only bring us happiness to some degree. Money alone will not bring us total and complete happiness. The equivalent of having money and being financially secure, means that money does have its value because it plays an important role in our daily lives, however, it is not the only factor in achieving happiness and being successful. It only means that if we are financially secure, then we are successful in the business world.

About the only time that money will completely makes us happy is when we use it to create new values for ourselves and for others, for example, money can help in the creation of new jobs for other people, thereby, creating happiness for those less fortunate, it is then that we will be rewarded with happiness for ourselves.

I'm not suggesting that we should give all of our money away, after all, everyone works hard for it, what I am suggesting here is that we should be using some of our money to create values for others, for example, new jobs, but without taking advantage of people's misfortunes. In other words, we will be creating values for society and at the same time, we will be rewarded with more money, and perhaps an enormous amount of happiness. I think it is a good deal not only for us, but for others as well, in other words, it's a win-win situation for everyone.

We all know that when we have plenty of money, we will be able to buy whatever our hearts desire, however, this action is only going to make us partially happy, but on the other hand, if we use some of that money to make a good deed or help someone in real need, then that will be real happiness because of the good feeling that we get from having done something good for someone else. Believe me when I say that those feelings will last a lifetime, in other words, we are always going to remember them. When we have plenty of money, we will have the power or the choice to help or not help others, now, that is power.

Again, success should be measured by how healthy and happy we are and not by money alone. As mentioned many times before, we are always looking for something which is going to help us find happiness, so why not look for happiness in enjoying, not only the materialistic and bigger things, but enjoying the little things that life has to offer us as well. Yes, the little things which are going to make us feel good all over again. By enjoying the little things in life, we will generate feelings of joy, laughter, and inner peace for ourselves.

Furthermore, we must be aware that some of the best things in life are free. For example, the feeling of being alive, the feeling of inner peace that we feel inside when we have done something good for someone else, the feeling of a nice gentle breeze touching our bodies enticing us to relax. All these things are free for everyone to enjoy, and we can never put a prize on that.

Just being able to breath should be enough for us to make us happy, but unfortunately, as human beings, we normally take everything for granted and it is because we are always in the pursuit of riches and therefore, we forget about the most important things which are going to make us happy the most, for example, joy, satisfaction, laughter and inner peace.

Who is God?

Who is God and how did he become into existence? Is he an eternal God? We only know what the bible tells us, and the bible tells us that: at the beginning of time there was no physical universe, there was no space, and there was no matter. We are told that God created everything from the physical universe to everything which is visible and invisible. The bible also tells us that God created man in his image, in other words, we share the same basic appearance as God, for example, head, hair, eyes, ears, mouth and body, however, it does not mean that God is human. God is not human in flesh and blood, rather, God is a spiritual being. An all knowing, perfect, eternal God. God is the ruler of everything in existence.

Is God Responsible for Our Suffering?

Is God responsible for our suffering? Is he responsible for our personal problems that we had in the past, the present and the future? We all have those moments in our lives when we tend to blame God for our suffering, for our tragedies and for our sicknesses, but is it true? Personally, I really don't think that God is responsible for our sufferings. It's not God's will to make his children suffer, how can God be so heartless? It doesn't make any sense whatsoever, it's not logical to think that God wanted his children to suffer in any shape, way or form.

We must ask ourselves the following question: "What was God's intention when he created us, did he create us just so that we suffer? Now, let me ask you another question "do you, as a father or as a mother want your children to suffer? Of course not, I wouldn't want my kids to suffer either, on the contrary, I want them to be happy and healthy.

I believe the answer is crystal clear, God cannot be as heartless and senseless as to do such horrible things with his own children. Believe it or not, God was the creator of everything that ever existed, including us humans, but he must have a good reason for not interfering with our lives, and I believe that it's because he wanted us to have the freedom to decide for ourselves between right and wrong. We have the freedom to do as we wish and that is a beautiful thing, so we must be thankful that we are able to make our own decisions, but without any interference from God.

I will never blame God for our sufferings. On the contrary, we are responsible for our own suffering because we put ourselves in difficult situations, in other words, when we suffer it's because of our own doing. We must remember that for every action that we take, there will be a reaction. Everything that we have done in the past, present and future will cause something else to happen, and it can be a good thing or bad thing, therefore, we must be careful that we always do the right thing. We must remember that if we do good deeds, then we will be rewarded with good things in return, but on the other hand, if we do evil or bad things, then we are going to be rewarded with bad things in return.

Does God Communicate with Us?

I do believe that God is in constant communication with us, but how does he do it? Well, it's possible that God is always communicating with us through our dreams, our visions, our creativity, our moral guidance, our own suggestions and through our own reasoning. God can communicate with us in many ways, however, most often than not, we are not capable of capturing his messages because we are not paying attention. We go about living our lives not realizing that God is reaching out, he is trying to communicate with us all the time, but unfortunately, we choose to ignore him. Maybe it's because of our lack of self-awareness, lack of knowledge, or plain and simple, we choose to ignore him, period.

We must be aware that we are the creators of whatever happens to us. We create our own world; therefore, we create our own reality. God is, in my own opinion, a loving God, the problem here is that we refuse to listen to him. Remember that most of our problems, whether they are big or small, are created by no one else then ourselves, they were not created by God.

Chapter Thirty-One

Fog in Our Brains

What! Fog in our brain? Brain fog is also known as brain fatigue, it's a mental state of mind in which we experience episodes of mental confusion, lack of focus, or unable to recall certain things, for example, not remembering how we got home after work, forgetting words, names and addresses. A foggy brain affects our ability to think clearly. We feel confused, lethargic, disorganized, and unable to put our thoughts in order.

So, what triggers brain fog? There are several reasons as to why sometimes we feel disconnected, confused, and unable to find clarity, furthermore, sometimes we feel as if our brain is full of tiny rocks which prevent us from concentrating. Well, according to scientists, overtime, our brain begins to clog with toxic plaques. These tiny toxic plaques are called "Senile plaques," which sticks to our brain cells. These toxic plaques keep accumulating in our brains until our neurons can no longer communicate any information to the rest of our bodies. Basically, there are two types of toxic plaque "amyloid and tau" amyloid clumps into plaques while tau forms into tangles, so as we age, our brain is slowly clogged with sticky yellow plaque, and eventually, our brain is chocked by the buildup, and as a consequence, our neurons will begin to die, thereby, lowering our functionality more and more as time goes by. Neurons or nerve cells are specialized neurons, which are responsible for sending information throughout the human body, in both, chemical and electrical forms. In addition, there are other types of neurons, which are responsible for performing other tasks, for example, we have "sensory neurons" which carries information from our sensory receptor cells throughout the body and into our brain. We have "motor neurons" which are responsible for sending information from our brain to all the muscles of the human body. We also have "interneurons'' which are responsible for sending information between different neurons in our bodies.

Now we know that plaque is responsible for our mental decline as we age, but what causes plaque buildup in our brain to begin with, and what can we do to prevent that from happening? It's obvious that there are many factors that will contribute to the accumulation of plaque in the human brain, which is going to make us feel lethargic, tired, and unable to function properly throughout the day. Some of the factors which contribute to plaque buildup in our brains are as follows: lack of sleep, lack of exercise, lack of water and fluids, not eating the right foods, stress, anxiety, hormonal changes, medical condition, smoking, alcohol, and medications.

There is a way to prevent our brain from fogging up and to keep it healthy, and that is by making sure that we do some of the following: Getting plenty of sleep, and it's recommended that we get a minimum of seven hours of sleep per night, we need to eat more healthy foods, especially, foods which are rich with vitamins, minerals and nutrients. But even when we eat healthy foods, our bodies are deficient in many other vitamins, for example, B-vitamins and Omega-3's. Salmon will provide us with omega 3 but we need to eat more of it, at least 3 times a week, in addition, we need to eat other healthy foods, for example, fish, nuts, blueberries, vegetables, fruits and avocados. Furthermore, there are other things that we can do to prevent our brain from being invaded by fog, for example, we need to cut down on sugars and sweets, we need to work out more often, but we must do it on a consistent basis because exercising will boost our moods and memory, we need to meditate more often, especially, at times when we are feeling anxious, stressed or whenever we are experiencing anxiety. Laughter is a good natural source of stress reliever that will make us feel better, therefore, is important that we learn to laugh more often.

Whether we realized or not, our brain gets foggy and it happens more often than we realize. We all experience some type of brain fog from time to time, I know I have, in fact, I am feeling this way right now, and how appropriate, as I am attempting to finish this chapter, I am feeling as if I was in San Francisco across the Golden Gate Bridge. On the Northwest top of the hill where I can't see any part of the city, in other words, I feel like my brain is full of fog which means that I am unable to concentrate, and no matter how hard I try, nothing seems to work.

I have been trying hard to clear my mind from junk and debris, but with no avail, so my only choice was to stop writing, and instead, I went outside to get a bit of fresh air because I wanted to clear my mind from a state of fogginess which invaded my brain. As I was trying to clear my mind, I realized that I was feeling this way because I didn't have enough sleep the night before, and as a consequence my entire body was feeling the effects, my eyes felt tired and my feet felt as if they were a hundred pounds each, but as the day went bye, I was able to slowly regain more clarity. But how was I able to accomplish such a task? Well, I began by closing my eyes for a few minutes because it was important for my body and mind to be in total relaxation. I was able to slowly regain my mental and physical strength, so after thirty minutes of relaxation I was feeling reenergized and ready to rumble again. I must admit that my eyes were still feeling a little tired after I got back to writing, however, I was able to concentrate on my writing once again.

There's too many things which can affect how our bodies and brains will feel, therefore, we must be careful of everything that we do, including, what we eat and drink, in addition, there are other reasons as to why we feel mentally and physically tired throughout the day and it's because our environment is full of pollutants which clogs our brains with fumes which contains hundreds of different chemicals, and by the way, these chemicals fumes are invisible to the naked eyes, but occasionally, we are able to smell those them in the air, however, there is absolutely nothing we can do about that.

Whether we are aware of the situation or not, we are breathing high amounts of unhealthy air which is full of chemicals and pollutants. I am not surprised whatsoever about the fact that our outdoor air is contaminated with high amounts of smog which contains carbon dioxide, lead, arsenic, chemical gases, fertilizers, mercury toxic metals, plastic and many other vinyl's flowing in the air, no wonder we feel the way we do.

The conditions are not much better indoors, in fact, the inside of our homes are much more contaminated than the outdoors, and it has to do with the fact that we use vast amounts of chemicals to clean the inside of our homes. We might think that the air inside our homes is safer than the outside air, but unfortunately, that is not the case. The indoor air that we constantly breath is full of gases which are release when we use cleaning supplies, in fact, researchers are saying that indoor air is ten times more polluted than the outside, that is a shocker to me, I never image that our indoor air would be so much more polluted than the outdoors, but apparently it is. Many of the pollutants indoor air mold, acids, pollen, dust and bacteria, and these are just a few of the many pollutants that we have inside our homes, in fact, there could be well over a hundred different combinations of chemicals in the air at any given time, whether is outdoors or indoors.

But hold on, because it only gets worse, there is also chloride in our toothpaste and in our water, this cannot be good, or is it? In fact, researchers say that more than seven hundred chemical compounds have been found in our drinking water. There is a very good reason as to why me and my family have been drinking bottle water for the last forty years, but we must be aware that all drinking bottle water is not equal, especially bottle water which comes out of the faucets, but even though we drink bottle water, we must be careful not to leave our bottle water expose to the sun because the sun's heat will cause the bottle's own chemicals to react and melt into the water.

The foods that we eat are also full of preservatives, and if that wasn't enough, we are making the situation worse by not eating the right foods, plus the fact that we don't get enough sleep will take a toll on our bodies and brains. Some of us also, drink and smoke excessively, thereby, making the situation even worse. No wonder we are a nation of zombies, we do not sleep enough, we do not exercise enough, we do not eat the right foods and on top of that, we make it worse by inhaling thousands of chemicals from smoking. Wow! No wonder our brain feels foggy most of the time, and if all these chemicals were not enough, we are consuming more and more drugs now than ever before.

Sometimes I wonder if we really need all these drugs in our bodies which are made from bio-chemicals. I agree that sometimes we must take some of those drugs for certain medical conditions, but it's because we have no other choice, however, most of the time we don't need all those drugs, it's unfortunate that doctors prescribed them anyway and it's because we either pressure them to give us those drugs or they automatically give them to us even though we might not need them. It's no wonder that our brains are clogged from all the chemicals and pollutants that we breathe and eat daily. Again, we need to be careful what we put in our bodies.

The human brains was not designed to absorb all these drugs and chemicals, instead, it was designed to get its energy from natural brain foods. We can get most of the nutrients, vitamins, and minerals that our bodies need by eating healthy foods, including, nuts, fruits, and vegetables. We were designed to be vegetarians, but somewhere along the years, we stopped eating healthy foods and it all started about fifty or sixty years ago, when the food industries exploded with new ways of processing our foods. We are constantly feeding our bodies fried foods and processed foods, and therefore, we are unable to function properly as a result.

When our brain is in a state of fogginess, we will not be able to think clearly, we will not be able to achieve complete peace of mind, and consequently, we will not be able to achieve complete happiness. Again, how are we going to achieve clarity in our brain when our brain is hindering our abilities to think clearly, how are we going to get rid of our brain fog? Well, believe it or not, there is hope after all, just like there are thousands of chemicals in our environment and our foods, there are thousands of things that we can do to improve our lives. I know for a fact that clearing our brain from junk, debris, pollutants, and chemicals is not an easy thing to accomplish, but at the very least, we can start by making small changes to our diets.

Curiosity

Most people know that necessity is the mother of all inventions, which I believe to be true, but what about "curiosity," where curiosity fits in all this? Well, as human beings we are curious about everything, it's something that we were born with. our human curiosity is what separates us from the animal kingdom, although, sometimes I think that some animals are curious about certain things as well. Anyway, we are curious about who we are, where we come from, we are curious about whether God, heaven and hell do exist, we are also curious about what happens to us after we die. Do we go to heaven or do we go to hell? We are also curious about the planet, the sun and billions of stars and planets that exist throughout our galaxy and beyond, in fact, we are curious about the entire universe.

When we were children our curiosity was at an all-time high. We wanted to know everything about our surroundings, and it's perfectly understandable because everything is new to us, but as we get older, we want to know more, we want to know how everything works. But what about as full-grown individuals, is our curiosity the same as when we were children, does our curiosity diminish, or does it get stronger as we get older? I cannot speak for everyone, but my curiosity as an adult is bigger than ever before. It keeps on groin and groin and I am sure that it has to do with the fact that I am forever willing to learn new things, furthermore, I want to know how those things work, in fact, the older I get, the more I want to learn.

I strongly do believe that our curiosity keeps on growing as we get older, at least for most of us, and it has to do with the fact that we are never satisfied with what we know. We always want to learn more, and its because we are "intrapersonal intelligence" which means that we want to know everything.

Not everyone's curiosity is what it should be, but why is that? well, sometimes we fall into a state of complacence because it's a place where we feel comfortable, it's a comfort zone or a happy place where we feel safe and secure, and therefore, we don't want anything to interfere with that. We don't want to make any new changes which might interfere with the way we are feeling. One of the things that we must keep in mind is that complacence and resistance to learning new things is the enemy of innovation.

What would happen if we didn't have that curiosity which makes us want to venture out into the unknown? Well, most likely we will not learn much of anything; we will not be able to discover or conquer new things. I cannot even imagine how many great ideas would have been lost forever because of our lack of curiosity. When our curiosity is present, then a whole new world of new possibilities will open for us, so we must always keep that in mind.

We must remember that people who are adventurous and curious about everything, will find excitement in everything they do, in other words, their lives will not be boring because they will be too busy looking for answers, in addition, they will be much happier than those who are not. Curiosity will enhance our learning abilities, and at the same time, it will activate the hippocampus which is responsible for consolidating information from short-term to long-term memory. Furthermore, curiosity is important because it will put our minds in active mode and when that happens, we will start to ask ourselves lots of questions, and consequently, we will start searching for answers related to those questions.

Again, I have an inquisitive mind, I like to know how everything works. I like to know how everything is made, I want to know what other people are thinking and what they are saying, furthermore, I like to know what they are doing, not because I am being nosy per say, but because my curiosity is enormous, and I cannot stand not knowing what is going on within my surroundings.

I considered myself an individual with a strong desire to learn something new every single day and it's because I have an inquisitive mind with an enormous desire to explore new things, additionally, I want to expand my horizons and gain as much knowledge as I possibly can. Curiosity is the main ingredient for learning new things, so people who are curious about life itself or are curious about how most things work, will seek answers to their questions, but why do we sick answers? Well, because people like me, with an inquisitive mind, want to know everything that there is to know under the sun and beyond.

Remember that knowledge is going to enable us to accomplish more of our goals much faster, in addition, knowledge is going to help us find happiness much faster. We must understand that knowledge is power and if we have the power, we will be able to know what to do in almost every situation. When we have the knowledge, we will be able to become successful in almost everything that we do. We will be able to use our wisdom and intelligence to help us make better decisions for ourselves, furthermore, knowledge is going to allow us to improve our relationships with others.

Just imagine for a minute about all the things that we wanted to do in the past, but we were not able to do them because of our lack of knowledge or understanding. Having the knowledge is going to allow us to live a more fulfilling life, plus we will be able to spend more quality time doing the things that we care the most about. Most of our goals and dreams will become a reality, but only if we have the curiosity to learn new things. Never forget that our curiosity is going to open the doors for new opportunities.

Our Curiosity is going to take us into a whole new world full of wonderful surprises, for example, we are going to find out that things are more interesting than what we thought they were, and it's because we are going to be able to see them from a new perspective. When we are curious, we want to be more engaged in learning how everything works, allowing us to live a more fulfilling and happy life.

We must never prevent our minds from learning new things, otherwise, they are going to fall into a dormant state of mind and when that happens, we will not be able to function at full capacity and it's because we are depriving our mind from learning new and exciting thing, in other words, we are depriving our mind from new information. We should never let our curiosity vanish into thin air, especially in our old age because as we get older, our minds need more stimulation than ever before. Curiosity is going to help us to keep our mind young and sharp for a long time, but only if we let our curiosity run wild. We must never let our curiosity expire or let it go to sleep. If our curiosity is in a dormant state of mind right now, then we need to wake that curiosity and let it explore new things because it will transform our ordinary lives into a more enjoyable life. When we put our curiosity into motion along with a little imagination, then our knowledge is going to multiply by tenfold.

The best thing about people with a high degree of curiosity is that they always seem much happier than those who rely on the familiar, their lives will always be more meaningful, their experiences will last longer than those who don't use their curiosity to explore new things. Maintaining a consistent curiosity in our daily lives will allow us to get rid of preconceived ideas.

By waking up our curiosity, we will be creating new ideas which is going to bring new and exciting changes in our lives. Old ideas are boring because they lack excitement, but on the other hand, new ideas will bring us new hope and excitement into our lives. Always remember to let your curiosity out of the bag, do not let it become dull and boring. We must use our curiosity to explore new things that we always wanted to explore but never had the opportunity to do because the lack of curiosity was missing from your life. Remember that new ideas will stimulate our minds, plus it will keep our mind sharp and young for many years to come.

A Plan of Action

There's isn't a formula in place out there that will fit or help everyone in accomplishing their personal goals and dreams because everyone is different. Everyone have different ideas, and everyone needs are not the same needs as everyone else, so having said that, we must do whatever we need to do in order to accomplish our goals, but first, we must ask ourselves the following question: "what makes us happy or what are some of the things which is going to makes us get excited about life? Once we know or have an idea of the things which will make us happy, then we must decide if we are going to pursue those them or not, and if we decide to pursue those goals, then we must jump out of our chairs and go after those dreams. It's a matter of how much we want something. We must keep in mind that no one will come to our rescue, no one will be able to accomplish our dreams for us but ourselves. We must keep in mind that we are responsible for creating our own destiny. Again, we must remember that there is no specific solution that will work for everyone because we all have unique minds. In other words, no two minds are exactly alike, what makes one person happy, it might make another person unhappy.

If we want to improve our lives, then we must remember that we need to create a plan of action and that we must follow with physical action. There are two types of actions, the first is mental and the second is physical. The mental type of action does not require any physical work on our part. The second type of action is the hardest of the two because it requires actual physical action, it requires movement on our part, and it's not an easy task for most humans to accomplish. Furthermore, as human beings we tend to get lazy from time to time and so we fall into complacency and it's because we feel secure and satisfied with what we have. Sometimes we want to accomplish the most with as little energy as possible, in other words, we try to take the path of least resistance. One important factor that we must consider when we are trying to accomplish our goals is that "nothing will happen until something moves" so, if we don't move, then nothing is ever going to happen.

Furthermore, in order to have a plan of action, we must first have a clear vision of what we want to accomplish, then we must have the desire, the motivation, the courage and the strength which is require in order to carry out those plans. We must remember that a plan is just a plan, and that if we don't put those plans into action, then nothing is going to happen. Remember that making plans and putting them into action is in fact a marriage of the two. We can make all the plans that we want, but these plans are never going to materialize unless we put them into action. Furthermore, a plan without execution is a plan destined for failure.

We must remind ourselves that people don't want to hear that we have plans for the future, instead, they want us to show them that we are capable of executing those plans. We must demonstrate not only to ourselves, but we must demonstrate to others that we are indeed capable of doing what we say we are going to do; it's a simple philosophy to live by. We can no longer afford to seat and wait on the sidelines waiting for others to do most of the work for us. We can no longer wait for our dreams to become a reality without moving a finger. Now is the time to stay active through intense action. Now is the time to remind ourselves that we can transform our dreams into reality through action, instead of inaction.

We must push ourselves to the best of our abilities. We must find the burning desire to create or build our own destiny. We must be ready and willing to become achievers by moving forward with our dreams and without any hesitation.

To be successful in achieving our dreams, we need to think about our old bad tendencies so that we don't repeat them in the future. We need to arm ourselves with positive thoughts, self-confidence, self-control, and a strong will to succeed. Furthermore, we need to leave our self-destructive behaviors behind. We must not forget that we must invest our time and energy on finding our true-selves, and at the same time, build our own true character.

Greed Money and Power

Should we be ashamed of ourselves for accumulating huge amounts of money, power, and materialistic things? It is said that America is the richest country on Earth, where even poor people are considered rich when compared to some of the people from third world countries. I believe that we shouldn't be as ashamed in trying to better ourselves, after all, it's the American dream to become financially independently.

Most of us want to make as much money as possible, we all want to make it big. We want to have it all, and again, it is the American dream, but not just the American dream, it is the dream of every man and woman on the face of the planet to become financially independent. The hope of someday becoming rich is what keeps most people driving forward. The hope of someday becoming rich, famous, and powerful is the driving force which keeps most humans on the go.

We are obsessed with the accumulation of all these things, but the saddest thing of all is that the more we have, the more we want, it seems that it's never enough, we are never satisfied with what we have. Greed will eventually destroy us if we are not careful, furthermore, it will prevent us from becoming the person that we were meant to be. Greed will destroy our relationships with those who we love, in other words, greed will rob us of our happiness, furthermore, greed can destroy everything good which we believe in. May I remind everyone that having dreams is not a bad thing because it is what motivates us. It is what drives us to better ourselves. It is not a sin wanting to better ourselves, mentally, physically, and economically, however, when we lose sight of who we are and our greed takes over our souls, then it becomes a sin. We must stay true to ourselves and not let greed destroy our good values, furthermore, we must never let greed, power and money take over our lives to the point where we are no longer ourselves, we must never let materialistic things destroy and steal our happiness.

Our dreams and goals should not be only about money and power. Our dreams should be about working hard and making the time to enjoy with our loved ones; that should be priority number one. Accomplishing our dreams and goals is a big part of our lives, but we must stay humble and at the same time, not sacrifice everything else because of our greed. It is okay to have money. However, we must not let money rule our lives entirely.

We must never measure our success by how much money we accumulate, instead, we should measure our success by our degree of happiness and by showing our true love for our family members, friends, and others.

One of the biggest things in life that I really appreciate about myself is my integrity, I believe in honesty and integrity because without any of those two things, we are not much of anything. Yes, greed will compromise our honesty and integrity and I am not saying that everyone who have money and power have no integrity or that they are dishonest, I am simply saying that some people become immune to those in real need. In other words, they have become immune to their pain. That is what money and power does to people, they become blinded by their ambition, and their judgment becomes impaired because of their greed. We must remind ourselves to stay humble every single day, we must be leaders of good things and not of bad things, we must treat others with respect. Greed, money, and power can and will be the path to self-destruction when it is not kept under control.

Normally, money is on everyone's mind, at least most of the time, therefore, we must not stay focused on the accumulation of money. We must not focus all our energy on money alone because if we do, it will eventually destroy us. Again, we must not be driven by pure greed, money, and power. We must be aware of how we conduct ourselves in all facets of our lives. We must not find ourselves falling in the grasps of greed that we forget everything else which is important in our lives. Money is a necessity, we all know that, but unfortunately, some people will become invaded by greed and they will forget about what is important... happiness. Greed is only good up to a certain point, and beyond that point, it will become a destroyer of all good things.

What makes people become so greedy? Perhaps, is the fact that most people were poor when growing up and consequently, they don't want to be poor any longer, so now, all they have on their minds is to accumulate as much money as possible. It is by pure instinct that people feel the necessity to accumulate as much money as possible, furthermore, they think that no matter how much money they have, it's never going to be enough.

Throughout history, humans have been driven by pure greed, power, and money. Greed is fueled by the lack of certain things which are necessary for our survival. Any time there's scarcity of something which is essential for our survivor, there will be greed, for example, food, water, gold, or silver.

Our entire economic system is based on money, and as I said before, money is going to give us the ability to buy whatever we want, furthermore, we probably wouldn't survive for too long without money, and it's because it will allow us to buy, not only materialist things, but food and water as well. Yes, money is the driving force of the world. We are never going to feel safe if we don't have the money to be able to survive when in hard times. We must remember that money and power it's never going to make us completely happy, therefore, we need something else which is the love from our family and friends, now! That is what I call being rich. My question is: "if we have plenty of money, why not share a little with those less fortunate?" I know, I can just hear people inner thoughts saying to themselves...if people are poor is because they are lazy, and in some cases, it's true, however, not everyone is lazy, so we must keep that in mind. The reality is that some people will come up with excuses not to share a little bit of their money with others less fortunate. We must remember one thing, and that is that we are all somehow connected, we all need each to survive.

How to Position Ourselves for Success

It's unfortunate that most people will spend their entire lives without accomplishing much success, in other words, they will fail in achieving most of their goals and dreams, but why is that? Again, I hate to keep repeating myself over and over, but it's the only way for us to learn, so having said that, I am going to start by saying that too many people will not be able to accomplish most of their goals and dreams, and it's because there are many internal and external powerful forces that we are not aware off which is preventing us from becoming successful. Internal forces are much easier to defeat because they are forces which are under our control, however, we will need to have the right knowledge or the know-how in order to defeat them. Now, external forces is a whole different story. External forces or obstacles were designed and put into place by others in order to sabotage our plans or to prevent us from becoming successful. Those are the ones which are beyond our control, so therefore, those will be difficult for us to defeat, not impossible, but difficult, and it has to do with the fact that we don't have the right knowledge or the know-how, plus the fact that we are forever making excuses for ourselves for not trying. Sometimes we don't have the desire to succeed, other times, we don't have a plan of action in place or we become invaded by laziness and I am sorry for saying that, but it's the truth.

The main reason as to why we fail often in accomplishing our goals is because we are not aware of these powerful forces which is preventing us from becoming successful. Sometimes our intentions to succeed are good, however, we are not aware that these powerful forces are working against us and it's all by design. These powerful outside forces are part of everyone's daily lives and if we are ever going to be successful in defeating them, then we need find out what these powerful forces are.

One inside force which is preventing us from becoming successful is fear... fear is something that will stop us death in our tracks. When we become overwhelmed by fear, we will lose control of ourselves, our minds will become foggy and because of that, we will not be able to think clearly, so, what is the solution? Well, we must learn to overcome our fears, and it's only by taking charge of every situation that we are going to be able to overcome our fear. We must not let our emotions of fear take control over our lives. Another internal powerful force that can potentially prevent us from becoming successful is our old beliefs and it's because our beliefs play an important role in our lives, in fact, our beliefs make us who we are as a person. We must never limit ourselves from achieving success because of our erroneous beliefs. It's important that we learn new beliefs, however, we need to make sure that those beliefs are the right beliefs.

Other outside external powerful forces which is prevent us from becoming successful or reaching our goals is our environment, but how can our own environment prevent us from becoming successful? It's actually simple, for example, when we associate ourselves with negative people, and those people are forever complaining about everything, then their negative way of thinking will influence our way of thinking and occasionally we will become those negative people ourselves. We should try our best to never put ourselves in such a negative environment.

There are other powerful forces which is going to prevent us from achieving success, for example, new technologies, social and demographic factors, lack of information, and lack of skills, but perhaps, the biggest outside force which is going to prevent us from achieving our goals is the "roadblocks" which are put into place by others, and because we don't know how to overcome those obstacles, then it's obvious that we are going to fail miserably in trying to accomplish our goals. So, what is the solution here, are we supposed to lay down and play dead, how are we going to overcome such roadblocks or obstacles? Well, there's only one way which is going to help us defeat those obstacles and it's by using our two most powerful weapons, our knowledge and our imagination.

Chapter Thirty-Two

It's Time to Expose Our Hidden Talents

We all have hidden talents or secret talents, but discovering our hidden talents it's not an easy thing to do and it's because we don't know what they are, so how do we tap into our hidden talents? Well, sometimes it takes someone else to point out that we have certain abilities or that we have a special hidden talent, and it's because we tend to overlook our skill. it's only then that we will realize that we indeed have a special gift. The best way to find out what our hidden talents is by experiment with different things, for example, if we like music, then perhaps, we can discover that we indeed have a gift for playing an instrument or be a singer, if we like dancing, then maybe we can become a professional dancer. If we are good with numbers, then we can become a mathematician. If we are good with words and we have good social skills, then becoming a public speaker or a lawyer might be the way to go, maybe we have a talent for writing or even cooking, perhaps we can discover that we like science or working with computers.

There are plenty of other things that we can try in order to find out what we are really good at, for example, art, drawing, photography, film maker, comedy or acting, furthermore, we can try sports, for example, baseball, basketball, football, hockey, golf, bowling, skiing, snowboarding, skydiving, bike riding, running or swimming. It's important that we experiment with different things every single day, specially, things that we never done before. The possibilities are endless, we just need to find out what we are good at and go for it, but without any hesitation.

Some hidden talents which we have are easier to identify, but others are a little trickier, however, it's after us to find out what our hidden talents are, and once we find out what they are, then we need to further develop those talents by practicing them on a day by basis, so that we can fully masters them, and at the same time, maybe we can use some of our talents to help change the world.

We have many hidden talents that we haven't been able to discover and develop, and may I mention that some are easier to develop than others, but they are all there, hiding inside us, waiting to be put into action. Again, we have many hidden talents, and even though some people might believe the opposite, the fact of the matter is that we do have many hidden talents inside ourselves. We must never allow ourselves to think otherwise, furthermore, we must never let someone else tell us that we don't have such special talents because we all have them, the problem lies in that we have yet to figure out what they.

We have other hidden talents which are not so easily identifiable, for example, we have a tremendous amount of knowledge, we have imagination, we have creativity, we have perseverance, we have will power and we have determination. All these hidden talents are waiting to be discovered. They are inside us waiting to be unleash and put into action, and if we are ever going to step up into the next level of super humans, then we need to start using these precious hidden talents, but we must start using then right now because there is no better time than the present, we must not wait until tomorrow to start using our hidden talents.

One of my hidden talents that I knew I had ever since I was a kid was the desire to help other people in any way that I could, but now I want to use some of my other hidden talents which I have to help change the way other people think and act and hopefully I will be successful in accomplishing such a task. The way I'm planning on helping other people to be the best they can be is by letting them know that: they too, have many hidden talents which are waiting to be unleashed. We all have secret talents that we never knew we had, but we must learn to unlock them, they are in there, and if we look hard enough, we will find them.

When we were born, we were given the same opportunity, in other words, everyone was given the opportunity to be able to thrive, to grow, and to develop their own hidden talents. Our talents were given to us for a reason, they were given to us so that we put them into good use, and now is the best time to put them into action. We must remember that we only lived once. It's important to remember that time is precious, therefore, we must not waste it on unproductive tasks which have no value to ourselves or others. Unproductive tasks which have no merit should not be in our thoughts because they will be a waste of our time and energy on our part, let me put it in a different perspective. It is like planting a fruitless tree which is not going to produce any fruit for us to eat, so why plant it, well, maybe it will be useful for shade in the summertime.

My suggestion to everyone is to: not wait until it's too late to make a change, and no matter how young or old we are, it's never too late to experience something new. Most often than not, people like to wait, and wait, and wait some more to make a change, but that change never comes, and therefore, nothing ever happens. Most people will tell themselves "I will start using my talents tomorrow," but unfortunately, tomorrow never comes.

We must stop our procrastination. We must throw it into outer space and never again think of being procrastinators. Now! we all know that the non-procrastinators do whatever it needs to be done in order to better themselves, they don't wait for something good too happened to them, instead, they go out and make it happen, and it's only because they put all of their hidden talents into action, in addition, they leave their laziness behind. Some people say that good things will come to those who wait; however, I happen to believe that: if I want something good to happen to me, then I must go and make it happen.

Again, we must never wait for others to make changes for us. Because it's not their job to make those changes for us, we are the only ones responsible for everything that happens in our lives, so we have no other choice, but to do it ourselves, and we can accomplish it by putting all of our resources into action mode.

We can make ourselves happier by using our hidden talents, but first, we must know what makes us happy. What is going to motivate us to transform our life from the life we currently have to the life that we were meant to have. Again, we must ask ourselves "what makes us happy?" does money make us happy, and if not, then, what else is going to make us happy, perhaps, it will be a combination of many things that is going to make us happy.

For me personally, money will not bring me complete happiness. Money is essential for surviving, but it's not the most important thing in my life. Lack of money can certainly make some people miserable, but for me, it's not all about the money. There are more important things in my life other than money, for example, the feeling of freedom, the feeling of success, and the feeling of accomplishing some of my goals. I try not to get too attached to money because I know that money has wings, in other words, money comes and goes. Sure, whenever I find myself with extra money, it does make me happy, but that type of happiness is only temporary. My real happiness comes from helping others to help themselves. Also, it makes me happy knowing that there is plenty of love, harmony, and caring among my family and friends because that is what life is all about, finding real happiness, I am happy when I see others happy, and I will not deny that.

Whatever we want out of life it's something that we should never wish for, instead, we must use our hidden talents and then we must work hard to get what we want out of life. We must remember that we do not get out of life what we wish for. We only get out of life what we work for. We all wish for a better life, but sometimes we are not willing to work for it, and that is something that we all need to work on. We must remember that if we work hard, we will accomplish most of our dreams. We must keep in mind that smart people who use their hidden talents must work hard to get what they want.

There will be plenty of wonderful feelings when we finally learn to use our hidden talents, for example, we will be much happier doing what we loved to do, plus the fact that others will be able to benefit from our talents because they were given to us, not only to benefit ourselves, but to benefit other as well, and that in it-self is a tremendous feeling of joy. I can go on and on talking about all the benefits that we get we use our talents to help make the world a better place, so go ahead, let your imagination run wild, do not be afraid to explore your inner self for answers, but whatever you decide to do, make sure that it's something that you love to do, something that you will enjoy doing for the rest of your life. Happy trails to all.

Staying Motivated with Positive Thinking

Positive thinking is an immensely powerful tool that we can all use when in times of despair, but unfortunately, sometimes we forget that we have the power of positive thinking. Positive thinking comes from self-motivation, and motivation comes from within our-selves, furthermore, our motivation comes from the people that we love, because without the love from others, the help, and the encouragement from the people that we love, our goals are going to be that much more difficult to obtain.

How do we stay motivated? Well, staying motivated 24-7 is not an easy thing to accomplish because we are good at making plans for ourselves, but we are terrible at executing them, but why is that? Well, the only reason that I came up with is because our feelings and emotions get in the way. They will prevent us from making most of our plans become a reality, and it's because our feelings and emotions are always competing with our desire to make our plans come true, and it has to do with the fact that our feelings and emotions will win most of the time, but only if we let them.

I cannot remember how many times I found myself making plans only to postpone them for a later day, perhaps it was because of the way I was feeling at that time, my feeling and emotions were all over the place, perhaps, I was feeling physically and mentally exhausted to the point where I had to stop whatever I was doing, however, once I stopped, it was difficult to come back and continue doing what I was doing, so it's important to remember to stay motivated at all times.

One way for us to stay motivated is to remind ourselves every single day that we need to stay motivated no matter how many roadblock we might encounter on our way to accomplishing our goals. I understand that staying motivated is not an easy thing to do, in fact, nothing that we ever do is easy, it's one of the most difficult things to overcome, but nevertheless, we must stay strong and focus our attention to what is important to us. We must constantly remind ourselves that we need to stay motivated, so that we can keep our eyes on the big prize.

There will be many distractions along the way that will prevent us from staying motivated, for example, the feeling of not belonging, the feelings of not being loved by the people that we love, including our spouses, our parents, and our kids, all this things are distractions that prevent us from staying motivated. In addition, it will be difficult for us to stay motivated when we are stuck in a job that we don't enjoy doing, or perhaps is the lack of not having a job, furthermore, it will be difficult for us to stay motivated when we are sick, or when we have some type of incurable disease.

These are examples of why it's so hard for us to stay motivated, but it's at times like this, when we are feeling lonely, hopelessly, depressed and we feel as if nothing in this world will be able to help us to overcoming our feelings of despair and isolation. This is the time when we must put ourselves back into action mode, back into a positive thinking mode and back into finding something that will help us to stay motivated. We must understand that we are humans and that from time to time, we will fall into despair, but we must not dwell on it for too long because then it will be even harder, but not impossible to try and make a comeback.

We must search for things that will make us feel good all over again, something that will help us bring our motivation and our self-confidence back. We must look for the things that will make us feel good on the inside and not the ones that will make us miserable or unhappy, and I'm not talking about alcohol or drugs, although sometimes a glass of wine or a couple of beers will help us to relax, in other words, it will help us not to feel so intense.

Happiness is within us; we just need to do a little soul search and we will find it. We must do our absolute best to never fall into despair, but if we do from time to time, then we must keep in mind that after the storm, there will be calmness and sunshine, and if today was not a good day for our peace of mind and happiness, then we must remind ourselves that there will be sun tomorrow, so we must keep our hopes alive.

I know that some people might be annoyed by telling them about staying positive, they probably will say something like "yea, I am tired of people telling me about staying positive" and it's understandable, after all, they heard about staying positive most of their lives many time before, but somewhere along the line they stop believing in the miracle of staying positive, in fact, some people forgot about the real meaning of staying positive. I really believe that staying positive is the best medicine for some of our ailments, therefore, we must never forget that indeed staying positive does work, we just need to practice it on a day-by-day basis. It's like everything else, we must remind ourselves to keep using our positive thinking, or we have the option to stay where we are right now; with our negative way of thinking, but I can assure you that you will not be happy staying stationary.

Reaching for the Stars

What does it mean when I say reaching for the stars? It doesn't mean that we can literally reach out and touch them, it simply means that if we find ourselves lost in the middle of the desert, then we can find our way back home by simply following the stars. It means that we should set our goals or dreams extremely high because we are very capable of accomplish anything that we desire. But before we can reach for the stars, we need to take care of our mental and physical health first. We all have good intentions to succeed, but we must remember that good intentions is not enough. We need to take care of our physical bodies by exercising regularly; by getting enough sleep and by eating healthy food. It's important to take care of our physical bodies, but it's also important that we take care of our mental health. But how do we achieve mental health? Well, we can star with yoga, then follow by meditation. There's nothing more powerful than meditation to help us put our minds in a state of calmness and get rid of unnecessary junk.

Furthermore, if we want to reach for the stars, then it's important that we stay true to ourselves and not let anything or anyone stop us from reaching our true potential or deviate us from achieving our goals. Furthermore, we must not let greed get in our way and ruin our happiness and other people's happiness on our way to stardom. We can all reach our true potential as human beings; we can all be kind to each other, but without the need for destroying each other's dreams or cause pain and suffering to others along the way.

We have many powerful tools that God gave us to help us along our journey, but we must remind ourselves that we need to put them into action. For example, we have the power of our minds, we have the power of imagination, we have the power of reasoning, we have the power of observation, we have the power of desire, and we have the power of stimulation. We also have instincts, creativity, and perseverance. If we use all these tools that God gave us, we are going to be able to aim for the stars and spanned our universe.

Again, this arsenal of weapons was a gift from God. He gave us all the tools that we need in order to survive in our environment. God wanted us to learn from our mistakes so that we can become better human beings, better fathers, better mothers, better brothers, better sisters, and better friends. It's the most wonderful gift that any human being could ever ask for, but we must learn to use these magical powers which are hidden inside.

It's unfortunate that some of us are not willing to unlock our true potential, but there's always hope in the horizon. I'm hoping that someday, people will find themselves reading this book and hopefully they will be able to change their lives forever. Personally, I don't like to waste my days hoping for something good to come my way. I don't want to waste my days hoping that someone will come and rescue me from myself, I rather use my arsenal of weapons that I have at my disposal to rescue myself. I rather use my knowledge, my imagination, intelligence, my instincts, and my creativity to save myself from stagnation and from living a boring life; a life that wasn't meant for me.

We must not see things for what they are, instead, we must see them for what they should be. So, if we want to reach for the stars, we must not let any outside forces influence our state of mind. We must keep going forward, but without letting any outside forces influence our decision making, unless of course, it's something that it's going to help us achieve our goals.

What is Holding Us Back from Achieving Our Goals?

Why do we fail when we are trying to achieve our goals? What is holding us back? Everyone knows that achieving our personal goals is not an easy thing to accomplish, most often than not we will fail, and it's not because we want to fail on purpose. Most of the time we fail because there are too many unforeseen or hidden obstacles that we do not anticipate happening, but they do happen more than we can ever imagine.

In addition, there are other reasons as to why we fail when we are trying to achieve our goals, but perhaps, the number one reason which is preventing us from achieving our goals (again, I hate to keep repeating myself) is our lack of knowledge. Lack of knowledge will stop us in our tracks, thereby, preventing us from becoming successful in accomplishing most of our personal goals. We must keep in mind that: "knowledge is power" and when we lack that knowledge to help us overcome the barriers that we will encounter along the way, most likely, we will fail.

Before we try to accomplish a personal goal, and it doesn't matter what that might be, we need to be well prepared, in other words, we need to learn as much as possible about whatever it is that we are trying to accomplish. We must never venture out in any business blindly because it could be expensive for us, monetary wise, we can end up losing our shirts. Plus, there will be other devastating effects, for example, our credibility will be challenged by others, including family members, furthermore, we will experience psychological negative effects, like, frustration, guilt, ashamed, in addition, our self-esteem will suffer. However, we must never dwell on our failures for too long, we must get up on our horse and try again, but this time around we must be careful not to fall off the horse.

There are other things besides having the knowledge that we need to be aware of when trying to accomplish our goals, for example, we must be one hundred percent committed, we must never quit too soon, we must stop our procrastination, we must not be afraid of failing, we must have reachable goals, we must try to stay away from negative people, instead, we must surround ourselves with knowledgeable and happy people who knows what they are doing. We must focus on one goal at a time, we must stay motivated 24/7, and finally, we must have a plan of action. If we paid close attention to the above suggestions, then we will have a good chance of succeeding.

I know from personal experience that bad things can happen when we are not well prepared because it has happened to me, many times before, but you know what? I never gave up, I kept on pushing until I was able to tear down those brick walls that were preventing me from achieving my goals. Now I know how to bring down most of the walls because I'm armed with knowledge. By obtaining and creating new knowledge I gave myself new opportunities to overcome most of my obstacles. I never gave up and because I never gave up, I was able to accomplish some of the things that I wanted. We must understand one thing, and that is that we know what we know and that is it, and unless we obtain new knowledge, we will not be able to become successful in achieving our goals.

Another reason as to why sometimes we fail in achieving our goals is because of our limited thinking which can prevent us from reaching our goals, but why is that? Well, because we are limited to what we can accomplish, and it is because we don't have the knowledge and the skills which are required to be successful. If we want to be successful, we must obtain new knowledge and new skills.

In addition, we must learn from other successful people. We must find out how they became successful, however, it's important for us to follow their lead. Sometimes knowledge is not enough, we must also know people who know people who know how to be successful. We need those people to teach us how to accomplish our goals. It's all about preparation. It's all about preparing ourselves with the right knowledge and the other tools which are required in order for us to be successful.

I want to make it crystal clear. When I am talking about people's limited thinking, I am not suggesting that people are ignorant, I am simply saying that they are limited in what they are able to accomplish and it's because they don't possess enough knowledge or information to put them over the top. Some people are unaware that in most cases, there's more than one solution to solving a problem, and in many cases, there will be 10 different solutions to solving such a problem, it's all about using our imagination. It's all about putting our knowledge to work for us, but the most important thing to remember here is that we must never give up, we must never surrender when we are faced with obstacles which will prevent us from achieving our dreams.

We must keep in mind that every time we failed at something was because we did something wrong or perhaps it wasn't the right time for us. Sometimes we must sit back and reflect about all the possibilities, and then, we must learn new things so that we can come up with new solutions to help us reach our goals.

Furthermore, there will be a time when we will fail, but not because we did something wrong, but because whatever we were trying to accomplish was not under our control, we did everything right, however, we failed miserably, but not because of our own doing, instead, it was because sometimes there are outside powerful forces that we can't control, and I want to make it clear, whether we like it or not, we will encounter outside forces from time to time which will prevent us from reaching our goals, however, we must never give up because there will be other opportunities coming our ways, and remember that there is always a different way to accomplish what we want. We need to improve our awareness when dealing with outside forces that we can't control, in other words, we must be careful when putting our trust and faith in other people because they will either make us or break us.

Now, moving on to other things which have the potential to hold us back when trying to accomplish our goals, and these are things that we normally don't think about, for example, anxiety, phobias, lack of motivation, lack of self-awareness, and lack of action. Furthermore, when we fail at something, we must ask ourselves the following question: "why are we failing?" did we do something wrong, and even if we did everything right, somehow, we still manage to fail.

We must overcome our weaknesses, but first, we need to figure out what those weaknesses are. We must ask ourselves, "who or what is stopping us from reaching our goals?" If we find out that the only thing stopping us from accomplishing our goals is none-other than ourselves, then, we need to find out why, maybe it's because we are feeling powerless, maybe we have feelings of anxiety, or perhaps, we have past feelings of failure.

I'm going to write a little something about how I was able to accomplish better results when trying to reach some of my goals. You see, it all started when I was about five or six years old, I knew back then what I wanted out of life, I knew what I wanted to accomplish and even though I have not yet accomplished most of my goals, I have never given up on my dreams. Nothing has been easy for me, nothing has been given to me for free, I had to earn everything on my own and

I am not talking about money, rather I am talking about acquiring as much knowledge as possible.

One of the things which helped me to overcome most of my obstacles in my life was the knowledge that I accumulated throughout the years. I gain all this knowledge by reading hundreds of books on different topics. From psychology, philosophy, neurology, biology, science, history, and many other books on self-improvement. I also read several bibles from different religions. Some of my favorite books that I like to read is about how the human brain works. How it works and how we can learn to develop and evolve our brain even farther than ever before. In some of these books I was able to uncover the power of my mind and even though I have not completely mastered its powers, I am totally aware of the many miracles which our brain is capable of creating, but only if we just give it a chance. I have learned to think correctly and do the right things most of the time. In addition, I learned that it doesn't matter how much knowledge you or I may have, if we don't put that knowledge into action, then it will be all for nothing. I learned that we must use this knowledge correctly and in the right situations. Again, knowledge without action is nothing more than just a dormant knowledge.

It's obvious that sometimes we will fail in achieving our goals, it's something that we must be aware of at all times, also, we must be aware that it's a human reaction to feel down every time we fail. Our failures can and will prevent us from reaching total happiness, but nevertheless, failure is a good thing because it will help us to learn from our mistakes. Failure is a big part of our lives, it's something that no matter how hard we try, we will fail at one time or another, but we must never let those failures defeat us forever.

We must continue to search for the truth, we must never rest or give up until we have, if not complete understanding of ourselves, at the very least, we must try to better understand ourselves a bit more, and at the same time, we need to understand how other people think. In addition, we must increase our awareness of the things which are holding us back. One of the things which is holding us back is the lack of motivation to excel in becoming who we were meant to be.

Sometimes we do have the motivation to excel, however, other times we don't want to even try because we are afraid of failing and it all has to do with the fact that we fail many times in the past. Motivating myself is a big part of me because when I do fail from time to time, it just makes me want to succeed even more, so I keep on trying until I'm able to achieve some type of success. Partial success is better than no success at all.

We must never give up on ourselves or the things that are important to us, we must not stop caring for our families, we must renew our love for our spouses, our children, and our friends because when we stop caring and we stop learning new things, we stop producing good values for ourselves, our families, and the community. We must never give up, in addition, we must never stop caring about the people that we love because happiness could be just around the corner, also, we must never stop caring about the things that we used to like or enjoy doing.

If we want to accomplish total and complete happiness, then we must arm ourselves with the right tools, the right skills, and the right knowledge. We must take advantage of all these tools which are available to us because these tools is the key to living a happy and successful life, it's the key to a successful marriage and other relationships. Like said before, and perhaps, many times before. There will be an abundance of roadblocks that will prevent us from achieving our goals and dreams, but only if we let them. We must wake up from our "I do not care anymore attitude." We must not give up on those feelings of good sensations. We must all work on increasing our abilities so that we can achieve a happier and more fulfilling life.

When I was in the tenth grade; one of my dreams was to become a professional photographer, so I studied photography for three years, but unfortunately, I wasn't able to get my photography career going because there was always something which prevented me from achieving such a dream of becoming a professional photographer. More than thirty years went by, but my dreams of becoming a photographer never faded away. I was about fifty years young when I finally had the opportunity to pursue my photography career, so, I decided to go to college for two years and learn digital photography, I made up my mind that I was going to become a professional photographer. After 2 years of college, I achieved my dream of becoming not just a photographer but a good photographer. I'm mainly a landscape, nature, and wildlife photographer, but I don't mind photographing people as well. You see, I never gave up on achieving one of my goals, I never gave up on my dreams and neither should you.

Another one of my dreams was to write a book and that is what I am doing right now. This book has been in the makings for about forty-three years and I am sure that most of you are probably wondering, but why did it take so long? Again, there were many obstacles which prevented me from achieving some of my goals. One of the main reasons that prevented me from writing my book was the lack of knowledge and lack of writing skills. Like I said before, I started to write my book about forty years ago, but back then I was not ready, my education was not where I wanted it to be, my writing skills were not as good as they are right now and may mention that my writing skills are not by any means perfect, but I didn't let that stop from doing.

I knew back then what I wanted to write about, however, I could not accomplish such a task because whatever I wanted to write about would not translate very well into writing. I could not put my ideas into writing no matter how hard I tried, but now I'm a little bit more efficient in putting my thoughts into writing, I'm not completely there yet, but my skills are five times better than what they were forty years ago.

Around the same time that I decided to become a professional photographer, I decided to start writing my book again, and I did accomplish a lot, I was able to complete half of my book and that gave me the inspiration to keep going, to keep learning and to keep gaining new knowledge, and I did. Again, I'm not completely there yet, but my skills are much more polish now than ever before. So, you see, I never gave up on any of my dreams. It was not the only two dreams which had. I have other goals and dreams that I want to accomplish, but they are still in the making, in other words, I have not given up on any of my dreams. As long as I'm alive, I will never, ever will give up on them.

As you can see by now, there are so many reasons as to why we fail when trying to accomplish our goals. I hate repeating myself, but we fail because we don't always do the right thing at the right time, we fail because we procrastinate most of the time which is a human condition, we fail because of the fear of failing, we fail because we get discouraged when things do not work out as planned, we fail because of too many unrealistic goals at the same time, we fail because we are trying to accomplish the wrong goals, we fail because we don't know what we want, we fail because we don't always follow through, we fail because we keep changing our minds about what we really want, we fail because we lose our focus, and we fail because our inability to act.

So, now we know why we fail when trying to achieve some of our goals. We all know that achieving our personal goals is not an easy thing to do. Most of the time we will fail, and it's not because we want to fail on purpose, it's because of the above reasons, however, by now you must know or have an idea as to why we fail most of the time in accomplishing our goals.

We should never get discouraged; we should never let bumps on the road stop us from moving forward. Sometimes we don't want to go through the pain and suffering from failure, and I know that achieving our goals is a difficult thing to obtain, however, we must not quit at the first sign of trouble, we must resist the temptation to quit. Again, I have been there many times before, more than I like to admit, but again, I never gave up.

Sometimes we come up with an idea, or we want to accomplish a certain goal, and that is okay, it's a natural thing to do, we get super excited about it at the beginning, but then the cold reality kicks in, we realized that we don't know how to make that idea become a reality and it's because we are lacking the knowledge, we are lacking the skills, and we are lacking the energy which is required in order to make it happen, so, what happens next? Well, we simply end up giving up, plain and simple.

As humans beings, we are forever looking for something new to do or something new to explore, we always want to try something new, something that perhaps is going change our lives forever, however, overtime the fizzed that we first had when we first thought about that idea starts to disappear, we start to lose interest and it has to do with the fact that we realized that it's going to take a tremendous amount of effort and energy on our part, and overtime, we just simply give up. We give up on our dreams because we don't want to waste our energy on something that we might not be able to achieve.

We all have many goals and dreams that we want to accomplish within our lifetime. Some of those goals and dreams are small and they don't require much effort on our part; they are easier to obtain then our bigger goals. Our monumental goals are the ones that will be difficult to obtain because it will take a tremendous amount of effort on our part.

I keep on mentioning throughout this book about how important it is for us to not underestimate the power of imagination, yes, we can use the power of our imagination to figure out how we will be able achieve our goals, when we put our imagination into action, everything will be possible. One word of advice, never try to achieve your bigger goals first, be smart about it, be reasonable and only go after your smallest goals first, the ones that do not require too much effort. Once you achieve some of your smaller goals, then you can move on to bigger goals.

By taking on smaller goals, you will be able to gain valuable knowledge which you will be able to use for your bigger goals, in addition, you will build your self-confidence, it will help you tremendously in many ways, and it will teach you valuable lessons for the future. This is one way in which we can fight back and have success, and it's by going after the more achievable goals at first. Remember that there will are more things that will prevent us from reaching our goals, but the most important thing to remember is that you should always go after your goals and that you never give up, no matter what.

Here are a couple more reasons as to why we fail most of the time and it has to do with the fact that we are forever blaming other people for our failures and our misfortunes because it's the easiest thing to do, but what we might not realize is that whatever situation we find ourselves in, it's because we created that situation for ourselves, we have no one else to blame but ourselves. Another good reason as to why we fail so miserably is because we are too comfortable being where we are, and because of that, we don't want to try anything new.

Sometimes we don't want to try anything new because we don't want others to know that we failed in the past, and therefore, we don't want to try and fail again. Nobody likes to fail or be a failure, but we must not give up because it's only by failing that we will, eventually going to be successful. It's all about gaining valuable experience, and new knowledge that we use next time.

Don't ever be afraid of failing, don't ever give up, don't ever quit, does it make sense to you? It does to me. I'm an individuals who is not afraid of failing, well, maybe just a little afraid, but that will not prevent me from trying new things. One last thing. If we want to succeed in life, we must not get too concerned with some of the comments or remarks said to us by other people, they don't know us, they don't know what we want, and they don't know what makes us happy. Remember that the true purpose of our existence is to learn and grow as human beings, but most importantly, the true purpose of our existence is to find happiness. Anyway, get out of your current comfort zone and remember that it doesn't matter what other people think about us because in the end, what really matters is what we think, not what other people think. Happy trails to everyone and I hope that you will acquire plenty of knowledge so that you can bring happiness into your life.

About the Author

Genaro is a first-time non-fiction writer. He devoted most of his life studying philosophy, psychology, biology, health, and wellness.

In this book you will learn how the human brain works.
- You will learn to push your mind to higher levels of awareness.
- You will learn to expand your knowledge tenfold.
- You will learn how your thoughts are processed, and how they impact your life for better or for worse.
- You will learn to unlock your imagination.
- you will learn about your feelings and emotions.
- You will learn that decision-making does not have to be stressful.

- you will learn that you can still find happiness despite your afflictions.
- You will learn to create new values for yourself, your family, and others.
- you will learn to motivate yourself and to stop making excuses for yourself.
- You will learn to leave your past failures behind and reach for stars. You will learn to simplify your life by getting rid of your mental and physical junk.

www.ingramcontent.com/pod-product-compliance
Lightning Source LLC
Chambersburg PA
CBHW030901080526
44589CB00010B/99